Evaluation of Agri-Environmental Policies

SELECTED METHODOLOGICAL ISSUES AND CASE STUDIES

OECD
BETTER POLICIES FOR BETTER LIVES

Please cite this publication as:
OECD (2012), *Evaluation of Agri-Environmental Policies: Selected Methodological Issues and Case Studies* OECD Publishing.
http://dx.doi.org/10.1787/9789264179332-en

ISBN 978-92-64-17932-5 (print)
ISBN 978-92-64-17933-2 (PDF)

Corrigenda to OECD publications may be found on line at: *www.oecd.org/publishing/corrigenda*.

Foreword

Governments are increasingly aware of the importance of monitoring and evaluating agri-environmental policies. By establishing evidence-based policymaking, management and accountability, they can improve the design and implementation of their policies. The thirteen chapters in this volume were presented at the OECD Workshop on "Evaluation of Agri-Environmental Policies" held in Braunschweig, Germany on 20-22 June 2011. They cover a broad range of conceptual and practical issues related to evaluating policy measures for stimulating improvements in the environmental performance of agriculture. The focus is on policy instruments that target farming practices with the objective of enhancing agriculture's provision of public goods or raising environmental performance standards above the mandatory level specified by legislation

Acknowledgements

Dimitris Diakosavvas organised the Workshop and supervised the preparation of the Proceedings. The Secretariat would like to thank Alison Burrell for her excellent work as editor of this volume. The OECD Secretariat is indebted to the German authorities for hosting a successful Workshop and to all those who provided and presented chapters, acted as discussants and panellists, and contributed to the general discussions. Françoise Bénicourt, Michèle Patterson and Theresa Poincet provided assistance in preparing the final publication.

Table of contents

V. Market-based solutions to agri-environmental policy

Abbreviations

ADAS	Previously the government-run Agricultural Development and Advisory Service in England and Wales, now a privatised company known as ADAS
AE	Agri-environmental
AEM	Agri-environmental measure
AES	Agri-environmental scheme
AFI	Agri-environmental Footprint Index
ARMS	Agricultural Resources Management Survey
CAFO	Confined animal feeding operation
CAP	Common Agricultural Policy
CBA	Cost-benefit analysis
CEA	Cost-effectiveness analysis
CHP	Combined heat and power
CMEF	Common Monitoring and Evaluation Framework
Defra	Department for Environment, Food and Rural Affairs (England and Wales)
EF (farming)	Environmentally friendly (farming)
EFDPP	Environmentally Friendly Direct Payment Programme (Korea)
FADN	Farm Accountancy Data Network
FAS	Farm Advisory Service
GAEC	Good agricultural and economic condition
GIS	Geographical information system
GWh	Gigawatt hour
Ktoe	Kiloton of oil equivalent
LU	Livestock unit
MC(D)A	Multi-criterion (decision) analysis
MS	Member State (of the European Union)
MWh	Megawatt hour
NHP	National handicap payments
NUTS	Nomenclature of Territorial Units for Statistics
NVZ	Nitrate Vulnerable Zone

QAS	Quality assurance scheme
RDP	Rural Development Programme
RPA	Rural Payments Agency (England and Wales)
SMR	Statutory management requirement (with an EU Directive as its legal basis)
SPS	Single Payment Scheme (direct decoupled payment scheme under the EU's CAP)
UAA	Utilised Agricultural Area
USDA	US Department of Agriculture

Introduction

Alison Burrell

The thirteen chapters in this volume are a selection of the contributions presented at the OECD Workshop on "Evaluation of Agri-Environmental Policies" hosted by the Johann Heinrich von Thünen Institute, Braunschweig, Germany on 20-22 June 2011. During the Workshop, a total of twenty-four presentations as well as formal contributions from seven discussants were programmed. They covered a broad range of conceptual and practical issues related to evaluating policy measures for stimulating improvements in the environmental performance of agriculture. The focus was specifically on those policy instruments that target farming practices with the objective of enhancing agriculture's provision of public goods or raising environmental performance standards above the mandatory level specified by legislation.

Contributors drew on a wide range of experience from across the OECD area and beyond. Roughly half the presentations reported activities, results and issues arising in EU member countries, which share a common legal basis for agri-environmental policy and a common methodological framework for evaluating its performance. Other contributions – notably from Japan, Korea, Norway, the United States, Canada, Australia and Brazil – provided a more heterogeneous picture of agri-environmental policy that pinpointed interesting differences in objectives, instrument choice, implementation and results, not to mention differing stages of policy maturity and practical experience gained so far. Yet even among the EU member countries, there was considerable variety among the contributions in the issues that were seen as important or problematic, and in the way administrations have organised and implemented evaluation procedures.

In addition to country-specific reports of the implementation and *ex post* evaluation of agri-environmental measures, there were chapters on methodological issues and *ex ante* evaluation analyses, and these dimensions are also reflected in the papers selected for this volume.

Such a wide spectrum and richness of experience resulted in a valuable body of information and analysis from which all Workshop participants could learn something. Inevitably, the selection of papers included in this volume cannot do justice to the full range of material that was aired and discussed in the Workshop, although we are confident that the major issues and any common viewpoints that emerged during the Workshop are represented.

This introduction serves two objectives: first, that of presenting the volume as a whole and highlighting the content of the chapters included and, second, that of providing a few insights from the Workshop discussions and summarising any conclusions reached. To meet the second objective, it draws on the formal contributions of the discussants, subjective recall of the participants' comments from the floor in discussion sessions and the rapporteur's summing up. It follows that this introduction makes no claim to being a conventional executive summary, but rather it is a "curtain-raiser" to the thirteen chapters presented, each of which can be appreciated on its own merit with its own distinctive and valuable message.

The chapters are grouped into five sections. The first section, entitled "Framework for Agri-Environmental Policy Evaluation?" contains two conceptual chapters that together provide the broader context for agri-environmental policy evaluation and set the scene for the other chapters in the volume. The first chapter, by Keenleyside, Allen, Hart and Baldock, reviews the whole sequence consisting of agri-environmental policy design, implementation and evaluation, and systematically considers whether, at various key stages in this sequence, it is possible to formulate "best-practice" guidelines that could be generally applicable across OECD countries. This perspective provides an excellent reminder that each stage in the policy sequence depends on and feeds into other segments of the sequence. The task of policy evaluation – especially that of *ex post*, evidence-based evaluation activity, which is the subject of most of the chapters in this volume – comes towards the end of this sequence. It follows that the parameters according to which the evaluation will be conducted (policy objectives, the causal mechanisms assumed in the policy design (i.e. the intervention logic), and coherence with other policies) and the evidence that can be called upon (the available database including evaluation-relevant indicators) are at least partly pre-determined in earlier stages of the sequence. The evaluator's task is facilitated or severely hampered depending on how well these previous stages have been performed, to what extent the needs of the evaluation were borne in mind when previous stages were conducted and on how much information he has about the inputs used, procedures established and decisions taken in each of these earlier stages.

The specific question addressed by the chapter is the feasibility of providing guidance that is generally applicable and relevant across OECD countries, characterised as they are by somewhat diverse approaches to agri-environmental policy, a multiplicity of country-specific objectives and a heterogeneous mix of policy instruments in use. The authors find that at each stage in the policy sequence some useful general guidance *can* be formulated on matters of underlying principle, not to mention warnings issued about pitfalls to be avoided. However, the scope and level of detail of this guidance would not be the same for all interventions or all stages of policy design and implementation. A combination of general guidelines with specific examples, illustrating how the principles can be applied in concrete instances, is recommended.

The second chapter, by Burrell, was the basis for the keynote address of the Workshop. It focuses directly on the evaluation of agri-environmental policies, taking as its starting point the malaise often expressed by evaluators and end-users of evaluations regarding the rigour and relevance of current evaluation procedures. There are various interested parties on the evaluation scene: policy makers, farmers targeted by policy measures, scientists and the general public in its dual role as ultimate beneficiary of agri-environmental policies and as ultimate paymaster through the tax system. In fact, each of these stakeholders has different expectations from the evaluation process, and different priorities regarding timing, depth and degree of scientific rigour, not to mention different views on the most appropriate criteria for the evaluation judgement. It is inevitable that evaluation exercises designed to fulfil the needs or meet the criteria of one stakeholder group will be criticised as inadequate or possibly superfluous by other groups.

Burrell's chapter identifies three stylised types of evaluation – the "administrative", "scientific" and "economic" approaches – each of which provides a different kind of information in a different time-frame. After characterising each of these approaches, the chapter argues that rather than being competitors for "authenticity", each approach makes a valuable contribution in a specific context. It is essential that users understand the different roles played by these three types of evaluation, and avoid the trap of trying to draw from one approach the kind of conclusion that can only be supported by another of the approaches. It seems clear that, as long as there is a demand for the type of information best provided by each type of evaluation, they will continue to co-exist. It is therefore important that expectations and interpretative skills be aligned with a more realistic appreciation of what each of them can actually accomplish.

The second section consists of two chapters, grouped under the heading "Specific Evaluation Issues and Country Experiences". Each chapter explores in depth a particular issue currently facing evaluators, and illustrates it with detailed evidence from the authors' own country. The chapter by Höjgård and Rabinowicz draws on a recent comprehensive evaluation of the agri-environmental measures within Axis 2 of the CAP's Rural Development Programme (Pillar 2) in Sweden, conducted according to the Common Monitoring and Evaluation Framework (CMEF) – a standardised methodology drawn up by the European Commission for producing what would be classified, using Burrell's terminology, as an "administrative" evaluation, and categorised by Höjgård and Rabinowicz as an "institutionalised evaluation process."

Based on the rich detail of the Swedish case, the authors identify major weaknesses in the evaluation procedure they followed. These weaknesses include vague concepts, a frequent mismatch between questions posed and indicators demanded, insufficient availability of suitable methodology and lack of empirical data. In the words of the authors, "The single most important weakness relates to the fact that the questions, as they are phrased at present, seem "too big" or too complicated to be answered within the time and resource framework of the evaluation. The evaluation is about establishing to what extent positive environmental effects can be attributed to the support programme, which in turn amounts to answering two questions: how payments have affected the behaviour of farmers and how changes in farmer behaviour have influenced the environment. As pointed out before, reliable, science-based answers to both questions are often difficult to obtain." These remarks typify the frustration and scepticism that arise when expectations and judgement criteria that properly belong in the ambit of a "scientific" evaluation are hooked onto an administrative evaluation with its narrower constraints.

The authors make a number of strong recommendations, some of which identify improvements that could be made relatively easily within the current methodology, others of which indicate a stark choice for administrators between either relaxing some of the very constraining parameters of the current process or scaling down their expectations of what can be achieved within the given framework.

The dilemmas created by the short time-frame for the administrative evaluation, raised by the last two chapters, were further highlighted by discussant Leo Maier (European Commission), who mentioned that in a recent review of evaluations of agricultural policies carried out at EU level since 2008, those in charge of developing and implementing policies identified imperfect timing as the single most important reason in cases where feedback from evaluations was not used in the next round of the policy preparation process.

The second chapter in this section, by Claassen, focuses on a thorny issue in policy evaluations, namely that of quantifying additionality. The additionality of a policy measure refers to the extent to which the policy was a necessary condition for obtaining the targeted result.[1] In the context of agri-environmental payments, a policy measure has full additionality if all participating farmers needed the incentive provided by the scheme to change their farming practices or improve their environmental performance, and would not have done so in the absence of the payment. Additionality is low when a large proportion of payment recipients would have changed their behaviour or complied with the programme requirements even without the payment.

Clearly, when additionality is low, budget resources are being spent unnecessarily, although it should be stressed that this interpretation of the consequence of low additionality depends on the view that the rationale for the payment is to act as a trigger, i.e. to provide an *incentive to change behaviour*, and not simply to grant a *reward for a particular behaviour* regardless of what was its motivating factor.

Claassen reports on the first phase of a USDA project designed to investigate the additionality of agri-environmental payments targeting the adoption of conservation practices in the United States. He presents fascinating evidence from the ARMS (Agricultural Resources Management Survey) 2009 and 2010 results showing that, among the wheat and corn producers surveyed, considerable numbers adopted the targeted conservation practices *without* the stimulus of an incentive payment. The evidence is broken down over a number of different conservation practices. In the typical case, less than half of the respondents adopting a particular practice targeted under a payment scheme were actually receiving an incentive payment for doing so.

In the next phase of this research project, the statistical method known as Propensity Score Matching will be used with the ARMS database in an attempt to the quantify the degree of additionality among those farmers who both followed conservation practices *and* received agri-environmental payments.

A comparison of the issues of additionality and compliance reveals some interesting parallels. In the case of low additionality, farmers are paid for doing something they would have done in any case. In the case of low compliance, farmers are paid for doing something that in reality they do not do. Clearly, in the first case, the consequences for environmental performance are less negative than in the second, and in the second case there is also a legal implication since some kind of contractual undertaking has been broken. However, as regards the cost effectiveness of the policy the consequences are similar: in each case, the amount of *additional* benefit that is obtained per dollar spent under the policy is not maximised. For some time, economists have been studying the possibility of designing contracts that are self-enforcing, i.e. contracts that contain incentives such that non-compliance would never be a chosen strategy. It would be interesting to take an analogous approach to contract design with the aim of maximising additionality, i.e. to explore the possibility of designing contracts containing a disincentive for volunteers who are already behaving as required, or who would do so even without the payment.

The third group of chapters, under the heading "Lessons Learnt from Evaluations Performed," contains four chapters reporting the results of *ex post*, evidence-based evaluations of agri-environmental measures. The first two chapters report the results of evaluation studies of specific policy measures within the European Union's Rural Development Programme (Pillar 2 of the CAP), in Finland and Belgium. The third chapter summarises a study of the environmental impacts in the United Kingdom of the cross compliance requirements accompanying the direct payments made to farmers under Pillar 1 of the CAP. The fourth chapter looks at the transitional direct payments paid to Korean rice farmers who switch to environmentally friendly farming methods.

The chapter by Aakkula *et al.* deals with agri-environmental policy impacts on water quality and biodiversity in Finland. The authors studied trends in various indicators of nutrient load (nutrient balances and soil test P value), and trends in nutrient fluxes (based on observed discharge and nutrient concentration) from 22 agricultural rivers, concluding that the P load has continuously declined in recent years whereas the N load in nearly all river basins has increased, although not uniformly across regions. To study biodiversity, trends in five complementary indicators covering a wide range of farmland flora and fauna were monitored, and three case studies of particular measures were also performed. Positive environmental impacts of several specific agri-environmental measures are confirmed. The authors find that trends in landscape structure pose the most important threat to biodiversity, in particular the decreasing incidence of open semi-natural areas that remain uncultivated due to land use "rationalisation" aiming to increase arable area. They consider this trend demonstrates "policy incoherence" between agri-environmental policy on the one hand, and agricultural policy on the other.

Discussant Pierre Dupraz commented that "the impressive Finnish evaluation framework probably has no equivalent in the world", and it is clear that the authors dispose of an excellent database, which permits them to draw a number of robust and detailed conclusions about trends in the interaction between agriculture and the environment in Finland. Yet despite this – especially regarding the nutrient load question, less so as regards biodiversity – the links between observed trends and agri-environmental policy measures are not strongly established, not least due to the acknowledged lack of a counterfactual.

The problem of unambiguously identifying policy impacts when a counterfactual is lacking was already referred to in the chapters by Burrell and by Höjgård and Rabinowicz, and here we see that data abundance (quantity and detail of observation) cannot substitute for a counterfactual, which depends essentially on how the dataset is structured (*who* is included, *when* observations are made, and *how* the dataset is partitioned). This chapter, and others that follow, highlight the need to structure data collection more purposefully in such a way that it can be exploited in order to isolate policy impacts.

The chapter by Van Zeebroeck and Van Gijseghem reports the impacts in Flanders, Belgium, of two types of measure implemented within Pillar 2 of the CAP. First, the environmental effects of measures to support farm investment that targets farm modernisation and diversification into non-agricultural activities are assessed. The environmental impacts considered are reductions in CO_2 emissions and in ammonia emissions, the amount of water recycled and reduced energy consumption. Concentrating on the period 2007-mid-2010 and on 44 types of on-farm investment with intended impacts on the variables just listed, and using a set of relevant indicators linking investment types to *expected* results via a set of technical coefficients, the study finds sizeable expected impacts of these measures. Second, the impacts of agri-environmental measures on farmland bird populations (numbers, species diversity and breeding) were measured based on two separate monitoring initiatives. Comparing several bird biodiversity indicators across monitoring sites with different levels of agri-environmental adoption, and controlling for a number of other habitat variables unrelated to agri-environmental policies, a relatively small but significant effect of agri-environmental measures on several bird biodiversity indicators is found.

Each of these approaches finds its own solution to the counterfactual problem. In the first case, because the study starts with the database of all the relevant investments funded and quantifies the expected effects directly using technical parameters, the *ceteris paribus* conditions (with-policy versus without-policy, everything else held constant) are effectively imposed, *and* the savings in emissions and water and energy use can be directly linked to the policies. The only quibble one might have is that these impacts are not independently observed *ex post* (did they really materialise?), but of course the challenge of measuring the effects *ex post* and singling out any change in emissions specifically due to the policy measures is insurmountable.

In the second case, the use of multivariate regression and the availability of appropriate data for controlling for other non-policy factors allow the *ceteris paribus* impacts of the policies to be identified. The drawback here, which is fully acknowledged by the authors, is that the analysis is based on one cross section dataset obtained during four months in 2010, so the dynamic aspect is missing and we cannot judge whether the quantified impact of policy measures on bird populations and density, as reported in the study, is the long-run cumulative impact of the policy measures (which it almost certainly is not). The authors recommend that the 14 monitoring areas on which the cross section study was based should be re-sampled annually. If this is done, a dynamic picture over time can be constructed.

These two solutions to the counterfactual problem are specific to the particular measures being evaluated and the type of data available. However, they show that, at least in some cases, *ad hoc* solutions to the counterfactual problem can be found. This observation does not weaken the general argument that the evaluation task would benefit greatly if a more systematic approach were taken from the beginning of the policy design and implementation sequence to ensuring that the information needed for constructing a counterfactual at the evaluation stage will be available.

The third chapter in this section is a summary of a multi-authored report of over 200 pages prepared for Defra, United Kingdom, which evaluates the environmental impact on farms in England of the first four years of applying the cross compliance conditions attached to the Single Farm Payment (SFP) under Pillar 1 of the European Union's Common Agricultural Policy. The summary concentrates on a few main findings, and provides a long list of recommendations. Interested readers are strongly encouraged to download the full report.

The main findings are that the compliance level is generally high and that some measures have indeed stimulated significant changes and benefits, although lack of additionality was noted for one measure. A further dimension in this chapter, which is not part of the evaluation design in the previous two chapters discussed, is the contribution in the form of primary evidence from participants themselves via a representative farmer survey (300 respondents), two farm advisory workshops, and various interviews with administrative stakeholders. This input allows the authors to identify, among the main lessons learnt, the need for farmers to be convinced of the rationale for and the public good benefits of some of the cross compliance measures, the importance of improving the clarity with which requirements are formulated, and the need for more help to farmers with some record-keeping tasks. These elements are considered to be important for a better functioning of the policy and attainment of results.

Although participant perceptions and reactions are not a substitute for objective observation and verification of impacts, direct input from participants can be crucial when it comes to interpreting 'hard' statistical findings and making recommendations about what needs to be changed or improved. Yet the use of such surveys seems to be at the discretion of the evaluator. For example, there appear to be no formal guidelines in the CMEF about whether or when this kind of participant feedback *must* form part of the evidence base, nor how extensive or representative such a survey should be. On the negative side, the dangers of trying to glean insights from samples that are too small or unrepresentative, and then applying them to all participants, are all too obvious. Clearly, within the typical time- and resource-constrained "administrative" evaluation, the risk of collecting and interpreting this kind of input inappropriately must be great. However, since the administrative evaluation aims to cover issues like implementation and farmer uptake in some detail, it seems counter-intuitive to evaluate such performance aspects *without* primary input from participants themselves. In short, more thought needs to be given to this dimension of the evidence base available to evaluators, and some guidelines would be useful

The fourth chapter in this section, by Kim and Banfill, reports on the Korean experience with transitional direct payments. These payments, made over a three-year period, are intended to provide an incentive for farmers to switch to environmentally friendly farming techniques, categorised as "certified organic systems" and "certified no-pesticide systems." There has been steady growth in the number of farming households, and the number of hectares, enrolling in this programme since its inception in 1999. The authors also show that the total number of farming households certified as *using* these more environmentally friendly production systems has also been steadily growing, indicating that once the payments cease the greater part if not all the farmers who have switched continue to farm in an environmentally friendly way.

The evaluation exercise reported in this chapter is based on an opinion survey of policy officials (local and regional administrators involved in implementing the scheme) and policy beneficiaries (farming households). The level of commitment to the scheme among both types of respondent is high. A striking result is that an even higher proportion of officials than of farmers thought that the payment rate should be increased. The chapter contains no evidence on the scheme's environmental impacts *per se*. However, since the object of the conversion is certification, it can be assumed that the environmental impacts are real enough and that they are monitored directly by the relevant certification bodies.

The fourth section, entitled "New Methodologies and Evaluation Approaches", contains three chapters proposing new conceptual or technical approaches for tackling a particular difficulty encountered by evaluators. The first chapter, by Schouten, Polman, Westerhof and Opdam, addresses explicitly the *spatial dimension* involved in determining the extent to which agri-environmental measures achieve their objectives. The importance of the spatial configuration of agri-environmental actions and results is often ignored by analysts because of the lack of tools – and data – for capturing it adequately, and yet it may be crucial. For example, in this volume, the chapter by Van Zeebroeck and Van Gijseghem reports a positive impact of agri-environmental schemes on bird abundance and diversity *only if* there is a *density* of AE measures in the landscape surrounding a land parcel.

The chapter by Schouten *et al.* starts by recognising the importance of spatial habitat network patterns for biodiversity preservation and the need to be able to assess a specific *landscape pattern* for its potential to conserve biodiversity. They propose a spatially explicit, agent-based simulation model as a tool for evaluating, at landscape level, the potential of agri-environmental policies to conserve biodiversity. The model is used to compare two different policies in a rural area of the Netherlands: agri-environmental payments at a fixed rate per hectare for all land parcels where farmers agree to adopt habitat-conserving land use practices, and flexible, spatially differentiated payments determined by each parcel's potential to contribute to habitat networks. In the first case, all parcels offered are accepted into the scheme, whereas in the second case eligible farms tender parcels (with their bids based on farming income foregone) and the policy-implementing authority selects those bids that maximise the effectiveness of the habitat network, until exhaustion of the budget.

The results show that, for the same budget outlay, the spatially differentiated payments result in a much smaller area being contracted but with an increase of up to 10% in the effectiveness of the spatial configuration of the plots for habitat conservation. By taking the spatial coordinates of the plots into account, the dual goals of sustainability and agricultural productivity, as enshrined in the green growth agenda, can be more finely balanced and the potential trade-off between them narrowed.

Although the case study provided is an *ex ante* evaluation of the two policies, the model might perhaps be used to provide a hypothetical – ideal – benchmark against which the outcome of agri-environmental payments is evaluated *ex post*. Clearly, the challenge is to develop this approach to spatially explicit analysis in ways that will allow spatially defined information to be taken into account more routinely not only *ex ante*, when designing agri-environmental policy mechanisms, but also *ex post*, when evaluating them. On a more cautious note, discussant Janet Dwyer raised the issue of the transaction costs of implementing such a scheme in practice, whilst others expressed some scepticism regarding the feasibility of obtaining appropriate data in the general case to analyse it.

The chapter by Chabé-Ferret and Subervie addresses the question of how to estimate the impacts of a voluntary agri-environmental payment from farm-level data. Specifically, what is the appropriate counterfactual with which to compare the outcomes observed *ex post* on participant farms? The chapter demonstrates why "naïve" methods, such as comparing outcomes on participant farms with pre-scheme base-year outcomes on the same farms, or comparing post-scheme outcomes for participant farms scheme with those of farms remaining outside the scheme, will give biased – typically, upward-biased – estimates of policy impacts. In the first case ("time-trend bias"), the effect of any other factors that have systematically affected the outcome between the base year and the evaluation year will also be picked up and erroneously attributed to the policy measure. In the second case ("selection bias"), the effects of any farm characteristics that both pre-dispose the farm to volunteer for the scheme *and* affect the environmental outcome will be included in the estimate of the direct effect of the policy.

Using farm-level data from a specially constructed data set compiled from several sources, the authors investigate the impact in France of the measure AES 0301 (requiring the planting of cover crops during winter) for farms that enrolled for this scheme during the programme period 2000-2006. The authors demonstrate the use of two estimation techniques designed to deal with the second type of bias. First, they use a matching estimator, which 'twins' farms within the scheme with farms outside the scheme according to a set of observable characteristics, and effectively compares the outcome on each participant farm with that of its "twin" outside the scheme. Second, they illustrate the use of the difference-in-difference matching estimator, which takes account of the possibility that the decision to participate may also depend on some unobservable characteristics likely to affect the targeted outcome. Their example shows that the "naïve" measure of the average increase in cover crops due to the policy (16.22 additional hectares) includes a bias of 30.3% from selection bias according to observable farm characteristics, and a further bias of 3.6% from selection bias according to unobservable characteristics, leaving a "true" causal impact of 10.66 ha, or only about two-thirds of the naïve estimate.

Commenting on the need for a relevant counterfactual if policy effects are to be rigorously identified, discussant Leo Maier reported that a review of recent evaluations of rural development measures prepared for the European Commission showed counterfactual analysis through comparison groups had been used in a practical way in about one-third of the programme areas. Half of them used unmatched samples, while the other half used some sort of matching technique. However, he advised a cautious interpretation of these statistics as regards the true extent to which the counterfactuals contributed to the overall evaluation results, and their scientific quality. Nonetheless, he was confident that "the importance of counterfactual analysis is increasingly being recognised on a wide scale in applied agri-environmental evaluation in the European Union."

In conclusion, this very accessible article is recommended as required reading by all researchers and evaluators intending to estimate policy impacts from micro data.

The third chapter in this section, by Christopoulos and Vlahos, presents an evaluation tool known as the Agri-environmental Footprint Index (AFI), designed to compare environmental performance and outcomes for participant farms with those of non-participants, particularly in situations where policies are characterised by multiple objectives (in the case studies, the chapter differentiates between objectives that were explicitly stated in the legislation and other unstated environmental objectives, recognised by stakeholders, to which the measures also contribute) and where hard statistical data on outcomes are not plentiful. The methodology combines the use of agri-environmental indicators and multi-criterion decision analysis, and enlists the collaboration of local stakeholders and agricultural or environmental experts.

For the full details of how to implement this approach, the reader will have to go to other sources. What we see in the chapter included here are the results of applying the approach to two case studies in different parts of Greece: the evaluation of an agri-environmental scheme supporting organic olive production, and that of a scheme for reducing nitrate pollution from intensive arable farms. In neither case are the intended environmental effects confirmed, and there is interesting discussion about reasons for this.

A concern was expressed by discussant Pierre Dupraz about the potentially strong subjective element in the AFI methodology due to the weighting of indicators associated with different objectives. Indeed, the chapter itself does not give any information about the weights underlying the aggregated indexes on which the chapter's conclusions are based. Moreover, it was also pointed out in the discussion that, since potential selection bias was not corrected for, the somewhat disappointing results regarding the policies are not necessarily reliable. Nonetheless, the chapter makes a convincing contribution as a demonstration of a methodological approach intended to circumvent difficulties that are only too often encountered in practice.

The chapters in the last section, "Market-based Approaches to Agri-Environmental Policy", are a little outside the main theme of the Workshop, since they do not deal directly with policy evaluation. They both analyse the functioning of a cap-and-trade system. In such a system, the "cap" (a policy-determined lower limit for an environmental good, or upper limit for an environmental bad) is what delivers the environmental benefit, whereas the "trade" reallocates the cost burden of achieving the benefit over responsible agents (farmers, firms) in such a way that the total cost of achieving the cap is minimised.[2] Public intervention may be limited to providing the legal framework for fixing a cap and authorising trade in credits or permits, whilst large parts of the administration and monitoring may be 'outsourced' to non-governmental agencies, including legal entities governed by the participants themselves.

The first chapter, by Povellato and Longhitano, reports an *ex ante* analysis of a hypothetical scheme for the Veneto region of Italy designed to increase the allocation of land to meadows and grazing pasture (MG), thereby producing eco-services in the form of increased carbon sequestration. The idea here is that farms are responsible for providing an area of MG not less than a given percentage of their agricultural land area, but they can choose whether to provide it on their own farm or buy it from other farms that are able to produce a MG surplus at lower cost. This policy is compared with a situation where the mandatory minimum land allocation applies on each farm and no trade is allowed, and also with a more conventional agri-environmental scheme in which farms can volunteer to allocate a minimum area of farmland to MG in return for payments. Comparing the mandatory minimum allocation with and without trade, the latter achieves a greater total provision of the eco-service, but the income foregone per hectare of additional MG is far higher. For example, when the minimum provision of MG is set at 10% (15%) of each farm's area, the with-trade policy achieves over 10 (3) times as many extra hectares of MG per EUR 1 000 loss in gross farm income as the no-trade version. As for the additional MG provided in the region as a whole, the with-trade scenarios achieve increases relative to the baseline of 65% (142%), compared to increases of 148% (223%) without trade. Here again is another instance of a policy mechanism that permits the dual goals of sustainability and agricultural productivity, as enshrined in the green growth agenda, to be more finely balanced, reducing the potential trade-off between them.

The chapter by O'Grady reports on a relatively mature cap-and-trade system for water quality permits that has been functioning for over ten years in the South Nation River watershed in Ontario. The chapter describes in some detail the kind of institutional and legal infrastructure needed to underpin such a scheme successfully. In terms of both water quality improvements and participants' expressed satisfaction with the scheme, the record to date is impressive.

Considering these two chapters in a context where the main theme is the *evaluation* of agri-environmental schemes gives rise to various questions. First, does the cost saving due to minimising the total cost burden on participants via a market mechanism carry through into an overall improvement in cost-effectiveness once we also take into account the costs of organising the market and the transaction costs of participating in it, as well as the usual monitoring costs? Second, does this particular approach to organising the delivery of a scheme for enhancing environmental benefits have any implications for the ease with which the policy can be evaluated *ex post*, or change in any way the main thrust of the way it should be evaluated? Third, does the additional flexibility participants have to use the permit/credit market so as to optimise the way they comply with the requirements of the scheme improve participant satisfaction relative to other types of scheme, and does it affect compliance rates?

During the two and a half days of presentations and general discussion, a number of ideas and concerns recurred. The issue of the level at which agri-environmental payments are fixed was touched on by a number of speakers. According to WTO green box criteria for direct support (WTO, Agreement on Agriculture, Annex 2). direct payments to farmers within environmental programmes should be set so as to cover the extra costs or income foregone due to compliance with the programme. Some Workshop participants considered that programmes would be more effective if payments went beyond just covering costs and included an element of pure incentive, in order to overcome farmer inertia or risk-aversion. Others considered that simply remunerating farmer costs does not do justice to the market-failure rationale that underlies environmental policies, and it was argued that agri-environmental policies would be more cost-effective if the size of individual payments could be related to the size of the environmental benefit obtained. The reader will find the issue of payment levels touched upon in several of the chapters included here. Although this debate is not directly linked to the evaluation process, it would of course have implications for how policies are evaluated if payment levels were fixed according to expected or actual environmental benefits.

Another concern voiced by various participants was the lack of institutional capacity in national administrations for conducting evaluations to satisfactory standards. In theory, outsourcing the activity can increase the man-years and analytical resources available, but at a cost to institutional budgets. In any case, problems of data availability, and the burden of data collection and database management, would be likely to remain with public authorities. This concern was more typical of smaller EU member countries, faced with a heavy mandatory timetable for evaluating policies and a significant number of measures to evaluate. However, at a time when budgets are coming under pressure everywhere, it resonated with the majority of participants. How to streamline evaluations whilst at the same time improving their relevance and usefulness to the policy process is a challenge that *must* be revisited in this kind of forum in the near future.

The idea of designating control farms when setting up agri-environmental schemes was hotly debated. These farms could provide "counterfactual" data at the evaluation stage. Whilst the scientific merit of this idea was recognised (as well as a few technical challenges on the scientific side), issues like that of each eligible farmer's right to choose whether or not to participate in a voluntary programme and questions about remuneration were seen as practical difficulties.

Finally, a recurrent theme was the need to be able to draw on a stronger scientific base when attempting to identify and evaluate environmental benefits in a rigorous way. Some participants felt that science – scientifically robust empirically based knowledge about the environmental processes that agri-environmental policies aim to influence – is lagging behind the needs of policy evaluators. Others referred to issues of accessibility and transferability of scientific results into a form that could be used in evaluations. Various suggestions were made, including that of establishing a database of existing scientific studies and results that are relevant to issues encountered when evaluating agri-environmental programmes, and (in the European context) making stronger links between the needs of agri-environmental policy evaluators and research domains funded under the EU Framework research programmes.

Summing up, the Workshop brought together a lively and expert group of administrators, academics, scientists and policy analysts, closely involved in evaluating agri-environmental policies, at a very timely moment in the development of this activity. The variety of topics debated, the quality of the interventions and the insights obtained are well illustrated by the chapters in this volume.

Notes

1. The question highlighted by the issue of additionality – i.e. whether the impacts targeted by a policy measure would not have occurred otherwise and can therefore be attributed in full to the intervention – is not limited to voluntary policy measures involving payments to participants who "opt in." However, it acquires an extra implication in this case since the evaluator is trying to verify the link between additional expenditure and additional impact.

2. In theory, the cap may be set at the level of the region, watershed or other aggregate level, or – as in the paper by Povellato and Longhitano – at the level of the micro unit, i.e. the farm. In the first case, trade does not change the level of the total environmental benefit obtained, whereas in the second case, the scope for trade (i.e. the amount of initial surplus and deficit) will determine the size of the effective cap once trade has occurred.

I. FRAMEWORK FOR AGRI-ENVIRONMENTAL POLICY EVALUATION

Chapter 1

Design and implementation of agri-environmental policies: Are guidelines feasible?

Clunie Keenleyside, Ben Allen, Kaley Hart and David Baldock[1]

This chapter explores the feasibility of framing guidelines for designing and implementing agri-environmental (AE) policies of general relevance across OECD countries. It discusses various aspects of the design and implementation sequence: definition of objectives, the importance of policy coherence, the role of the reference level, the types of empirical evidence needed for sound design, implementation and evaluation, the role of the reference level, targeting, implementation and ensuring compliance, policy evaluation, institutional capacity and financial administration. It argues that potentially useful, general guidance may be feasible regarding many aspects of the process, but that its scope and level of detail would not be the same for all interventions or all stages of policy design and implementation. Given the diversity of circumstances and AE policy experience in OECD countries, guidelines should be accompanied by specific illustrative examples.

Agri-environmental (AE) policies are becoming increasingly important for stimulating agriculture's provision of non-marketable environmental public goods in OECD countries. AE policy mechanisms include incentive payments, taxes, standards and tradable permits. The OECD has recently published guidelines on the appropriate choice of AE policy mechanisms (OECD, 2010).

This chapter explores the *feasibility* of providing guidelines on the design and implementation of AE policies that would be generally applicable across OECD countries. Such policies seek to influence the decisions and behaviour of large numbers of individual farmers in many different situations, and to achieve a wide range of environmental benefits. It is not an easy task to design and implement policies that will do this well, particularly for agri-environmental incentive schemes where farmer participation is voluntary. The provision and application of guidelines could help to improve the environmental impact, cost effectiveness and long-term benefits of these policies, and would be a means of sharing best practice among OECD countries.

This document is not intended to elaborate such guidelines, but rather to consider where general guidance would be applicable and relevant for OECD countries. The policy mechanisms considered include binding environmental standards, environmental taxes and agri-environmental incentives, with an emphasis on payment systems and cross-compliance mechanisms. Published OECD guidelines also consider tradable permits, but these are not widely used at present in an agricultural context, and are not considered in the discussion below.

The chapter addresses the following issues of agri-environmental policy design and implementation:

- *Environmental objectives*: what is the policy trying to achieve?
- *Policy coherence*: how well will it work with other agricultural and environmental policies?
- *Reference level for payments*: what is the baseline level of management expected of farmers?
- *Evidence base*: is the problem clear and is the land management to solve it understood?
- *Design and targeting*: what changes in farming practices are required, where are the priority farms and what are the appropriate incentives?
- *Implementation and ensuring compliance*: what is the most efficient way of engaging farmers and ensuring they carry out the management required?
- *Policy evaluation*: is the policy working, what has failed, how can it be improved?
- *Institutional capacity and budgeting*: are the financial, personnel and other resources in place to manage and evaluate the policy?

We outline the key decisions at each stage, the factors to be taken into account and the feasibility of providing guidance to inform these decisions across the diverse environmental, agricultural and institutional situations in OECD countries. Illustrative examples are used, mainly from Europe, where there is 25 years' experience of implementing AE policies, and where 21 OECD countries (plus Estonia) now offer AE payments to farmers across the whole of their territory. The chapter concludes with a discussion of the overall feasibility of providing guidelines on the design and implementation of AE policy mechanisms.

1.1 Environmental objectives

The objectives of government interventions should be clear and specific. A strategic policy framework setting out the government's goals and justifying the need for the intervention is a good starting point. Once strategic objectives are set (often as national priorities or targets – or supra-national ones, as in the European Union) at the highest level of the framework, more detailed objectives relating to policy operation and performance that apply to specific instruments such as regulations, taxes or incentive payments can be elaborated.

Objectives set within a strategic policy framework

In the case of AE policy, government action is justified where environmental public goods from agriculture are clearly undersupplied in response to market incentives alone and intervention is needed to ensure that farmland provides the level of environmental services society wants. Governments may use a range of policy mechanisms, including regulation, taxes and incentive payments, to achieve the required environmental management on farms.

Irrespective of the AE policy mechanism chosen, the different levels of objectives should be defined as clearly and precisely as possible at the outset of the design process. There are several reasons for this.

- Even if they are complex or multi-layered, clear objectives are needed to underpin the intervention logic, to determine the actions required of farmers and to inform the design and implementation of the chosen policy instruments.
- An explicit definition of objectives and their reflection in the policy mechanisms provides the basis for a correspondingly clear and robust monitoring and evaluation system. If objectives are not clearly defined it is difficult to choose appropriate indicators with which to measure progress and to evaluate policy effectiveness.
- The success of most interventions, and especially payment schemes where the farmer has to make an active decision to participate, depends at least partly on the farmer having a clear understanding not just of "what" is required, but also "why." This should be clear in the objectives and the design that flows from them.

Many factors constrain the choice of objectives and the priority given to them, including international obligations, their economic impacts, the budget available and the capacity for measuring outcomes on the ground. For example, the European Union's obligation under the Council of Europe's Bern Convention led to strategic legislation requiring EU Member States to identify the Natura 2000 network of nature protection sites, and to ensure that these sites are managed to secure the long-term survival of Europe's most valuable and threatened species and habitats. At the level of operational objectives, a combination of regulation and AE payments are the key tools for improving the conservation management of farmland within Natura 2000. At this level, criteria relating to cost effectiveness and the budget become important. At site level, detailed environmental performance objectives are defined for the management of protected habitat and species, and implemented through site-specific environmental standards and AE payments. It is crucial to be able to measure impacts at this level.

Objectives are defined and quantified more precisely in some policy frameworks than in others. For example, the strategic objective of ensuring a certain level of environmental quality for all surface waters and ground waters in the European Union is translated into quantified national objectives for Member States, which in turn must take action to control nitrate run-off from farmland so that the pollution load of both ground and surface waters does not exceed 50 mg/l of nitrates. Some of the operational and performance objectives to achieve this are quantified, others are more descriptive (Box 1.1).

Box 1.1. Examples of operational objectives to reduce diffuse nitrate pollution in the European Union

Within identified Nitrate Vulnerable Zones there are mandatory standards (for example, for farmed land a maximum of 170 kg nitrogen per hectare per year from livestock manure), supplemented by detailed codes of practice. A range of different agri-environment payments support additional practices that help to reduce the risk of diffuse pollution, such as conversion of arable to grassland, and the creation of riparian buffer strips. In these cases proxy objectives (reducing the quantity of agricultural nitrates applied to farmland within a catchment) are used as a means of achieving the overarching objective (achieving a defined standard of water quality).

The objective of an environmental tax or regulatory standard, which applies to all farmers with few exceptions, may be relatively simple and quantifiable. For example, a tax on inorganic fertiliser at a given rate may be intended to reduce usage by a specified proportion. By contrast, agri-environmental incentive policies offer a wide range of schemes in which farmers may or may not choose to participate. Here, the strategic objectives may be more broadly framed, while the operational objectives define the scope of the intervention. To illustrate this, the intervention logic for EU agri-environment payments under the CAP is shown in Figure 1.1, and the objectives and targets of a UK scheme in Table 1.1.

Figure 1.1. Intervention logic for EU agri-environment payments

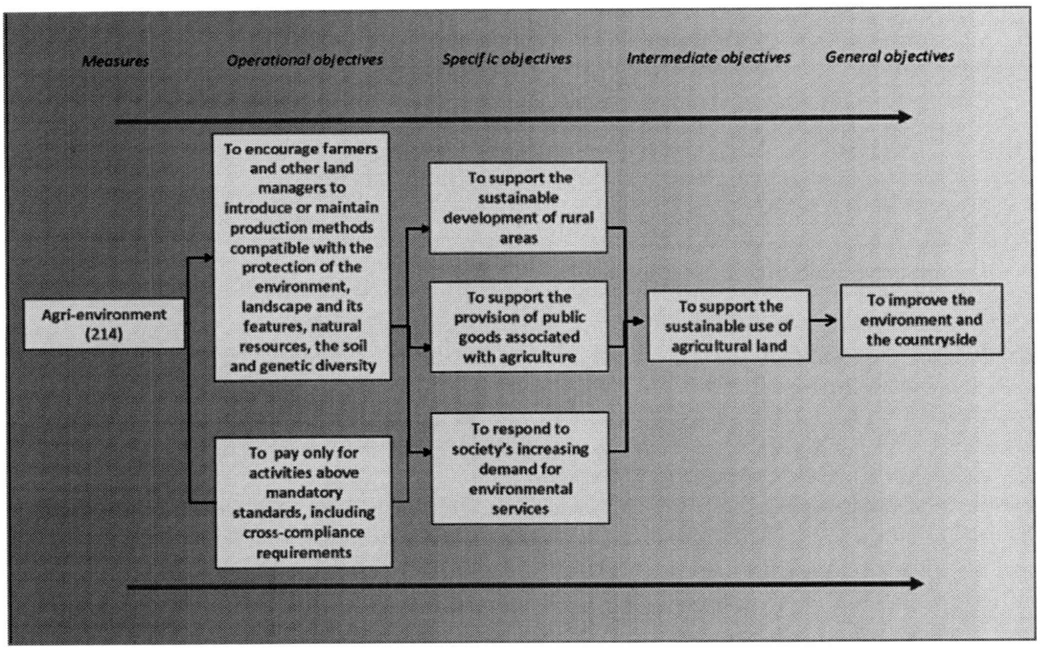

Source: Based on Cooper *et al.* (2009).

One of the most important considerations in defining objectives is the capacity to measure (directly or using indicators) the intended policy outcomes, particularly the environmental impacts. This should shape the way in which objectives at all levels are defined. It influences the whole process of policy design, from defining the management requirements for farmers to setting up databases. Lack of clarity and precision in the objectives makes it difficult to define and prioritise interventions, quantify and allocate financial and other resources, and ultimately to defend the policy.

Ideally, environmental performance objectives would also be specified at farm level, but in practice this is not always done for agri-environmental incentives, even though its omission can cause problems for subsequent policy evaluation. Detailed performance requirements are more likely to be quantified at farm level for regulatory standards or for cross-compliance obligations because they affect the majority of farmers and must be enforceable through transparent legal processes.

Table 1.1. Objectives and targets for the Environmental Stewardship scheme in England

	Targets
Primary objectives	
Wildlife conservation (biodiversity)	Improved quality of the farmed countryside for wildlife. Maintenance and restoration of nationally and internationally important wildlife sites in order to safeguard their value (including Sites of Special Scientific Interest (SSSIs) and Natura 2000 sites). Enhanced implementation of Article 10 of the Habitats and Species Directive, the Gothenburg Protocol and the Kyiv Biodiversity Resolution to halt the loss of biodiversity in Europe by 2010, through helping to halt and ultimately to reverse the decline in farmland species and habitats identified as a priority in the England Biodiversity Strategy.
Maintenance and enhancement of landscape quality and character	Maintenance and enhancement of characteristic landscape features, restoration of characteristic landscape features appropriate to the local area. Maintenance and enhancement of the local distinctiveness of the landscape, restoration and creation of locally distinctive landscapes.
Protection of the historic environment	Protect the historic environment, including archaeological features and traditional farm buildings.
Promotion of public access and understanding of the countryside	New or improved public access routes, links and areas where their need has been identified (*de minimis* state aid). Greater public enjoyment and understanding of the countryside, its history, landscape, wildlife, culture and agriculture (de minimis state aid).
Natural resource protection	Enhancement of the quality of inland and coastal water bodies including ground water in line with objectives for Water Framework, Habitats, Ground Water and Bathing Water Directives Stabilisation of nitrogen and phosphate losses from agriculture Soil conservation, maintaining and restoring their healthy functions in line with the objectives of the national Defra Soils Action Plan and future Soil Strategy.
Secondary objectives	
Flood management	More land availability for flooding (to assist in flood risk management). Relevant resource protection measures that will also reduce the likelihood of localised flooding incidents. Promotion of (sustainable) coastal defence management.
Genetic conservation	Conservation of traditional and locally distinctive breeds of farm animal and varieties of fruit tree where their conservation also contributes to the primary objectives of the Environmental Stewardship Scheme.

The objectives of policy may change over time in response to external factors (e.g. climate change) or new political demands, or as a result of improved knowledge. For example, the US federal commitment to wetland protection has evolved from a strategic policy objective of "no net loss" to one of 'overall gain' in the quality and quantity of the wetland area. AE payments have been used to slow the rate of wetland loss on farmland within the ecosystem management approaches introduced for the Great Lakes, Chesapeake Bay, the Florida Everglades, the Gulf of Mexico and numerous other watersheds (OECD, 2009). In Europe, the objective of CAP agri-environment payments has shifted from limiting the negative environmental impact of agricultural intensification in selected "environmentally sensitive areas" in the 1980s, to using payments to achieve a broad range of environmental policy commitments and aspirations.

Multiple environmental objectives

Although there is a case for pursuing individual objectives with specific individual measures, this may not be appropriate when a large number of agri-environment objectives would mean a proliferation of different measures. Therefore, multi-purpose interventions have a role despite the potential hazards involved.

For example, it can be argued that the most significant environmental public goods associated with agriculture are water quality, water availability, soil functionality, climate stability (reducing greenhouse gas emissions and improving carbon storage), air quality, agricultural landscapes, farmland biodiversity, and resilience to flooding and fire (Cooper *et al*, 2009). The relative importance of the different strategic objectives associated with the long-term provision of these goods will differ both between and within OECD countries, varying with political preferences, regional and local bio-geographic conditions, climate and agricultural systems. In practice, the operational objectives of agri-environmental interventions will often seek to achieve several of these objectives simultaneously.

Many of the changes in farming practices sought through agri-environmental measures can contribute to more than one performance objective. For example, keeping vegetative cover on arable fields during the winter reduces the risk of soil erosion, but if the winter cover is a leguminous crop it will also provide winter food for farmland birds and reduce the quantity of mineral nitrogen needed for the next crop, thus helping to minimise pollution of surface waters. Thus, three different objectives are targeted (soil erosion, biodiversity and water quality) but articulating the different objectives separately makes it easier to prioritise them. This may be necessary to address locally specific environmental problems and opportunities. In Europe some farming systems are better than others in providing multiple environmental public goods, notably low-intensity livestock and mixed systems, traditional permanent crops and organic systems (Cooper *et al.*, 2009). In such cases, where the environmental benefits are clear the operational objective of intervention may be to support the whole farming system, not just individual practices.

Secondary objectives

In some cases, secondary objectives, of an economic or social nature, may exist alongside the primary environmental one. Meeting secondary social objectives alongside primary environmental objectives can be very effective, but the intervention measure must be carefully designed. For example, the United Kingdom's *Tir Gofal*[2] agri-environment scheme provided an incentive for farmers to use locally grown oak timber for gates, not only because it was appropriate in the landscape but also to improve the management of local native woodlands (a specific objective in itself) and to support jobs within the rural community. Secondary objectives are rarely evaluated (often because they are not clearly articulated) although they may prove to be significant.

Feasibility of providing guidelines on setting objectives

General guidance on the need for objectives, and on their structure and definition, is potentially applicable to all policy interventions in OECD countries. It could focus on identifying different types of objectives (e.g. strategic, operational, performance) and on designing related tools such as a logic of intervention. It could seek to clarify the relationship between the policy objectives and the monitoring and evaluation of policies. It should be feasible to provide guidelines at this level that are applicable across OECD countries, covering the need to define AE objectives, the process of doing so, and the levels and types of objective that may be appropriate. Providing more detailed guidance on setting specific objectives may be less feasible because of the wide range of conditions within the OECD area, but examples could be given.

1.2 Policy coherence

The need for policy coherence

It is important that government policies do not conflict with each other, and it is desirable in terms of both cost effectiveness and efficiency that opportunities for synergy between different policies are exploited. At worst, policy conflicts can negate the benefits of one policy, inhibit the implementation of one or both, and lead to criticisms of inefficient use of public funds and poor effectiveness. It is important to screen for policy coherence at an early stage in the design process, as soon as the framework of objectives has been established, because it is difficult and often impossible to remedy policy conflicts after the intervention is established.

This issue gains in pertinence and complexity due to the fact that AE policies typically involve two domains that are often viewed as separate in more conventional policy making, namely those of agricultural and environmental policy. Ideally, the screening for policy coherence should be performed over policies *within* each of these areas, *across* the two policy areas viewed jointly, and at *a more detailed level between measures* in both areas in respect of instrument choice, type of incentive and the scale at which the measure is intended to operate.

In terms of governance, internal policy coherence is usually sought by an appropriate institutional division of responsibilities (for example, between government departments). External policy coherence is sought through formal arrangements for joint working (such as inter-departmental working groups, or public and stakeholder consultation processes). This applies also to AE policy, where the potential for policy incoherence as well as the range of issues at stake is considerable. AE policy mainly uses agricultural policy instruments for influencing farmer behaviour as the principal means of meeting environmental policy objectives, which necessitates that careful attention be paid to policy coherence. Moreover, in some situations, environmental pressures or the undersupply of environmental public goods are a direct or indirect consequence of long-established agricultural policies (like specific forms of income or commodity support, which may drive intensification, such as the encroachment of arable areas into grasslands, or high stocking densities).

Policies should be designed to avoid conflict. For example, agri-environment payments to support low-intensity land management systems (such as traditional mixed cropping, agro-pastoral systems, and dryland cropping) could be thwarted if farmers are offered more attractive investment support to intensify production or install irrigation systems. It is important to recognise that greater coherence can improve synergies, as when, for example, policy support for marketing and product development includes elements specifically tailored for farmers pursuing practices that deliver high levels of environmental benefit, or to help them develop niche-market sustainable products;

Failure to achieve coherence can be costly, as illustrated in the European Union before 2005, where livestock support payments per head of cattle or sheep over a long period had led directly to environmentally unsound overgrazing of semi-natural habitats in the United Kingdom and Ireland. Agri-environment schemes addressed this by paying farmers to reduce livestock numbers, but the payments to compensate for income foregone as a result of removing the animals had to cover not just the lost market income but also the lost headage subsidy. In this case, one part of the CAP budget was being used to 'buy-off' another part of the budget. The issue was resolved when most CAP support payments were decoupled from production in 2005.

The need to scrutinise for coherence applies to all combinations of policy instruments including payment schemes, whose detailed implementation is often locally flexible and may not be subject to the advance scrutiny that applies to regulatory standards or changes in property rights. Still, it may sometimes be impossible to achieve complete policy coherence, especially when one policy has a much broader scope or geographical coverage than the other and the target groups include a wide range of farm types and circumstances.

The effect of governance on policy coherence

Environmental and agricultural policies may be implemented together or in parallel by different levels of governance (federal, regional or local) or by different agencies at the same level responsible for different environmental issues (for example water supply and quality, soil conservation, habitat protection). Clarity of roles and relationships in policy formation may be particularly important where agri-environmental interventions with almost identical objectives operate across several geographical and administrative boundaries. For example, there are different environmental standards and agri-environment payments all targeted at reducing diffuse agricultural pollution of the River Danube as it flows through Germany, Austria, Slovakia and Hungary.

Despite nationally diverse combinations of governance structures and institutions in each OECD country, some general principles and issues can be identified. Coherence between agencies should be addressed not just at the first stage of setting policy objectives (for example, those of a national agri-environment payment scheme, or local conservation management agreements in a nature reserve or national park), but also at the stages involving policy design, data collection and "farm-gate" implementation. The aim should be to avoid conflicts and to exploit opportunities for synergy at all scales down to the level of the individual farmer, who may be confused or discouraged by apparently unrelated government incentives and requirements applying to the same land. This takes time, requires considerable effort, and depends on establishing good communications between institutions not necessarily used to working together. The benefits include more efficient promotion of shared objectives and improved acceptance by farmers.

Coherence of data

A common problem is the lack of coherence or complementarity between the agricultural and environmental data sets needed for effective policy targeting and implementation, and for subsequent policy monitoring. This is particularly true for map-based information where different authorities may each use their own definitions, sample frames, mapping systems and databases to collect environmental and agricultural information that has to be collated and integrated for the effective design and targeting of AE policy mechanisms. Such problems may be surprisingly difficult to resolve, such as when the environmental GIS data identifying the location of priority habitats cannot be transferred to the agricultural GIS system used to target habitat-specific agri-environment payments. Prior planning and coordination could help to obviate such issues. For example, in designing the *Caring for Our Country* agri-environmental scheme, the Australian government addressed the problem of coherence through inter-departmental committees and a National Plan for Environmental Information.

Feasibility of providing guidelines on policy coherence

It should be feasible to elucidate the *process* of screening for policy coherence, and to identify some of the common problems encountered, particularly when setting up AE policies for the first time. However, given the considerable heterogeneity of governance, administrative capacity and data across OECD countries, it is not possible to provide detailed guidance on how to *achieve* policy coherence in specific situations, although a range of examples (both successful and failed) could be helpful.

1.3 The reference level for agri-environmental payments

Why the reference level is important

A clear understanding of the definition and role of the reference level implicit in a policy is important for both policymakers and farmers, particularly in the context of payment schemes. The reference level effectively defines a farmer's property rights, stipulating what may or may not be done in managing farmland. There are no set rules for where property rights (or the reference level) should be set, nor is there a *prima facie* reason for granting or denying property rights to one particular group of farmers or another, despite the fact that the allocation of property rights has economic consequences for the individual farmer.

Box 1.2. The concept of the reference level

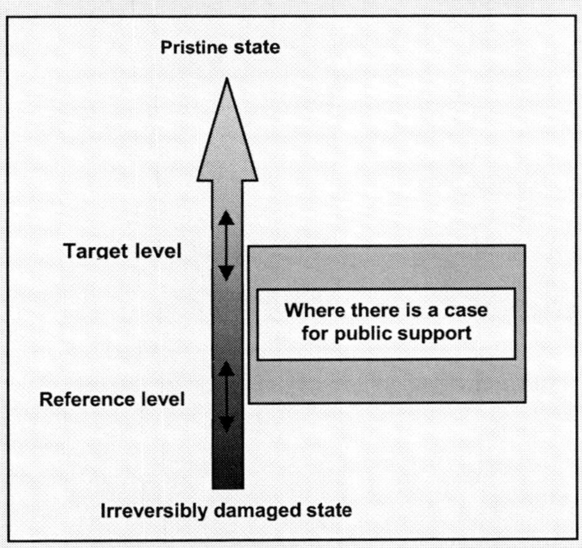

The concept of the "reference level" as a cost allocation mechanism was developed by OECD in the 1990s, recognising that, to achieve environmental outcomes more ambitious than those required by law, farmers will often need a financial incentive to influence how they use their land, labour and capital (Bromley and Hodge, 1990).

The reference level serves to distinguish between those costs associated with the achievement of environmental outcomes that must be borne by the land manager, and those that should be remunerated (OECD, 1998; Scheele, 1999).

Source: Cooper *et al.* (2009).

The impact of the reference level on agri-environment payments

The reference level defines what environmental goods and service a farmer is obliged to provide without remuneration, regardless of whether he opts to receive agri-environment payments for provision beyond that level. The question of where to set the reference level is rarely determined by desired environmental outcomes or the biophysical characteristics of land. Rather, it is largely a matter of legal tradition, political history and choices, and considerations of equity and fairness. This explains why reference levels may be set at different levels in different countries. A farmer in one country may receive an agri-environment payment for an action that, in identical circumstances, is a legal requirement in another country (Box 1.3).

In the European Union, the reference level underlying agri-environment payments (which are available within Pillar 2 of the CAP) incorporates the "cross-compliance" standards that apply to the receipt of direct income support payments under Pillar 1. If cross-compliance obligations are not met, then the farmer risks losing some or all of the agri-environment payments (in addition to the Pillar 1 payment and any specific penalties for breaching regulations). The reference level may also include other national or regional legislation, which is not part of cross-compliance.

Box 1.3. Example of the effect of different reference levels

Suppose that, when the reference level is set 'low', a farmer who owns land that provides a habitat for rare species has the right to plough it up for conversion to a more profitable land use, thereby destroying the habitat. If regulations are introduced that require the habitat to be maintained in line with standards laid down in legislation, the reference level is raised. Without the regulation, although there is a right to plough, the farmer nevertheless may be willing to allocate factors of production towards the preservation of the habitat in return for a payment that is sufficient to cover the income forgone. With the regulation, the destruction of a habitat is not within the property rights of the farmer, who therefore has to bear the opportunity costs of being denied conversion.

Table 1.2. EU Framework of issues and standards for Good Agricultural and Environmental Condition

Issue	Compulsory standards	Optional standards
Soil erosion Protect soil through appropriate measures	Minimum soil cover Minimum land management reflecting site-specific conditions	Retain terraces
Soil organic matter Maintain soil organic matter levels through appropriate practices	Arable stubble management	Standards for crop rotations
Soil structure Maintain soil structure through appropriate measures		Appropriate machinery use
Minimum level of maintenance Ensure a minimum level of maintenance and avoid the deterioration of habitats	Retention of landscape features, including, where appropriate, *hedges, ponds, ditches trees in line, in groups or isolated, and field margins*	Minimum livestock stocking rates or/and appropriate regimes *Establishment and/or retention of habitats*
	Avoiding the encroachment of unwanted vegetation on agricultural land Protection of permanent pastures	Prohibition of the grubbing up of olive trees Maintenance of olive groves and vines in good vegetative condition
Protection and management of water *Protect water against pollution and run-off, and manage the use of water*	*Establishment of buffer strips along water courses (implemented by 2012)* *Where use of water for irrigation is subject to authorisation, compliance with authorisation procedures*	

Note: Standards shown in *italics* were added in 2009.
Source: Annex III of Council Regulation (EC) No 73/2009).

The reference level varies from country to country, and also potentially between farms within the same country, depending on their circumstances. Relevant factors include regional differences in regulations, the farm's location relative to designated areas for water or soil protection or nature reserves, and the type of farming (for example, mixed farms will have to comply with regulations aimed at both arable and livestock systems). The reference level will also vary over time, as new regulations are introduced.

There might appear to be an incentive for governments to set relatively demanding reference levels as a way of redistributing the costs of providing environmental goods between the public and private domains. However, to do so has obvious risks. First is the possibility that farmers choose not to comply with high regulatory levels after comparing the real cost of compliance against the perceived risk of detection and penalties. The second is that some farmers are discouraged from volunteering for agri-environment payment schemes because the financial reward is perceived as insufficient to justify the cost and effort required to meet, additional demands above already demanding reference level standards (Jones, 2008).

Feasibility of providing guidelines on the reference level

It would be feasible to provide *general guidance* on the function of the reference level in the context of agri-environment payment schemes, explaining its background and rationale, and how the reference level works in practice, to ensure that public money is not used to provide incentives for what is already a legislative requirement. However, it would not be feasible to provide *detailed guidance* on the specific scope and content of the reference level in different OECD countries because of major differences in their environmental, agricultural and regulatory contexts. Concrete examples of best and weak practice could be given.

1.4 The evidence base

All policy interventions should be based on sound evidence that helps to shape the framework of objectives and interventions, define the reference level, support the justification for using public funds, inform the choice of instruments and their targeting and, not least guide, the actions of those managing the land. Further evidence for evaluation purposes should also be gathered throughout the period in which the intervention is implemented (see the discussion below on policy evaluation).

Environmental evidence

The correct analysis of the environmental and related agricultural situation and problems to be addressed forms the background to any successful scheme design (IEEP, 2002). Most policy interventions should be underpinned by environmental evidence, including biological, landscape, physical, and resource (soil, water) data, particularly where they relate to existing regional, national, or supra-national policies and targets. This evidence can help to:

- identify the characteristics and location of environmental problems and opportunities associated with agricultural land management that need to be addressed through some form of policy intervention;
- define the operational objectives of the policy (for example, by assessing the scale of diffuse pollution by fertilisers, or identifying the type and location of soils most prone to erosion);
- provide evidence of the efficacy of proposed management interventions based on pilots or field trials (for example, techniques to restore degraded heathland, or the effect of different grazing regimes on breeding success of threatened ground nesting birds); and

- provide a baseline against which the degree of achievement of objectives can be measured (for example surveys of the distribution and populations of farmland butterflies).

Environmental data sets may be held by several different organisations – government departments, research institutes, universities and sometimes NGOs (for example, the British Trust for Ornithology in the United Kingdom and the Audubon Society in the United States have collated bird census data for many decades). Reliable experimental evidence may be available to differing degrees for certain environmental issues. There tends to be good data from water and soil research institutes on measures to control agricultural pollution or soil erosion, but limited experimental evidence to support on interventions for habitat and species management, although observational scientific studies can be informative in their place.

Where habitats or landscape elements are the main focus of agri-environmental management, it is important that the evidence base not only covers the extent and location of such features but also their condition, the environmental problems that may be affecting them and the most appropriate conservation management (whether for maintenance, restoration or enhancement). The appropriate agricultural management of semi-natural features may be very different from that required to address the negative environmental impacts of certain types of farming over a wider area. In both cases gathering evidence may require technical data collection techniques such as water sampling, soil nitrogen monitoring or vegetation surveys.

By contrast, the extensive agricultural datasets at farm level available in most OECD countries tend to provide little environmental information. For example, the EU Farm Structure Survey provides detailed time series data on the distribution of the *type of farming* (crops and livestock) but very limited information on the *intensity* of land management, which is often the aspect of most interest to the designer of AE policies. However, such datasets can provide some insight into farm structures and broader trends in farm management, for example trends in expenditure on agro-chemicals and other inputs. There is generally very little information available in most countries on the condition of different habitats or landscape features, with the exception of those in some designated protected areas.

Socio-economic evidence

Participation in most AE payment schemes is voluntary for farmers. Therefore, understanding the dynamics and socio-economic characteristics of the farming businesses and systems being targeted is an important element of the evidence base, because these factors can have a powerful influence on participation rates and uptake of relevant management practices. The farmed environment of OECD countries is highly variable both within and between countries, reflecting market demands, historic structures, existing and previous policies. Information on cropping systems, rotations, input use, stocking densities, profitability and farm structure should be accessible from agricultural data. Also important, but easily overlooked, is an understanding of farmer attitudes, land use history, and current land tenure, which may be much more difficult evidence to obtain. In most cases, agricultural expertise, previous experience within extension services and local knowledge will be needed to capture this information. This is another reason for involving stakeholders at an early stage in the design process, including representatives of the farmers at whom the scheme is targeted.

Individual farmers' attitudes have been shown to be particularly important in the success or failure of voluntary schemes. For example, uptake of some agri-environment in-field options has been low in some of England's agri-environment schemes despite their having attractive payment rates, in contrast to wider uptake of options that are easier to implement and can be separated from normal farming operations. A recent survey of farmers indicates that this difference may be due to the way farmers perceive their role as land managers, regarding environmental management and farming as two separate activities rather than an integrated whole. The evidence base supporting the design of AE policy mechanisms should therefore account for such drivers and attitudes, where possible, particularly in setting payment rates and using advisory efforts to broaden uptake of particular management options.

Scale of data

The scale of the data required depends on the objectives of the policy, the environmental features and problems to be targeted, and the geographical scope of the scheme. Horizontal schemes, covering a whole territory or region, will require data covering a wide geographical range. Such schemes tend to operate at a lower level of complexity and the data requirements may be less onerous. Zonal schemes, where efforts are focussed on more narrowly defined areas, often have more complex data needs. Although they may require less geographically widespread data, it will be needed at a much greater resolution and level of detail. In the case of zonal schemes, evidence may also be necessary to define those zones or areas in which to focus implementation (see section on targeting) if they are not already predefined by other national and supra-national designations.

Availability of data

The evidence base for AE policy design is likely to be incomplete, quite fragmented, out-of-date and not specific to the task for which it is required. Often there will be insufficient time or resources to gather more evidence before the policy is implemented. In countries where AE policy mechanisms are being designed for the first time, evidence may be particularly scarce. To make the best use of limited data and to fill gaps in knowledge it is often necessary to rely on expert judgement and advice. Care needs to be taken to ensure a balanced approach in gathering such evidence, and advice should be sought across a range of stakeholders and partners.

Research institutes and NGOs are often valuable sources of expertise. For example, the advice of specialist ornithologists was sought in designing an AE payment to protect nesting sites of the 1 500 pairs of a globally threatened grassland bird, the corncrake, which return to the Czech Republic to breed each spring. Sharing knowledge and experience with other countries or regions may also be useful way of filling gaps in the evidence base, especially if farming systems and environmental problems are similar. Farmers themselves should not be ignored as a valuable source of detailed information. Many farming systems are complex and may have developed over a long period, in some cases in conjunction with the semi-natural habitats and wild species targeted by AE payment schemes.

Feasibility of providing guidelines on the evidence base

General guidance, supplemented by illustrative examples, could be provided on the scope, type, scale and potential sources of evidence required for designing and implementing AE payment schemes in OECD countries, and examples could be given. However, due to the diversity of data collection systems, farming and environmental problems, it would be rather difficult to specify the data sets required, or to comment on their availability or suitability.

1.5 Design and targeting

Designing for long-term environmental impact

It is rare that any AE policy is backed by sufficient resources to meet all its objectives across the whole territory for an indefinite period of time. Policy design has to take account of the time scale required for environmental management to take effect, as well as the need to encourage long-term provision of environmental benefits, and changes in farmers' attitudes beyond the duration of a particular payment scheme. This will have an impact on the duration of AE contracts, which may be as short as one year or as long as twenty years.

Targeting agri-environmental interventions helps to optimise cost-effectiveness and environmental efficiency by focusing resources and effort on the problems, opportunities and areas where the environmental objectives and targets are most likely to be achieved.

Depending on the nature of the AE policy a range of different targeting approaches may be required. Broadly speaking there are three types:

- targeting specific environmental objectives or features to be *protected or managed through the scheme;*
- spatial targeting, relating to the *geographical extent and zones* in which schemes are to be implemented; and
- structural targeting, relating to specific *farm types* to be covered.

Prerequisites for targeting are a clearly defined policy framework with a hierarchy of objectives, and the availability and accuracy of a suitable evidence base.

Targeting environmental objectives

Targeting environmental objectives refers to the process of refining the operational objectives into specific performance objectives at farm level to be attained by regulation, taxes or payments. This has largely been covered in the discussion of the hierarchy of objectives and will not be discussed in further detail here, apart from noting that both spatial and structural targeting rely on well defined and clearly targeted performance objectives. Regulations, taxes and horizontal AE payment schemes, which apply across the whole territory, may have little if any spatial or structural targeting and may be entirely targeted at performance objectives.

Spatial targeting

Spatial targeting is mainly concerned with focusing resources (especially funding and staff time) into a defined geographical area to deal with specific environmental issues (Vojtech, 2010; Allen and Reid, 2005). As resources become increasingly limited within national budgets, it may not be feasible to meet or attempt to meet all scheme objectives equally across a territory (Allen, 2007). The target area may already be defined by national or other designations (as in the case of Nitrate Vulnerable Zones in the European Union where there is a high risk of nitrate pollution from agriculture, or the Natura 2000 network of protected habitats) or target areas may be defined by locally specific environmental criteria (as in the case of water-dependent ecosystems in the Murray-Darling Basin in Australia).

The application of resources to geographically defined areas is a defining feature of zonal AE payment schemes, which can be closely tailored to local conditions and particularly suited to more demanding and complex land management activities involving greater restrictions on farm management. For example, the Higher Level tier of the Environmental Stewardship agri-environment scheme in England target areas where specific environmental objectives have been defined using a combination of existing designations, known locations of features, administrative boundaries and expert advice. Farmers within these target areas are actively approached and encouraged to apply for the scheme.

Defining target areas may not be a straightforward process, and spatial targeting often requires additional administrative effort to implement the scheme. When target areas are geographically rather than administratively based, data availability or compatibility may be limited due to lack of coherence between environmentally defined areas and administrative boundaries. For example, the latter may follow mountain ridges or main rivers, dividing large-scale habitats and catchments. Another difficulty in defining target areas is reaching a consensus amongst stakeholders. The early involvement of stakeholders in the design process, and the management of their expectations, is an important consideration.

Spatially targeted schemes can cause frustration among farmers outside the target area, especially where the border is not based on immediately obvious geographical differences, who may feel they are being denied an opportunity to participate (IEEP, 2002). On the other hand, where regulations or taxes are zonally targeted, it may be the farmers within the target area who feel that their land management is being unfairly restricted. Hence, the early involvement of stakeholders in the design process and the management of their expectations are important considerations.

Structural targeting

It may be necessary to target different farming sectors, types of farm or tenure systems in order to address the main drivers (economic, environmental and social) of scheme uptake. Farm businesses from different sectors vary markedly in their profitability and motivation, and may have quite different attitudes to AE payments depending on the perceived impact on farm management and farm income. For example, it may be appropriate to target payments at small economically marginal livestock farms, where a high proportion of the farm is semi-natural grazing that provides high levels of environmental benefits (such as in the Iberian Peninsula) and where AE payments may help to maintain both environmental benefits and farm income.

Regulations often apply to all farmers in an administrative region but compliance efforts may have to be structurally targeted, especially when the regulations are first introduced. For example, small and medium-sized dairy farms may cause proportionally more water pollution problems than their larger counterparts, simply because they have lacked the resources to invest in appropriate manure storage facilities. Similarly, large profitable arable farms may be a more appropriate target for payments to manage a proportion of their productive land for wildlife, because economies of scale apply to both the habitat provision and the impact on total farm income.

Appropriate scale of the intervention

The effectiveness of AE payment schemes often relies on the participation of many farmers within a given area, each contributing a small component towards a larger objective. This may involve management at catchment scale for soil and water protection, at landscape scale for the maintenance of cultural landscapes with small, mixed farming systems, or at habitat scale for the management of large scale open habitats as feeding and breeding grounds for raptors or the provision of habitat networks across farmland. In some cases, single contracts with a group of farmers may be the only option for achieving the objective; for example, this may be needed in the case of common land where many farmers have user rights only, often for grazing, but neither own nor rent the land. More often it will be desirable to bring multiple, and preferably contiguous, farms into AE payment schemes to achieve impacts at the desired scale. Although this is far from easy when participation is voluntary, some OECD countries have already used different methods of encouraging collective action.

For years, farmers have recognised the benefits of marketing co-operatives. Co-operatives can also be used to organise collective participation in AE schemes using a variety of structures, as illustrated by Dutch environmental co-operatives (Franks and McGloin, 2006). As environmental co-operatives have moved beyond being simply groupings of farmers with a shared commercial interest to engaging a much wider community of stakeholders, they have become more similar to the Landcare groups that developed from the initial Landcare movement of 1986 in Victoria. This movement built strongly on voluntary participation to improve soil management and environmental stewardship (Hodge and Reader, 2007).

Co-operative implementation of this kind could be applied not just to AE payments for land management but also to payments for providing agri-environmental training, advice and information.

Costs and benefits of targeting

The voluntary nature of many AE policy mechanisms means that their effectiveness depends largely on farmer participation. Ensuring that the land management options are attractive enough to be taken up at a sufficient scale is critical to scheme success. The way AE policy mechanisms achieve targeting is a complex and resource intensive exercise both for the administrative body and the farmers implementing the scheme. Complexity, transaction costs, and administrative capacity are therefore important elements to consider throughout the design and implementation of targeted AE policies.

The benefits of successful targeting are improved achievement of environmental impacts, both in scale and intensity, as well as greater efficiency and effectiveness. A concentration of effort can have specific benefits, including the potential for a positive impact on farmers' attitudes, when a large proportion of farmers within an area or a group of specialist producers participate.

Feasibility of providing guidelines on targeting

General guidelines could be provided on the principles and types of targeting used in AE policies, the positive range of targets and the potential benefits, illustrated by specific examples.

Guidelines, accompanied by examples, could be provided for OECD countries on the types and principles of targeting involving agri-environmental interventions, the possible range of targets to be considered and the potential benefits for achievement of policy objectives.

1.6 Implementation and ensuring compliance

Implementing an effective and efficient agri-environment payment scheme is not a simple task. The details of implementation will depend on many local factors and circumstances but some key elements of the process will be common to most situations. There are valuable lessons that have been learned in practice, both from countries such as the United States, where a range of models have been applied, and Europe, where there is experience of implementing an essentially similar model adapted to circumstances as different as those of Germany and Bulgaria.

Administration

It is beyond the scope of this analysis to consider all the different administrative structures and processes required to implement regulations, taxes and payment schemes. Here we cover only the main components of the processes required to administer AE payment schemes.

The administrative processes required for implementation can be grouped into three main functions:

- inviting applications from farmers, selection of successful applicants, setting up and servicing long term contracts;
- payment and compliance monitoring; and
- evaluation of effectiveness (environmental and financial) and review of scheme design.

The first two functions often are separated administratively for reasons of financial accountability, being allocated either to different organisations (in the European Union, typically a government agricultural department and a separate payment agency that handles all government payments to farmers), or to two separate departments of the same organisation. The aim is to ensure the absence of any link between staff setting up and servicing contracts with farmers and staff dealing with payments. This is a sound general principle.

Managing large numbers of agri-environmental contracts will usually require databases designed for the purpose. The case of map-based information was already mentioned in Section 1.1 in the context of data coherence. It is equally important for implementation and management. Reliable and consistent mapping systems at farm level are important both for defining the terms of the contract with the farmer, and monitoring uptake and effectiveness of targeting. The scale of spatial specificity will, at a minimum, be the farm boundary but more often will need to be individual parcels or precise locations within parcels (for example, to identify where buffer strips should be placed to control diffuse pollution or to locate important habitats that need protecting). This means that most contracts should be accompanied by maps, or at least detailed reference to specific parcels of land. However, the data held by agriculture departments rarely shows environmental features in sufficient detail, if at all. Another common and time-consuming problem, often not apparent until implementation is underway, is the existence of discrepancies between a farmer's records, government records and actual measurements on the ground defining the size and precise location of land parcels within the farm. Ideally, these discrepancies should be resolved before the contract is set up, to provide an accurate baseline against which payments can be made and compliance assessed. Many countries now use GIS based mapping systems, which are particularly useful if mobile IT equipment allows them to be taken onsite and shown to the farmer.

Training, advice and information

The role of training, advice and information is to ensure efficient and environmentally effective implementation of agri-environment payment schemes. It is easy to underestimate the need for training and advice, particularly when the scheme is being implemented by agricultural authorities already in contact with the target population of farmers. However, both the implementing authorities and the target farmers need to recognise that agri-environment payments are a completely different concept from more familiar agricultural support policies. Farmers may initially find it difficult to accommodate the shift in focus from production to environmental objectives. In some circumstances, the management required may not only be unfamiliar but also viewed as contrary to their perception of "good farming", especially if it involves new techniques or less intensive farming practices that are perceived as old-fashioned or inefficient. This barrier needs to be overcome, not only in the minds of farmers but most importantly in the attitudes and knowledge of their agricultural advisers, and of the staff administering and monitoring the scheme. Cultural acceptance of environmental management by the farming community has a significant influence on uptake. Ensuring that farmers understand why they are being asked to change their management and what outcomes are sought requires considerable proactive advisory, information and training effort. This is especially important at the start of a programme but should continue throughout, addressing the needs of each new intake of farmers. Farmers need to be confident that measures have been assessed, are technically proficient and are applicable to them.

The value of pilot schemes

Testing the design and implementation of AE policy mechanisms through pilot schemes is valuable for refining the policy and identifying potential problems, particularly for voluntary AE payment schemes. Pilot schemes take time and resources, but they help to avoid potentially expensive long-term problems, and to improve efficiency and cost-effectiveness. They also familiarise staff and farmers with the new policy, giving them and other stakeholders an opportunity to provide feedback in order to refine the final design. Pilot schemes normally operate for a year in several different areas selected to provide a representative range of farm types, environmental objectives and administrative structures. The example of Bulgaria's experience illustrates the potential value of using pilot schemes (Box 1.4).

Box 1.4. Bulgaria's experience of developing an agri-environmental pilot measure

Valuable lessons were learnt about capacity building, in both institutions and the farming community, as Bulgaria prepared its first agri-environment scheme in 1999.

- Farmers were very keen to "try" the agri-environment scheme, but the majority could only be expected to implement one agri-environment action (from a possible nine) because at the start of the programme the level of training and know-how among farmers, their advisers and the administrators was insufficient.
- There was good co-operation and partnerships were forged between government and NGOs for the development of pilot projects, but also a lack of specific experience in the process of implementation, monitoring, evaluation, etc.
- The late establishment of an agri-environment division in the Ministry of Agriculture meant that when the scheme was implemented most of the newly appointed experts lacked experience in agri-environment and needed time to adjust.
- Not enough resources were allocated for the targeted development of pilot projects.

Source: Based on Kazakova (2000).

Dealing with changing needs and circumstances

A significant degree of uncertainty about results is inevitable in agri-environment payment schemes, and the need to maintain the desired management over a period of many years makes it even more important that implementing agencies have some flexibility. Among the sources of uncertainty are the voluntary nature of farmer participation, and the fact that farmers' behaviour, even if they enter an agri-environment contract lasting many years, cannot always be predicted since it is influenced by many factors.

During the life of a scheme, therefore, the implementing authority will need to make adjustments to the scheme and to individual contracts, whilst ensuring rigour in the pursuit of environmental objectives, and transparency and accountability in the use of public funds. At the start of a contract, the management or outcomes required might need adjustment in order to fit the environmental opportunities of the farm; to some extent, this can be foreseen by offering several variants of a single management requirement. A classic example is where farmers are paid to delay mowing species-rich hay meadows so that the plants can set seed; the dates at which mowing starts will be significantly earlier for farms at low altitudes than for farms in the mountains, where the growing season begins later. Yet, despite such refinements, in some years extreme weather conditions will mean that details such as grazing regimes, and dates of sowing or harvesting of crops, will have to be altered for all farmers. Over the longer term, many participants will see changes in profitability of their main enterprises, size and structure of the farm, and availability of labour, all of which may require contractual changes or revision of payment rates whether at the level of the scheme as a whole or individual farm contracts.

Perhaps the most important success factor is the flexibility to alter the design of a scheme if it is not working, and to do this quickly in response to feedback from implementation staff, before the problem becomes a disincentive for farmers to participate.

Communication with farmers and stakeholders

The benefits of effective communication between the managing authority, other stakeholders and the farming community are obvious at the design stage and in the initial phases of implementation, when time and resources must be allowed for it. What is less well recognised, but equally important, is to maintain this communication as a two-way process for the life of the scheme. This provides opportunities for farmers to raise concerns and seek advice, improves management at farm level, and conveys the message that society is interested in how farmers are meeting these new environmental objectives – an important message when most farmers will enter an agri-environment contract for many years, but during that time their only contact with staff will be occasional visits from field inspectors looking for compliance failures.

Ensuring compliance

The success of intervention depends on farmers complying with the requirements. Compliance is normally encouraged by formal inspection and by the provision of advice and information to the wider farming community, farm advisers and individual farmers. The choice of methods for checking compliance, penalising failure and remedying consequential harm will vary, depending on the type of intervention and the specific environmental objectives, and on national cultures. Cost and synergies of agri-environmental inspections with other forms of farm inspection are important considerations. Identifying compliance failures may involve administrative checks (of written notifications, discharge permits, tax documents, livestock movements, dates of ploughing and harvesting), on-farm visual inspections of the location and the state of areas under environmental management (stocking rates, habitat condition), and off-farm sampling and scientific analysis (river samples tested for nitrates and prohibited pesticides, aerial photographs). The proportion of farmers checked by different methods will vary; it is generally higher at the start of a scheme (for example, in pilot schemes, 100% of participants are likely to have on-farm compliance checks). Subsequently, the sample selected may be much smaller and based partly or wholly on risk factors, which can be measured in various ways (for example, in relation to previous non-compliance or the magnitude of the environmental consequences of potential non-compliance).

Penalties may vary from written warnings and advice to partial or complete withdrawal of payments and cessation of payment contracts. In the case of breaches of regulations and tax requirements, financial penalties may be on a fixed scale, applied by judicial action and possibly including financial or land restitution (for example, restoration of protected habitats that have been drained or ploughed up). Publicity within the farming media of cases of compliance failure and the penalties applied is often used as a means of encouraging other farmers to improve their own compliance. This will only be effective if farmers perceive the risk of detection and consequential financial penalties to exceed the costs of compliance.

Feasibility of providing guidelines for the implementation process

Guidelines could be provided on the stages and processes of implementing AE payment schemes, which would be useful for most situations in the OECD, irrespective of the agricultural and environmental context. It may not be feasible to provide similar guidance on the implementation of regulatory and taxation instruments, because this would have to address the specific context in each country.

1.7 Policy evaluation

The main purpose of a monitoring and evaluation programme is to obtain information on the success or failure of a given policy in achieving its principal objectives (IEEP, 2002). This section of the report considers only the monitoring and evaluation of agri-environmental incentive policies, because they are rather distinctive. By contrast, the evaluation of regulatory measures in this sector raises fewer specific questions.

Monitoring and evaluation lies at the heart of AE policy, as shown in Figure 1.2.

Figure 1.2. The cycle of agri-environmental policy making

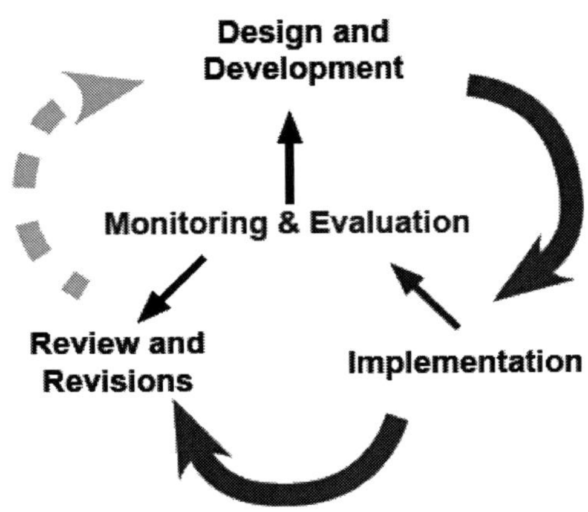

Source: Redman and Hemmami, 2008.

The monitoring component provides information on progress over time in programme implementation using indicators of financial inputs (payments committed), outputs (farms with agri-environmental contracts), results (as a minimum, the area of land under specific types of environmental management) and impacts (for example, changes in farmland bird populations, area of land subject to soil erosion).

The evaluation component provides in-depth analysis of the impact of measures against *quantified* performance objectives, using data from the monitoring process and other relevant sources of information (IEEP, 2001). Environmental impact evaluation needs to take account of:

- the time lag between changes in management and the measurable changes in environmental condition (often several years);
- varying baseline conditions at farm level, for example in water quality, or the state of semi-natural habitats and landscape features; and
- extraneous influences on the chosen indicators (for example, fluctuations in plant or animal populations caused by weather or disease).

Indicators are a useful evaluation tool for measuring progress, but only if they relate directly to clearly defined objectives. The Common Monitoring and Evaluation Framework of the European Union includes five main types of indicator:

- input indicators are commonly used to monitor progress in terms of the payment of the funds to farmers;

- output indicators monitor the uptake of specific measures (for example, number of new agri-environment contracts with farmers, number of hectares supported, etc.);
- result indicators relate to the direct and immediate effects of the measure on the management of the farm (for example, area of land receiving pesticides, area of land with a particular crop, number of newly planted trees, length of soil erosion barrier, etc.);
- impact indicators look beyond the immediate "results" at the long-term effects on the environment (for example, improvements in water quality); and
- baseline indicators are an important reference point for the evaluation of impacts of single measures and programmes as a whole.

Monitoring and evaluation programmes must be devised as part of the policy design (not afterwards), as shown in Figure 1.3, and should be conducted throughout the implementation process. It is important to design data systems that meet both administrative and monitoring requirements. The availability of AE payments to all farmers in an area means that it is not always possible to compare two sample populations of farms, one of which is implementing the policy and one which is not. It is therefore important to collect baseline data when farms enter the scheme and subsequent time series evaluation data for the same farms.

Figure 1.3. Position of monitoring and evaluation in development of AE schemes

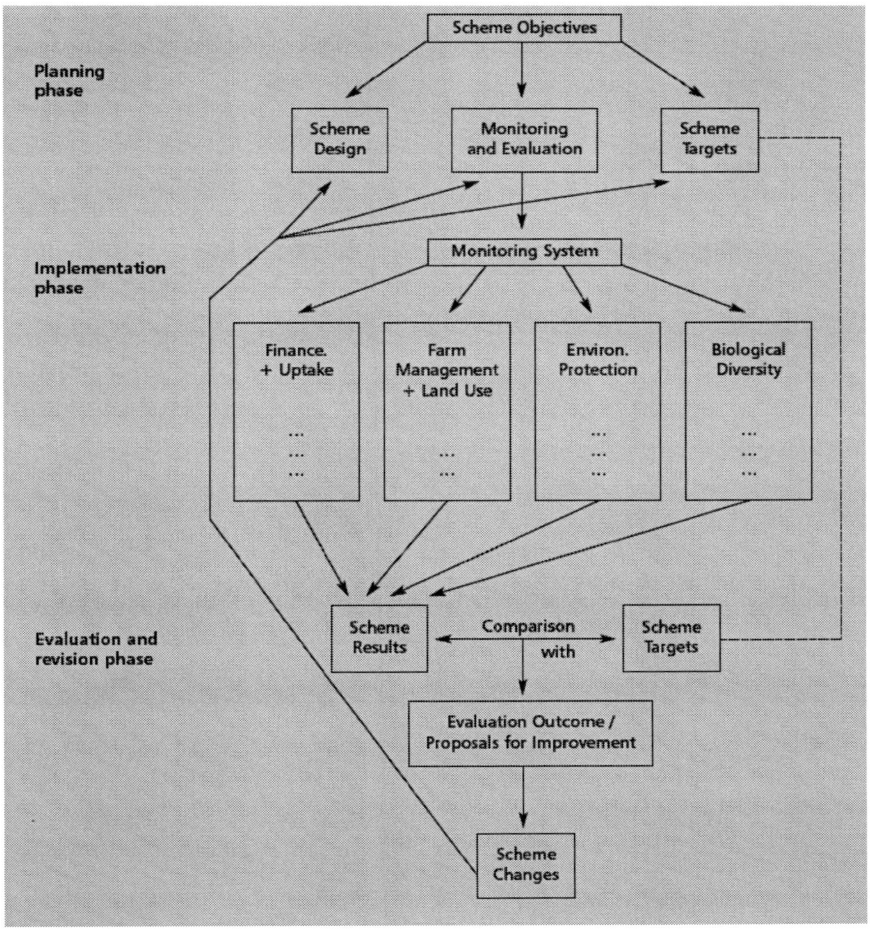

Source: IEEP (2002).

Monitoring and evaluation programmes should provide *ex ante* and *ex post* assessments of current and future policy mechanisms, and also guide policy adjustment in response to needs (for example, problems of uptake) that become apparent during implementation. Rational appraisal of agri-environmental policy requires a comparison of costs and benefits (Pearce, 2005), as well as a broad range of other criteria to assess the true value of the policy (Jones, 2005). These are likely to include socio-economic, agricultural and environmental aspects, and cover the relevance of objectives, effectiveness in contributing to the achievement of objectives, and efficiency in terms of the cost effectiveness of resource transmission into results and impacts. The monitoring methodologies and data systems should themselves be reviewed from time to time, as needs change and techniques improve.

1.8 Institutional capacity and budgeting

Agri-environmental regulations and taxation are likely to be administered by the relevant authorities, such as the central or regional government departments responsible for ensuring water quality, habitat protection and tax collection. AE payment schemes are normally but not necessarily administered by government agricultural authorities, centrally or regionally. Environmental agencies may be equally or more suited to the task, depending on circumstances.

Introducing new regulations or taxes is likely to involve increasing institutional capacity (staff, IT systems, sampling and laboratory services) and will certainly require staff training. In addition to these costs, resources will be required for making farmers aware of the requirements of the intervention and possibly for training farmers and farm workers for specialist tasks, like techniques for handling and disposing of agricultural pesticides. Resources will also be allocated to compliance monitoring and policy evaluation.

Similar increases in institutional capacity are needed to implement an AE payment scheme, as well as the budget resources to fund annual payments to farmers over many years (typically, there will be a new intake of farmers every year and individual contracts will last from 3-10 years). In the European Union, the two main administrative bodies required are a *managing authority* and *paying agency*. They have very distinct functions, and are usually established separately, sometimes by adding to the role of an existing agency (the paying agency, for example, may already be responsible for other types of payments to farmers). It is important that the lead organisation for implementing an agri-environment scheme has credibility with farmers, and that implementation is efficient and timely when schemes are first introduced, since any delays and problems with implementation (especially payment) tend to diminish farmers' goodwill, with potentially serious consequences for future uptake. Both agencies will have to cope with seasonal peaks in workload, because some essential field inspections can only be done during summer, and the annual application "window" for AE contracts is usually short, because farmers need a decision before they plant the next season's crops.

The managing authority is the lead organisation for developing and implementing the overall agri-environment programme, and should have sufficient administrative capacity, a well-developed regional/local network, and easy access to specialised expertise in other government agencies, technical and research institutions, and NGOs. The responsibilities of the managing authority in EU-funded payment schemes are defined in regulations[3].

The paying agency is specifically responsible for the administration and control of the agri-environment payments to farmers, including monitoring compliance, applying penalties and tracking and reporting on expenditure. Agri-environment payments will be a completely new function for most agencies, and existing administrative systems rarely have the spare capacity or skills needed. The paying agency will have to cope with the detail of agri-environment contracts, such as identifying small parcels of land or measuring vegetation and other features during compliance checks. Capacity building is likely to require new staff, equipment and skills to set up and use agri-environment recording systems (GIS and databases), process applications, set up contracts with farmers, carry out seasonal compliance visits, make payments and record information for monitoring.

Excellent co-ordination or liaison procedures are important for successful and coherent implementation of agri-environment schemes. Many different people and organisations are involved and it is vital that all understand not just 'what' needs to be done but also "why", "how", "when" and "where". Failure of communication not only slows progress down, but may allow other, unwanted messages to reach farmers. There will be frequent communications between the managing agency and the paying agency, especially in the early stages but it is important to communicate more widely too. Effective co-operation between the Ministries of Agriculture and Environment is desirable for all agri-environment schemes. The value of multi-stakeholder support for the development of agri-environment payment schemes has already been referred to in Section I.2, and this should continue during implementation. Feedback on the progress and acceptance of measures, as well as on possible administrative problems, is vitally important and can be gained through regular meetings of an agri-environment working group or consultative committees.

If they have no previous experience with agri-environment schemes, advisory and administrative staff have many of the same needs and problems as farmers in understanding the agri-environment concept and putting it into practice. They must, however, be fully trained, confident, and committed before the scheme is launched. It is particularly important that all front-line staff have credibility with farmers and can discuss whole farm management, not just agri-environmental. It is easy to underestimate the time and resources needed for initial and on-going training of the staff involved (and the importance of training the trainers, in a large scheme). Training programmes need to be developed well ahead of scheme implementation. Since considerable parts of the scheme may be region-specific, the capacity of staff and project officers at a regional and local level often needs strengthening most.

1.9 Conclusions on the feasibility of providing guidance

This analysis of the key stages in designing and implementing different types of agri-environmental interventions has shown that it is likely to be feasible to provide potentially useful guidance on many aspects of the process with relevance for most OECD countries. However, the scope and level of detail of this guidance would not be the same for all interventions or all stages of policy design and implementation. European examples have predominated in this chapter.

The processes of designing a policy framework, setting objectives, ensuring policy coherence and determining the reference level are expected to be common to many interventions in all OECD countries, and it should be possible to elaborate guidance on the underlying principles and processes involved for regulatory, taxation and payment schemes.

Similarly it should be feasible to provide guidance on the principles and processes of targeting, managing and evaluating AE payment schemes that would be useful in most situations in OECD countries, irrespective of the current structure of agricultural support payments (if any) and the priority environmental objectives adopted. Less specific, but nevertheless useful, guidance could also be given on the issues to be considered in building up institutional capacity to implement payment schemes. Similar guidance on regulatory and taxation interventions may also be feasible but has not been assessed in this chapter.

Given the diversity of circumstances and experience of AE policies in OECD countries and the many different potential audiences for a guidance document, it would be helpful to accompany guidelines with specific examples, illustrating how the principles are applied and illuminating the details of the design and implementation process.

Notes

1. Institute of European Environmental Policy (IEEP).
2. See *wales.gov.uk/topics/environmentcountryside/farmingandcountryside/farming/agrienvschemes/tirgofal/?lang=en.*
3. See Article 75 of Council Regulation (EC) No 1698/2005, which lists the specific functions of the managing authority for EU-funded agri-environmental incentive schemes, and underlines that the supreme responsibility for their management and implementation resides with the managing authority even "...when a part of its tasks is delegated to another body."

References

Allen, B.R. and C.M. Reid (2005), *Using spatial frameworks to target agri-environment schemes. The landscape ecology of sustainable landscapes*. Proceedings of the thirteenth annual IALE (UK) conference, 12–16 September 2005.

Allen, B.R. (2007), "Maximising the benefits to arable biodiversity from the effective targeting of agri-environment schemes", *Aspects of Applied Biology*, Vol. 81, Delivering Arable Biodiversity.

Bromley, D.W. and I. Hodge (1990), "Private property rights and presumptive policy entitlements: reconsidering the premises of rural policy", *European Review of Agricultural Economics,* Vol. 17, No. 2 pp. 197-214.

Cooper, T., K. Hart, and D. Baldock (2009), *The Provision of Public Goods Through Agriculture in the European Union*, Report Prepared for DG Agriculture and Rural Development, Contract No 30-CE-0233091/00-28, Institute for European Environmental Policy: London.

Franks, J.R. and A. McGloin (2006), *Co-operative Management of the Agricultural Environment,* Report 0009 for the Rural Economy and Land Use (RELU) Programme, University of Newcastle.

Hodge, I. and M. Reader (2007), *Maximising the provision of public goods from future agri-environment schemes,* Land Use Policy Group, Peterborough.

IEEP (2001), *Preparing for the Implementation of Agri-Environment Schemes in Central and Eastern Europe:* proceedings expert seminar, Bratislava, 8-9 December 2000, organised jointly by Avalon, Daphne Institute of Applied Ecology, Institute for European Environmental Policy.

IEEP (2002), *Developing agri-environmental programmes in Central and Eastern Europe - a manual.*

Jones, D. (2005), *Evaluating agri-environmental policy in the OECD in Evaluating agri-environmental policies: design practice and results,* OECD Publications, Paris.

Jones, G. (2008), "Small farms – major embarrassment or key to policy delivery?" *La Cañada,* N°22 Winter 200, European Forum on Nature Conservation and Pastoralism, *www.efncp.org.*

Kazakova, Y. (2000), *Implementation of agri-environmental schemes in Bulgaria* in IEEP (2001) *Preparing for the Implementation of Agri-Environment Schemes in Central and Eastern Europe*: proceedings expert seminar, Bratislava, 8-9 December 2000, organised jointly by Avalon, Daphne Institute of Applied Ecology, Institute for European Environmental Policy.

OECD (1998), *Agriculture and the environment: issues and policies,* OECD Publications, Paris.

OECD (2009), *Environmental Performance Reviews 2nd cycle*, set of the conclusions and recommendations approved by the OECD Working Party on Environmental Performance Reviews (2001-2009).

OECD (2010), *Guidelines for Cost-effective Agri-environmental Policy Measures*, OECD Publishing, Paris.

Pearce, D. (2005), "What constitutes a good agri-environmental policy evaluation?" in OECD (2005) *Evaluating agri-environmental policies: design, practice and results,* OECD Publications, Paris.

Redman, M. and M. Hemmami (2008), *Developing a National Agri-environment Programme for Turkey*, IEEP, London; Buğday Association for Supporting Ecological Living, İstanbul, Turkey

Scheele, M. (1999), *Environmental services provided by agriculture: the setting of environmental targets and reference levels,* Conference Paper, "Non-Trade Concerns in a Multifunctional Agriculture", Gran, Norway.

Vojtech, V. (2010), "Policy measures addressing agri-environmental issues", *OECD Food, Agriculture and Fisheries Working Papers*, No.24, OECD, Paris.

Chapter 2

Evaluating policies for delivering agri-environmental public goods

Alison Burrell[1]

This chapter provides a conceptual framework for discussing methodological and practical issues arising in the context of evaluating policies for delivering agri-environmental public goods. It distinguishes three stylised types of evaluation – the "administrative", "scientific" and "economic" approaches – each of which provides a different kind of information in a different time-frame. The scope for each approach to perform its role more efficiently and usefully is explored, as well as the underlying difficulties and constraints.

Over the last two decades, policies for stimulating the provision of environmental public goods in rural areas have claimed a growing share of government money allocated to agriculture in OECD countries. In parallel with this trend, there has been a sharp rise in the number of formal evaluations of these policies commissioned by administrations, often within a legally defined timetable that stipulates regular policy appraisals.[2] At the same time, the number of more *ad hoc* policy evaluations conducted by academics and NGOs has also increased markedly. Given this existing body of work and much on-going effort, it is a good moment to examine and compare the approaches taken to evaluating agri-environmental policies in different contexts and countries, and to explore in more depth the evaluation issues that arise specifically in the case of agri-environmental policy.

This chapter aims to provide a conceptual framework for such a discussion. It begins by restating the formal definition of a public good and discussing how it has been applied to the agricultural sector in developed countries. The definition of an agri-environmental public good used in this chapter is also given.

The perspective taken here for discussing the main methodological and analytical challenges arising when evaluating agri-environmental policies is a comparative one. However, instead of comparing evaluation methods between countries or types of intervention, it contrasts three stylised types of evaluation activity – what I call the administrative, the scientific and the economic approaches to evaluation. Each has its role and purpose, and each gives rise to specific methodological problems. The idea is not to establish a hierarchy among these three approaches, but to explore how each of them might perform its role more efficiently and usefully. Concluding remarks are intended to stimulate discussion on future improvement strategies.

2.1 Definition of a public good and implications for its provision in a private market

A public good has the following characteristics: it is non-rival[3] and non-excludable,[4] and is valued by individuals and hence by "society." For some public goods, the presence of the first two properties may depend on the context of their provision and use. For example, the property of non-rivalness is lost when the good is so heavily consumed that congestion or over-use begin to reduce its availability to others. Some public goods can be made excludable albeit at a very high cost.

A public good will not be provided by an individual for his own private use unless his private benefit from consuming the good exceeds the cost to him of providing it. Many of the "classic" public goods involve massive infrastructure and prohibitive operational costs. Examples are a national highway system or a television network. Although the public good services they offer are valued by each of us as individuals, no single individual can provide them for himself. And if he were able to do so, their non-excludability would create a multitude of free-riders who would also benefit from them without sharing the cost. Goods with these characteristics, sometimes also called "collective goods," are typically funded by government out of tax revenue and provided free of charge, or at minimal cost, at the point of use.

An alternative method of collective provision for smaller-scale public goods occurs when a number of individuals agree among themselves to finance the provision of goods or services with public-good characteristics for the exclusive use of the group as a whole. Such an arrangement implies that excludability *vis-à-vis* non-members of the group can be enforced. Goods provided in this way are called "club goods" and are often cited to demonstrate that reliance on government for public good provision is not always necessary.

As well as these stand-alone public goods, which are not provided at all without a collective decision to do so, public goods may also occur as positive externalities of other economic activities, where their provision is a *by-product* of the decision to produce a private good. In this case, the public good will be produced without anyone having taken the decision to produce it or having to pay for its provision. However, it will be provided in quantities that are sub-optimal from the social point of view, since the benefit of the externality that is enjoyed free of charge by others is not taken into account by the economic decision-maker when deciding how much of the private good to produce. Table 2.1 summarises these two cases.

Table 2.1. Comparison of private and optimal provision of a public good

Type of public good	Fully separable (stand-alone) public good *i*	Public good *i* occurring as a positive externality linked to production of good *j*
Market result without government intervention	Good *i* is not produced as a private good at all unless $PB^i \geq PC^i$	Good *i* is produced as long as $PB^j \geq PC^j$, but at a socially sub-optimal level
Socially optimal result (*in theory* achievable by intervention)	Provision as a collective good is socially optimal as long as $\Sigma_k PB^i_k \geq PC^i$	Socially optimal level of provision occurs when $PB^j + \Sigma_k PB^i_k = PC^j$

Notes:

PB= private benefit, PC= private cost.

It is assumed that K individuals (*k*=1,…,K) derive individual benefit from the public good. In both cases, the condition for socially optimal provision balances the social benefit (i.e. the sum of the benefit of all individuals) against the cost of provision.

The condition for the stand-alone public good assumes that it is of a fixed size, and compares total social benefit with total cost of provision.

The condition for determining the optimal provision of the public-good externality (and hence also of the provision of the private good j) should be interpreted as a *marginal* condition: provision should be expanded up to the point where the *marginal* social benefit (which is the marginal private benefit to the producer of producing j + the sum of the marginal benefits derived by third parties from externality i) equals the *marginal* cost of producing the private good j.

2.2 Public goods in agriculture

It has been known for generations that agriculture produces public goods. Nineteenth century poets extolled the countryside as a place for peaceful reflection and restoration of the soul. For decades, a favourite textbook example of a reciprocal positive externality has been an agricultural one: that of the beekeeper whose bees pollinate (free of charge) the fruit trees of the neighbouring fruit grower, whilst the fruit grower's orchard provides (also free of charge) the nectar needed for the production of honey. The value of the benefit of the externality conferred is not taken into account in the decision-making of either the honey producer or fruit grower, but the benefit of the externality received is crucial for the viability of both private production activities.

At the end of the 1990s, the policy debate surrounding the multifunctionality of agriculture gave prominence to the idea of public goods as positive externalities of agricultural commodity production. The proposition was that the existence of these socially valued but non-remunerated joint products of agricultural production activity justified supporting the price of farm outputs above the minimum cost of getting them onto the market (whether from domestic or imported production), and that to reduce this support would – by precipitating a decline in agricultural commodity production – also reduce the provision of the valued public goods. Conversely, if society wished to have more of these positive externalities, the rate of support to commodity production should be increased. This view makes sense only if the public good externalities are joint, non-separable outputs with agricultural commodities such that a subsidy for commodity output results in both more output and more public good.

The multifunctionalists' position in favour of farm price support was progressively abandoned for two reasons. *First,* it turned out that there are actually very few examples of positive externalities whose production is technically interdependent with that of agricultural commodities. In fact, it is much easier to demonstrate jointness between commodity production and negative externalities.[5] For example, at current production levels in developed countries, an increase in commodity output is far more likely to result in more nitrate pollution and soil erosion than in more biodiversity.[6] *Second,* market price support is a subsidy coupled to production, and hence it is in the WTO amber box of restricted-use measures. It was not likely that other WTO members would agree to make an exception for market price support purporting to remunerate the provision of public good externalities.

These two reasons largely explain the move away from seeing agricultural public goods as externalities of commodity production. In fact, the same reasons underpin the idea, already operational in the agri-environmental measures adopted in some OECD countries in the early 1990s, of treating agriculture's public goods as separable "stand-alone" outputs whose provision can be directly stimulated by targeted policies. The absence of technical interdependence between agricultural public goods and commodity production allows policy interventions to encourage public good provision but *without* creating incentives to increase commodity production. This offers scope for agri-environmental measures that will not be contested as trade-distorting.

There has been much discussion about what exactly qualifies as an agricultural public good.[7] On the short list are items such as wildlife conservation and biodiversity (including preservation of rare of farm animal breeds), maintenance of landscape quality and character, protection of natural resources (soil, water and air quality), flood control and carbon storage. All these items can uncontroversially be characterised as public goods and all of them are associated with benefits to the rural environment. More debate on what counts as an agricultural public good has surrounded various items on the long list, such as the maintenance of rural populations and rural economic activity, national food security and animal welfare. Since these more controversial items fall outside the focus of this chapter anyway (they are not *environmental* public goods), it is not necessary to rehearse the debate here. Rather, we state explicitly the definition of agriculture's environmental public goods adopted in this chapter.

The agri-environmental public goods that are targeted by the policies whose evaluation is the subject of this chapter are non-rival, non-excludable outputs or services that are valued by society and whose provision enhances and preserves the natural rural environment, local ecosystems and the natural resource base linked to farming. Yet, precisely because of their non-rivalness and non-excludability, and despite society's positive willingness to pay for them, *markets do not exist* for them. A further important defining characteristic for the purposes of this chapter is that their supply can be increased through the actions of farmers – that is, farmers typically have both the *property rights* over the use of the resources needed to supply these agri-environmental public goods and the *requisite skills* for managing their provision alongside their farming activity.

Although this definition covers the quite heterogeneous short list of public goods presented above, it is nevertheless quite narrow. For example, it rules out what might be seen more as *consequences* of farming activity (such as keeping population in rural areas or contributing to national food security), which do not depend on the actions – other than producing food – of any single farmer, but rather on the total amount of farming activity taking place or the number of farmers engaged in it. Under the definition used here, the provision of public goods depends on decisions taken by individual farmers to do things over and above simply producing food, or to produce food in a certain way.

2.3 Policies for delivering agri-environmental public goods

Interventions that aim to improve the environmental footprint of farming can be classified according to the mechanism used, and by whether they merely ensure the basic environmental standards expected by society or encourage farmers to go beyond those standards.

Regulations that prescribe minimum levels of environmental performance or ban certain environmentally harmful practices, and that apply to all farmers, set the parameters for the basic standard of environmental preservation that society expects as a norm. In the following discussion, these measures will be treated as part of the counterfactual against which the impact of policies for delivering environmental public goods should be measured. Regulatory norms stand apart from the other types of intervention identified below in that no public money is devoted to incentivising farmers to adopt or comply with them. Instead, compliance is achieved by the threat of legal sanctions, in the spirit of the polluter pays principle. Therefore, they are not included among the policies whose evaluation methodology is examined in this chapter. This does not mean that the environmental effectiveness of these regulations should not be monitored on a regular basis.

Cross compliance measures require farmers to refrain from or to adopt particular farming practices, for the most part motivated by environmental considerations, as a condition of their receipt of income support payments. Debate has raged in the past over how best to describe these payments. Are they really incentive payments targeting environmental benefits, to which farmers respond or not depending on whether they wish to make more room for public good provision in their farming activities? Or does the main objective of these payments remain farm income support that is *also*, and almost incidentally, used to obtain some leverage over the choice of farming methods and bring producers up to a common level of good agricultural practice?

Fortunately, this issue does not have to be settled here. What seems clear is that cross compliance requirements cannot be considered as part of the benchmark defining the minimum environmental performance level expected from all farmers by society. This is because, *first*, the payment system to which cross compliance is attached does not always apply to all farmers or farming activities, and *second*, there is the (theoretical) possibility that eligible farmers can opt out of the payment system and thus avoid compliance. However, for farmers within a cross compliance scheme, these requirements have to be considered as part of the counterfactual against which *additional* incentive measures for further enhancing environmental performance should be measured.

Agri-environmental payment schemes are measures designed to target the provision of agricultural public goods beyond the level defined by the regulatory benchmark norms and cross compliance requirements. Generally, these publicly funded schemes are voluntary for farmers and involve them responding to an incentive payment by opting into a contract of some years' duration. For compliance with the WTO definition of a green box measure, the payment should be set at a level that merely compensates the farmer for extra costs incurred, including income foregone. In practice, the payment might be determined according to the real costs on each farm, the estimated cost on the "average" farm, or (quite rarely[8]) the expected environmental benefit. Each of these options has implications for the amount of farm-specific information needed in order to set up the contract, as well as for the profile of the typical farmer-volunteer – that is, whether volunteers tend to be those whose participation would secure the greatest environmental benefits or those whose opportunity cost of participation would be lowest. There is a risk that poor uptake of the measure results in a low density of coverage, which can reduce the overall environmental impact) if the payment is set too low.

Schemes for creating markets in environmental externalities are initiatives that follow the general cap-and-trade principle. Examples are water quality trading schemes[9] (found in the United States, and also in Australia, Canada and New Zealand), and the scheme for trading "mineral rights" (effectively, nitrogen and phosphorous surpluses or deficits relative to an allowable farm-level surplus) that has operated for over a decade in the Netherlands.[10] It is the collective "cap" and its binding allocation to individuals that provides the environmental benefit. However, the trade allows the total economic cost of applying the cap to the polluting economic activities to be minimised, or in other words permits a given environmental benefit to be achieved at the lowest cost to the polluting industries. Government participation in these programmes may involve putting in place the overall regulatory framework required for imposing the cap. Typically, some financial assistance in setting up the trading scheme is needed, and maybe on-going assistance with running costs. How to evaluate such interventions is not explicitly discussed in this chapter. However, these programmes should also be regularly evaluated. Clearly, many of the issues touched on in this chapter are relevant to their evaluation as well.

2.4 Definitions of terms

Since markets do not exist for public goods, they have no observable price. Hence, their value in money terms has to be estimated. But the *valuation of a public good* is only one element of the *evaluation of a policy* designed to deliver it, and one that is often not performed in practice. Policy evaluation assesses a sequence of changes and their consequences occurring in different dimensions, at different points in time, and at different degrees of "remoteness" from the initial policy stimulus, in order to establish what effect it has had.

The discussion of this sequence below adopts the terminology used by the European Commission's framework for evaluating rural development policies (CMEF).[11] Other evaluation approaches adopt analogous classifications, but the terminology may differ.

The consequences of the policy intervention can be classified as:

- *outputs* (actions financed and accomplished with the money allocated to the intervention) (e.g. number of enrolled participants, number of farm visits);
- *results* (direct consequences for programme participants) (e.g. changes in farm practices, environmentally friendly on-farm investment, farmers' participation in training); and
- *impacts* (longer-lasting effects of the intervention with direct or indirect relevance to the programme's long-term objectives and their attainment) (e.g. improved water quality, reappearance of skylarks in arable areas).

This classification can be used in the context of both *ex ante* and *ex post* evaluation, although most of the discussion in this chapter relates to *ex post* evaluation.

Ex post evaluation involves evidence-based judgements and recommendations. A major task of the evaluator is therefore to assemble the available evidence on the consequences of the policy. The selection of relevant evidence should be guided by a conceptual "model" of the various causal pathways through which the intervention is expected to operate, the key links in the expected chain of effects and the outcomes expected. This conceptual roadmap (the *intervention logic*) is implicit in the design of the policy and would have already been elaborated and tested for internal consistency during an *ex ante* evaluation of the intervention.

Its role *ex post* is to guide the evaluator in his choice of what evidence to review and what criteria to use for assessing the success of the programme.

2.5 Three stylised approaches to evaluation

The large and growing volume of evaluation studies can be classified into three main categories according to why and by/for whom the evaluation is performed, which in turn tends to determine the approach taken, the type of information provided and the challenges faced. This classification is presented in Table 2.2.

Table 2.2. Three evaluation stereotypes, according to methodological approach

	Type of evaluation		
	Administrative	**Scientific**	**Economic**
Purpose	• account for the use of public money • verify that the targets as specified by the policy objectives were achieved • streamline the delivery of policy	• improve understanding of natural systems and causal mechanisms • provide advice on instrument choice and ways of improving the impact of policy mechanisms	• examine social justification of policies • analyse behavioural responses to policies • advise on improving overall policy design (including incentives, value for money)
Timing	Short term (1-4 years after the start of the policy)	Longer term (five or more years after the start of the policy)	Ideally, requires input from a scientific evaluation, so >5 years, but pressure to provide full economic evaluations more rapidly
Focus	• monitoring of outputs, results • ideally would also assess impacts, but often not feasible given time-frame	• existence and magnitude of impacts • causality between policy and impacts observed	• social value of impacts and their relationship to full social cost • conclusions depend on prior confirmation of causality
Approach	• use of indicators measuring changes in key variables over the evaluation period	• detailed measurement of environmental changes • scientifically rigorous attempts to establish causality	• various approaches to valuing environmental benefits • cost-benefit analysis • simpler methods for comparing costs and benefits
Issues and challenges	• need to collect baseline data before the policy is implemented • additionality • time horizon may be too short to verify desired impacts • can results be good predictors of impacts?	• availability of baseline data, research design • high resource cost of field data collection • what is the counterfactual/ control? • uncertain dynamics in the causal chain • scaling up from surveys to whole population, from individual farms to region	• valuation of benefits in money terms • importance of measuring policy transaction costs • need to identify and value unintended consequences • need to assume time horizon for future cost and benefit flows • choice of method for comparing costs and benefits

Three stylised groups of stakeholders/practitioners are also involved.

Administrators and officials of public bodies directly responsible for a policy need fairly rapid feedback on its progress so as to correct mistakes at an early stage. They also need information on its first-round results in order to accommodate the relatively short time-horizon of the political process. Their needs are closely driven by their institutional setting.

Scientists (ecologists, environmentalists, biologists, water scientists, landscape ecologists and so on) are interested in uncovering the dynamics of the natural processes that the intervention is intended to affect, and the causal links between policy and outcome. An environmental policy intervention can be seen as an experiment that provides an excellent opportunity for them to gain scientific knowledge about underlying relationships in the natural world, and about the speed and sensitivity of responses inherent in these relationships. At the same time, the information they acquire through this investigation is extremely valuable for improving the policies themselves at a later stage. Given the biological lags involved and the slow cumulative nature of some of the responses expected to agri-environmental interventions, it may be impossible to evaluate the full impact until an appropriate number of years have elapsed since the start of the policy. Of course, this time-frame does not fit well with the needs and the timetable of the administrators.

Finally, *economists* explore the social justification for a policy by examining the trade-off between its benefits and costs in a society-wide context. The validity of any conclusion they can draw depends on the prior confirmation of causality. That is, it only makes sense to compare benefits with programme costs if those benefits have indeed been produced by the policy intervention. As well as the expected direct and indirect consequences of the policy, the economist must also value in money terms any unintended side-effects. An 'economic' evaluation needs input from both the other types of evaluation in Table 2. When done rigorously, a full economic of evaluation involves the longest delay with respect to the start of the policy. Unfortunately, this does not shield economists from pressures to evaluate policies far more rapidly.

While waiting for the scientific evidence on whether environmental benefits have been achieved, economists often study society's willingness-to-pay (WTP) for the expected environmental benefits *on the hypothesis* that these benefits are indeed produced. It is reassuring for the administrators if WTP turns out to be greater than what has been allocated or spent from public funds. But, until impacts are verified, this is hardly more than an *ex ante* evaluation, and is certainly not a substitute for an evidence-based appraisal of whether the policy actually changed anything in the real world.

Inevitably, the various practitioners and users of these different approaches to agri-environmental evaluations do not always share each other's point of view or fully appreciate each other's priorities. The delay that is usually necessary for a rigorous scientific or economic evaluation is too long for the administrator's timetable. Scientists and economists may be dismissive of some of the cruder assumptions made in a more rapid evaluation conducted for administrative purposes, failing to realise that maintaining the momentum of the policy process is essential to change, and that policy-making routinely involves more uncertainty and a higher margin of error than scientific research.

However, despite such differences, these groups tend to share some common goals. Moreover, within *each* of the three stereotypic evaluation approaches shown in Table 2.2, there are currently a number of issues and areas where issues still have to be resolved and challenges have not yet been met. The following sections look at the most important of these challenges for each type of evaluation.

2.6 Current challenges and issues

"Administrative" evaluation

The main constraint faced by the administrative evaluation is its limited time-frame[12]. This poses several problems for the evaluation of agri-environmental schemes. *First*, it affects the type of data that can be used. Berriet-Solliec *et al.* (2011) point out the hierarchical nature of different types of data, in terms of reliability and quality, which they consider begins at the lowest level with opinion surveys (where the respondents may be participants, experts or official authorities), followed by historical or geographical comparisons, and several levels higher, culminates in the results of randomised trials. It seems inevitable that the sooner the evaluation is performed, the lower the availability of "high reliability" data.

Second, many of the environmental benefits targeted require a number of years to emerge. For example, targeted increases in bird populations are reported from various studies in the United Kingdom for periods taking 7-10 years, whereas water and soil quality improvements resulting from policy interventions may need some decades (Boatman *et al.*, 2008). Kleijn (2006) refers to evidence that "on intensively used farmland, the restoration of species-rich communities following the re-instatement of more extensive management may take considerably longer than six years." These long time lags mean that administrative evaluations have to rely extensively on indicators that capture outputs and results, since evidence of longer-term environmental benefits tends to fall outside the time-frame.

The important issue of additionality[13] arises in the outputs-results segment of the chain of linked effects leading from outputs to impacts. It has a major bearing on the cost effectiveness of the programme: when additionality is low, then a large part of the payment costs was not necessary to achieve the results. Such a finding cannot be neutralised or offset by subsequent information on impacts. Even when the links in the next stage of the causal sequence – those between results and longer-term benefits – are verified, they cannot be attributed to the policy if the changes in land use choices, farm practices, attitudes and so on that led to the increase in benefits would have happened in any case without the policy stimulus.

In their survey of over 200 evaluation studies, Boatman *et al.* (2008) report various estimates of additionality where the source of evidence is mainly farmer (participant) interviews or geographic comparisons. The rates of measured additionality vary enormously between projects. It is interesting to note that farmer interviews produced estimates of both high and low additionality, suggesting that this source of evidence on additionality does not necessarily yield biased results. More generally, uncertainty regarding additionality is just one problem caused by the lack of a counterfactual scenario showing what would have happened in the absence of the policy (this is discussed further below).

The "administrative" evaluation relies on evidence supplied in the form of indicators measuring the current situation of the variables targeted in terms of results and possibly also impacts, and their changes since the start of the policy. Oñate *et al.* (2000) define three key operational attributes for agri-environmental indicators: *reliability* (extent of scientific support for the relationship between the indicator variable and the targeted environmental benefit), *relevance* (degree of pertinence of the indicator variable and its associated benefit to the policy goal), and "*realisability*" (data availability).In general, the extent to which the indicators available to evaluators fulfil these criteria vary enormously.

A pre-requisite for the meaningful interpretation of indicators is the availability of baseline data measuring the levels of those same indicators prior to the start of the programme. In their assessment of an agri-environmental programme for maintaining and enhancing dry-cereal landscapes in north western Spain, Oñate *et al.* (2000) found that availability of *reliable* and *relevant* data from existing sources was severely limited by problems of scale and content, and that a great deal of new data had to be collected at farm level. In these circumstances, the construction of a baseline retrospectively is not easy and may not produce reliable results. Ten years later, this situation is still common. Until collection of appropriate (in terms of content and level of observation) baseline data is included as a *necessary initial step* in the setting up of all agri-environmental programmes, the full value of indicators as evidence will not be realised.

The implications of a short time-frame for the type of evidence that can be considered prompt the question: Can results be good predictors of impacts? Clearly, a minimum requirement for this is the availability of robust prior evidence on the causal links between on-farm changes and environmental impacts, and this is often lacking. Kleijn (2006) states that for most EU schemes targeting biodiversity, knowledge about the causal links between various management prescriptions and species abundance does not exist. Programme design is "largely inspired by traditional agricultural practices that used to be associated with high levels of biodiversity." When this is the case for a targeted environmental benefit, the scope for predicting from results (changes in practice) to impacts (long-term environmental benefits) may be severely limited.

In cases where substantial scientific evidence exists on the causal links between results and impacts, mathematical models can be used to simulate potential benefits.[14] However, a caveat is needed here: what has been observed in the general case may not hold for a given area with particular local characteristics. Site- and area-specific factors can be important for determining the effects of management practices on targeted benefits.[15] Therefore, unless the model is sophisticated enough to allow the "average" causal relationship to be modified through the inclusion of other conditioning variables describing site and regional characteristics, model predictions may be quite misleading.

A final question then is the following: when changes in the appropriate indicators of results are available, measured correctly from the relevant baseline data, together with an intervention logic based on proven replicated evidence on longer-term causal links, is this sufficient to predict that environmental benefits will be enhanced? The answer is already given above: any prediction made on this basis may well be valid for the 'average situation' yet could be quite unrepresentative for the area or type of farm where the intervention has been undertaken.[16]

The above discussion supports the recommendation of Boatman *et al.* (2008, p.122): "We suggest that, whilst the short-term indicative evaluation methods are undoubtedly useful for the policy review cycle as well as directing on-going learning and experimentation, they should be used in conjunction with, and not as replacements for, direct and longer-term evaluation of scheme impacts on the ground".

"Scientific" evaluation

The focus of the "scientific" evaluation is to verify the existence of intervention impacts (environmental benefits), measure their extent and establish causality between changes in farm practices and increased benefits. This is an important step for establishing the success of the policy measure. Its validity depends on the exercise of the same rigorous standards applicable to any scientific investigation. Yet evaluations often fall short of meeting these standards,

Kleijn and Sutherland (2003) reviewed 62 *ex post* evaluations investigating the impacts of EU agri-environmental programmes that targeted biodiversity. They concluded (p.947) that "in the majority of studies, the research design was inadequate to assess reliably the effectiveness of the schemes. Thirty-one per cent did not contain a statistical analysis. Where an experimental approach was used, designs were usually weak and biased towards giving a favourable result."

A common reason for bias in this type of study is the use of an inappropriate counterfactual. The counterfactual is the situation that would have prevailed without the policy. The rigorous identification and measurement of policy impacts requires it to be done by comparing performance after implementation of the programme against the counterfactual. For policies like statutory regulations that are compulsory for everyone without exception, the counterfactual is a wholly hypothetical state of the world that has to be reconstructed using a model and with the aid of a number of assumptions. By contrast, for voluntary measures where the uptake is partial, some farmers remain outside the scheme. At first sight it might seem that their behavioural choices and the environmental benefits they generate could provide the counterfactual for the farms in the programme. However, the fact that their choice is voluntary may create what is known as *selection bias*. Without proof to the contrary, farmers opting into the scheme did so because they had certain characteristics relevant to the scheme that are not shared by farms remaining outside. Perhaps they were already using management practices close to those required by the scheme, or already had higher environmental performance on their farms, or were situated in areas more conducive to realising environmental benefits. The difference between their performance and that of non-scheme farms confounds two effects: the impact of the scheme *and* the underlying differences that determined their choice to opt in.

Another simple but invalid choice of counterfactual is the pre-policy situation of those farms opting in. Here too the difference between their situation at the start of the programme and x years later confounds two types of impact: that of the policy and the combined effect of all the other changing factors that may have influenced environmental outcomes on their farm over time (other policies, (micro-)climate change, unusual weather effects and so on). The problem this time is that, in this kind of non-experimental context, it is not possible to impose *ceteris paribus* (that is, hold other factors constant) over the time period in order to isolate the effects of the policy.

Selection bias might be greatly reduced by collecting baseline data for farms in and outside schemes and comparing the *changes* between the two groups over a number of years, or comparing changes in biodiversity between areas with and without schemes, or by pairing with-scheme and control sites having similar environmental conditions for comparison, or by using statistical methods like propensity score matching[17] to create an artificial control group. These approaches require appropriate data and skilled analysis.

Kleijn and Sutherland (2003) go further than any of these strategies in proposing the following ideal experimental design: the designation of control sites that are similar to scheme sites in every respect except for the changes obligated by the programme, ensuring "sufficient replication" of both types of site, and the collection of baseline data for both. Boatman *et al.* (2008) challenge the feasibility of this proposal, not least because of the difficulty of finding suitable control sites that are neither coercively excluded from the programme nor atypical in respect of characteristics that are relevant for the programme.

Another problem affecting the scientific measurement of environmental impacts of agri-environmental measures is that the *causal dynamics* between initial management change and (full) environmental impact is often unknown. Initial responses may be delayed for several years and response paths are unlikely to be linear. This raises the question of *when* and *how often* to monitor environmental impacts on farms within an agri-environmental programme. Various studies recommend that not only should baseline data be collected before the scheme starts but also that repeated surveys should be carried out over the life of the scheme (and beyond). Regular monitoring would help to establish the time profile of the environmental impact, which would contribute to knowledge and may lead to better policy design in the future. However, frequent on-farm monitoring, not to mention the technical and practical difficulties inherent in measuring certain environmental changes in the field, inevitably place a heavy data-collection burden on research budgets.

To control cost, data collection is usually carried out for a sample of farms. This raises the issue of scaling up from the sample to the whole group in order to measure the total effect of the programme. Unless the sample has been selected randomly or using a stratified sampling technique, the appropriate set of raising factors (weights) for aggregating benefits over all farms in the scheme is not a straightforward issue. In any case, it may well not be appropriate to apply standard stratification schemes, with weights depending on factors like farm size and type of farming, when aggregating environmental impacts.

Finally, according to the definition of agri-environmental measures adopted in this chapter, the decision on whether and how to produce agri-environmental public goods is taken by the *individual* farmer who responds to payment incentives to modify his management and resource use decisions. It also implies that evaluation of policy impacts should look at the link between individual decisions and the resulting environmental benefits. However, there is also a collective, spatial element in the provision of many agri-environmental public goods. Critical mass, synergies between the decisions of individual farmers, the extent and manner in which individual actions are coordinated and the spatial design of the intervention within an area – such factors may also determine the effectiveness of individual farmer decisions. This raises the question of the appropriate level or spatial scale at which effects should be measured and analysed.

For example, maintaining a given landscape usually requires the participation of a number of farmers in the same small area, as does improving water quality in a watershed. An individual farmer's contribution to preserving certain wildlife populations depends in part on design features such as the provision of wildlife corridors over wider tracts of neighbouring land. The value of schemes to improve public access across farmland can depend on whether paths are coordinated to link with and extend existing local path networks (Boatman *et al.*, 2008). Scientific evaluations based on individual farm data need to find a way of incorporating such synergistic effects: are they simply an exogenous contextual element to be controlled for, or are they endogenous aspects of the policy that should be included in what is to be evaluated?

"Economic" evaluation

An economic evaluation introduces monetary values into the evaluation framework. The most comprehensive type of economic evaluation is a cost-benefit analysis (CBA), in which all present and future costs and benefits arising from the intervention are valued in money terms.[18] These monetary flows, which are distributed over time, are converted to their equivalent value at a single point in time using a discount factor and then aggregated.[19] If the net value of the aggregate is positive, then the policy is judged to make a positive contribution to social welfare. The information obtained from "scientific" evaluations about the size and flow of benefits over time is clearly an important input into this calculation.

This ambitious methodology poses various challenges. *First*, agri-environmental benefits, which by their nature are not marketable and hence have no easily observed market price, have to be valued in money terms. Economists have been busy with this issue for years. Currently, the two most frequently used approaches are *stated preference* (SP) methodologies (survey respondents are asked directly for the value they attach to particular non-marketed benefits)[20] and *revealed preference* (RP) techniques. Among the latter are approaches where actual choices are analysed in order to infer the value of associated unpriced benefits (e.g. the travel cost method, hedonic pricing) and choice experiments. Choice experiments ask participants to choose between (usually hypothetical) options in which different levels of non-marketed attributes are "bundled" together. When the resulting data are processed using complex econometric techniques, the implicit value attached to each attribute can be extracted. Both SP and RP approaches have strengths and weaknesses, as well as their own partisans and detractors. These methodologies are still being refined in order to improve their general performance and their flexibility in particular situations. Such approaches aim to estimate society's *valuation of the benefit* in money terms. In certain cases, given the nature of the benefit, an approach involving *foregone costs* can be used (for example, the saving in water purification costs due to measures enhancing water quality).

Second, a social CBA requires all costs and benefits arising from the policy to be included. This involves not only direct programme costs (agri-environmental payments themselves), but also so-called policy-related transaction costs (PRCTs) (e.g. administrative costs, legal costs of setting up agreements with farmers and non-remunerated farmer costs like the opportunity cost of extra time spent on administrative and recording tasks).[21] Studies have found that these other cost components can be high relative to size of the payment, and may depend quite strongly on the design and delivery of the programme. Appropriate data on all relevant cost items is often absent and costly to obtain.

Third, all unintended consequences of the policies - whether beneficial or harmful – need to be identified and valued. For example, if landscape rehabilitation due to an agri-environmental programme stimulates farm tourism in the area that generates multiplier effects in the local economy, this should also be included as a benefit since it will not be covered by the valuation of the landscape improvement *per se*.[22]

Fourth, an assumption has to be made about what happens to the flow of benefits at the end of the agri-environmental contract (Pearce, 2005). The most optimistic assumption is that the farm continues to be managed as when it was under the contract; the most pessimistic is that farm practices and land use choices quickly revert to their pre-contract status. For contracts of long duration and if a high discount rate[23] is used, it may make little difference which assumption is made. For a ten-year contract and a discount rate of, say 2%, it *will* affect the calculation of present value of the benefit significantly.

The difficulty of imputing a monetary value to non-marketed benefits increases the appeal of two other techniques for economic valuation, namely *cost effectiveness analysis* (CEA) and *multi-criterion analysis* (MCA) (Pearce, 2005). In both cases, economic information is used for costs, which are compared with benefits measured in some physical unit. For example, CEA applied to a programme targeting biodiversity maintenance might measure the increase in hectares of High Nature Value (HNV) farmland, or the increase in nesting pairs of a threatened bird species, per euro of cost. This criterion only makes sense for single-impact programmes, or where multiple impacts can be aggregated into a meaningful total in some non-monetary unit of measurement.

MCA is used for multi-objective programmes. Experts give scores to a programme according to how far they think it has met each of its objectives. These scores are then summed over objectives, using as weights the experts' preferences or priorities to reflect the relative importance of each objective. The resulting composite score can then be treated as the "impact" and compared with cost as for CEA. With both CEA and MCA, the question remains open as to whether all costs should be taken into account, as in CBA, or only budget costs. In practice, usually only the latter are considered.

Pearce (2005) argues strongly for the superiority of a full cost-benefit analysis. His main arguments are that (a) CBA uses citizens' valuations (expressed through their stated or revealed preferences) to value public good impacts, rather than the preferences of experts, and is therefore more "accountable" than MCA; (b) CBA indicates whether the project provides a net benefit to society and should be implemented or not, whereas CEA and MCA can only rank a set of alternatives, on the assumption that *one* of them will be implemented. In fact, none of them might pass the CBA test. Proponents of MCA react to (a) by questioning whether non-experts are sufficiently well informed on agri-environmental issues for their preferences to be as valid as those of experts. As for (b), this argument carries much more weight as regards *ex ante* evaluations, where no policy commitment has been made yet.

Finally, only CBA can evaluate a programme in a value-in/value-out perspective, since to compare the value of resources and benefits achieved, a common metric – money – is indispensable.

This issue might look like a squabble among economists. In fact, it has real operational importance, since these alternative methodological approaches have different interpretations and answer different questions. Users need to realise that they are not interchangeable options for obtaining the same kind of answer.

2.7 Concluding remarks, future directions

A review of the state of today's evaluation methodology and the way it is applied pinpoints various areas where received ideas can be challenged, and some new initiatives are needed.

Closer links between ex ante and ex post evaluations

The *ex ante* evaluation of a policy is the moment when, logically, its objectives should be clarified, its intervention logic defined and the questions that are pertinent to its evaluation should be formulated. Once this is done, it is possible, still in the *ex ante* perspective, to identify the data needed both to establish the baseline and to monitor the policy after implementation. Once the policy is adopted, this would serve as the blueprint for data collection procedures.

The *ex ante* evaluation would logically form the starting point for the *ex post* appraisal. And yet, in the more typical case, institutional *ex ante* evaluations are not available to *ex post* evaluators and therefore highly relevant information cannot be exploited. *Ex post* evaluators may have to reinvent a statement of the policy objectives or reconstruct the intervention logic – at least, versions that are precise enough to act as an operational basis for an evaluation – by inductive processes. Key mechanisms and responses that were seen as crucial to the operation of the policy when it was evaluated *ex ante*, may have to be re-identified *ex post*.

The fact that the *ex ante* appraisal was conducted under conditions of greater uncertainty than prevail a few years later, and that the version of the policy finally adopted may not correspond in all details to the one that was formally appraised, does not mean that *ex ante* evaluations are worthless to *ex post* evaluators. If the policy as implemented has been modified from the one first appraised, this could easily be recorded in a codicil to the original *ex ante* evaluation, explaining the rationale for the modification and specifying any changes it implies for data collection needs. Better coordination between these two types of evaluation is strongly recommended.

One-size-fits-all approach?

It has often been observed that the type of stylised formal evaluation framework applied in the European Union for administrative evaluations is not used in other countries. Reactions to it are certainly mixed. Blandford *et al.* (2010) note that practitioners' perceptions of the formal EU framework range from seeing them as "box-ticking exercises" to appreciating them as useful attempts at improving the efficiency of policies. Whatever one's view, it is clear that the agri-environmental measures to be evaluated are themselves far from being as standardised as the methodology for evaluating them, prompting questions like: Is a high degree of methodological standardisation counter-productive? Is a uniform time-schedule for evaluating impacts appropriate to agri-environmental measures? Given the slow emergence of many agri-environmental benefits, is it realistic to expect that *ex post* evaluations after a few years can measure long-term impacts required by the CMEF?

An alternative view can be illustrated by the interesting – but perhaps outlying – case of the US Conservation Reserve Programme (CRP) as described by Hellerstein (2005). The main objective(s), rules for eligibility and range of likely impacts of this programme have all been evolving steadily over the 25 years of its existence. As Hellerstein puts it, "as we increase our understanding of how the CRP (and other conservation programmes) affect the bio-physical environment, so will our ability to carefully determine the value of these programmes. Given the geographical breadth of these programmes, and their sometimes subtle impacts, acquiring such information is not inexpensive."

It is hard to imagine how the evaluation of such a policy might be made to fit into the stylised framework of the European Union's CMEF. Yet, as documented by Hellerstein, a sustained stream of empirical studies and appraisals, some performed in-house at the ERS and others conducted outside, have built up over time a rich picture of what the CRP has delivered in different sites with respect to different, locally prioritised, conservation objectives. And the evidence continues to accumulate, adding to scientific understanding of the interaction between human decisions and rural environmental outcomes. Having said this, one can also ask whether, given increasing budget stringency and a greater clamour for accountability, a more formalised approach to evaluating at least some aspects of such programmes might become more commonly demanded in the US policy context.

Balance of resources and follow-up?

As already stated, each type of evaluation approach has its role and purpose. Discussion of the inherent superiority of one or another is pointless. However, it is useful for administrations and the research community to ask themselves periodically whether the balance of resources deployed over the three approaches is delivering the maximum benefit to the policy process, to the policy participants and to the ultimate stakeholders. Moreover, do the different types of exercise, with their different time-frames, each receive their appropriate share of the attention and effective follow-up from policy-makers?

The issue of whether or not policy evaluations are followed up or ignored is hot one. If administrative evaluations are not taken up because their message is distorted or incomplete because of efforts to adhere to a rigid methodology, what can be done about it? If scientific evaluations are not acted upon, is it because they come too late, because the conclusions are expressed in scientific jargon and not well communicated, or for other reasons? If evaluations are not being exploited to upgrade policies and policy-making, then this is an area for improvement where everyone should benefit.

Interpretation and use of economic techniques

It is tempting to see the economists' main challenge in terms of valuing non-marketed items. However, other important challenges arise when recommending and communicating techniques for combining economic information so as to yield valid conclusions that are useable for evaluating policies. Given the various techniques available, policy makers need clear and objective guidance on the different kind of information each provides, and how they can best be used. It is clear that the choice made is not always an appropriate one, and that the chosen technique is not always correctly interpreted by end-users.

For Pearce (2005), "Any rational evaluation of agri-environmental policies, of which agri-environmental schemes are the chosen example here, must compare costs and benefits…" – a compelling view. A cost-benefit study, which establishes whether a project will yield a net social benefit, can make its greatest effective evaluation contribution *ex ante*, since this is the moment where policy makers have most degrees of freedom for avoiding policy failures. Nonetheless, when performed *ex post*, CBA can also deliver useful information from which much can be learned.

Short of this, however, evaluations quite often settle for measuring a project's cost effectiveness. This approach leads to a comparative measure for ranking different policy options. By contrast, the usefulness of CEA for a *single* policy in isolation, as it is frequently used in practice, can be seriously challenged. For example, is it helpful to the policy-maker to know that in a project for restoring ancient hedgerows as field boundaries, the cost was X euros per metre of hedgerow? Is the figure "reasonable" or not? What can we compare it with? If the objective of restoring the hedgerows is to enhance landscape amenity and biodiversity, and preserve cultural heritage, which are valued by society, how can such a ratio help us to evaluate it? Maybe the policy-maker will compare the cost per metre with an independent estimate of the social value of hedgerows per metre. But doing this simply brings cost-benefit analysis in by the back door, and in a most non-rigorous way. The policy maker needs to be informed about the strengths and limitations of these different approaches.

Alternatively, it might be argued that, in an *ex post* context, CEA could have a role to play in comparing the performance of the same scheme between regions, or over time. This strategy would deploy the CE ratio in a comparative context where it belongs. But what conclusions can we draw from a comparison revealing that cost per metre is higher in region A than in region B? Maybe the benefits deriving from hedgerows are also valued more highly in region A (it may be closer to urban centres, and the countryside may be more extensively used for recreation and tourism).

In conclusion, weighting outcomes and costs according to price (i.e. measuring them in money terms) has the great advantage of allowing them to be aggregated. A second advantage is that the aggregates have a straightforward and easily understood interpretation as costs and monetised benefits. Still, it does not follow that using economic information in evaluation studies always leads to sensible answers to the specific questions asked, nor that the use of assumed or speculative monetary coefficients when more robustly based prices are missing always leads to better conclusions. Economists could be more critical of the way they use these measures, making sure that any short-comings or caveats are well explained to end-users, and relying more on sensitivity analysis in cases of valuation uncertainty.

Notes

1. Economic consultant.

2. For example, for some years the European Union's rural development legislation has required independently performed *ex ante*, mid-term and ex post evaluations of all its co-funded rural development programmes. Evaluations are performed at the level of individual programmes. At a more synthetic level, Oréade-Brèche (2005) provides an overviewing appraisal of EU agri-environmental measures for a ten-year period. Policies for assisting agriculture in the European Union's less favoured areas, which also have strong environmental objectives, were assessed at EU level in 2006 (see IEEP, 2006).

3. A good is non-rival when its consumption by one individual does not reduce the quantity available for consumption by other individuals.

4. A good is non-excludable if, when it is produced, no one can be prevented from using it.

5. See, for example, Hodge (2008).

6. As with most generalisations, this one also is not universally true. Many OECD countries have policies in place for maintaining extensive, low-input farming in marginal areas where the abandonment of agricultural activity may well increase soil erosion and reduce wildlife populations. Indeed, the heterogeneity and site-specificity of the link between agricultural activity and environmental values is another reason why blunt policy

instruments such as price support are inappropriate for stimulating public good provision in agriculture.

7. For recent discussion, see Cooper *et al.* (2009), McVittie *et al.* (2009).

8. Reasons why this is rarely done include uncertainty about the size of the potential environmental benefit, methodological difficulties involved in valuing it unambiguously in money terms, and the possibility that this method of calculating the payment could infringe the relevant WTO green box criterion.

9. See Selman *et al.* (2009).

10. See Komen and Peerlings (1998), Peerlings and Polman (2008).

11. Common Monitoring and Evaluation Framework (European Commission, 2006).

12. Boatman *et al.* (2008, p.121) describe how in the United Kingdom during 1992-2003 ("a period of intense experimentation with these schemes") the evaluation focus shifted from longer-term reviews to shorter-term monitoring and "early, indicative performance measures". In their view, "this has reduced our ability to actually measure scheme impacts for UK agri-environmental schemes". However, it may also have allowed lessons to be learned more quickly and hence benefited scheme design and delivery. They also note that, because of this shift, more weight is given to expert judgement and "other predictive methodologies" and less to repeat surveys as sources of "evidence." These observations appear to be applicable also beyond the United Kingdom.

13. Additionality refers to the extent to which the observed changes (e.g. behavioural changes of farmers enrolled in the scheme) are due to the programme, or whether they would have occurred in any case.

14. See, for example, Boatman *et al.* (2007).

15. For example, even "the location of a buffer strip in relation to the pollutant source or pathway is of paramount importance in determining its performance in protecting water quality" (Boatman *et al.*, 2008, p.106)

16. Pearce (2005) argues strongly against using "results" as proxies for "impacts" in agri-environmental evaluations. Results are to be treated as a means to an end, not the end itself, and "Failure to make this distinction has led to some confusion in the literature" (p.76).

17. Propensity score matching is recommended when selection bias is present in non-experimental data where there are few "natural pairings" between the with-scheme and control groups, and/or natural pairings are difficult to identify because of a large number of potentially relevant pre-treatment characteristics. However, it is not without its own technical problems.

18. For a recent example, see Boatman *et al.* (2010).

19. They may be aggregated in unweighted form, or with distributional weights attached to particular items that reflect society's preferences between social groups who may benefit from the policy or have to bear its costs.

20. See, for example, Pruckner (1995), Loomis *et al.* (2000) for studies based on stated preferences (contingent valuation methodology), and Hanley *et al.* (1998), Scarpa *et al.* (2007) for studies using choice experiments.

21. For some relevant literature, see OECD (2007), Falconer and Saunders (1999), Nilsson (2007), Mettepenningen *et al.* (2009).

22. Cost-benefit studies of publicly-funded projects usually also take into account the marginal cost of obtaining tax revenue. Empirical studies show that the cost to society of EUR 1 of tax-payer money is greater than EUR 1.

23. Rate at which society trades off a benefit occurring in the present against one received in the future. An annual discount rate of 5% means that EUR 100 today is valued as equivalent to EUR 105 in a year's time. The lower the discount rate is the more willing society is to defer some benefits to the future.

References

Berriet-Solliec, M., P. Labarthe, C. Laurent and J. Baudry (2011), "Empirical validity of the evaluation of public policies: Models of evaluation and quality of evidence", paper prepared for the 122nd EAAE Seminar *Evidence-Based Agricultural and Rural Policy Making: Methodological And Empirical Challenges of Policy Evaluation*, Ancona, 17-18 February 2011.

Blandford, D., R. Boisvert, and B. Hill (2010), "Improving the evaluation of Rural Development Policy. Guest Editorial, Special Issue: Evaluating Rural Development Policy", *EuroChoices*, Vol. 9, pp. 4-9.

Boatman, N., S. Conyers, H. Parry, S. Pietravalle and C. Ramwell (2007) *Estimating impacts of ELS on key biodiversity indicators and diffuse pollution of surface waters by nutrient,* Final Report to Defra, project MA01041.

Boatman, N., C. Ramwell, H. Parry, N. Jones, J. Bishop, P. Gaskell, C. Short, J. Mills and J. Dwyer (2008), *A review of environmental benefits supplied by agri-environment schemes.* FST20/79/041, Report to the Land Use Policy Group, United Kingdom.

Boatman, N., K. Willis, G. Garrod, and N. Powe (2010), *Estimating the Wildlife and Landscape Benefits of Environmental Stewardship*, Final Report for the Food and Environment Research Agency, Defra, United Kingdom.

Cooper, T., K. Hart, and D. Baldock (2009), *The Provision of Public Goods Through Agriculture in the European Union*, IEEP, London.

European Commission (2006). *Handbook on Common Monitoring and Evaluation Framework, Guidance document and Annexes*, Directorate General for Agriculture and Rural Development. Available at *ec.europa.eu/agriculture/rurdev/eval/index_en.htm.*

Falconer, K. and C. Saunders (1999), "Transaction costs for SSSIs and policy design", *Land Use Policy* Vol. 19, pp. 157-166.

Hanley, N., R.E. Wright and V. Adamowicz (1998), "Using choice experiments to value the environment", *Environmental and Resource Economics*, Vol. 11, pp. 413-428.

Hellerstein, D. (2005), "Conservation policy and agriculture in the US: valuing the impacts of the conservation reserve program", Chapter 13 in OECD, *Evaluating Agri-Environmental Policies. Design, Practice and Results.* OECD Publications, Paris.

Hodge, I. (2008), "To what extent are environmental externalities a joint product of agriculture? Overview and policy implications", in OECD, *Multifunctionality in Agriculture: Evaluating the Degree of Jointness, Policy Implications*, OECD Publications, Paris.

IEEP (2006). "An Evaluation of the Less Favoured Area Measure in the 25 Member States of the European Union", Report prepared by the Institute for European Environmental Policy for DG Agriculture, November 2006.

Kleijn, D. and W.J. Sutherland (2003), "How effective are European agri-environment schemes in conserving and promoting biodiversity?" *Journal of Applied Ecology,* Vol. 40, pp. 947-969.

Kleijn, D. (2006). Guidelines for the evaluation of AE schemes. Wageningen University. Available at: *www.ncp.wur.nl/NR/rdonlyres/EA88E46A-1B26-4A04-AF51-4FBB5AC50619/52783/ Guidelines_evaluation_ae_schemes2.pdf*

Komen, M.H.C. and J.H.M. Peerlings (1998), "Restricting intensive livestock production: Economic effects of mineral policy in The Netherlands", *European Review of Agricultural Economics,* Vol. 25, pp. 110-128.

Loomis, J., P. Kent, L. Strange, K. Fausch, and A. Covich (2000), "Measuring the total economic value of restoring ecosystem services in an impaired river basin: results from a contingent valuation survey", *Ecological Economics* Vol. 33, pp. 103-117.

McVittie, A., D. Moran, and S. Thomson (2009), "A review of literature on the value of public goods from agriculture and the production impacts of the single farm payment scheme", Report for the Scottish Government's Rural and Environment Research and Analysis Directorate (RERAD/004/09), Scottish Agricultural College.

Mettepenningen, E., A. Verspecht and G. Van Huylenbroeck (2009), "Measuring private transaction costs of European agri-environmental schemes", *Journal of Environmental Planning and Management*, Vol. 52, pp. 649-667.

Nilsson, F.O.L. (2007), "Transaction costs of agri-environmental policy measures: the case of Swedish permanent grasslands. Swedish University of agricultural Sciences". Working Paper Series 2007:6. Sweden: SLU.

OECD (2005). *Evaluating Agri-Environmental Policies. Design, Practice and Results.* OECD Publications, Paris.

OECD (2007), *The implementation costs of agricultural policies*, OECD Publications, Paris.

OECD (2010), *Guidelines for Cost-effective Agri-environmental Policy Measures*, OECD Publications, Paris.

Oñate, J.J., E. Andersen, B. Peco, and J. Primdahl (2000), "Agri-environmental schemes and the European agricultural landscapes: the role of indicators as valuing tools for evaluation", *Landscape Ecology*, Vol. 15, pp. 271–280.

Oréade-Brèche (2005), *Évaluation des mesures agro-environnementales : Rapport final*, Report for the European Commission.

Pearce, D. (2005), "What constitutes a good agri-environmental policy evaluation?" Chapter 3 in OECD, *Evaluating Agri-Environmental Policies. Design, Practice and Results.* OECD Publications, Paris.

Peerlings, J.H.M. and N. Polman (2008), "Agri-environmental contracting of Dutch dairy farms: the role of manure policies and the occurrence of lock-in", *European Review of Agricultural Economics*, Vol. 35, pp. 167-191.

Pruckner, G. (1995), "Agricultural landscape cultivation in Austria: An application of the CVM", *European Review of Agricultural Economics*, Vol. 22, pp. 173-190.

Scarpa, R., D. Campbell and W.G. Hutchinson (2007), "Benefit Estimates for Landscape Improvements: Sequential Bayesian Design and Respondents' Rationality in a Choice Experiment", *Land Economics*, Vol. 83, pp. 617-634.

Selman, M., Greenhalgh, S., Branosky, E., Jones, C. and J. Guiling. (2009), *Water Quality Trading Programs: An International Overview*, WRI Issue Brief #1. Washington DC: World Resources Institute.

II. SPECIFIC EVALUATION ISSUES AND COUNTRY EXPERIENCES

Chapter 3

Evidence-based agri-environmental policies: The Swedish experience

Sören Höjgård and Ewa Rabinowicz[1]

This chapter discusses the evaluation of agri-environmental measures within Axis 2 of the CAP's Rural Development Programme, focusing on methodological aspects. The evidence analysed is based on experiences from the recent mid-term evaluation of the Swedish Rural Development Programme, which is dominated (70%) by Axis 2 measures. The authors identify major weaknesses in the present evaluation procedure and suggest appropriate remedies. The weaknesses include, inter alia, vague concepts, insufficient availability of suitable methodology and lack of empirical data. A number of strong recommendations for improvement are formulated, which would jointly improve the objectivity and scientific rigour of the methodology as currently applied.

Agri-environmental schemes for the protection of the environment are common in many OECD countries. In the European Union, such schemes come under Axis 2 of the Rural Development Programme (RDP) (EU, 2005). Axis 2 accounts for 44% of the EU's RDP spending. Due to co-financing requirements, additional funds are allocated to those measures from member states' (MS) budgets. Altogether, about EUR 96.3 billion[2] will be spent for the period 2007-2013 on agri-environmental policies in the European Union. Hence, it is highly relevant to ask what those policies are actually delivering. The need to show value-for-money for European citizens is further accentuated by the present economic crisis and taking into account the many competing demands on the EU budget.

There is an extensive scientific debate about the efficiency of agri-environmental schemes as well as about the relative merits of the alternative designs of such schemes (see, for instance, the discussion in Primdahl *et al.*, 2010). As part of the RDP programmes, Axis 2 measures are subject to an institutionalised evaluation procedure based on a set of common evaluation questions and indicators (see Council Regulation (EC) No 1698/2005). Accordingly, these evaluations should have the potential to contribute to this debate and to inform formulation of efficient environmental policies. Additional usefulness of this evaluation procedure could come from the broad coverage of countries and regions, which follows from the fact that all MS are obliged to carry out the task. This should help to correct the geographical bias found in the existing scientific literature on the subject. For instance, a widely quoted review article by Kleijn and Sutherland (2003) is mainly (76%) based on studies from just two countries (the United Kingdom and the Netherlands).

It is therefore very pertinent to ask whether the present evaluation procedures are up to the task and, if not, what needs to be revised. Kleijn and Sutherland (*op cit*), commenting on the obligatory EU evaluations, state that "most of the evaluation studies simply examine uptake patterns of different schemes in the programme." According to Primdahl *et al.* (2010), who analysed the methods applied in a selected sample of evaluations of agri-environmental schemes, "common sense methodology" was the most commonly used (51%) followed by qualitative assessments (34%). Moreover, the results of these evaluations appear not to be referred to very much in the relevant scientific literature, which raises doubts as to their quality. Rather than providing an appraisal of past evaluations, our discussion below focuses on the common evaluation procedure as such, as it is presently designed, and examines prospects and preconditions for this procedure to generate science-based analysis. The chapter builds on experiences from the evaluation of the Swedish RDP where Axis 2 accounts for 70%.

The outline of the chapter is as follows. Section 3.1 describes Axis 2 of the RDP. In section 3.2, the European Union's Common Monitoring and Evaluation Framework is presented. Section 3.3 reports the evaluation of the Swedish RDP: questions, methodology, data and conclusions and recommendation. Section 3.4 summarises the results of the evaluation. Section 3.5 assesses major weaknesses of the evaluation procedure, Section 3.6 outlines suggested improvements. Overall conclusions are given in Section 3.7.

3.1 The agri-environmental measures and the CAP

The European Union's agri-environmental schemes are a part of the RDP, also known as the second Pillar of the CAP. The first Pillar consists of market instruments (tariffs, export subsidies and domestic market interventions), which aim at supporting the prices of agricultural commodities and stabilising markets, and the direct farm payment system (the Single Payment Scheme, SPS). The CAP has been constantly changing and the present design is the product of this evolution, which has involved a weakening of the role of price supports and the introduction of direct farm payments decoupled from production. These payments constitute the single most important instrument of the CAP and account for almost three quarters of the CAP budget. To qualify for SPS entitlements, farmers are required to keep agricultural land in "Good Environmental and Agricultural Condition" (GAEC) and respect relevant Statutory Management Requirements. These requirements are together referred to as cross-compliance conditions (Council Regulation EC No. 1782/2003). Because environmental requirements are attached to the SPS, those payments operate to some extent as a rudimentary environmental support and interact with environmental supports in Pillar 2.[3]

Pillar 2 is much smaller than Pillar 1 (about 25% of Pillar 1)[4] in terms of spending but has been gaining in importance over time. In contrast to Pillar 1, Pillar 2 requires co-financing from national budgets, at the rate of about 50%, but poorer MS pay less. Pillar 2 is devoted to promoting rural development and consists of four axes. The MS can freely choose from a menu of eligible measures. However, there is a lower limit for the share of each Axis in each MS's total RDP budget. For Axis 2, the lower limit is 25% of RDP spending.

Table 3.1. Budgetary allocation per axis for the Swedish programme for 2007–2013, million euro (before the 2010 revision) and corresponding shares in the European Union

Axis	Swedish budget mn euro	Percentage of Swedish budget	Percentage of budget in EU
Axis 1 – to improve the competitiveness of the agriculture and forestry sector	555	14	34
Axis 2 – to improve the environment and the countryside	2 702	69	44
Axis 3 – to improve the quality of life in rural areas and encourage the diversification of economic activities	326	8	13
Axis 4: LEADER	264	7	6
Technical assistance	70	2	3
Total	**3 917**	**100**	**100**

Source: Financial plan, 2007, The Swedish Department of Agriculture, 2010.

Table 3.1 shows the distribution of payments in Sweden and the corresponding shares in the European Union. Clearly, the Swedish allocation differs significantly from that of the rest of the European Union, with Swedish spending focusing much more on environmental support and considerably less on farm competitiveness.

Axis 2 aims at improving the environment and countryside by means of support to land management. The most important measures are agri-environmental payments. These include payments to encourage extensification of farming, low-intensity pasture systems, organic farming, preservation of landscape and historical features, and conservation of high-value habitats and their associated biodiversity. The payments are intended to compensate farmers for the additional costs, or income foregone, from adopting such practices and are usually paid on a per hectare basis. Below, these measures are presented in more detail.

Axis 2 in Sweden

Since measures in Axis 2 aim at protecting the natural environment, it may be of interest to start with a short description of environmental problems related to Swedish agriculture. Agriculture accounts for only a tiny share of GDP and employment in Sweden: less than 0.5 and 2%, respectively. Sweden is a large country and conditions for agricultural production differ considerably between the northern and the southern parts. The intensity of agricultural production and, consequently, the type of environmental problems encountered vary according to geographical location. Land use in Sweden is dominated by forestry. Arable land accounts for only 11% of total land use (5% in northern Sweden). Loss of biodiversity, nutrient leaching and use of pesticides are considered to be the major environmental problems, while soil erosion does not represent a major threat. Loss of biodiversity is strongly linked to abandonment of marginal agricultural land in forest-dominated regions.

Axis 2 consists of five different measures. The sole justification in Sweden for payments with respect to natural handicaps (codes 211-212) is preservation of biodiversity by preventing marginal land from turning into forest, which already completely dominates the land use in the regions in question. Accordingly, this measure is considered an environmental support. The greatest share of the budget, however, goes to measures under codes 214-216, which account for almost 80% of the budget.

The architecture of Axis 2 in Sweden is immensely complicated, as is illustrated in Table 3.3 with measure 214 as an example. As can be seen, this measure consists of eight different payments.

Table 3.2. Budgetary allocation to measures within Axis 2 in Sweden

Measure	Total budget (m euro)	Percentage of budget
211-212 Natural handicap payments to farmers in mountain areas and to farmers in other areas with handicaps	562	21
214-216 Agri-environment payments and support f or non-productive investments	2 106	78
227 Support for non-productive investments – forestry	34	1
Total, Axis 2	**2 702**	**100**

Source: The Swedish Board of Agriculture.

Table 3.3 Payments within measure 214, Agri-environmental payments in Sweden

	Payments for…	Indicative budget share %
1.	…biodiversity and cultural heritage in semi-natural grazing lands, mown meadowland and wetlands	32.9
2.	…valuable natural and cultural environments in the agricultural landscape and reindeer herding areas	5.8
3.	…regional priorities	5.2
4.	...traditional cultivated plants and livestock breeds	0.4
5.	...reduced nutrient leaching from arable land	6.1
6.	...environment protection measures	1.7
7.	...organic forms of production	18.7
8.	…extensive ley management for a better environment and an open landscape	29.1

However, not even this breakdown does full justice to the details of the Swedish RDP. Several of the payments listed in Table 3.3 are divided into further categories and even sub-categories. Payments for biodiversity in semi-natural grazing lands are differentiated according to land use, land type and environmental quality level. Payments for valuable cultural elements in the agricultural landscape are differentiated between point elements (12 different categories) and line elements (nine different categories). Regional priorities, a payment administered at the county level, is subdivided in 22 categories, etc. It may be noted that the subdivision often concerns payments that are small in terms of their initial budget shares, resulting in very small amounts of money to be paid. Those tiny payments coexist with large schemes such as organic forms of production and extensive ley management. It is not uncommon that the same piece of land receives several payments with different objectives and conditions attached to them.

3.2 The Common Monitoring and Evaluation Framework (CMEF)

The evaluation of these measures in each MS is required to be conducted by evaluators that are independent of the authorities responsible for the design and monitoring of the programme. The work is guided by the CMEF (European Commission, 2006), which includes a set of common evaluation questions that are to be answered with information provided by a set of common indicators. To be useful for the evaluation, the indicators should follow naturally from the intervention logic for the measures, i.e. the chain of causality hypothesised to run from the supported measures to the objectives. A schematic illustration of the intervention logic for Axis 2 is presented in Figure 3.1.

Figure 3.1. Intervention logic for Axis 2 measures

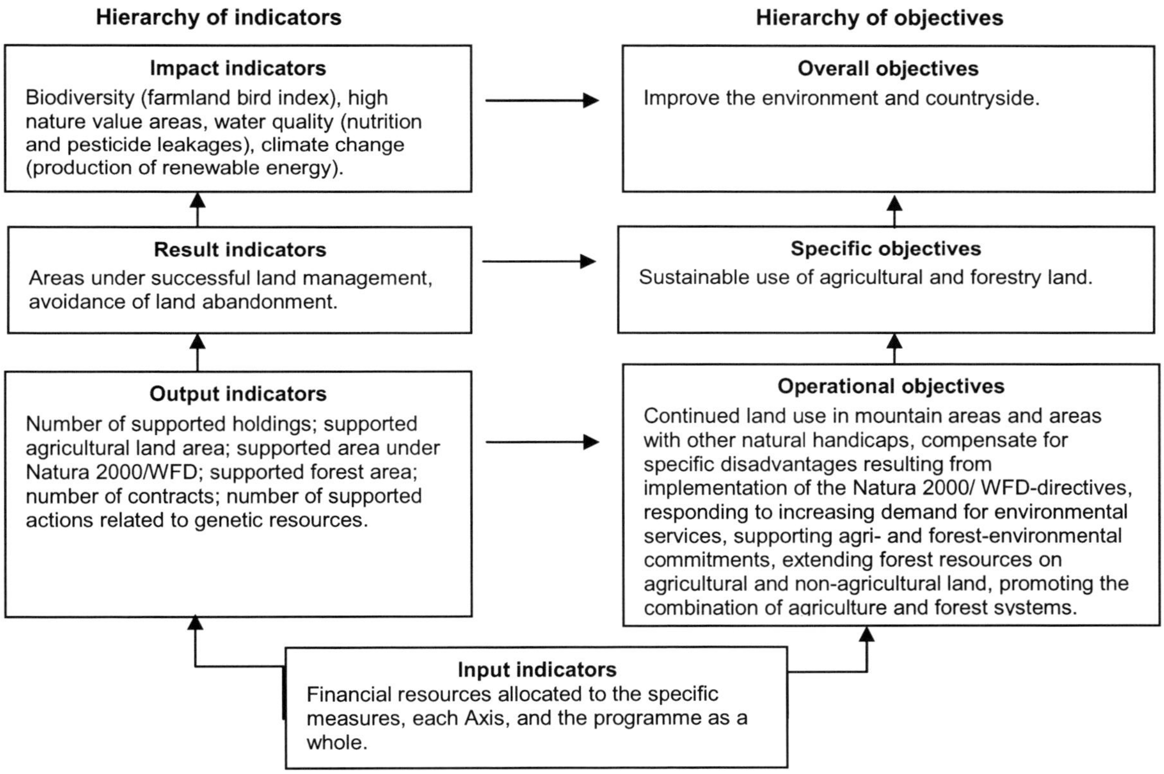

Thus, the implementation of the measures is assumed to result in the attainment of some operational objectives, deemed essential for attaining the specific objectives, which in turn are essential for the attainment of the overall objectives. As the causal links are hypothetical (in the Swedish RDP, while there is some reference to economic theory, references to biological or ecological theories as the rationale for the choice of measures are lacking), firm theoretical foundations for these hypotheses are needed. The economic rationale for Axis 2 is the provision of public goods. Those goods are, however, produced jointly with agricultural commodities. For instance, raising beef cattle may provide both a private good (meat) and a public good (biodiversity). Private and public goods are not produced in fixed proportions, however, and the environmental payments aim, by and large, to favour the latter, i.e. lower the intensity of agricultural production. Hence, the evaluator needs to establish both how farmers respond to the payments, which is not easy, and how changes in their behaviour affect the environment. For the latter, theories from other fields (biology, ecology, etc.) are needed and, as it turns out, they are not always conclusive. For instance, different species thrive in different types of habitats, (Kleijn *et a*l., 2006; Wretenberg *et al.,* 2006; Kleijn *et al*., 2009) implying that the overall effect may be difficult to assess. The complicated architecture of Axis 2 with one measure having several objectives, and vice versa, adds to the difficulties.

The common indicators

Separate indicators are attached to each level of the hierarchy of objectives. At the first level, there are the *input indicators*, which quantify the financial resources allocated to each intervention. At the next level are the *output indicators*, which quantify the number of beneficiaries (farms, farmers, projects, area, etc.) and the total volume of investment for each beneficiary. At the third level, the *result indicators* measure "immediate effects of the intervention and provide information on changes in, for example, the behaviour, capacity or performance of direct beneficiaries". It is clarified that information is to be collected from *supported* enterprises only (cf. European Commission, 2006). Thus, the result indicators provide information on changes in the target variables but not necessarily how much of this change that can be attributed to the intervention. At the fourth level are the *impact indicators*. These are intended to measure the effects attributable to the respective interventions. Considering measures that are relevant for Axis 2, they should measure changes in biodiversity, high nature value areas, nutrient balances, and production of renewable energy in supported enterprises (regions). It is noted that their quantification requires counterfactual analysis.

The common evaluation questions

The evaluation questions are divided into two main groups: measure-specific questions (around four per measure) and horizontal questions where the latter are related to the programme as a whole.[5] Both types of questions should be answered with the information provided by the *impact indicators* (cf. European Commission, 2006 – Guidance note B). Questions that are asked for the main measures applied in Sweden (211-212 and 214-216) are as follows:

Measure codes 211-212: Handicap payments

- To what extent have compensatory allowances contributed to ensuring continued agricultural land use in mountain areas?
- To what extent have compensatory allowances contributed to the maintenance of a viable rural community in mountain areas?
- To what extent has the scheme contributed to maintaining or promoting sustainable farming systems?
- To what extent has the scheme contributed to maintaining the countryside and improving the environment?

Measure codes 214-216: Agri-environmental payments

- To what extent have agri-environmental measures contributed to maintaining or promoting sustainable farming systems?

- To what extent have agri-environmental measures contributed to maintaining or improving habitats and biodiversity?
- To what extent have agri-environmental measures contributed to maintaining or improving water quality?
- To what extent have agri-environmental measures contributed to maintaining or improving soil quality?
- To what extent have agri-environmental measures contributed to mitigating climate change?
- To what extent have agri-environmental measures contributed to maintaining and improving landscapes and its features?
- To what extent have agri-environmental measures contributed to improving the environment? Distinguish between the contribution of agri-environmental measures implemented demanding site-specific measures, and less demanding measures which are widely applied.

It should be observed that the questions are very general and apply, in the case of measure 214, to the measure as a whole, which obviously complicates the evaluation process.

3.3 Evaluating agri-environmental schemes in Sweden: Data and methodology

The evaluation of the agri-environmental measures in Sweden proved to be a considerable challenge. The major difficulties were related to three issues: the design of the evaluation procedure (clarity of concepts and scope of questions, see the previous section), the availability of appropriate analytical methods, and the availability of data. All three are interconnected but here we focus on data and methodological issues.

The effort to evaluate the programme amounted to answering the questions listed above. In the case of measure 214, this was done at the level of the payments listed in Table 3.2, which is already a considerable simplification.

The ambition was to use a counterfactual approach, as prescribed by the CMEF guidelines. This implies a comparison between a supported group of farms and a control group. If supports were distributed randomly, the control group could be a random selection of non-supported farms. When this is not the case, the control group should be as similar as possible to the intervention group in all other respects. For instance, the control group could be created by matching farms using the criterion that they should be equal in all observable variables hypothesised to influence the probability of being granted support (propensity score matching). Given longitudinal data on the development of the target variables for members of the intervention and the control group, panel data methods could then be used to control for the effects of unobserved confounders (provided that differences in unobserved confounders could be assumed to be constant, or to develop according to some linear trend over time; see Wooldridge, 2002, or Greene, 2003).

Occasionally, it was possible to apply this type of methodology for the evaluation of measures in other axes (investment support in Axis 1). In the case of Axis 2, however, it was difficult to apply econometric techniques for two reasons. *Firstly*, data on the development of the target variables are lacking in official registers. *Secondly*, in many cases the measures are extended to all farmers as broad schemes, implying that it is practically not possible to construct a control group.

Data

It is suggested (European Commission, 2006, Guidance note I) that data on the evolution of the target variables and farm characteristics hypothesised to influence this evolution could be obtained from the Farm Accounting Data Network (FADN), the EUROFARM and the EUROSTAT databases, complemented by national or regional registers and surveys. The problem with the FADN database is that it is biased towards larger farms and includes only about 1.6% of all EU farms (FADN home page).[6] Accordingly, it is unlikely that a sufficient number of farms can be identified to conduct the matching process for the construction of the control group. In addition, at least in Sweden, the FADN farms are a rotating panel. For these reasons, FADN is not very suitable for panel data analysis. Oenema *et al.* (2011) argue that FADN ”should preferably be avoided" as a data source for producing agri-environmental indicators (of which indictors related to RDP are a part) since it is entirely based on economic data and is less representative of the farm population as a whole.

As to the Eurofarm and Eurostat databases, they are constructed like the FADN from data in national registers in the respective MS. In the Swedish case, with two exceptions (the TUVA and NILS databases), national registers only contain information on different types of land uses at farm level. Accordingly, there is no information on the evolution over time of the variables actually targeted by the environmental measures in Axis 2 (biodiversity, high nature value areas, water quality, and climate change).

Moreover, though national registers may contain information not included in the FADN and Eurostat data collections, there is the problem that (at least in Sweden), because of privacy considerations, access is restricted. This implies that merging information from these registers with information on which enterprises that have been granted support from the RDP must be performed by Statistics Sweden. In our experience, this is very time-consuming and costly.

As to Axis 2 measures, the TUVA database contains data on different species of vascular plants, as well as cultural values (i.e. man-made features of the environment such as traditional barns, hedgerows, and stone walls) in meadows and pasture lands in Sweden obtained through a nationwide inventory in 2002-2004, while NILS contains data on different species of insects in some of the meadows and pasture lands included in TUVA. Unfortunately, since both data bases contain cross section data only, they are hardly sufficient for analysing the effects of the environmental measures. Now, because of the difficulties in measuring the ultimate target variables, "driving force indicators" based on a so-called the Driving Force-State-Response framework (OECD, 1999) might be used as substitutes. Driving forces are factors, such as land use trends, that cause environmental changes. It was, therefore, contemplated to utilise the longitudinal information on different kinds of agricultural land use contained in the other national registers to identify the effects of Axis 2 measures on these driving force indicators. However, closer inspection revealed that data on what types of land use that applied to a particular farm in a given year to a large extent had been generated from information contained in the farm's application for support from the RDP. That is, the coverage of data on land use is not independent of the payments granted, which makes it hard to draw conclusions regarding the effects of payments on land use.

Surveys are only suitable for the generation of cross section data since asking respondents retrospective questions is likely to result in recall errors. One might, of course, consider repeating the survey (with the same respondents) on an annual basis. However, this is likely to lead to attrition (observations lost due to respondents refusing to participate after some time). Also, given the time-frame of the evaluation, repeated annual surveys would not be feasible for generating the data needed. Finally, the information elicited by means of surveys may be difficult to interpret since responses could be affected by strategic considerations. In addition, environmental effects may become visible only after a number of years, or be spread out over long distances (Oltmer *et al.*, 2000). Accordingly, it is difficult if not impossible for the evaluators to rely on surveys to collect supplementary data from farmers and the evaluation has to rely on pre-existing sets of data.

Methodology

As already mentioned, it was difficult to identify control groups and apply econometric techniques to Axis 2 measures. The complexity of the programme, with many interacting, not fully observable, factors adds to the difficulties. Agri-environment schemes display strong inter-linkages among measures and objectives whereby a single measure may contribute to multiple objectives and a single environmental objective may be achieved by several measures (Finn *et al.*, 2009). Accordingly, the same tract of land usually receives several different payments with different objectives attached, implying that different payments are interacting with each other. This means that it is often implausible to evaluate the programme measure by measure (or rather payment by payment as environmental measures often include several different payments) and then add the results. Moreover, those payments interact also with the supports in Pillar 1 because of the jointness in production and because of the cross compliance conditions attached to the SPS.

This can be illustrated with the natural handicap payments (NHP). Their major justification is to prevent marginal agricultural land from going out of production and the accompanying loss of biodiversity. NHP are extended to almost all (over 90%) farmers and agricultural land in the eligible regions. Extensive ley management payments and biodiversity payments for semi-natural grazing lands are to a large extent paid to agricultural land in the same regions. In addition, the cross compliance conditions attached to SPS payments have to be taken into account. In Sweden, SPS payments go both to arable land and to semi-natural grazing land. Under GAEC requirements, farmers receiving SPS are required to keep a minimal stocking density of grazing animals (to promote biodiversity). The profitability of meat production has to be considered as well in addition to the Nordic Aid scheme (price support to milk production), which is paid to most NHP areas (north of the 62nd parallel).

Under those circumstances, disentangling the result (change in land use) and the impact (improvement of biodiversity) of *just* NHP from the influence of other measures and factors is extremely difficult and not feasible without using a modelling approach. Evaluation using simulation models is performed as follows: first, the model is solved and validated for a given base year; second, the policy scenario (i.e. the counterfactual) (in this case, *removal* of a given support or of the programme as a whole) is determined and, finally, a comparison between the results of the base run and those of the policy run is made.

There are, however, several difficulties involved in applying simulation models for evaluation purposes. *First*, there are often no off-the-shelf-models available. Existing models have to be adapted, but this is possible only to a very limited degree given time and resource constraints. *Second*, aggregate agricultural sector models do not lend themselves easily to a precise assessment of many, small heterogeneous schemes. *Third*, key parameters of many simulation models, such as elasticities, are often derived from heterogeneous external sources and their reliability is uncertain. They may, nonetheless, strongly influence the results and hence the outcome of the evaluation. In the case of environmental support, the elasticity of land supply with respect to net return per hectare is often of crucial importance as the support is primarily paid to land. *Finally*, agricultural sector models provide an estimate of the behavioural changes (*results*) the support is intended to induce and need to be supplemented with estimates of the environmental effects (*impacts*) caused by these behavioural changes. This is often accomplished by linking farm output or input to environmental indicators such as nutrient or energy balances, (Sinabell *et al.*, 2010). Combined economic and environmental models, whether linked or fully integrated, are preferable but are difficult to achieve on a large (country) scale. Drechsler *et al.* (2007) discuss differences and similarities between ecological and economic modelling, arguing that integration of approaches is possible but not without problems. The major advantage of using economic-ecological models is that the environmental implications of behavioural changes may differ considerably according to location and it is much easier to take this into account in economic-ecological models than in pure economic models. Hence, it may be difficult to make an informed judgement if the location cannot be identified.[7]

These problems were to a large extent encountered in the evaluation work in Sweden where the agricultural sector models CAPRI and AgriPoliS were used to analyse the results of environmental support, and the impact on water quality was analysed using the models SOILNDB and ICECREAMDB. Spatial comparisons between areas receiving support and not receiving support were made using GIS.

CAPRI is a regionalised comparative static sector model of agriculture in the EU and in the rest of the world, the latter being modelled in a more rudimentary way.[8] CAPRI was used to assess the impact on land use, farm incomes, nutrient balances and greenhouse gas emissions at an aggregate level, i.e. the effects of all measures 214-216 and measure 211-212 *and* the joint effects of both measures – in other words, of the entire Axis 2 support. Hence, the assessment of the environmental benefits from keeping land (especially grazing land) in production was only done at the general level. Because CAPRI is not a spatial model, it was, of course, not possible to identify *which* land has been saved from afforestation. Detailed simulation results are presented in Annex 1 of Wissman *et al.* (2010).

In these simulations, the policy instruments NHP, payments for semi-natural grazing lands and payments for extensive ley management were individually modelled (as addition to SPS or area payments for the activity in question). All remaining environmental payments were conceptualised as an intensity-reducing payment available to farmers who choose the extensive technology option in the model. Data on input indicators for all individual payments at the NUTS3[9] level were aggregated to the CAPRI regions (NUTS2) and the modelled instruments. The elasticity of land supply with respect to net return per hectare was based on van Meijl *et al.* (2006) and regionalised for the CAPRI regions using the CLUE model (Verburg *et al.*, 2010). Transformation elasticities for switching between arable land and grazing land were based on Golub (2006). In the policy experiments, only the Swedish agri-environmental programme was removed, implicitly assuming that the agri-environmental support continues in other MS but not in Sweden, which may seem a questionable assumption. However, the alternative (elimination of all environmental payments in the whole of European Union) would amount to an evaluation of the entire environmental support in the European Union, a task beyond the capacity of the team.

AgriPoliS is an agent-based, spatial dynamic agricultural model available for two NUTS3 regions, one in northern and one in central Sweden, both covered by NHP. The model contains an environmental module linking changes in land use to changes in biodiversity (farmland birds). In addition, the impact of structural change on landscape diversity is modelled.[10] The following payments were modelled: NHP (differentiated after region and land use), extensive ley management and semi-natural grazing land payments (base level only). All other payments were ignored (i.e. calibrated into the baseline). Simulations were made by Brady (see Annex 2 to Wissman *et al.*, 2010). The model was used to assess effect on land use, farm incomes, structural change nutrient balances and biodiversity (farmland birds).

The CAPRI and AgriPoliS models are complementary. However, because of the differences in, inter alia, modelling approach and geographical coverage, the results were somewhat difficult to merge. The main adaptation to the shock of removing the support in the CAPRI simulations was the adjustment (decline) in land use, especially semi-natural grazing land. In the AgriPoliS simulations there was no effect on land use. Instead, structural change in the form of the merging of smaller farms into larger units accelerated.

The SOILNDB and ICECREAMDB models (see Mårtenson *et al.*, 2010) were used to calculate nutrient leakage (nitrogen and phosphorus respectively) from arable land in Sweden divided into 22 leakage regions. The models are purely biological and do not estimate behavioural changes. Instead, the implications for nutrient leakage of lower input use are traced out. Moreover, those implications can take time to materialise. Hence, the results should be interpreted as expected long-term effects.

GIS (Geographical Information System) data were used to compare supported and unsupported areas with respect to several environmental qualities, such as the number of vascular plants per square metre based on an inventory of environmental features available from the TUVA database. Note that these data are cross sectional and, therefore, do not allow the evaluator to control for unobserved confounders, implying that it may be questioned how much of the differences between supported and unsupported areas should be attributed to the support.

Inevitably, in spite of all the hard work, the result of the evaluation is more of an overview than an in-depth assessment. The programme is very complicated and should in principle be evaluated at an appropriate level of complexity. The very justification of specialised small schemes is the fact that they are supposed to deliver unique benefits. OECD (2010) also argues that "many of the environmental effects are site-specific, reflecting heterogeneous agricultural and environmental conditions, and thus some impacts cannot be extrapolated." Since an evaluation of the programme in all its detail was not possible given the time and resource limitations, the validity of the conclusions is limited.

3.4 Results of the evaluation

Because this chapter focuses on methodological issues, only a short summary of the results will be provided highlighting recommendations about methodology. The major results can be summarised as follows.

Given that other agri-environmental payments continue to be paid out, the natural handicap payments NHP (measure codes 211-212) have limited consequences for land use and income in the regions concerned. By slowing down the rate of structural change in agriculture, the payments to farmers in mountain areas and in other areas with handicaps are contributing to higher employment in agriculture. However, this may be at the expense of future competitiveness. This lower rate of structural change is probably having a positive effect on the preservation of man-made landscape features, but biodiversity does not appear to have been markedly affected.

Agri-environmental payments were evaluated, as pointed out above, at the level of the categories identified in Table 3.3. The payments for "biodiversity and cultural heritage in semi-natural grazing lands, mown meadowland and wetlands" have contributed to more pastures and grazing animals remaining in production. The payments for upkeep of wetlands and the special measures for pastures and meadows are contributing to the continuing upkeep of land with high biological value. Areas receiving payments compared with areas outside the scheme appear to have a more favourable environmental status, but the differences are small and not always in favour of the areas receiving payments. The payments for organic forms of production are contributing to decreasing the use of pesticides, which can help in promoting biodiversity in certain cases. The effects of the payments for "valuable natural and cultural environments in the agricultural landscape and reindeer herding areas" on biodiversity are unclear, although it is probable that they contribute to the upkeep of a greater number of elements. In summary, this indicates that the payments have contributed to the conservation of biodiversity.

The payments for "extensive ley management for a better environment and an open landscape" may potentially have negative effects, particularly in combination with the payments for biodiversity and cultural heritage in semi-natural grazing lands, mown meadowland and wetlands and the natural handicap payments to farmers in mountain areas and to farmers in other areas with handicaps. The payment for extensive ley management (cultivated grassland) admittedly keeps the countryside open, but also contributes to homogenisation in the form of increasing the share of cultivated grassland in a landscape already dominated by cultivated grasslands.

A number of different schemes, especially payments for reduced nutrient leaching, contribute to decreasing nutrient leaching from arable land and pesticide use. The schemes that are most effective, measured per hectare, concern wetlands in the case of nutrient leaching and buffer zones in the case of decreasing phosphorus emissions. The payment decreasing the use of pesticides most is that for organic forms of production.

No agri-environmental payments directly target the mitigation of climate change. The impact of agricultural production on climate change is a very complicated matter and there are many gaps in knowledge about emission processes. Based on results from the CAPRI model, it can be concluded that if all payments in Axis 2 were eliminated, emissions would decrease somewhat because the payments contribute to more agricultural land being used and more grazing animals being kept. Elimination of all measures in Axis 2 (implying an assessment of the overall impact of the environmental programme) would furthermore result in a decrease of agricultural land by 8%, mainly owing to a strong decrease (about half) in pastures (semi-natural grazing land).

Comparison between broad, less demanding schemes and site-specific payments was only possible in a limited number of cases, where computer simulations could be used. Targeted payments were found to be more efficient. For instance, the computer simulations carried out regarding the effect of organic production and the measurements performed in the field show that this payment had little or no effect on decreasing plant nutrient losses from agricultural land.

3.5 Major weaknesses of the procedure

The single most important weakness relates to the fact that the questions, as they are phrased at present, seem "too big" or too complicated to be answered within the time and resource framework of the evaluation. The evaluation is about establishing to what extent positive environmental effects can be *attributed* to the support programme, which in turn amounts to answering two questions: how payments have affected the behaviour of farmers and how this has influenced the environment. As pointed out before, reliable, science-based answers to both questions are often difficult to obtain. Unless suitable methodology and appropriate data are available, reliable answers cannot be produced. In other words, there is a considerable danger that the evaluation is not producing much new information beyond what is already known through monitoring and previous scientific research.

There is a shortage of data for analyses of environmental effects.[11] As pointed out before, FADN is of limited value in this context. The major reason is that it seems not to have kept up with changing societal preferences and, in particular, with changes in the CAP. The concept of FADN was launched in 1965 for the purpose of monitoring the impact of the CAP on farm income. At that time the (emerging) CAP was driven by annual price reviews while the predecessor of Pillar 2 played a marginal role. At present, there is no direct link between adjustments to Pillar 1 (SPS and market regulations) and the evolution of the income of farms of different types. At the same time, the RDPs are regularly revised. The process of mid-term evaluation is, for instance, supposed to produce recommendations for policy alterations.

As pointed out before, because of the difficulties in measuring actual environmental effects, driving force indicators based on the Driving Force-State-Response framework were used as substitutes for assessing the effects of the measures in Axis 2. However, while the use of driving force indicators may lend credibility to the intervention logic, the problem that a given driving force may affect different objectives in opposing directions (and to varying degrees in different MS) still remains. Moreover, what counts at the end of the day are the actual improvements in the environment and there is not enough focus on providing evidence, such as field data, that this actually the case.

Looking especially at the evaluation questions, it can be observed that the link between evaluation questions and the indicators is occasionally weak. For instance, most questions for measures 211-212 and the first question for measures 214-216 cannot be answered using the information provided by the impact indicators. Partly this is due to the scope of the questions. At the same time, there are indicators that are not related to any questions. Moreover, many of the ambiguities are caused by the use of vague concepts and overlapping questions. For instance, what is the difference between "maintaining a viable rural community" and "maintaining the countryside" or "promoting sustainable farming systems" and "improving the environment"? What does "promoting sustainable farming system" entail in addition to biodiversity, water quality, soil quality, landscape improvement and climate mitigation, to which separate questions are devoted? Concepts such as soil and water quality could also be more precisely defined. Without guidance it is likely that different evaluators interpret the concepts differently, implying that they might not investigate the same effects. This, in turn, could compromise the comparability of results. In other cases, the questions do not seem relevant for evaluation of the impacts on the objectives. For instance, why is it of interest to investigate to what extent agri-environment payments have contributed to viable rural communities in certain areas when the overall objectives are preservation and enhancement of biodiversity, high nature value areas, water quality or to counteract climate change? Again, without clear guidance, different evaluators may interpret the questions differently, which could compromise the comparability of results.

As the main rationale for policy evaluation is to contribute to the revision or improvement of the policy design in order to achieve higher efficiency, it is surprising that no questions are asked about efficiency or effectiveness, and that the common indicators are not designed to elicit such features. In the general instruction in Guidance note B, "Judging" section (European Commission, 2006), the evaluator is asked to assess the efficiency and effectiveness of the programme. However, it is not clear what is intended and whether those questions can be answered in a meaningful way using the information in the impact indicators.

The existence of a positive willingness-to-pay on the part of the user constitutes an intrinsic quality of a good, whether private or public. It could be argued that this requirement should also apply to those public goods whose provision Axis 2 payments are aiming to stimulate. However, none of the evaluation questions asks for evidence that taxpayers would be willing to pay for the agri-environmental programmes. It is implicitly assumed that willingness to pay, or at least some form of societal appreciation, exists. Research in Sweden (Hasund *et al.*, 2010) shows that there is considerable difference between what kind of agri-environmental amenities consumers are willing to pay for and what amenities are supported by the payments. This implies that societal appreciation should not be taken for granted.

3.6 Suggested improvements

The evaluation of the Swedish RDP resulted in a number of recommendations with respect to the design of the programme as well as the monitoring and evaluation procedure. Here, we focus only on the latter.[12]

It seems reasonable that agri-environmental policies in the European Union should be assessed jointly. The provision of European environmental public goods is the strongest justification of having a common policy for agriculture in the Union (see, for instance, Declaration of agricultural economists, 2009). However, the argument is only valid as long the policies applied actually deliver environmental benefits and do so in an efficient way. A common evaluation process could contribute to achieving this and thus increase the credibility and legitimacy of the CAP. In addition, common evaluation and monitoring may offer several advantages, such as gaining additional experience and increasing the reliability of the results. As argued in the introduction to this chapter, common evaluations can also contribute to improved geographical coverage. To exploit those advantages, it must be possible to aggregate or at least compare the national results. Ideally, meta-studies should be conducted. The interest in meta-studies, especially in relation to environmental impacts, has been growing (see, for instance, Batary *et al.*, 2010; Oltmer *et al.*, 2000). It seems a reasonable ambition to synthesise results of the common evaluations in that way. Such a synthesis is not possible, however, if national experts are *in reality* answering different questions and using very different evaluation methods.

The common evaluation questions should be precise (i.e. not require, or be open to, interpretation by the evaluator) and rely on well-defined concepts. This may seem an obvious demand yet, as demonstrated above, many of the questions are vague and the concepts used are often unclear as well. Overlapping questions should be avoided since this creates confusion as to their proper interpretation. The link between evaluation questions and impact indicators must be strengthened. As demonstrated in the previous sections, there are indicators without questions and questions for which no indicators are produced. Also, some of the indicators seem to be of questionable relevance for the end objectives. This implies that concepts that are not readily interpretable should be defined, that evaluation questions should ask directly, and only, for the information contained in the impact indicators. In addition, the common impact indicators should be defined so that they quantify the effects intended by the measures. The evaluator is also of the opinion that there is an imbalance between the large number of output and result indicators and the few impact indicators within Axis 2. More (national) impact indicators need to be introduced. In particular, there is a need to develop more indicators of biodiversity. Pollinating insects were suggested as one possibility to be further investigated. Development of indicators for soil quality was suggested as well. The evaluator proposes that the work on developing new impact indicators be coordinated with increased collection of field data.

Common methodological standards should be prescribed and enforced. They should consist of well-established evaluation practices designed to provide relevant science-based evidence for the question at hand. If, in spite of reasonable and documented effort, a solid answer for some questions cannot be produced, the evaluators should be allowed to abstain from answering those questions. To some extent, ambitions to create a common methodology are already in place. Reliance on control groups is, for instance, encouraged in the CMEF as pointed out before. But this is still a recommendation not an obligation.

Enforcing common methodological standards has obvious advantages but may create some problems as well. On the other hand, as pointed out during the OECD Braunschweig workshop,[13] it could be argued that standardisation and harmonisation risk reducing the analysis to issues that are strictly measureable and quantifiable. Moreover, "unanswerable" questions may produce highly important answers. This is a valid critique but asking evaluators unclear questions and accepting vague answers is not a valid solution.

Instead, it could be advisable to distinguish between short-term evaluation questions and long-term *research issues* where evaluation is complicated by gaps in basic knowledge, and allocate them to separate activities. When scientists are in disagreement, it is not reasonable to expect evaluators to produce a reliable answer in a limited time. Development of advanced economic-ecological models (see below) and improvement of methodology for valuation of non-market benefits like biodiversity preservation could be seen as cases in point. More standardised procedures for "simple questions" could be designed alongside coordinated joint research programmes for long-term issues. Prescribing and enforcing a common methodology (see above) would be facilitated by such a division of responsibilities. Furthermore, "scientific" and "quantitative" should by no means be seen as synonymous.

Evaluation of impacts on the environment is especially cumbersome, as demonstrated in previous sections, due to difficulties in identifying control groups and the presence of many interacting factors. Such difficulties are often resolved by relying on modelling approaches. However, suitable off-the-shelf-models are not universally available. Even existing models have to be adapted, which is only possible to a very limited degree taking into account the time and resource limitations. Hence, this type of methodology needs to be developed in advance and in a co-ordinated way to ensure appropriate coverage (countries, regions, evaluation questions). Those circumstances need to be taken into account when designing monitoring and evaluation procedures.

Given the lack of empirical data, there should be efforts to develop a co-ordinated data generation process in MS. Especially with respect to the assessment of environmental impacts, the systematic collection of field data needs to be increased. Since environmental effects arise at a larger scale than the individual farm, data collected from farmers will not be sufficient for evaluating the effects of the agri-environmental supports. Boccaccio *et al.* (2009) argue that field monitoring of environmental impacts of spending is rare in the MS, and recommend that the assessment of the level of success should be based on the measurement of impact and not on the level of uptake. We agree with this recommendation.

Existing databases should, moreover, be better utilised and adjusted to serve evaluation purposes. The FADN system is at present designed to provide data on farm income development and it is biased towards bigger farms. The usefulness of this information for the evaluation of rural development policies is limited. Accordingly, it seems reasonable to redesign FADN for the needs of the RDP. Adjustment of the FADN for the purpose of evaluation of Axis 2 (and other rural development policies) should imply revision of both the selection of farms and the choice of variables.

The recommendations above relate mainly to the issues of how to design and answer the evaluation questions. An equally important issue is what kind of questions the evaluation should seek to answer. The major rationale for any policy evaluation is to inform potential policy revision. To be useful in that respect, the evaluation procedure should focus much more strongly on assessing efficiency. When possible, the evaluation questions should address the results of the measures undertaken in value terms (not be content with establishing whether or not they have succeeded in increasing output in physical terms) and provide cost-benefit ratios. When market values for the benefits are missing, cost effectiveness of measures aiming at achieving the same objectives should be assessed. In particular, comparisons of cost efficiency between measures aiming at similar objective should be provided in a comprehensive and systematic way. Cost-benefit analyses of the environmental support schemes are complicated by the difficulties of valuation of non-monetary benefits. Eliciting the willingness to pay from the population for goods such as biodiversity is a non-trivial matter (see, for instance, Rosen, 1974; Freeman, 1979; Bateman *et al.,* 2002). Indeed, including the development and adaptation of appropriate methodology for valuations of environmental non-market goods in joint the research programmes, as argued above, could be a good solution. Need for methodological improvement is, however, no reason, for completely abstaining from including societal valuations as part of the policy evaluation. Otherwise, there is no evidence that the policy is actually delivering a *public good.* It would be reasonable to provide some kind of "proof" that society values what is provided. Needless to say, such evidence or willingness-to-pay studies can hardly replace science-based assessments of whether policies are designed and operated optimally.

3.7 Conclusions

This chapter discusses the evaluation of agri-environmental measures within Axis 2 of the CAP's Rural Development Programme, focusing on methodological aspects. The evidence analysed is based on experiences from the recent mid-term evaluation of the Swedish Rural Development Programme, which is dominated by Axis 2 measures. We identify major weaknesses in the present evaluation procedure and suggest appropriate remedies. The weaknesses include vague concepts, a frequent mismatch between questions posed and indicators demanded, insufficient availability of suitable methodology and lack of empirical data.

We make a number of recommendations for improvement, which can be summarised under five headings as follows. First, the common evaluation questions that govern the process should be precise and not require, or be open to, interpretation by the evaluator. Second, the evaluation procedure should focus more strongly on efficiency and not be limited to establishing whether or not the measures have succeeded in increasing participation. Moreover, when possible the benefits should be assessed in monetary terms. Third, modelling approaches are often used to resolve the problem of missing control groups. Suitable off-the-shelf-models are, however, not universally available. Hence, this type of methodology needs to be developed in advance and in a coordinated way to ensure appropriate coverage (MS, regions, evaluation questions). Fourth, given the notorious lack of suitable empirical data on environmental variables of interest and at an appropriate measurement scale, there should be efforts to develop a coordinated data generation process across member states. Existing databases should, moreover, be better utilised and adjusted to become more useful for evaluation purposes. For example, the FADN could be redesigned with respect to selection of farms and the type of data collected in order to make a contribution to the evaluation of environmental and other rural development policies.

Notes

1. Swedish University of Agricultural Sciences.
2. Cf. *europa.eu/legislation-summaries/agriculture/general _framework/160032_en.htm.*
3. It should be noted that the monitoring and evaluation mentioned in the introduction, and the methodology critiqued in this chapter, refer specifically to Pillar 2 measures.
4. Cf. *europa.eu/legislation_summaries/agriculture/general_framework/160032_en.htm.*
5. If a MS were to apply all measures in the RDP menu, the evaluation would have to answer 171 questions (c.f. European Commission, 2006 – Guidance note B).
6. In the Swedish case, it includes 1 000 of a total of approximately 72 000 farm enterprises (Statistics Sweden, 2010).
7. See also OECD (2010) for a review.

8 For detailed information, see Britz and Witzke (2008).

9. NUTS = Nomenclature of Territorial Units for Statistics. This nomenclature establishes three levels of territorial division within the European Union, level 1 being the division into Member States. There are 271 (1303) regions at NUTS2 (NUTS3) level.

10. For a detailed description of the model, see Kellerman *et al.* (2008).

11. For a detailed discussion of the farm data needed for agri-environmental reporting and calculation of environmental indicators, see Oenema *et al.* (2011).

12. For other details see SLU (2010).

13. By Ian Hodge, University of Cambridge, United Kingdom, in his role as discussant.

References

Batary P, A. Baldi, D. Kleijn, and T. Tscharntke (2010). "Landscape-moderated biodiversity effects of agri-environmental management: a meta-analysis", in *Proceedings of the Royal Society. B* (published online November 2010).

Bateman I.J., R.T. Carson, D. Brett, M. Hanemann, N. Hanley, T. Hett, *et al.* (2002), *Economic Valuation with Stated Preference Techniques. A Manual.* Edward Elgar, Cheltenham, United Kingdom.

Boccaccio L, A. Brunner, A. Powell (2009), "Could do better", *BirdLife International*, May , pp. 1-45.

Boyle K, N. Kuminoff, C. Pameter, J. Pope (2010), "The benefit Transfer Challenges", *American Review of Resource Economics,* Vol. 2, pp. 61-82

W. Britz, P. Witzke (2008), "Table of Contents, *CAPRI* model documentation 2008", *www.capri-model.org/docs/capri_documentation.pdf*

Declaration of agricultural economists, (2009). *available at www.reformthecap.eu/posts/declaration-on-cap-reform*

Drechsler, M., V. Grimm, J. Mysiak, F. Wätzold (2007), "Differences and similarities between ecological and economic model for biodiversity conservation", *Ecological Economics*, Vol. 62, pp. 232-241.

European Commission (2006), *Rural Development 2007-2013*, Handbook on Common Monitoring and Evaluation Framework – Guidance document. European Commission, Directorate General for Agriculture and Rural Development. Available at: *www.ec.europa.eu/agriculture/rurdev/eval/guidance/document_en.pdf*

European Union (2005). Council Regulation (EC) No. 1698/2005 of 20 September 2005 on support for rural development by the European Agricultural Fund for Rural Development (EAFRD). Official Journal of the European Union, L277/2. Available at *eur-lex.europa.eu/LexUriServ/LexUriServ.do?uri=CELEX:32005R1698:EN:NOT.*

Finn, J.A., F. Bartolini, D. Bourke, I. Kurz, D. Viaggi (2009), "*Ex post* environmental evaluation of agri-environment schemes using experts' judgments' and multicriteria analysis", *Journal of Environmental Planning and Management*, Vol. 52, pp. 717-737.

Freeman, A.M. (1979), "Hedonic prices, property values and measuring environmental benefits: A survey of the issues", *Scandinavian Journal of Economics*, Vol. 81, pp. 154-173.

Golub, A., T.W. Hertel, H.L. Lee (2006), "Modeling land supply and demand in the long run", Prepared for the ninth annual conference on global economic analysis, Addis Abeba, Ethiopia, 15-17 June.

Greene, W.H. (2003), *Econometric Analysis* (fifth ed.), Prentice Hall. Upper Saddle River, New Jersey, United States.

Hasund, K.P., K. Mitesh, C.J. Lagerkvist (2010), "Valuing public goods of the agricultural landscape: a choice experiment using reference points to capture observable heterogeneity", *Journal of Environmental Planning and Management* (published online November 2010).

Kellermann, K., K. Happe, *et al.* (2008), "AgriPoliS 2.1 - Model Documentation", Halle, Germany, IAMO [*www.agripolis.de/documentation/agripolis_v2-1.pdf*].

Kleijn D., W.J. Sutherland (2003), "How effective are european agri-environment schemes in conserving and promoting biodiversity?" *Journal of Applied Ecology,* Vol. 40, pp. 947-969.

Kleijn, A.D., R.A. Baquero, Y. Clough, M. Diaz, J. Esteban, F. Fernández, *et al.* (2006), "Mixed biodiversity benefits of agri-environment schemes in five European countries", *Ecology Letters,* Vol. 9, pp. 243-254.

Kleijn, D, F. Kohler, A. Báldi, P. Batáry, E.D. Concepción, Y. Clough, *et al.* (2009), "On the relationship between farmland biodiversity and land-use intensity in Europe", *Proceedings of the Royal Society B: Biological Sciences,* Vol. 276, pp. 903-909.

Mårtensson, K., H. Johnsson, K. och Blombäck (2010), Läckage av kväve från svensk åkermark för år 2007 och 2008 beräknat med PLC5-metodik. Avdelningen för biogeofysik och vattenvårdslära, SLU. Teknisk rapport 138.

Neumann, B, M. Lütz, B. Schüpbach, E. Szerencsits (2009), "Spatial modeling for the development of agri-environmental programs", *Regional Environmental Change*, Vol. 9, pp 197-207.

OECD (2010). *Linkages between Agricultural Policies and Environmental Effects. Using the OECD Stylized Agri-environmental Policy Impact Model.* OECD Publishing, Paris, available at: *dx.doi.org/10.1787/9789264095700-en.*

Oenema, O, B. Amon, C. van Beek, N. Hutchings, M. Perez-Soba, S. Procter, *et al.* (2011), "Farm data needed for agri-environmental reporting", *Eurostat Methodologies and Working Papers*, Publications Office of the European Union, Luxembourg.

Oltmer, K, P. Nijkamp, R. Florax, F. Brouwer (2000), "A Meta-analysis of Environmental Impacts of Agri-environmental Policies in the European Union", *Tinbergen Institute Discussion Paper, TI 2000-083/3*, Tinbergen Institute, Amsterdam, The Netherlands.

Primdahl, J, J.P. Vesterager, J.A. Finn, G. Vlahos, L. Kristensen (2010), "Current use of impact models for agri-environment schemes and potential for improvements of policy design and assessment", *Journal of Environmental Management*, Vol. 91, pp. 1245-1254.

Rosen, S. (1974), "Hedonic prices and implicit markets: product differentiation in pure competition", *Journal of Political Economics*, Vol. 82, pp. 34-55.

SLU (2010), "Halvtidsutvärdering av landsbygdsprogram för Sverige 2007-2013", Sveriges lantbruksuniversitet (Swedish University of Agricultural Sciences), Uppsala.

Sinabel, F., E. Schmid, P. Zulka (2010), "Agri-environmetal indicators in sector models: the case of nutrient balances and biodiversity", OECD Workshop on OECD Agri-environmental Indicators: Lessons learned and Future Directions, March 2010, Leysin.

van Meijl, H., T. van Rheenen, A. Tabeau, and B. Eickhout (2006), "The impact of different policy environments on agricultural land use in Europe", *Agriculture, Ecosystems and Environment* Vol. 114, pp. 21–38.

Verburg, P.H., D.B. van Berkel, A.M. van Doorn, M. van Eupen, H.A.R.M. van den Heiligenberg, (2010), "Trajectories of land use change in Europe: a model-based exploration of rural futures", *Landscape Ecology*, Vol. 25, pp. 217-232.

Wissman, J, E-L Päiviö, H. Andersson (2010), "Axel 2 – utvärdering av åtgärder för att förbättra miljön och landskapet", Swedish University for Agricultural Sciences, Uppsala. Available at: *www.agrifood.se.*

Wooldridge, J. (2002), *Econometric Analysis of Cross Section and Panel Data*, MIT Press. Cambridge, Massachusetts.

Wretenberg, J, T. Pärt, A. Berg (2006), "Changes in local species richness of farmland birds in relation to land use changes and landscape structure", *Biological Conservation*, Vol. 143, pp. 375-381.

Chapter 4

Additionality in US agri-environmental programmes for working land: A preliminary look at new data

Roger Claassen[1]

The United States' agri-environmental (AE) policy for working land relies largely on voluntary programmes. Agri-environmental payments result in additional environmental gains only if they prompt the adoption of practices that would not have been adopted without these payments. Little is known, however, about additionality in US programmes. Recent data from the Agricultural Resources Management Survey (ARMS) show that some producers have adopted conservation practices without payments, either because they are profitable on their farms (conservation tillage) or because targeted practices are required by state regulations (nutrient or manure management). It is also possible that some recipient farmers might adopt practices even without payments. In future research Propensity Score Matching (PSM) will be used to estimate the extent of additionality in US agri-environmental programmes. Potential barriers to this research include small sample size and the complexity of US agri-environmental programmes.

Voluntary payment programmes form the core the US Federal effort to encourage resource conservation and environmental quality on US farms (Claassen and Ribaudo, 2006). Spending in these programmes was more than USD 5 billion in fiscal year 2010—the highest (inflation adjusted) level since 1960 (Claassen, 2011). Since 2002, much of the increase has been in working land programmes—voluntary payment programmes designed to assist producers in the adoption of environmentally sound practices such as conservation tillage, nutrient management, integrated pest management, field-edge filter strips, and other practices that are compatible with on-going agricultural production. Since 2002, funding for these programmes has increased ten-fold from USD 200 million per year in 2002 to nearly USD 2 billion per year in 2010.[2]

The effectiveness and efficiency of voluntary payment programmes are difficult to assess. To understand these programmes in terms of meaningful environmental outcomes, the evaluator must understand a long chain of events, many of which are difficult to observe and measure (Smith and Weinberg, 2004). In terms of water quality, for example, voluntary payment programmes can encourage farmers to adopt nutrient management, field-edge filter strips, riparian buffers and other practices that can reduce nitrogen runoff from farms. Reducing runoff may decrease the amount of nitrogen that is transported to water bodies, lowering nitrate concentrations in downstream water and limiting associated water quality problems like eutrophication and hypoxia (Goolsby, 1999; Ribaudo and Johansson, 2006). Improved water quality can lead to an increase in fish and wildlife populations, for example, which can lead to improved opportunities for recreational and commercial fishing.

One property of this causal chain that has received comparatively little attention is "additionality" in voluntary payment programmes. Simply stated, a payment yields additional environmental benefit only if it prompts the adoption of a conservation practice or practices that would not have been adopted in the absence of the payment. Environmental benefits will be realised from expenditures in voluntary payment programmes only if payments made to farmers leverage the adoption of conservation practices that would not have been adopted otherwise.

Interest in additionality is based on the fact that some farmers may have adopted agricultural conservation practices without the benefit of cost-sharing or incentive payments (Lambert *et al.*, 2006). There are a number of reasons why this could occur. First, agricultural conservation practices can yield private benefits and may be adopted by some farmers because they are profitable, regardless of their environmental benefits. Nutrient management can be profitable, for example, if fertiliser costs can be reduced without a commensurate reduction in crop yields or increase in other production costs. Conservation tillage can reduce the cost of labour, fuel and machinery and, in many cases, can be applied without reducing crop yields. Some practices may also be required by state or local regulation. For example, some states require livestock producers to develop and apply nutrient management plans (Ribaudo *et al.*, 2003). Payments associated with the adoption of required practices are clearly non-additional – they do not prompt adoption of practices that would not have been adopted in the absence of payments.

Recently available data on conservation practice adoption payments on US wheat and corn farms may facilitate research on additionality. The new data, collected as part of the Agricultural Resources Management Survey (ARMS), may support analysis using Propensity Score Matching (PSM). Potential barriers include small sample size and information on US working land programmes, in which many implementation decisions are made at the state or local levels.

4.1 Practice adoption and payments

Data collected by the US Department of Agriculture as part of the Agricultural Resources Management Survey (ARMS) show the extent of adoption and related adoption incentive payments for a selected group of common conservation practices used on farms that grew wheat in 2009 and farms that grew corn in 2010. ARMS is a nationally representative sample of farms providing extensive data on land use, crop and livestock production, production expenses, government payments, producer demographic characteristics and other aspects of agricultural production.

Table 4.1. Conservation practices and practice groups

Practice group	Practices
Buffer practices	Field-edge filter strips Field borders Riparian buffers
Soil conservation structures	Terraces Grassed waterways Grade stabilisation structures Water and sediment basins
Conservation tillage	No-till Mulch till Ridge-till
Integrated pest management	Integrated pest management
Nutrient and manure management	Comprehensive nutrient management Manure management

Source: Economic Research Service, USDA.

For a sub-sample of surveyed farms, drawn from selected states,[3] ARMS also includes a crop-specific, field-level survey, which provides a wealth of data on production practices, including tillage, nutrient management, pest management and selected structural and vegetative practices (Table 4.1). In addition to being asked whether the practice was in use on the surveyed field, respondents in the 2009 (wheat) and 2010 (corn) surveys were asked when the practice was installed or first used and whether cost-sharing or an adoption incentive payment was received.

Figure 4.1 shows the percentage of surveyed fields where at least one practice in a given practice group is in use and the percentage of fields where the producer received a payment associated with adoption of the practice(s). Because our study is about the role of incentives in conservation practice adoption decisions, we consider only those conservation practice adoption decisions made by the current producer (the survey respondent). Structural and vegetative practices (e.g. terraces, filter strips) that were installed before the beginning of the current farmer's tenure are excluded from our data. USDA has been promoting and sharing the cost of installing soil conservation structures for more than 75 years, so these structures were in place on many surveyed fields before the beginning of the current producer's tenure.[4] We assume that management practices are re-adopted annually. When the reported date of initial adoption precedes the current producer's tenure, the date of initial adoption is assumed to be the first year of the current producer's tenure and it is assumed that the current producer did not receive a payment for initial adoption.

Figure 4.1a. Conservation practice adoption and payments, by practice group[1], 2010 corn survey

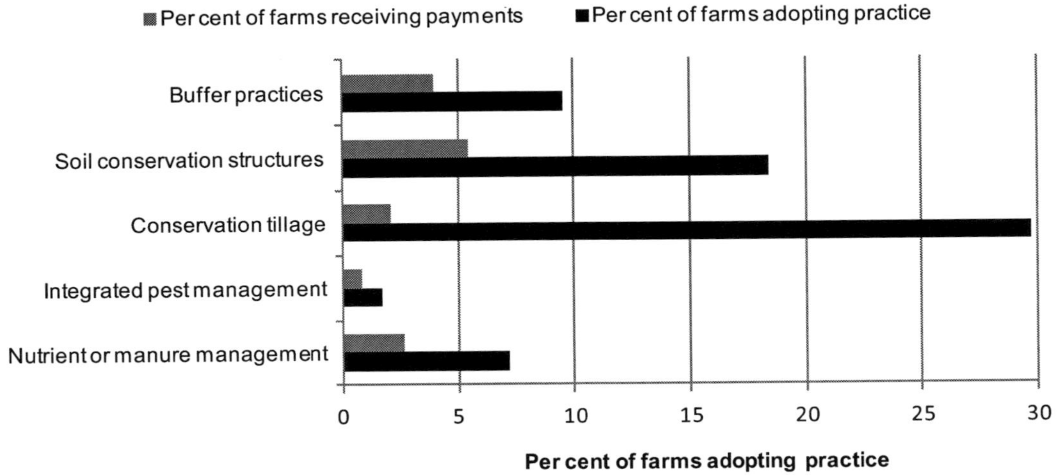

Figure 4.1b. Conservation practice adoption and payments, by practice group[1], 2009 wheat survey[2]

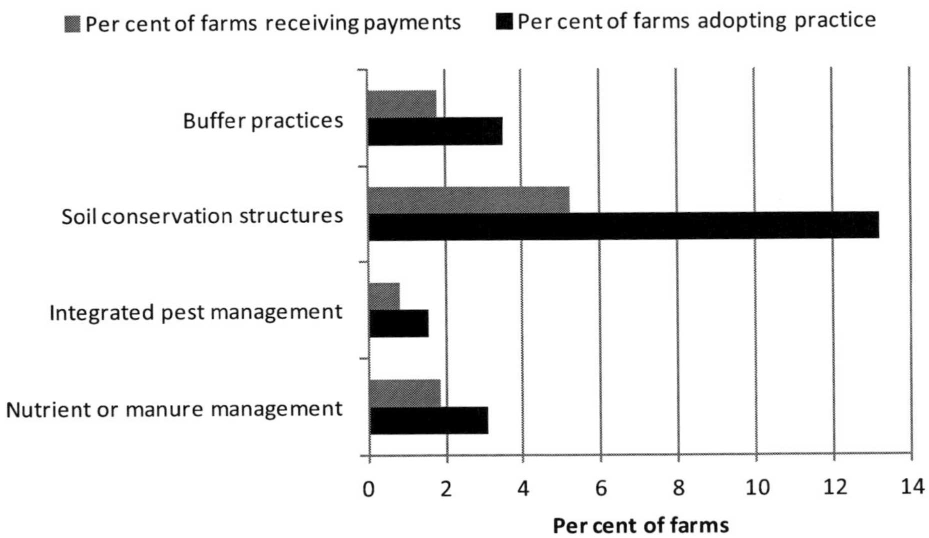

Notes:

1. See Table 4.1 for definition of practice groups.
2. Farmers in the wheat survey where not asked about conservation tillage payments.

Source: *Agricultural Resources Management Survey*, 2009 and 2010.

In the corn fields surveyed in 2010, practice adoption ranged from 3% for integrated pest management to more than 30% for conservation tillage. Soil conservation structures had been installed by the current producer on 18% of surveyed fields, while buffer practices and nutrient or manure management had been adopted on roughly 10% of surveyed fields. For wheat fields surveyed in 2009, adoption rates ranged from 4% for buffer practices to 14% for soil conservation structures (the wheat questionnaire did not include questions about conservation tillage payments).

Practices that were adopted with the assistance of conservation payments generally accounted for 50% or less of total adoption on fields in the 2010 corn survey, although the percentage receiving payments varied widely across practices (Figure 4.2a). Very few corn producers who adopted conservation tillage said they received a payment for doing so. For buffer practices, soil conservation structures, and nutrient and manure management, 30-40% of producers said they received payments. In the 2009 wheat survey, the percentage of producers adopting conservation practices who also received conservation payments was generally higher than in the corn survey (Figure 4.1b). For buffer practices and manure/nutrient management, more than 50% of producers reported receiving adoption-related payments. More than 40% of wheat producers reported receiving payments related to soil conservation structures.

Because some respondents have been farming surveyed fields for decades, some practice adoption decisions made by the current producer were made decades ago. It is not clear that decisions made 20 or more years in the past are comparable to more recent decisions about conservation practice adoption and conservation programme participation. Increasing farm size and specialisation, technical change and the evolution of conservation policy suggest that additionality research should focus on more recent conservation practice adoption and payments.

Policy evolution suggests that the 2002 Farm Act, which represents a major change in US agri-environmental policy, could serve to define the beginning of the period for analysis of additionality in conservation payment incentives. Beginning in 2003, funding for USDA working land conservation programmes increased sharply. Working land programmes encourage conservation practice adoption on land in agricultural production, including all of the practices that were asked about in the 2009 and 2010 ARMS surveys.

Because these programmes reward management practices that address a broad range of resource concerns, the funding increase effectively shifted US agri-environmental policy away from a long-standing focus on soil conservation and structural practices, to a broader set of environmental objectives and greater emphasis on management practices. In the corn survey, less than one-half of buffer practices and soil conservation structures in place on surveyed farms were adopted in 2003 or later (Figure 4.2a). Likewise, less than half the respondents who reported payments related to buffers, soil conservation structures and conservation tillage reported that these payments were received for practices adopted in 2003 or later (Figure 4.2a). For nutrient management and integrated pest management, however, most of the adoption and all of the reported payments occurred in 2003 or later (Figure 4.2a). A similar pattern is seen in the wheat survey, although payments for buffers and soil conservation structures were more likely to occur in the post-2002 period, particularly for buffer practices (Figure 4.2b).

Figure 4.2a. Conservation practice adoption and payments, by practice group and adoption year, 2010 corn survey

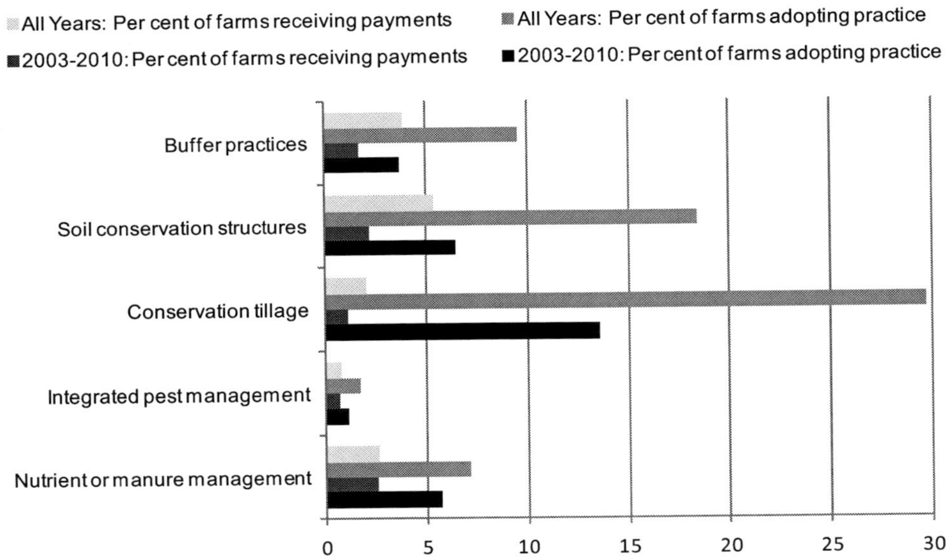

Figure 4.2b. Conservation practice adoption and payments, by practice group[1] and adoption year, 2009 wheat survey[2]

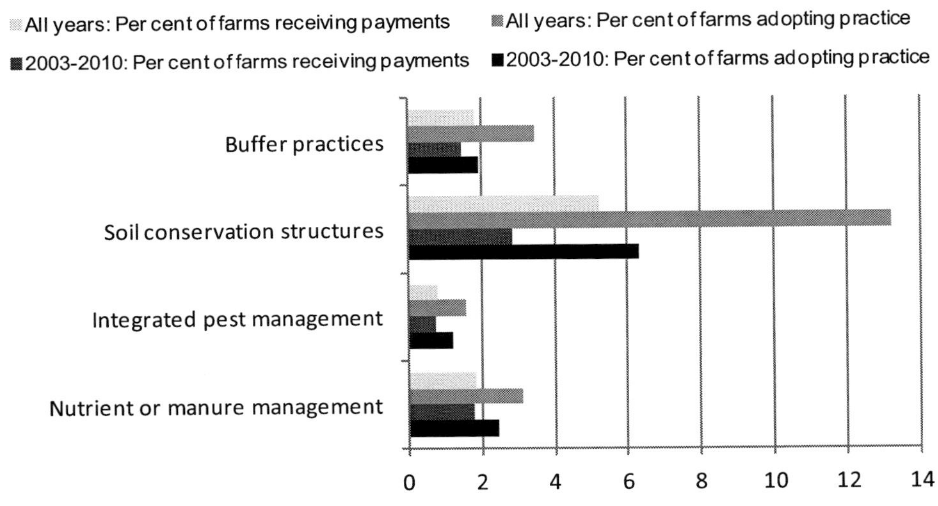

Notes:

1. See Table 4.1 for definition of practice groups.

2. Farmers in the wheat survey where not asked about conservation tillage payments.

Source: *Agricultural Resources Management Survey*, 2009 and 2010.

4.2 Propensity Score Matching and ARMS data

A common statistic used to evaluate the effect of a "treatment" provided by a government programme is the average effect of treatment on the treated (ATT). In the conservation programme context, the ATT is the expected effect of a payment (treatment) on an environmental or related outcome on farms where producers received payments for the adoption of a conservation practice. The ATT is defined as:

$$ATT = E[(Y(1)|D = 1] - E[Y(0)|D = 1],$$

where $D = 1$ indicates the receipt of a payment, $Y(1)$ is the outcome of interest when a payment is received, and $Y(0)$ is the outcome of interest when a payment is not received. For example, the outcome could be the nitrogen fertiliser application rate and the treatment could be a payment for adoption of a nutrient management plan (which might, among other things, include provisions that effectively reduce a producer's nitrogen application rate). In this example, $E[(Y(1)|D = 1]$ would be the expected nitrogen application rate when a nutrient management payment has been received, for a farm that did, in fact, receive a payment for adopting a nutrient management plan. This expectation can be estimated straightforwardly from survey data. The other term, $E[Y(0)|D = 1]$ would be the expected nitrogen application rate when a nutrient management payment has not been received, for a farm that did, in fact, receive a nutrient management payment. This expectation cannot be estimated from survey data because it does not reflect the farmer's behaviour. That is, farmers who receive payments for practice adoption *do* adopt the practice. Under certain conditions, however, this counterfactual outcome can be estimated by matching farms that did receive a payment to an observationally equivalent farm (or farms) that did not receive a payment. In the nutrient management example, the nitrogen application rate on a farm that received a payment for nutrient management would be compared to the nitrogen application rate of a very similar farm (or farms), that did not receive a payment for nutrient management.

Propensity Score Matching (PSM; see Heckman *et al.*, 1998; Caliendo and Kopeing, 2008) is a frequently used matching method. In PSM, matches are based on the propensity of a given individual to receive a specific treatment, or, in our application, the probability that the producer receives a payment for practice adoption. Propensity scores can be estimated econometrically using a discrete choice model (e.g. logit or probit). The probability of receiving a payment for practice adoption is modelled as a function of the field, farm, and farmer characteristics believed to influence the receipt of a practice adoption payment. While these methods are relatively new to agricultural economics, a number of applications exist (e.g. Lynch *et al.*, 2007; Pufahl and Weiss 2009; Chabe-Ferret and Subervie, 2011; Mezzatesta *et al.*, 2011).

The validity of PSM as a policy evaluation method rests on two assumptions (Caliendo and Kopeing, 2008). The first assumption (often referred to as "unconfoundedness," "selection on observables," or the "conditional independence assumption") is that farms that did not receive payments (non-payment farms), but that are observationally equivalent to a farm that did receive a payment (the payment farm), are assumed to make the same decisions about all production and conservation practices that the payment farm would have made in the absence of the payment. If that is true, differences in outcomes for the payment farm and matched non-payment farm(s) can be attributed solely to the payment. Although this assumption cannot be formally tested, its plausibility rests on the extent to which available data is rich enough to determine whether farms are observationally equivalent with respect to the likelihood of receiving a conservation practice adoption payment.

The second assumption is often referred to as "overlap" or "common support." Farms available for matching must have a non-zero probability of receiving conservation payments and a non-zero probability of not receiving conservation payments. Satisfying this condition insures that farms in the payment group will not be compared to non-payment farms that are inherently different. Farms with relevant field, farm, and farmer characteristics that lie outside a specified range of common support for payment and non-payment farms are not used for matching. In terms of policy, for example, this assumption excludes non-payment farms from the comparison group if they are ineligible for conservation payments (in general or for a specific practice) or face regulations that do not apply to payment farms.

To make high quality matches, the data describing farms (used to estimate the logit or probit treatment model) must be rich enough to account for all factors affecting conservation practice adoption, the willingness to seek payments from a conservation programme, and the likelihood that farms would be selected by the programme agency to receive payments. Previous research on conservation practice adoption shows that a range of factors are relevant, including field characteristics (e.g. productivity, erodibility), climate (average temperatures and rainfall), farmer characteristics (e.g. age, education), and farm characteristics (e.g. farm size, primary products) (e.g. Caswell *et al.*, 2001; Fuglie and Kascak, 2002; Soule, 2001; Wu *et al.*, 2004). In this respect, the ARMS survey (including data that can be readily linked to the ARMS survey observations) is a very rich source. Field-level data includes information on all field operations, fertiliser and pesticide applications, land tenure, conservation practices, irrigation, soil erodibility and the presence of wetlands. The farm level survey includes information on farm size, commodities produced, production expenses, total government payments, land tenure (the proportion of land in the farm that is owned by the farmer), operator age and education, off-farm work, and many other characteristics of the farm, the farmer and the farmer's household. Because ARMS observations are geo-coded, each can be linked to nearby weather stations, providing a wealth of historical data from which climate variables can be defined (e.g. long term averages for precipitation and temperature). ARMS data can also be linked to databases supplying extensive information on soil properties (e.g. soil texture or water holding capacity) and highly developed indicators of soil productivity that account for multiple soil properties (e.g. Dobos *et al.*, 2008).

In many respects, producers who have adopted nutrient and manure management plans differ from those who have not adopted plans (Table 4.2, compare columns A and B to column C). Producers who received payments for the adoption of nutrient and manure management plans also differ from those who adopted plans without payments, albeit in fewer ways (Table 4.2). For example, farms adopting nutrient and manure management plans tend to be larger and to rely more heavily on livestock, and their farmers have a greater tendency to be full-time farmers who are relatively young and have more education (with at least some time spent at college). Farm size and education also appear to differ across farms adopting nutrient and manure plans with payments and those adopting but without payments. Differences are also observed for producers who install soil conservation structures (Table 4.3), buffer practices (Table 4.4), and integrated pest management (Table 4.5). For example, farms that adopt soil conservation structures (e.g. terraces) are more likely to be in areas with greater precipitation and on higher productivity land (which may be a function of precipitation).

Small sample size is a potential limitation in terms of teasing out differences between producers who receive conservation payments and those who do not. Because the overall sample sizes are modest (2 906 usable observations for the combined wheat and corn sample), the number of farms in the sample that actually received a payment for conservation practice adoption may or may not be adequate to separate payment from non-payment farms. For the combined wheat and corn sample, 103 farms reported receiving nutrient or manure management payments in 2003 or later, 41 reported receiving payments for soil conservation structures, 38 for buffer practices, and 57 for integrated pest management. (A third year of data, from the 2011 survey of sorghum and barley producers, is available in May 2012.)

Table 4.2. Characteristics of farms adopting nutrient and manure management, 2009 wheat and 2010 corn (plans adopted 2003-10)

	Adopted with pay			Adopted without pay			Non-adopter		
Characteristic	**Estimate**		**CV%**	**Estimate**		**CV%**	**Estimate**		**CV%**
Farm	**A**			**B**			**C**		
Average Acreage	2 187.82	BC*	12	1 136.18	A	31	1 461.83	A	5
Average value of production (USD)	562 317.04	C	18	997 478.06	C	39	344 343.40	AB	5
% livestock	0.34	C	14	0.45	C	29	0.21	AB	8
% crops	0.66	C	7	0.55		24	0.76	A	2
Average government payments (USD)	41 199.11	BC	20	14 544.42	A	20	16 394.26	A	5
Average proportion of land owned	0.50		15	0.66		9	0.60		5
Field									
Proportion owned	0.48		20	0.49		33	0.57		4
Proportion irrigated	--		--	--		--	0.04		12
Proportion highly erodible	0.27	C	31	0.13		47	0.08	A	9
30-year average precipitation (mm)	636.77	C	8	735.02		14	759.77	A	1
30-year average max temperature (°C)	14.02	BC	5	15.91	A	4	16	A	1
30-year average min temperature (°C)	1.49	C	48	2.99		25	4	A	3
Average soil productivity (index)	0.41		9	0.45		14	0.43		2
Average erodibility index (ton/acre/year)	10.22		19	9.78		10	8.74		12
Farmer									
Proportion primarily farmers	0.94	C	4	0.95	C	5	0.81	AB	3
Average age of operator (years)	52.71	C	3	52.05	C	5	57.33	AB	1
Education:									
Proportion HS graduate	0.22	BC	29	0.51	A	26	0.39	A	6
Proportion with some college	0.55	BC	21	0.18	A	38	0.31	A	8
Proportion college graduates	0.21		35	0.21		39	0.25		10
Average off-farm income (USD)	36 853.77	C	21	24 810.36	C	37	52 566.02	AB	6
Average farm income (USD)	83 672.59		42	--		--	34 586.96		16
N	103			65			2 738		

Notes:

* Letters designate difference from estimates in other columns (denoted A, B, C from left to right) in the same row at p<=0.05.

-- = Coefficient of variation greater than 50%, estimate not reported.

Source: *Agricultural Resources Management Survey*, 2009 and 2010.

Table 4.3. Characteristics of farms adopting soil conservation structures 2009 wheat and 2010 corn (adopted 2003-10)

	Adopted with pay			Adopted without pay			Non-adopter		
Characteristic	**Estimate**		**CV %**	**Estimate**		**CV %**	**Estimate**		**CV %**
Farm	A			B			C		
Average acreage	1 204.47		25	1 309.37		19	1 479.71		4
Average value of production (USD)	343 266.04		25	276 783.62	C	13	357 648.38	B	5
% livestock	0.33		39	0.20		27	0.21		7
% crops	0.67		19	0.80		7	0.76		2
Average government payments (USD)	19 899.74		22	--		--	16 566.71		4
Average proportion of land owned	0.52		17	0.56		16	0.60		6
Field									
Proportion owned	0.34	C*	37	0.52		22	0.57	A	5
Proportion irrigated	--		--	--		--	0.04	A	11
Proportion highly erodible	0.27		44	0.24		45	0.08		9
30-year average precipitation (mm)	891.50	C	4	822.34	C	14	753.01	AB	1
30-year average max temperature (°C)	17.69		5	16.39		2	16.33		1
30-year average min temperature (°C)	5.74	BC	10	4.34	A	7	3.86	A	3
Average soil productivity (index)	0.61	BC	8	0.49	A	7	0.43	A	2
Average erodibility index (ton/ac/year)	7.71		22	10.89		18	8.73		12
Farmer									
Proportion primarily farmers	0.83		11	0.81		11	0.82		3
Average age of operator (years)	62.87		9	56.96		5	57.10		1
Education:									
Proportion HS graduate	0.38		43	0.32		28	0.40		6
Proportion with some college	#		#	0.47		23	0.30		9
Proportion college graduates	0.35		41	--		--	0.25		10
Average off-farm income (USD)	60 572.88		37	49 247.42		7	51 908.37		6
Average farm income (USD)	--		--	24 619.74		40	34 858.90		16
N	41			93			2 772		

Notes:

* Letters designate difference from estimates in other columns (denoted A, B, C from left to right) in the same row at p<=0.05.

-- = Coefficient of variation greater than 50%, estimate not reported.

= not reported, insufficient number of farms reporting.

Source: *Agricultural Resources Management Survey*, 2009 and 2010.

Table 4.4. Characteristics of farms adopting buffer practices[1], 2009 wheat and 2010 corn (adopted 2003-10)

	Adopted with pay			Adopted without pay			Non-adopter		
Characteristic	**Estimate**		**CV %**	**Estimate**		**CV %**	**Estimate**		**CV %**
Farm	**A**			**B**			**C**		
Average acreage	785.21	C*	23	603.89	C	30	1 484.34	AB	5
Average value of production (USD)	361 800.90		26	--		--	354 313.17		5
% livestock	--		--	0.34	A	32	0.22	A	7
% crops	0.96	BC	3	0.60	A	22	0.76	A	2
Average government payments (USD)	26 082.11		40	18 041.16		36	16 627.10		5
Average proportion of land owned	0.48		39	0.51		20	0.60		5
Field									
Proportion owned	0.61		38	0.60		32	0.56		5
Proportion irrigated	--		--	--		--	0.04	A	12
Proportion highly erodible	--		--	--		--	0.09		9
30-year average precipitation (mm)	917.82	BC	2	833.09	AC	14	754.75	AB	1
30-year average max temperature (°C)	15.39	C	2	16.56		11	16.37	A	1
30-year average min temperature (°C)	4.36		8	4.50		28	3.90		3
Average soil productivity (index)	0.65	C	4	0.62	C	8	0.43	AB	2
Average erodibility index (ton/ac/yr)	5.86	C	21	7.15		15	8.82	A	12
Farmer									
Proportion primarily farmers	0.93	C	5	0.87		11	0.81	A	3
Average age of operator (years)	56.37		8	58.59		12	57.21		1
Education:									
Proportion HS graduate	--		--	0.60		31	0.39		6
Proportion with some college	0.58	B	40	--		--	0.31	B	8
Proportion college graduates	--		--	--		--	0.25	A	10
Average off-farm income (USD)	42 873.13		22	38 588.22		30	52 207.26		6
Average farm income (USD)	71 172.43		34	25 741.43		172	34 330.16		16
N	30			28			2 848		

Notes:

1. Filter Strips, Riparian Buffers, Field Borders.

* Letters designate a significant difference from estimates in other columns (denoted A, B, C from left to right) in the same row at p<=0.05.

-- = Coefficient of variation greater than 50%, estimate not reported.

Source: *Agricultural Resources Management Survey*, 2009 and 2010.

Matching methods must also account for policy factors that could affect the likelihood that a given farmer receives a payment for a given practice. Agri-environmental policy poses a major challenge for matching because it involves a complex mix of Federal, state and local programmes. Agri-environmental priorities are often set by state or even local authorities. Many states have AE programmes and regulations, particularly for confined animal feeding operations (CAFOs) (Ribaudo *et al.*, 2003). Even federal programmes are often tailored to meet local resource conservation and environmental needs. In the Environmental Quality Incentives Program (EQIP), for example, decisions about which resource issues to target and which practices to support are made largely at the state level, but priorities and practices supported can vary among local jurisdictions within a state.

Table 4.5. Characteristics of farms adopting integrated pest management, 2009 wheat and 2010 corn (adopted 2003-10)

	Adopted with pay			Adopted without pay			Non-adopters		
Characteristic	**Estimate**		**CV %**	**Estimate**		**CV %**	**Estimate**		**CV %**
Farm	**A**			**B**			**C**		
Average Acreage	1 907.27		19	2 688.67		43	1 461.19		5
Average value of production (USD)	669 396.23	C*	23	--		--	350 927.47	A	5
% livestock	0.14		42	0.25		28	0.22		7
% crops	0.86		7	0.75		10	0.76		2
Average government payments (USD)	50 617.24	C	15	--		--	16 469.28	A	5
Average proportion of land owned	0.42	C	17	--		--	0.60	A	5
Field									
Proportion owned	0.48		26	--		--	0.56		4
Proportion irrigated	--		--	--		--	0.04		11
Proportion highly erodible	0.49	C	21	--		--	0.08	A	9
30-year average precipitation (mm)	692.36		9	580.70	C	14	758.79	B	1
30-year average max temperature (°C)	14.74	C	2	16.67		12	16.36	A	1
30-year average min temperature (°C)	2.56		24	--		--	3.93	A	3
Average soil productivity (index)	0.48	B	12	0.37	AC	9	0.43	B	2
Average erodibility index (ton/ac/year)	12.09		24	13.83		40	8.73		12
Farmer									
Proportion primarily farmers	0.97	C	2	1.00	C	0	0.81	AB	3
Average age of operator (years)	52.99	C	3	62.39		10	57.21	A	1
Education:									
Proportion HS graduate	--		--	0.62	A	37	0.39	A	6
Proportion with some college	0.37		29	--		--	0.31		8
roportion college graduates	0.54	BC	24	--		--	0.25	A	10
Average off-farm income (USD)	28 443.76	C	18	46 767.16		32	52 203.16	A	6
Average farm income (USD)	--		--	--		--	33 849.34		16
N	57			26			2 823		

* Letters designate a significant difference from estimates in other columns (denoted A, B, C from left to right) in the same row at p<=0.05.

-- = Coefficient of variation greater than 50%, estimate not reported.

Source: *Agricultural Resources Management Survey*, 2009 and 2010.

Enrolment in USDA conservation programmes is also competitive (Cattaneo *et al.*, 2005). Producers seeking payments must apply for a specific programme, providing a proposal for the application of specific practices in specific fields. Farmers may differ in their propensity to seek funding, perhaps because of differences in general attitudes about government, differences in familiarity with USDA in general or conservation programmes in particular, or differences in willingness to install or use conservation practices as prescribed by government conservation practice standards. Because farmer proposals for funding often exceed available funding, programme managers select proposals according to likely environmental benefits and costs, creating another set of factors that must be controlled for in the matching process (e.g. soil erodibility, proximity to water, and other factors believed to affect the environmental impact of an action taken on a given farm or field).

Clearly, this patchwork of policies must be considered in the estimation of propensity scores and the selection of matching methods. Because there are multiple programmes and regulations, not all of which are at federal level, an alternate approach is to match the payment farms with non-payment farms within the same geographic area, such as a state or region, where policies are likely to be the same or very similar for all surveyed farms. For example, matching large livestock farms in different states would be inappropriate if one state requires nutrient management plans but the other does not. Comparing producers in a regulated state to producers in a non-regulated state may result in underestimating the additionality of payments made in the unregulated state and/or overestimating additionality in the regulated state. It may be difficult, however, to find good matches for large farms (which are few in number) without reaching across state boundaries.

Table 4.6. Number of observations for selected regions, 2009 wheat and 2010 corn (practices adopted 2003-10)

		Nutrient and manure management			Soil conservation structures		
State or region	**Number**	**Payment**	**No payment**	**No adoption**	**Pay**	**No payment**	**No adoption**
Heartland	900	19	17	864	17	49	834
Northern Crescent	361	17	27	317	5	8	348
Northern Great Plains	615	19	4	592	2	5	608
Prairie Gateway	469	8	8	453	12	18	439
Fruitful Rim	205	13	4	188	2	3	200
Basin and Range	186	21	2	163	0	3	183
		Buffer practices			**Integrated pest management**		
State or region	**Number**	**Payment**	**No payment**	**Payment**	**No payment**	**Payment**	**No payment**
Heartland	900	20	9	20	9	20	9
Northern Crescent	361	3	6	3	6	3	6
Northern Great Plains	615	1	2	1	2	1	2
Prairie Gateway	469	1	3	1	3	1	3
Fruitful Rim	205	0	3	0	3	0	3
Basin and Range	186	3	1	3	1	3	1

Source: *Agricultural Resources Management Survey*, 2009-2010.

Table 4.6 shows the number of surveyed producers who reported adopting surveyed conservation practices during 2003-10 by Farm Resource Region[5] and practice group. Overall, 97 of the 159 producers who developed and began implementing nutrient or manure management plans between 2003 and 2010 reported receiving payments related the adoption of these plans (61%). The percentage of plans funded varied significantly across regions. In the Northern Crescent, only 17 of 44 farms that reported adopting nutrient or manure management plans also reported receiving a payment (39%). This region includes much of the Great Lakes and Chesapeake Bay watersheds (Wisconsin, Michigan, Northeastern Minnesota, Northeast Ohio, New York, most of Pennsylvania, and part of Maryland) where concern about nutrient runoff from livestock operations is high and many states have already enacted some type of nutrient management requirement.

Even if regulation is driving some adoption of nutrient and manure management plans, it does not necessarily mean that payments for these practices are not additional. The payments may be reaching a segment of producers who are not subject to the regulation, e.g. smaller, non-CAFO livestock farms. In the Northern Great Plains, Fruitful Rim, and Basin and Range regions, however, 53 of 63 farms that reported nutrient or manure management plans also reported receiving payments (84%). These regions include most of the West, portions of Texas and all of Florida. In these areas, it appears likely than nutrient and manure management plans would not be developed in the absence of payments. Nonetheless, payments are additional only if the adoption of practices on payment farms leads to better environmental outcomes. For example, this could include lower fertiliser application rates, more post-planting application of nitrogen fertiliser, or reduced application of nitrogen fertiliser in autumn for nutrient management plans.

4.3 Conclusion

United States agri-environmental policy relies heavily on voluntary incentive payments to encourage farmers to use more environmentally sound practices and improve the environmental performance of their farms. The additionality of these programmes has never been formally considered, due in large part to the lack of high quality data on practice adoption and associated payments. The 2009 (wheat) and 2010 (corn) ARMS surveys are among the first to include data on conservation practice adoption and related payments for US farms.

While the ARMS data provide a rich source of information about farms and farmers, a relatively small number of surveyed farms report adopting one of more of the practices listed in our four practice groups (with the exception of conservation tillage), a smaller number reported adopting practices in recent years (2003 or later), and fewer still report receiving payments associated with this adoption. The number of survey respondents that received a conservation payment for adoption of at least one practice in a given practice group ranges from 30 (buffer practices) to 103 (nutrient and manure management).

Perhaps the best opportunity to study the role payments in practice adoption and associated outcomes is in the case of payments for nutrient and manure management. For these practices, the majority of adoption has occurred in recent years (2003 or later) and a majority of farmers who report nutrient or manure management plans also report receiving a payment associated with adoption, although the proportion of farms reporting payments varies widely across regions. Nutrient management plans can also be tied to specific outcomes that are also surveyed in ARMS, including fertiliser application rates, timing and method, manure and legume crediting, and soil and plant tissue testing.

Finally, the complexity of US policy presents a major barrier to research on additionality. Although our simple analysis of regional differences in adoption of and payments for nutrient management does not necessarily imply that differences are due to inter-state policy differences, it does suggest that spatial variables should be considered in the estimation of propensity scores and consideration of common support. Nonetheless, the Northern Crescent includes large parts of the Great Lakes and Chesapeake Bay watersheds—places where the effect of agricultural nutrients on water quality has long been a major concern. Given inter-regional differences in the number of surveyed farms that have adopted practices with and without payments, however, the extent to which conservation payments are additional may vary across regions for some practice groups, particularly nutrient and manure management.

Notes

1. US Department of Agriculture, Washington D.C., United States.

2. Data are obtained from USDA budget summaries (for various years), published by the Office of Budget and Policy Analysis, US Department of Agriculture, *www.obpa.usda.gov/budsum/budget_summary.html.*

3. 2009 wheat survey included California, Colorado, Idaho, Illinois, Kansas, Michigan, Minnesota, Missouri, Montana, Nebraska, North Dakota, Ohio, Oklahoma, Oregon, South Dakota, Texas, and Washington; 2010 corn survey included Colorado, Georgia, Illinois, Indiana, Iowa, Kansas, Kentucky, Michigan, Minnesota, Missouri, Nebraska, New York, North Carolina, North Dakota, Ohio, Pennsylvania, South Dakota, Texas, and Wisconsin.

4. For roughly 40% of respondents (in both the wheat and corn surveys) who reported one or more structural or vegetative practices, the practices were installed before the beginning of the current farmer's tenure.

5. A map showing Farm Resource Regions can be found in the Annex.

References

Caliendo, M. and S. Kopeing (2008), "Some Practical Guidance for the Implementation of Propensity Score Matching" *Journal of Economic Survey,* Vol. 22, No.1, pp. 31-72.

Chabé-Ferret, S. and J. Subervie (2011), "Estimating the Causal Effects of French Agro-Environmental Schemes on Farmers' Practices," Paper presented at the OECD Workshop on the Evaluation of Agri-Environmental Policies, Braunschweig, Germany, 20-22 June.

Caswell, M., K. Fuglie, C. Ingram, S. Jans, C. Kascak (2001), *Adoption of Agricultural Production Practices: Lessons Learned from the U.S. Department of Agriculture Area Studies Project,* Agricultural Economic Report, AER-792, Economic Research Service, U.S. Department of Agriculture, January, 110 p.

Cattaneo, A, R. Claassen, R. Johansson and M. Weinberg (2005), *Flexible Conservation Measures on Working Land: What Challenges Lie Ahead?* Economic Research Report, ERR-5, Economic Research Service, U.S. Department of Agriculture, June.

Claassen, R. (2011), "USDA Conservation Spending on Working Agricultural Lands Bucks Long-Term Trend," *Amber Waves*, Vol.9, No.3.

Claassen R. and M. Ribaudo (2006), "Chapter 5.1—Conservation Policy Overview," in *Agricultural Resource and Environmental Indicators, 2006,* Economic Information Bulletin, EIB-16, Economic Research Service, U.S. Department of Agriculture, July, pp. 168-174.

Dobos, R., H. Sinclair and K. Hipple (2008), *User Guide National Commodity Crop Productivity Index (NCCPI) Version 1.0*, National Soil Survey Center, Lincoln, NE, Natural Resources Conservation Service, U.S. Department of Agriculture.

Fuglie, K.O. and C.A. Kascak (2001), "Adoption and Diffusion of Natural-Resource-Conserving Agricultural Technology", *Review of Agricultural Economics*, Vol.23, No.2, pp. 386-403.

Goolsby, D., W. Battaglin, G. Lawrence, R. Artz, B. Aulenbach, B. Hooper, R. Keeney and G. Stensland (1999), *Flux and Sources of Nutrients in the Mississippi-Atchafalaya River Basin: Topic 3 Report*, U.S. Department of Commerce, National Oceanic and Atmospheric Administration.

Heckman, J., H. Ichimura and P. Todd (1998), "Matching as an Econometric Evaluation Estimator," *The Review of Economic Studies,* Vol. 65, No.2, pp. 261-294.

Lambert, D., P. Sullivan, R. Claassen and L. Foreman (2006), *Conservation Compatible Practices and Programs: Who Participates?,* Economic Research Report, ERR-14, Economic Research Service, U.S. Department of Agriculture, January.

Lynch, L., W. Gray and J. Geoghegan (2007), "Are Farmland Preservation Program Easement Restrictions Capitalized into Farmland Prices? What Can Propensity Score Matching Analysis Tell Us?" *Review of Agricultural Economics*, Vol. 29, No.3, pp. 502-509.

Mezzatesta, M., D. Newburn and R. Woodward (2011), "Additionality and the Adoption of Farm Conservation Practices," unpublished manuscript, August.

Pufahl, A. and C.R. Weiss (2009), "Evaluating the effects of farm programmes: results from propensity score matching," *European Review of Agricultural Economics,* Vol. 36, No.1, pp. 79-101.

Ribaudo, M., N. Gollehon, M. Aillery, J. Kaplan, R. Johansson, J. Agapoff, L. Christensen, V. Breneman and M. Peters (2003), *Manure Management for Water Quality: Costs to Animal*

Feeding Operations of Applying Manure to Land, Agricultural Economic Report, AER-824, Economic Research Service, U.S. Department of Agriculture, June.

Ribaudo, M. and R. Johansson (2006), "Water Quality—Impacts of Agriculture", in Agricultural Resource and Environmental Indicators, Eds. K. Wiebe and N. Gollohan, *Economic Information Bulletin*, EIB-16, Economic Research Service, U.S. Department of Agriculture, June, pp. 33-42.

Smith, K. and M. Weinberg (2004), "Measuring the Success of Conservation Programs," *Amber Waves*, Vol. 2, No.4, pp. 14-21.

Soule, M.J. (2001), "Soil Management and the Farm Typology: Do Small Family Farms Manage Soil and Nutrient Resources Differently than Large Family Farms?" *Agricultural and Resource Economics Review*, Vol. 30, No.2, pp. 179-188.

Wu, J., R.M. Adams, *et al.* (2004), "From Microlevel Decisions to Landscape Changes: An Assessment of Agricultural Conservation Policies," *American Journal of Agricultural Economics*, Vol. 86, No.1, pp. 26-41.

Annex 4.A

ERS farm resource regions

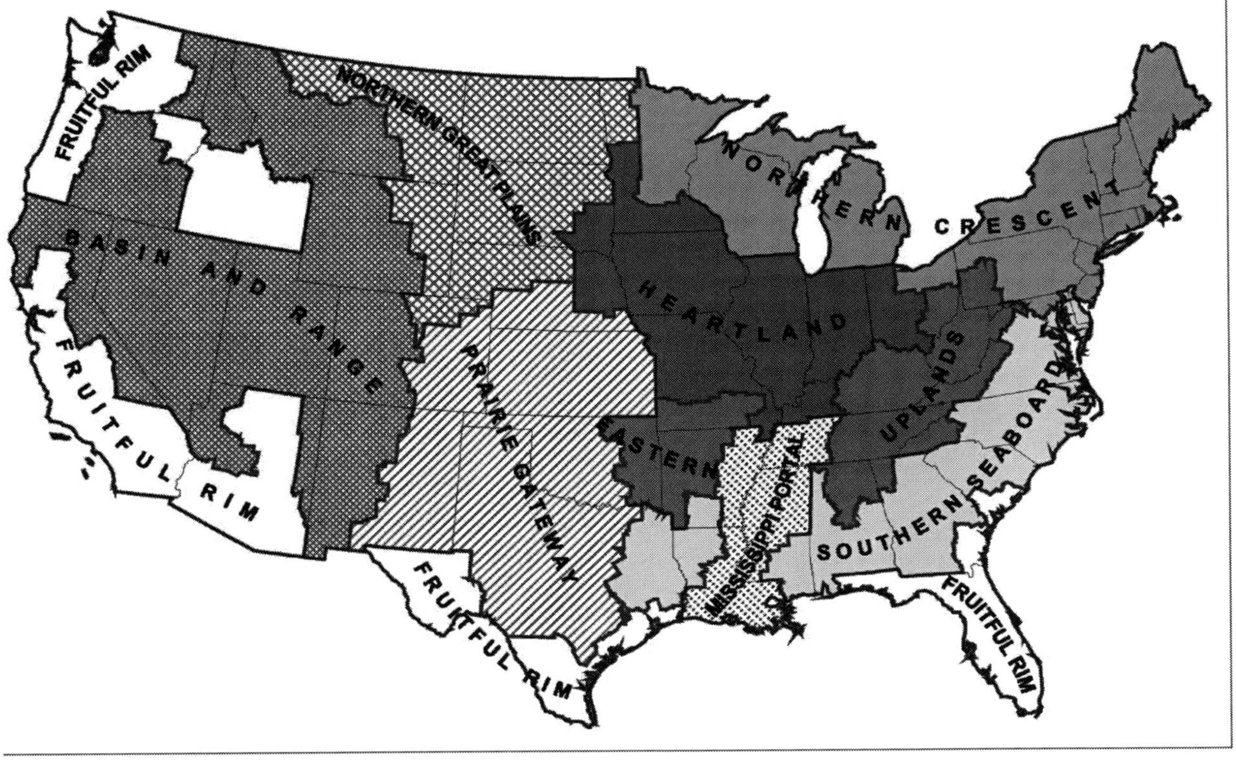

Source: U.S. Department of Agriculture, Economic Research Service (2000), *Farm Resource Regions*. Economic Information Bulletin, EIB-760, September.

III. LESSONS LEARNT FROM EVALUATIONS PERFORMED

Chapter 5

Follow-up study of the impacts of agri-environmental measures in Finland

Jyrki Aakkula, Mikko Kuussaari, Katri Rankinen, Petri Ekholm, Janne Heliölä, Terho Hyvönen, Laura Kitti and Tapio Salo[1]

This chapter summarises recent findings on the impacts of agri-environmental (AE) measures (2008-13), with special attention to water loading and biological diversity. Indicator trends, and comparisons between sites subject and not subject to AE measures, were analysed. Measures with the most potential for reducing nutrient loading are those targeting fertiliser rates, nature management fields and plant cover. Biodiversity has benefited from farmer contracts regarding traditional biotope management, organic production, raising local breeds and so on, as well as non-productive investments like establishing constructed wetlands.

Agricultural nutrient loading has decreased because of lower artificial fertiliser use, but nutrient leaching from manure around clustered animal production units is increasing and requires measures targeted to manure composition and disposal. The greatest threat to biodiversity derives from trends in landscape structure. Due to regional heterogeneity, the objectives, measures and support levels of the AE scheme should be customised more according to the region, production sector and individual farm, by means of farm-specific environmental management plans.

Modern societies direct various kinds of expectations to farming. Apart from producing food commodities, agriculture should also contribute to the maintenance of managed and open landscapes, environmental quality, rural viability and so on. Obviously, agricultural nutrient loading and greenhouse gas (GHG) emissions affect the quality of the agricultural environment. Biological diversity, in turn, interacts closely with agricultural production techniques, cultivation methods and land use. In developed countries, the significance of environmental goods and services as a joint product of farming has been growing in the past two decades and the importance of the public good aspect shows no sign of fading. For these reasons, it is essential that the relationship between agriculture and the environment is properly examined and the impacts of policy measures applied are carefully followed up.

Since 1995, Finnish agri-environmental (AE) policy has centred around the AE measures contained in successive EU rural development programmes, which are part-financed from the EU budget. The present Agri-Environment Scheme (AES) is included in the Rural Development Programme for Mainland Finland (2007–13), which both as such and through the legislation that it is based on requires the follow-up of the impacts of the measures. One element in this work is the follow-up study on the impacts of AE measures (so called MYTVAS 3) implemented in 2008-13, financed mainly by the Finnish Ministry of Agriculture and Forestry and in part by the Finnish Ministry of the Environment. The study is conducted by a consortium coordinated by the MTT Agrifood Research Finland (MTT) and, together with MTT, comprises the Finnish Environment Institute (SYKE), University of Helsinki (HY) and Finnish Game and Fisheries Research Institute (RKTL).

The aim of the MYTVAS 3 follow-up study is to find out how the AE measures have influenced the state of the agricultural environment, how the measures have influenced the preconditions for farming activities and how the AES should be developed in order to improve its effectiveness. A major focus is on the impacts of AE measures on nutrient loading to waterways and on biological diversity.

This chapter summarises preliminary key results of the MYTVAS 3 follow-up study and uses them to assess the effectiveness of the AE measures. In order to do this, it first describes at a general level the content of the current Finnish Agri-Environmental Scheme. A further aim is to discuss the possible policy implications of the observations and the conclusions drawn from them.

It should be borne in mind when assessing the results presented or making recommendations for new or revised measures that the follow-up data may indicate that *something* has taken place but not necessarily the exact cause of the event. It is not always possible to show that certain trends are specifically the outcome of applying the measures in the present AES. The time lag between adopting a measure and the observed impact is often long, and the cause-effect relationships are complex or partly unknown. In addition, other aspects of agricultural policy and changes on the market influence the state of the agricultural environment either directly or indirectly.

5.1 The current Finnish agri-environmental scheme and the monitoring of impacts

The objective of the current Finnish Agri-Environmental Scheme is to encourage sustainable agricultural and horticultural production so that the environmental burden caused by production is reduced from its current level. AE payments aim to diminish the negative environmental impact of agriculture, secure the biodiversity of agricultural environment and the cultural landscape in rural areas, and maintain the preconditions for agricultural production even in the long term. The burden on the environment and particularly on surface and ground water is diminished by increasing the use of plant nutrients, decreasing the risks caused by the use of pesticides, ensuring the biodiversity of the agricultural environment, and caring for the fauna, the flora and the rural landscape. Objectives also include a reduction in the erosion of arable land, an increase in the diversity of soil fauna and the amount of humus and the maintenance of the productivity of soil or its increase.

Structure and measures of the Finnish Agri-Environment Scheme

The Finnish Agri-Environment Scheme consists of basic measures, additional measures and special measures. Payments vary according to measures and assisted regions. The purpose of basic measures is a systematic monitoring of farming and its environmental protection, the fertilisation of field crops and horticultural plants according to soil fertility and the needs of the plant species in question, the allocation of wider headlands and of broader set-aside margins alongside water channels than what is required by the Water Law, and biodiversity and landscape preservation. The basic measures are obligatory for all farmers who participate in the AES.

In addition to basic measures, the AES includes a number of more demanding measures that are optional for farmers depending on the assisted region in question. There are additional measures for both regular field crops and horticultural plants. Additional measures include reduced fertiliser rates, adjustment of nitrogenous fertilisers for field crops, enhanced vegetal cover on arable land during winter, cultivation of catch crops, observation of nutrient levels, diversification of farming, extensive grassland production and the application of manure during the growing season.

The compensation for basic and additional measures is paid on the farm's entire arable land area eligible for AE payments, provided that both cross-compliance requirements and minimum requirements are complied with. The minimum requirements include the maximum limits for nitrogenous and phosphate fertilisers as well as the conditions for the use of plant protection products.

Special measures are those with a particularly significant impact on the quality of the agricultural environment. They can concern, for example, the establishment of a buffer zone or the creation of a multi-functional wetland, field cropping on underground water basins, treatment methods for runoff waters, organic production, rearing of native breeds, farming of original plant species or management of traditional biotopes. The compensation paid in the context of special measures is linked to area or animal unit. It is also possible to include non-arable land in some agreements.

Farmer participation in the AES is extensive. In March 2010, about 58 100 farms, or 90% of all farms (64 000), were committed to the basic AE measures defined for the programming period 2007-13. About 70% of these farms were cropping farms and 30% were livestock farms, with a total committed area of 2 112 000 hectares (about 92% of the Finland's total cultivated arable land).[2] In 2009, the total payment for basic measures was EUR 220 million and the total payment for additional measures was EUR 72 million. Total compensation paid in the context of special measures was EUR 48 million in 2009, making the grand total of AE payments about EUR 340 million.

Monitoring of impacts

The MYTVAS 3 follow-up study aims to continue the efforts of previous follow-up studies. The object of the first MYTVAS follow-up study (MYTVAS 1), which took place between 1995 and 1999, was to study the impact that the various measures associated with the AES had on the environment and the environmental burden caused by agriculture. The MYTVAS 1 study was complemented with a project during which the financial significance of AE payments was monitored.

The final report of the MYTVAS 1 study (Palva *et al.*, 2001) concluded that the use of nitrogenous and phosphate fertilisers had decreased and was, in most cases, approaching the (then) baselines defined for AE payments. However, phosphate fertiliser application rates were not yet adjusted precisely enough to correspond to soil fertility needs. The leaching of nitric nitrogen was estimated to have decreased 4-15% in different areas, which was mainly attributed to a decrease in application rates for nitrogenous fertilisers and livestock manure. Furthermore, it was estimated that phosphorus leaching was lower by 5-13% mainly due to the introduction of reduced tillage and spring ploughing. On the contrary, soluble phosphorus levels persisted or rose slightly, principally because the reduction of the set-aside obligation in 1994 led to a decrease in the use of green fallowing and an increase in cereal cropping.

A financial analysis revealed that the importance of GAEPS support (General Agri-Environmental Protection Scheme) for the total income of Finnish farmers was significant in all assisted regions, types of farming and farm size categories. It was estimated that 62% of GAEPS support covered the costs incurred by adopting the AE measures, and 38% remained as a financial incentive. Therefore, it was concluded that the termination of the AES would mean serious financial difficulties for the majority of farms, unless a new, corresponding scheme were initiated (Koikkalainen *et al.*, 1999).

The MYTVAS 2 follow-up study (2000-06) analysed the impact on water bodies and biodiversity in two separate reports. The final report on the impact on water bodies (Turtola and Lemola, 2008) concluded that a more effective reduction of the environmental load imposed on water bodies would require the reallocation of future measures towards areas where that load is greatest, and that particular priority should be given to diminishing the burden in the livestock production areas in south-western and western Finland.

The final report on biodiversity impact (Kuussaari *et al.*, 2008) reached two main conclusions. First, the impact of AE measures had been positive, even if they had not been able to stop the impoverishment of the agricultural environment. Second, the management of traditional biotopes was considered to be the most important biodiversity-promoting measure among the special measures. The report concluded that the AES should be restructured, particularly with respect to obligatory basic and additional measures, and that AE measures should be complemented with new, more effective biodiversity conservation methods.

The results and conclusions of previous MYTVAS follow-up studies reflect the evolution of AE measures, AE policy and general agricultural policy. Initially, the AES was also a method of securing farmers' income when Finland's entry into the European Union in 1995 destroyed overnight the cornerstone of national agricultural policy, namely the price support system that rested on strong border protection (Aakkula *et al.*, 2006). Since then, societal demands concerning the environmental impact of the AES have been incrementally increased. These days, the Agri-Environment Scheme in particular and AE policy in general are expected to have a significant effect on the environment.

5.2 Nutrient loading and its impacts on water quality

A major goal of national water protection policy in Finland is to control agricultural nutrient losses, since crop production and animal husbandry are the largest sources of nutrients in surface waters. Phosphorus (P) is transported from fields in dissolved form or attached to eroded soil particles. Transport of this particulate phosphorus depends on, for example, soil texture, slope and vegetation cover, whereas transport of dissolved phosphorus is governed by soil phosphorus status, and methods and rates of fertilisation and manure spreading. Nitrogen (N) is mostly applied in easily soluble form, and its losses depend mainly on methods and rates of fertilisation and manure spreading. Soil contains large amounts of organically-bound nitrogen, so transfer also depends on decay of organic matter.

Maximum fertilisation rates for different crops are set in the basic measures of the AES. In special measures, there are additional options to reduce fertilisation. Further, manure use and handling are controlled by the EU Nitrate Directive and the AES (basic, additional and special measures). Erosion control measures in the AES include winter vegetation cover and reduced tillage. Constructed wetlands and buffer zones (15 m wide) defined in special measures also serve this purpose.

The MYTVAS 3 study monitored nutrient loading to the surface waters using two methods. First, we studied trends in selected indicators of nutrient load (nutrient balances and soil test P value). Second, we calculated trends in nutrient fluxes from agricultural rivers based on observed discharge and nutrient concentration. Changes in indicators and river nutrient fluxes were compared to changes in agricultural practices and water protection methods by regression analysis (Penttilä *et al.*, 2006). To distinguish effects caused by AE measures from those caused by other, partly independent factors, we controlled for changes in climate and land use in the analysis.

While implementing the AE measures on fields, the total area of cultivated fields has been changing due to other factors, like changes in CAP policy and market prices. Furthermore, changing climate is assumed to increase nutrient load by increasing runoff and temperature. So far, no increasing trend in annual or seasonal runoff has been detected (Korhonen, 2007). On the other hand, higher annual temperatures have been detected (Tuomenvirta, 2004), which may have increased soil organic matter decomposition.

Changes in indicators: Nutrient balances and soil phosphorus status

In the MYTVAS 3 study, development of a real nutrient balances[3] and soil phosphorus status (soil test P value) serve as indicators of nutrient loading from fields (Uusitalo, 2004, Rankinen *et al.*, 2007). Fertilisation and yield uptake are the main factors influencing nutrient balances. National and areal nitrogen and phosphorus balances were calculated for the period 1990-2009. Use of commercial fertilisers decreased considerably in Finland during 1990-2006. In 1990, average nitrogen and phosphorus use were 112 kg/ha and 30.7 kg/ha, respectively. In 2007-09, average nitrogen use was 73 kg/ha and that of phosphorus only 7 kg/ha.

Both nitrogen and phosphorus balances have been decreasing since 1990 (Figure 5.1), mainly due to decreasing commercial fertiliser use. In recent years, the yield uptake has also increased in southern Finland. At the same time, however, there has been a change in cropping; since 1995, the area of cereals has steadily increased and the area of fallow was at its peak during 1990-94 due to obligatory set-aside intended to reduce over-production.

Nutrient balances decreased most in the Vuoksi catchment. Nutrient balances were highest in the areas of high farm animal density. In the Bothnian Bay drainage basin, both nitrogen and phosphorus balances were above the mean for Finland. Even though the total number of farm animals is steadily decreasing in Finland, animal husbandry is intensifying in south-western and western Finland. In some areas, nutrients in manure alone were sufficient to cover crop need. The highest rate of phosphorus in manure was applied in the Bothnian Bay catchment (about 11 kg/ha). Nitrogen balance was higher than the average in the Archipelago Sea catchment. This is the only area where decreases in commercial N fertiliser use have not occurred since 1995.

The effect of decreasing phosphorus balance is gradually reflected in soil test P values, which were decreasing, except in the Archipelago sea catchment where the mean values were higher than elsewhere (Figure 5.2). In multiple regression analysis, soil test P values depended positively on the areal percentage of high-value crops, which usually have high fertiliser rates. The amount of manure spread on the fields also had a positive impact on the soil-test P value.

Figure 5.1. Change in nutrient balances in Finland

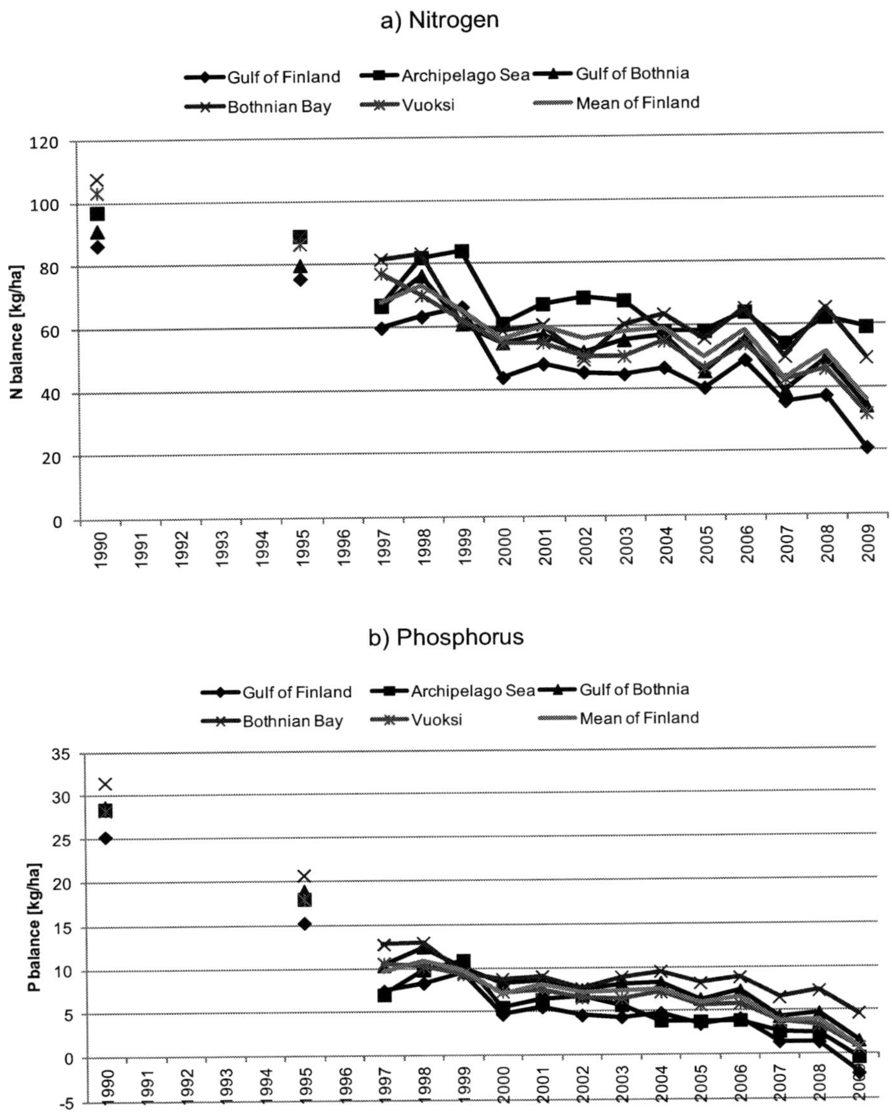

Source: Salo and Lemola (2010).

Figure 5.2. Change in soil test P values in Finland

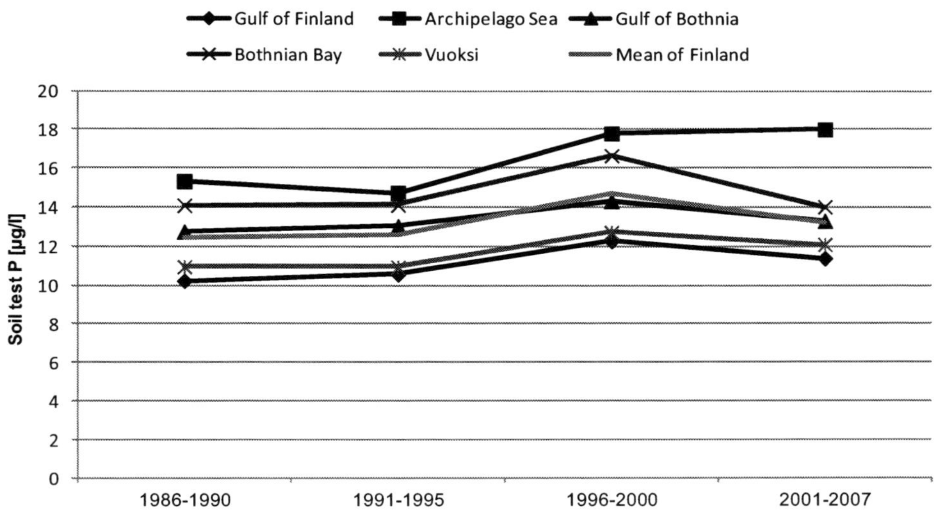

Source: Ekholm *et al.* (2010). Original data is from Viljavuuspalvelu (manufacturer of soil tests for farmers).

Changes in nutrient fluxes from rivers

We studied nutrient (N and P) loading and changes in land use and agriculture in 22 rivers discharging into the Baltic Sea. Areas of river basins ranged from 357 to 4 923 km^2, field percentage from 1.3 to 42.8 and lake percentage from 0.2 to 12.9. The remaining areas in the basins were mainly forests. Daily discharge and the concentrations of total phosphorus and total nitrogen were taken from the data base of the Finnish Environmental Institute. We divided the samples into four sets representing the periods 1985-89 (I), 1990-94 (II), 1995-99 (III) and 2000-06 (IV). Periods I and II served as background for the first and second AES periods (1995-99 and 2000-06, respectively). Nutrient concentrations were analysed in a regression model (Sjöblom, 2008). Daily nutrient loads were calculated from simulated concentration and observed discharge.

The highest nutrient load (tons/year) occurred in the large rivers discharging into the Bothnian Bay. Specific total-P load (kg/km^2/year) was clearly highest from the river basins with a high proportion of fields flowing to the Archipelago Sea. Specific total-N load (kg/km^2/year) from these river basins was also high (Figure 5.3).

To calculate trends in agricultural nutrient loads, we equalised the effect of discharge and removed the effects of municipal and industrial waste waters, waste waters from scattered settlements, and nutrient loads from forest treatment areas. Remaining nutrient flux originated mainly from agricultural areas. During 1985–2006, there was a decrease in phosphorus loads (on an average 17%) but an increase in nitrogen loads (27%). No decrease in phosphorus loads was found in the rivers discharging into the Archipelago Sea (Figure 5.4). The increase in nitrogen load was highest in the drainage basin of Bothnian Bay. The results were in accordance with the trend analysis by Ekholm *et al.* (2007).

Figure 5.3. Specific nutrient loads in drainage basins

a) Total nitrogen

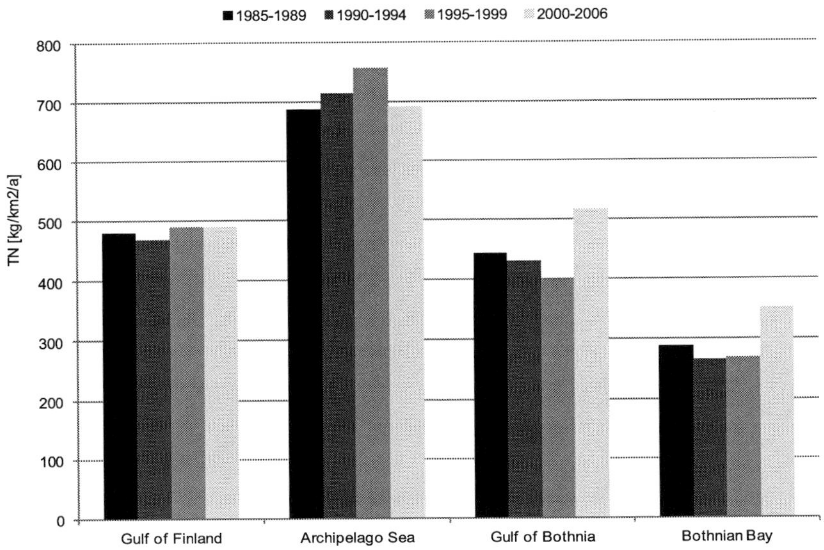

b) Total phosphorus

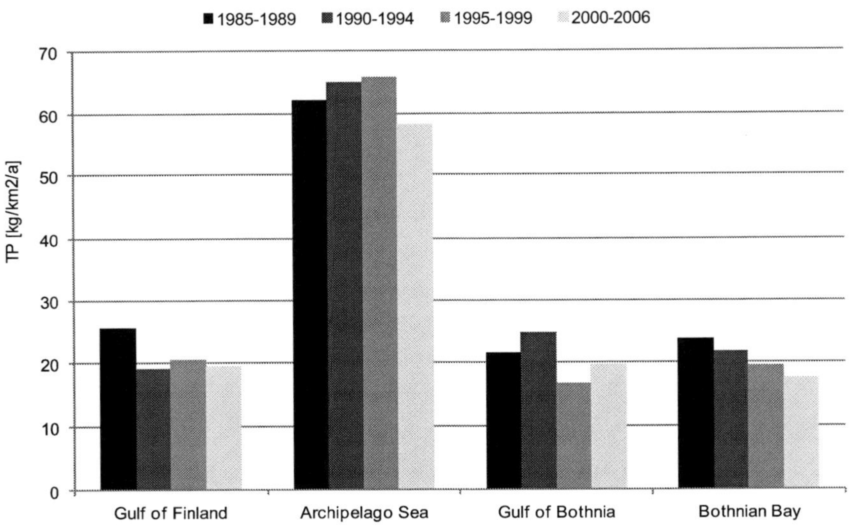

Source: Rankinen *et al.* (2010).

Figure 5.4. Change in nutrient loads from agriculture

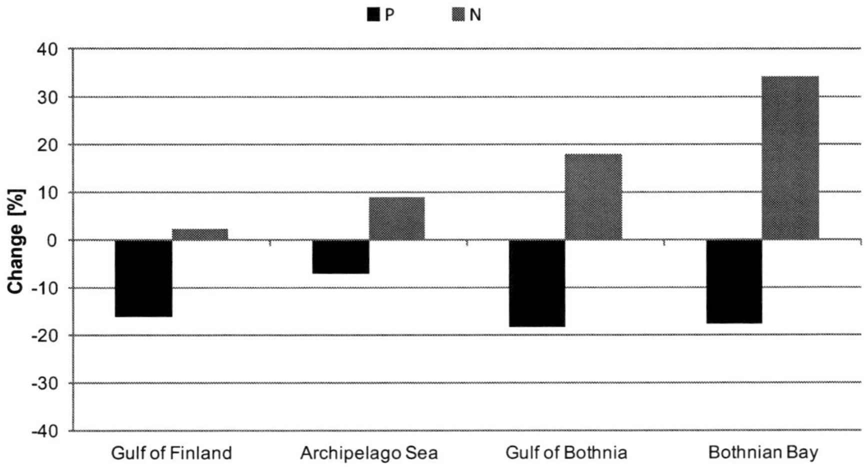

Source: Based on data published in Rankinen *et al.* (2010).

The Archipelago Sea is a sensitive sub-basin of the Baltic Sea, and its ecological state is largely governed by the nutrient loading from Finland. Nitrogen load into the Bothnian Bay has increased. Since this sub-basin is in a more pristine state with primary production being controlled by phosphorus rather than nitrogen, the increased nitrogen load there is not seen as a deterioration of water quality. However, excess nitrogen may be transferred from the Bothnian Bay to more southern sub-basins, which tend to be nitrogen-limited, i.e. primary production and the symptoms of eutrophication are principally governed by the availability of nitrogen.

A decrease in phosphorus load was mainly explained by more fallow area during some periods (1990-94), and the lower soil test P value. Grass cultivation may have served as an erosion protection method in erosion-prone fields in the drainage basin of the Archipelago Sea. Higher nitrogen loads seem to be due to a recent increase in field area and intensification of animal husbandry. Further, observed increase in temperature may have increased nitrogen load. On the other hand, most of the study catchment is located in the drainage basins of the Archipelago Sea and the Bothnian Bay, where N balances stayed above the average for Finland.

5.3 Biodiversity impacts

Two types of study have been conducted within the MYTVAS 3 project in order to examine the biodiversity impacts of the AES, namely monitoring of the trends in farmland biodiversity and case studies evaluating the impacts of specific AE measures.

Monitoring of farmland biodiversity

Monitoring of farmland biodiversity has focused on five complementary indicators: species richness of arable weeds, vascular plants and butterflies of open semi-natural habitats, abundance of farmland birds and components of landscape structure that affect farmland biodiversity. Below we briefly describe the approaches used to monitor these indicators and summarise the main observed trends.

Diversity of arable weeds in Finnish agricultural landscapes has been surveyed four times at intervals of about ten years: 1961-64, 1982-84, 1997-99 and 2007-09 (Salonen and Hyvönen, 2010). Each of these surveys has sampled 300-700 field parcels in 150-300 farms located in different parts of southern Finland. The last survey indicated a slight decrease in average weed species richness compared to the previous survey ten years earlier: in organic fields, a decrease from the average of 24 to 21 species/field parcel and from 16 to 12 species in conventional spring barley fields. The arable weed indicator (Hyvönen and Huusela-Veistola, 2008) showed that despite a slight increase in average weed densities, the index values of weeds for seed-eating birds and herbivore insects had decreased, whereas at the same time the index values of weeds for pollinator insects had continued to slightly increase (Figure 5.5).

Figure 5.5. Development of the Finnish arable weed indicator during 1960-2010

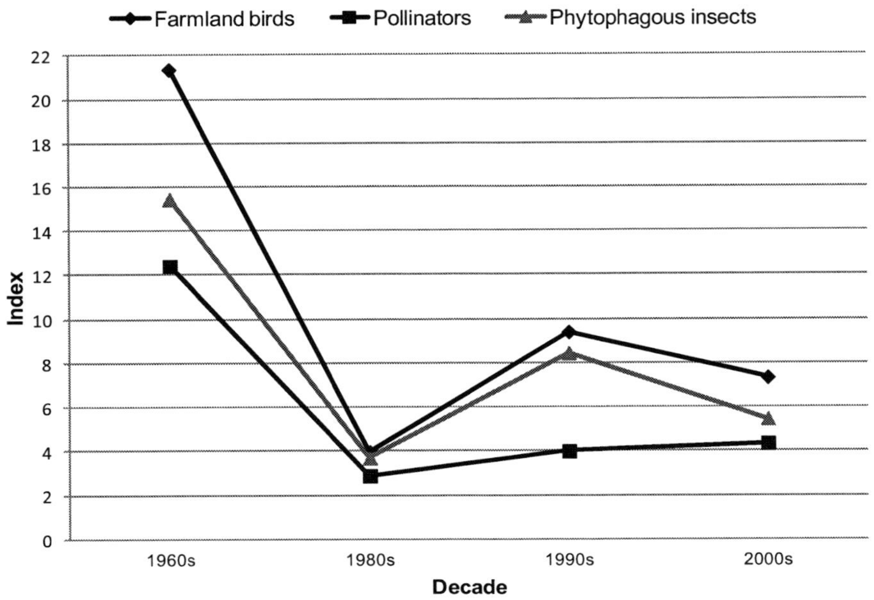

Source: Hyvönen and Huusela-Veistola, 2008; Salonen and Hyvönen, 2010.

The other four farmland biodiversity indicators were monitored within a common study design, which is based on a set of 58 agricultural landscapes distributed within four geographic areas in southern Finland. The landscape structure of the 1 km^2 study landscapes has been monitored since 1990, whereas vascular plants, butterflies and farmland birds have been monitored since 2001.

Somewhat differing trends have been observed in different indicators. In landscape structure the long-continued simplifying and generally negative trend for biodiversity still continued during 1990-2005. This was seen in a decreasing coverage of semi-natural habitats such as semi-natural grasslands and field margins in all studied geographical regions due to further agricultural intensification and the decline in traditional management of semi-natural grasslands (Kivinen *et al.*, 2008). The slight impoverishment of plant communities in field margins detected during 2001-10 (Helenius *et al.*, 2010) was probably related to the long-term negative trend in landscape structure. Also in butterflies the trend was on average slightly negative: one half of the species decreasing in number, whereas one third of the species increased during 2001-10 (Heliölä and Kuussaari, 2010). In contrast to plants and butterflies, the observed trends in farmland birds were generally positive. The long-continued impoverishment of farmland bird communities had stopped, and species of forest-field ecotones and farmyards had on average increased over the last ten years (Tiainen *et al.*, 2010). Farmland birds had probably benefited from the relatively high area of rotational fallows and long-term set-asides during the study period.

Case studies of the impacts of specific measures

Three case studies were conducted during 2007-09 to evaluate biodiversity impacts of specific Finnish AE measures. The main findings of these studies are briefly summarised below.

Constructed wetlands

The dual aim of wetland construction in the Finnish AES is to reduce the nutrient loading in waters and to promote maintenance of biodiversity. A total of 19 constructed wetlands were studied in the Uusimaa district in southern Finland in summer 2008 in order to evaluate the significance of this special measure for wetland biodiversity (Heliölä *et al.*, 2010a). Dragonflies were studied as an indicator group for species dependent on small-scale wetlands.

The results showed that this measure clearly benefits wetland biodiversity. Three main findings stand out (Heliölä *et al.*, 2010a). First, dragonflies were significantly more species-rich and abundant in the constructed wetlands than in other potential dragonfly habitats typically existing in the studied agricultural landscapes (i.e. different kinds of ditches; Figure 5.6).

Second, multiple regression models showed that the environmental variable best explaining the variation in species richness and abundance of dragonflies was the coverage of water plants with floating leaves. It had a positive effect on dragonfly species richness and abundance, whereas muddiness of water affected dragonfly abundance negatively. Third, the size of the wetland did not have a significant impact on dragonfly species richness, once other factors were taken into account This means that even small constructed wetlands can have a high species richness of dragonflies. This finding suggests that economic support would be well justified also for small constructed wetlands that do not have the capacity to significantly reduce nutrient loading.

Figure 5.6. Average species richness (+ standard error) and abundance of dragonflies in constructed wetlands and in the compared habitats, large and small ditches

Source: Heliölä *et al.* (2010a).

Buffer zones

The aim of establishing buffer zones with a minimum width of 15 m along waterways is primarily to reduce nutrient loading in waters but also to favour maintenance of biodiversity. The effects of buffer zones on biodiversity were studied in a case study of 21 buffer zones of differing age in southern Finland in summer 2009 (Heliölä *et al.*, 2010b). Vascular plants and day-active Lepidoptera (butterflies and moths) were studied as biodiversity indicators. Their species richness in buffer zones was compared to other linear uncultivated semi-natural habitats available in the study landscapes, i.e. forest edges and field margins, and particularly the field margin between the studied buffer zone and the neighbouring waterway.

There were two main results (Heliölä *et al.*, 2010b). First, the average species richness of both plants and Lepidoptera was lower in the buffer zones than in the neighbouring old field margins and other uncultivated semi-natural habitats within the study landscapes. Second, species richness of both study groups increased with the time elapsed after the buffer zone establishment (Figure 5.7).

Plant species richness increased linearly until it reached the level of species richness observed in the neighbouring buffer zones after about ten years, after which the increase levelled off. In Lepidoptera both species richness and abundance increased linearly throughout the studied buffer zone age classes. Also butterfly species richness reached the level of the neighbouring field margins after about ten years. Lepidopteran richness was also positively affected by nectar plant abundance and vegetation height. The results indicate that wide buffer zones can significantly promote farmland biodiversity, if they are kept in the same locations for at least ten years.

Figure 5.7. Plant and lepidopteran species richness in the >15 m wide buffer zones plotted against buffer zone age (black dots)

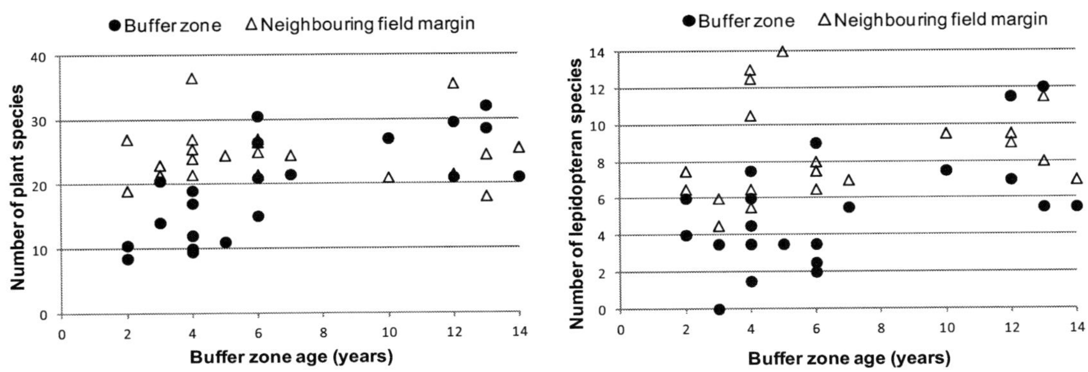

Note: Open triangles show the corresponding values for the neighbouring uncultivated old field margin.
Source: Heliölä *et al.* (2010b).

Long-term set-aside

The Finnish AES promotes establishment of green fallows and set-aside via a measure called environmental fallow, which offers economic support for the establishment of various kinds of green fallows including differently established long-term set-aside areas. The biodiversity effects of long-term set-aside were studied experimentally in a six-year field experiment during 2003-08 (Hyvönen *et al.*, 2010, Alanen *et al.*, 2011, Hyvönen and Huusela-Veistola, 2011). Here we report how two pollinator groups, bumblebees and day-active Lepidoptera, responded to the succession of set-aside cover consisting of three different seed mixtures: a standard mixture with competitive grasses and red clover and two alternative mixtures based on non-competitive grasses and nectar plants (Alanen *et al.*, 2011). The pollinators were monitored in 24 large treatment plots (50 m x 50 m) and on ten surrounding field margins.

The responses of the two pollinator groups to set-aside creation were distinctly different (Figure 5.8; Alanen *et al.*, 2011). Social bees, whose density peaked during the first year of set-aside succession, were more abundant on set-asides than on field margins during the entire experiment. In contrast, it took Lepidoptera three years to reach the abundance of the field margins, whereas the corresponding species richness level was not reached.

Both pollinator groups responded positively to the diverse seed mixture with nectar and pollen plants. The preference of the other two seed mixtures was similar in the two groups, the mixture with less competitive grasses generally outperforming the competitive grass mixture. The results indicate that pollinators in agro-ecosystems can be supported by long-term set-aside. Set-aside establishment by sowing a seed mixture of non-competitive grasses containing nectar and pollen plants can be recommended. It is possible to enhance bumblebees even on short-term set-aside. Lepidopterans, by contrast, responded much more slowly, their occurrence being strongly driven by the availability of larval food plants together with adults′ nectar resources. Supporting lepidopteran diversity therefore requires longer-term set-aside of at least several years.

Figure 5.8. Development of pollinator species richness and abundance in the long-term set-aside experiment over six years after set-aside establishment

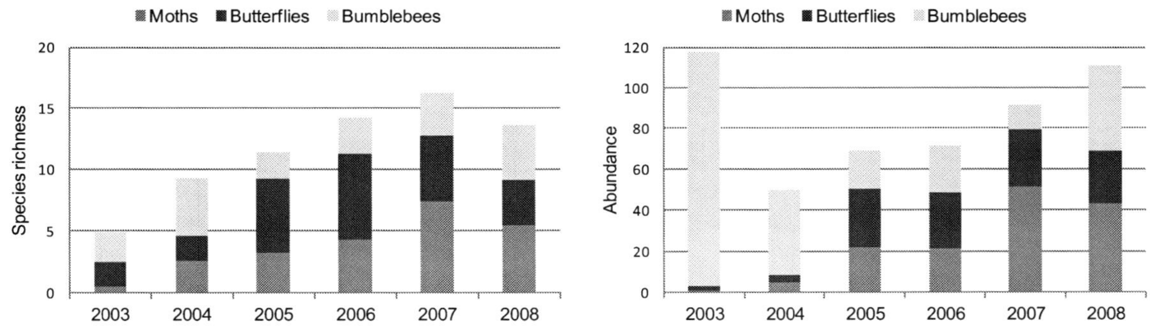

Source: Alanen *et al.* (2011).

5.4 Summary, discussion and policy implications

Nutrient load

In general, the agricultural nutrient load potential measured in nutrient balances has decreased constantly. The decrease can be attributed primarily to the reduction in the use of artificial fertilisers. There is, however, some evidence that especially clustered livestock production units in some regions pose an increasing problem because of nutrient run-offs from manure. Thus, it is important to develop measures that increase nutrient recycling particularly by making more efficient use of the nutrients contained in manure.

It can be concluded from SYKE's statistical modelling approach based on water quality and flow data that the flux of phosphorus from river basins to the Baltic Sea decreased during the analysis period (1985-2006) in all areas except the Archipelago Sea. The results are in line with the trend in soil phosphorus status, indicating that the content of readily soluble soil phosphorus had started to decrease in all catchment areas except that of the Archipelago Sea.

A partial explanation could be the relatively extensive farming area of high-value crops (potato, sugar beet, field-scale vegetables) in south-western Finland, combined with the fact that these crops have a considerably higher phosphate fertiliser allowance than herbaceous and cereal plants. Therefore, the reduction of the phosphate fertiliser allowance for special crops should be considered, as the maximum limits for these fertilisers are remarkably high compared to the average amount of phosphorus removed with yields.

On the contrary, nitrogen load increased in almost every modelled river basin, but particularly in Ostrobothnia. Apparently, the principal factors contributing to the rising nitrogen load are a local increase in the amount of arable land, the concentration of livestock production leading to local growth in manure volume, an increase in the surface application of manure in certain areas and the change in livestock feeding in a direction that tends to increase the nitrogen content in manure. Another potential explanation is the higher soil temperature, believed to accelerate the decomposition of organic matter. Since the surface application of manure is probably a factor behind the increasing rate of N leaching, the application of manure by injection during the growth season must be encouraged.

Interpretation of the results is made more difficult by the fact that the changes in N and P loads are caused by different reasons, as the behaviour of these two nutrients in the soil differs from each other. The monitoring data analysed is also problematic in some respects. A reliable definition of the phosphorus level trends determined on the basis of soil samples is made more complicated by the fact that the reliability of the soil samples available during the study period has not remained uniform over the years. Furthermore, the interpretability of results from the perspective of the effectiveness of AE measures is weakened, because the modelling did not account for the analysis of the impact of many key AE measures, such as low-tillage cultivation, riparian zones and constructed wetlands, as there was no regionally consistent data available for the entire study period.

The key problem with the agricultural nutrient load is the long-term differentiation of livestock production and plant production, which has undermined the practicality of nutrient use. For this reason, there is a need for future measures with which the use of nutrients contained in manure and the recycling of nutrients in general can be improved in a flexible way. In addition, more attention should be paid to requirements concerning manure application areas and animal density, because they are effective measures for regulating the number of animals on livestock farms and, consequently, the total amount of nutrients transferred through manure.

Biodiversity issues

Most special measures included in the Finnish AES aimed at conserving and increasing biodiversity have been effective as such, but the areas concerned have remained relatively small. The most important problem relates to basic measures which have a limited effectiveness from the perspective of biodiversity. The establishment of environmental fallows is the only basic measure with a significant impact on biodiversity, but even this measure is a voluntary one.

The management of field margins has only slightly increased the amount of open cultivated habitats and the maintenance of biodiversity and landscapes values has remained as an inefficient measure, because it does not include any obligation for a farm to carry out practical biodiversity-enhancing measures. Crop rotation is one measure through which the diversity of field cropping could be promoted.

The most important threat to biodiversity is the development of landscape structure, typically involving a decrease in the area of open or half-open semi-natural areas excluded from actual cultivation. The clearing of field margins and ecological islands located within crop fields, drainage arrangements aimed at increasing arable area and all other rationalisation measures of cultivated areas are reducing exactly those areas that are the most important from the perspective of the biodiversity of the agricultural environment. This poses a clear inconsistency between the objectives of the AE measures and the agricultural policy in general, because public funds are also employed to support the rationalisation measures of cultivated areas. For this reason, the assessment of biodiversity impacts should also be included when the rationalisation of holdings is planned.

Should it be relevant to increase the size of plots in order to remove technical obstacles to farming caused by ditches, etc., the headlands removed should be replaced with biodiversity strips or other similar uncultivated areas so that the mix of cultivated and uncultivated areas remains adequate within the farmed landscape. With careful planning, it would usually be possible to establish these replacement habitats in locations that are less valuable from the perspective of arable land use.

In practice, it is difficult to increase the acreage of areas excluded from arable land use, unless basic measures are accompanied by minimum area requirements. A suitable relative share of areas excluded from arable land use should vary be 5-20%, depending on location, landscape structure, type of farming, type of production and cultivation practices. In this context, particular attention should be paid to the increase in grazing, which is essential from the perspective of biodiversity. Most importantly, the use of natural grazing areas should be increased. The primary measure for achieving this is the special measure for the management of traditional rural biotopes such as semi-natural grasslands.

General observations and recommendations

The results of the follow-up studies show that the trends in the state of the environment vary according to region. Even if it is not possible to prove in an undisputable manner the impact of agriculture on the development in each region, it is clear that the production structure and the resulting farming practices play a critical role. For this reason, the measures and support levels associated with the AES should be increasingly adjusted to the needs of each region, type of farming and individual farm. As this is not easy to achieve, particularly with respect to basic measures, the priority of the AE payments should be placed on special measures. The tailoring of AE measures for each farm would require farm-specific environmental management plans that the farmer would draw up together with an authorised expert. The farm-specific environmental management plan would outline the environmental values and risks of the farm and assess the AE measures that would best promote the conservation of natural values and the management of environmental risks.

The truly successful tailoring of AE measures to each farm and region would require farm- and region-specific variation in support levels. A major problem from the perspective of incentives is the fact that EU rules define AE payments as compensation for the loss of income and additional costs incurred when measures are carried out. Even if a small incentive share were also allowed, it is not possible to determine the amount of payments on the basis of the environmental gains acquired through the measures. An inevitable result is the lack of cost-effectiveness of agri-environmental measures in producing environmental benefits. Therefore, future steps should be taken to establish a system in which compensation levels could be defined on the basis of the value of the environmental benefits acquired.

Notes

1. Jyrki Aakkula (MTT Agrifood Research Finland), Mikko Kuussaari (MTT Agrifood Research Finland), Katri Rankinen(MTT Agrifood Research Finland), Petri Ekholm (MTT Agrifood Research Finland), Janne Heliölä (MTT Agrifood Research Finland), Terho Hyvönen (MTT Agrifood Research Finland), Laura Kitti (MTT Agrifood Research Finland), and Tapio Salo (MTT Agrifood Research Finland).
2. In 2010, Finland had about 64 000 farms and 2 296 000 ha of total cultivated arable land.
3. "Areal" balance: Finland is divided into 15 administrative "areas" or Employment and Economic Development Centres.

References

Aakkula, J., P. Jokinen, M. Kaljonen and L. Kröger (2006), *Maatalouden ympäristöpolitiikan skaalat ja oppiminen.* In Finnish. Abstract: Policy learning and scales of agri-environmental policy, Helsinki: MTT Agrifood Research Centre. *MTT:n selvityksiä* 127.

Alanen, E.-L., T. Hyvönen, S. Lindgren, O. Härmä and M. Kuussaari (2011), "Differential responses of bumblebees and diurnal 1 Lepidoptera to vegetation succession in long-term set-aside", *Journal of Applied Ecology*, Vol. 48, pp. 1251-1259.

Ekholm, P., K. Granlund, P. Kauppila, S. Mitikka, J. Niemi, K. Rankinen, A. Räike, J. Räsänen (2007), "Influence of EU policy on agricultural nutrient losses and the state of receiving surface waters in Finland", *Agricultural and Food Science*, Vol. 16, pp. 282-300.

Ekholm P., K. Rankinen, R. Uusitalo, L. Vesikko, H. Rita and H. Sjöblom (2010), "Maan eroosio ja fosforikuormitus" in J. Aakkula, T. Manninen, and M. Nurro (eds.), "Follow-up study on the impacts of agri-environment measures (MYTVAS 3)", Mid-term report, *Maa- ja metsätalousministeriön julkaisuja* Vol. 1, pp. 22-29.

Helenius, J., M. Jauni, I. Herzon and I. Ollikainen (2010), Putkilokasvit (Vascular plants, in Finnish). In: Aakkula, J., T. Manninen and M. Nurro (eds.). Follow-up study on the impacts of agri-environment measures (MYTVAS 3), Mid-term report. *Maa- ja metsätalousministeriön julkaisuja* Vol. 1, pp. 57-60

Heliölä. J., S. Heikkilä and M. Kuussaari (2010a), Erityistuella perustettujen kosteikkojen merkitys hyönteisille (Significance of constructed wetlands for insects, in Finnish). in J. Aakkula, T. Manninen and M. Nurro (eds.). Follow-up study on the impacts of agri-environment measures (MYTVAS 3). Mid-term report. *Maa- ja metsätalousministeriön julkaisuja,* Vol. 1, pp. 79-90.

Heliölä. J. and M. Kuussaari (2010), Perhoset (Butterflies, in Finnish). In: Aakkula, J., T. Manninen and M. Nurro (eds.). Follow-up study on the impacts of agri-environment measures (MYTVAS 3). Mid-term report. *Maa- ja metsätalousministeriön julkaisuja,* Vol. 1, pp. 60-65.

Heliölä, J., L. Virtanen, L. Sandholm and M. Kuussaari (2010b), Suojavyöhykkeiden merkitys putkilokasvien ja suurperhosten monimuotoisuudelle (Significance of buffer zones for the diversity of vascular plants and diurnal Macrolepidoptera, in Finnish). In: Aakkula, J., T. Manninen and M. Nurro (eds.). Follow-up study on the impacts of agri-environment measures (MYTVAS 3). Mid-term report. *Maa- ja metsätalousministeriön julkaisuja* Vol. 1, pp. 94-104.

Hyvönen, T. and E. Huusela-Veistola (2008), "Arable weeds as indicators of agricultural intensity – a case study from Finland", *Biological Conservation,* Vol. 141, pp. 2857-2864.

Hyvönen, T. and E. Huusela-Veistola (2011), Impact of seed mixture and mowing on food abundance for farmland birds in set-asides. *Agriculture, Ecosystems and Environment,* Vol. 143, pp. 20-27.

Hyvönen, T., E. Huusela-Veistola, M. Kuussaari and E.-L. Alanen (2010), Viherkesantojen luontovaikutukset. (Effects of green fallows on farmland biodiversity, in Finnish). In: Aakkula, J., T. Manninen and M. Nurro (eds.). Follow-up study on the impacts of agri-environment measures (MYTVAS 3). Mid-term report. *Maa- ja metsätalousministeriön julkaisuja* Vol. 1, pp. 105-114.

Kivinen, S., M. Kuussaari, J. Heliölä, M. Luoto, J. Helenius and K. Härjämäki (2008), "Maatalousmaiseman rakenteen muutokset ja niiden merkitys lajiston monimuotoisuudelle"

(Changes in the structure of agricultural landscapes and their significance for biodiversity), in M. Kuussaari, J. Heliölä, J. Tiainen and J. Helenius (toim.), Maatalouden ympäristötuen merkitys luonnon monimuotoisuudelle ja maisemalle, MYTVAS loppuraportti 2000–2006. *Suomen ympäristö*, Vol. 4, pp. 112-127.

Koikkalainen, K., K. Haataja and J. Aakkula (1999), "Maatalouden ympäristötuen perustuen merkitys maatilojen taloudelle", in *Maatalouden ympäristöohjelma 1995-1999:n taloudellinen analyysi. Ympäristötukijärjestelmä ja tulevaisuus -tutkimuksen loppuraportti*, Helsinki: Maatalouden taloudellinen tutkimuslaitos (MTTL), MTTL:n tutkimuksia Vol. 90, pp. 7-41.

Korhonen, J. (2007), Suomen vesistojen virtaaman ja vedenkorkeuden vaihtelut. Finnish Environment, *Finnish Environment Institute* Vol. 15, p.120.

Kuussaari, M., J. Heliölä, M. Luoto and J. Pöyry (2007), Determinants of local species richness of diurnal Lepidoptera in boreal agricultural landscapes. *Agriculture, Ecosystems and Environment*, Vol. 122, pp. 366-376.

Palva, R., K. Rankinen, K. Granlund, J. Gronroos, A. Nikander and S. Rekolainen (2001), Maatalouden ympäristötuen toimenpiteiden toteutuminen ja vaikutukset vesistökuormitukseen vuosina 1995–1999. MYTVAS-projektin loppuraportti. Helsinki: Suomen ympäristökeskus (SYKE), *Suomen ympäristö* 478.

Penttilä, R., M. Lindgren, O. Miettinen, H. Rita and I. Hanski (2006), "Consequences of forest fragmentation for polyporous fungi at two spatial scales", *Oikos* Vol. 114, pp. 225-240.

Rankinen, K., T. Salo, K. Granlund and H. Rita (2007), "Simulated nitrogen leaching, nitrogen mass field balances and their correlation on four farms in south-western Finland during the period 2000-2005", *Agricultural and Food Science*, Vol. 16, pp. 387-406.

Rankinen K., P. Ekholm, H. Sjöblom, H. Rita, L. Vesikko (2010), Ainevirtaamat valuma-alueilla ja niihin vaikuttavat tekijät. In: Aakkula, J., T. Manninen and M. Nurro (eds.). Follow-up study on the impacts of agri-environment measures (MYTVAS 3). Mid-term report. *Maa- ja metsätalousministeriön julkaisuja* Vol. 1, pp. 122-129.

Salo T. and R. Lemola (2010), "Typpi- ja fosforitaseet", in J. Aakkula, T. Manninen and M. Nurro, (eds.), *Maa- ja metsätalousministeriön julkaisuja (*Follow-up study on the impacts of agri-environment measures((MYTVAS 3), Mid-term report, Vol. 1, pp. 30-41.

Salonen, J. and T. Hyvönen (2010), Rikkakasvillisuuden monimuotoisuus kevätviljapelloilla. (Weed diversity in spring-cereal fields, in Finnish). In: Aakkula, J., Manninen, T. and Nurro, M. (eds.). Follow-up study on the impacts of agri-environment measures (MYTVAS 3). Mid-term report. *Maa- ja metsätalousministeriön julkaisuja* Vol. 1, pp. 51-56.

Sjöblom, H. (2008), *Suomesta Itämereen laskevien jokien fosfori- ja typpikuormat 1961-2006 – arvio maatalouden kuormitusmuutoksista*. Yhdyskunta- ja ympäristötekniikan laitos, Teknillinen korkeakoulu. 129.

Tiainen, J., T. Seimola and J. Rintala (2010), "Pesimälinnusto" (Breeding bird fauna, in Finnish). in J. Aakkula, T. Manninen and M. Nurro (eds.), *Follow-up study on the impacts of agri-environment measures (MYTVAS 3)*, mid-term report, *Maa- ja metsätalousministeriön julkaisuja* Vol. 1, pp. 66-74.

Tuomenvirta, H. (2004), "Reliable estimation of climatic variations in Finland. Finnish Meteorological Institute", *Finnish Meteorological Institute Contributions,* No. 43.

Turtola, E. and R. Lemola (2008), "Maatalouden ympäristötuen vaikutukset vesistökuormitukseen, satoon ja viljelyn talouteen v. 2000–2006 (MYTVAS 2), Jokioinen: Maa- ja elintarviketalouden tutkimuskeskus (MTT)", *Maa- ja elintarviketalous 120.*

Uusitalo, R. (2004), "Potential bioavailability of particulate phosphorus in runoff from arable clayey soils", *Agrifood Research Report,* N°53, Jokioinen: MTT Agrifood Research Centre.

Chapter 6

Evaluation of agri-environmental measures in Flanders, Belgium

Michael Van Zeebroeck and Dirk Van Gijseghem[1]

Flemish rural development policy aims at improving the competitiveness of agriculture while enhancing the environment and the countryside by supporting land management. The quality of life in rural areas is encouraged by diversification of economic activities. The chapter focuses on the evaluation of the environmental effects of two types of rural development measures. First, the environmental effects of farm investment support measures targeting farm modernisation and diversification into non-agricultural activities were assessed. Second, the impacts of agri-environmental measures on farmland bird populations (numbers, species diversity and breeding) were measured based on two separate monitoring initiatives. Results of both evaluations are reported.

6.1 Rural development policy in Flanders

The Belgian region of Flanders can be characterised as a strongly urbanised region with a multifunctional use of the fragmented open space and an important role for the agricultural and horticultural sectors. As Member States implement EU rural development policy on a regional basis, Flanders adopted a specific Flemish strategy and programme for rural development. In this programme, particular emphasis was given to the quality of life in rural areas.

All measures within the 2006-2013 EU Rural Development programme can be classified under four central themes ("axes"), namely economics, environment, quality of life and diversification of the rural economy, and the furthering of the social cohesion through the LEADER approach. The total public funding for the programme for rural development In Flanders amounts to EUR 713.5 million. Of this, 64.5% is contributed by Flanders, and the balance comes from EU funding sources. The total Axis 1 budget in Flanders is 65% of the total RDP budget, which – together with Navarra (Spain), Guadeloupe (France) and Réunion (France) – is one of the highest RDP budget shares for Axis 1 within the European Union.

6.2 An impact indicator for environmental investment

Measures and methodology

Figure 6.1 shows that 47% of the programmed RDP budget is spent on two measures supporting investment in the agricultural sector: measure 121: modernisation of farms, and measure 311: diversification into non-agricultural activities. It can also be concluded from Figure 6.1 that investment support through measures 121 and 311 is given more weight in Belgium, and even more so in Flanders, than in other Member States.

Figure 6.1. Programmed public expenditure on measures 121 and 311 as a percentage of total programmed public expenditure, 2007-2013

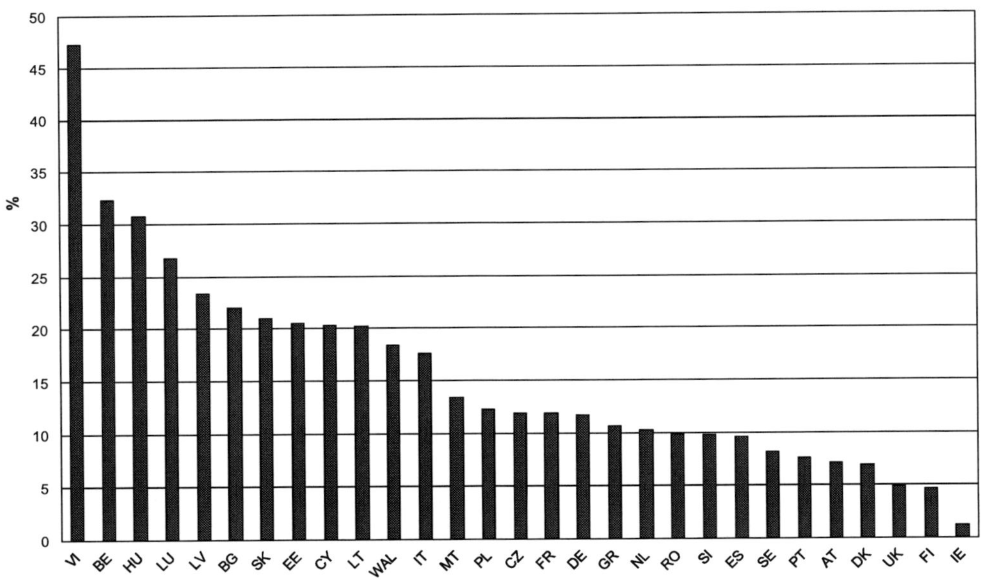

Both measures (121 and 311) are operated by the Flemish Agricultural Investment Fund (VLIF). The VLIF operates as an open system that offers capital and interest subsidies to all farmers who fulfil the minimum requirements. These minimum requirements are that the farm be viable (economic parameters are evaluated), the beneficiary has appropriate skills (diploma or experience), farm accounts are kept (bookkeeping is mandatory) and the farm achieves a minimum size.

Since 2000 there has been a graduated system for calculating the rate of subsidies: the more environmentally friendly the investments are, the more subsidy is granted. The current maximum rate for environmental subsidies is 38% of the investment cost (only for investments related to organic farming), and three other categories with rates of 28, 18 and 8%. Forty-four types of investment can be considered as investments with a direct positive environmental impact. They are all situated in the 28% and 18% categories, except for the subsidies for photovoltaic cells, which since 2010 have been placed in the 8% category due to budget restrictions. These 44 types of environmentally friendly investments include stables with systems for ammonia reduction, systems for purification, treatment and recycling of water, incineration plants for the use of bio-energy, photovoltaic cells, energy saving investments in greenhouse farming like energy screens, plants cogeneration of heat and power (CHP) and heat pumps.

A breakdown by theme of the total amount of VLIF expenditure committed to measures 121 and 311 for 2010 shows that 52.4% of the investment subsidies are foreseen for these 44 types of environmentally favourable investments. In absolute value, this amounts to EUR 44.7 million, which is more than double the Axis 2 expenditure in 2010 (EUR 21.5 million). The other large component of total expenditure committed to these two measures goes for structural investment and diversification (EUR 37.7 million, or 46.6% of the total). Investments related to animal welfare (EUR 512.7 thousand) and organic farming (EUR 290.5 thousand) account for only 0.6% and 0.3%, respectively, of the total.

Because the investment types that focus on improving the environment are important in Flanders, the evaluation of the impact of RDP measures 121 and 311 must take into account the environmental impacts as well as the economic impacts.

Environmental impact studies of best available technique (BAT) of the Flemish Institute for Technology Research (VITO) were used as a starting point for developing the environmental impact indicators needed to monitor the environmental impact of RDP farm investment support. The types of investment specific indicators are situated on the output indicator level.

There are qualitative and quantitative *output* indicators. Examples of qualitative indicators are the type of water purification system that is installed and the type of manure injection system that is subsidised. Examples of quantitative indicators are cubic metres of water purified per year and peak power of the installed photovoltaic cells. From the starting point of the quantitative output indicators, it is possible to calculate *impact* indicators with varying levels of accuracy. Only one of the four environmental impact indicators provided by the European Commission can be linked with the type of investment specific output indicators at our disposal, namely renewable energy produced in kilotons of oil equivalents (ktoe). There are, however, some more impact indicators that could be calculated out of the output indicators (in EU terminology they can be called programme-specific impact indicators):

- contribution to combating climate change: kilotons of CO_2 reduction;
- contribution to combating the acidification of the environment: kilotons of ammonia reduction;
- contribution to combating the water shortage: volume of water re-usage; and
- contribution to combating climate change: GWh of reduced energy consumption.

Calculation of the reduction in ammonia emission of the low ammonia emission stables can serve as an example of how we derived impact indicators from our output indicators. In the *ex post* evaluation of the RDP 2000-06 ("RDP I"), only a rough estimate of the contribution to ammonia reduction of the investment support could be calculated. This calculation was based on the number of subsidised stables, the type of animals in the stables, an average number of animals in the stables per animal category, the average production of ammonia per type of animal in classical stables and an average percentage reduction of 50% in ammonia emissions in low emission stables relative to that of classical stables.

In the new database for each subsidised ammonia reduction stable, two extra output indicators are defined that significantly increase the accuracy of the RDP 2007-2013 ("RDP II") ammonia reduction calculations: the number of animal places in the stable and the type of technique of ammonia reduction system that is installed. For the more precise calculation of ammonia reduction per low ammonia emission stable research results will be used that measured the kg of ammonia production per animal place per type of ammonia reduction technique per animal category.

Analysis and results

The database containing output indicators for each type of investment has been operational since October 2009. The indicators are included in the computer system for the administrative handling of the investment support. At a later stage, the output indicators of the investments approved under RDP II regulation since 2007 were also introduced in the system.

Figure 6.2 shows the results of the GHG emission reduction as calculated. Investment support for CHP gives rise to the greatest GHG emission reductions. In the second place comes the low ammonia emission stable for pigs, and in third place the investment support for the installation of the first energy-saving screen in greenhouses.

In the period 2007-08, a significant number of applications (submitted before January 2007) were also approved under the RDP 2000-2006 regulation. The environmental impact of these applications was determined by extrapolation from the environmental impacts of the applications approved under the RDP 2007-2013 regulation. Starting from these basic data on output indicators, it has been possible to calculate the energy saving for each year, and convert this into an annual GHG reduction by also taking in account the source of energy production before and after investment.

The results show that the VLIF investments for the period 2007-mid-2010 (approved under both RDP regulations) lead every year to savings in energy consumption of approximately 609 GWh or 7.5% of the total energy use for the agricultural and horticultural sectors in Flanders in 2006 (MIRA), and to savings in tap water consumption of approximately 993 000 m^3 or 1.5% of the total water consumption for the Flemish agricultural and horticultural sector in 2006 (MIRA).

The programme also played a significant role in this period in generating other environmental improvements, most notably:

- a saving in ammonia emissions of approximately 670 000 kg NH_3 per year (1.6% of the total ammonia emission of the agricultural sector in Flanders in 2006);
- renewable energy production of approximately 55 000 MWh (around 1% of the total energy consumption of greenhouse cultivation and 0.7% of the total energy consumption of the entire agricultural and horticultural sector in Flanders);and
- a saving in GHG emissions of approximately 541 000 tons of CO_2 equivalents per year (5.6% of the total GHG emissions in 2006 by the Flemish agricultural and horticultural sector; for CO_2 14% and for CH_4 and N_2O 1.6%).

Figure 6.2. GHG-reduction

ktons of CO_2 equivalent*

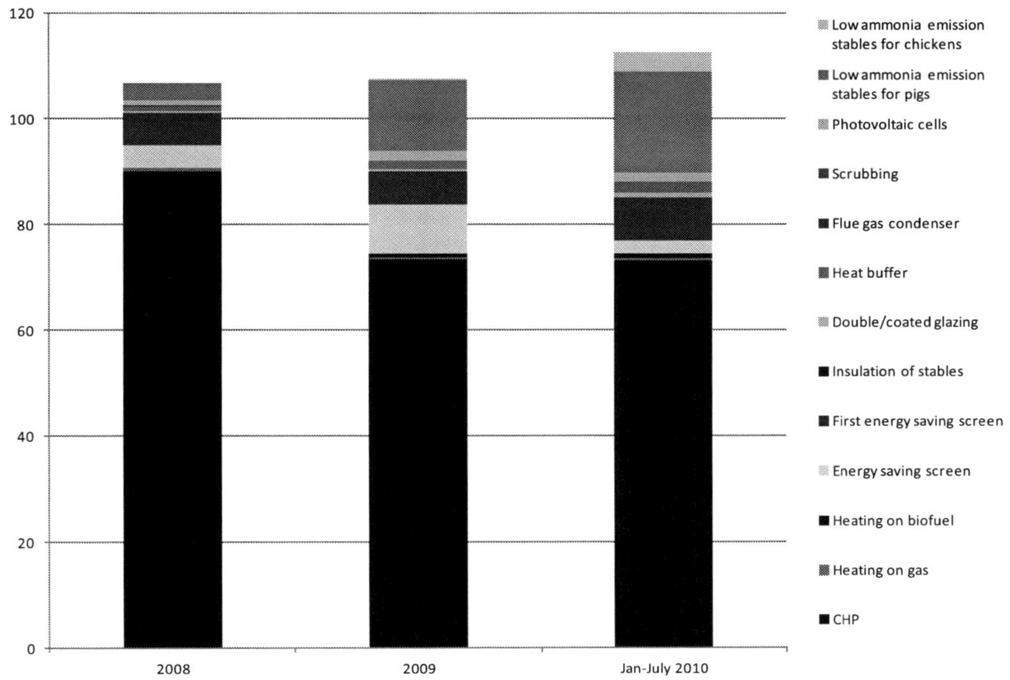

* Due to measures 121 and 311 approved under RDP II regulation in period 2007-mid 2010. The small number of applications that were approved in 2007 were included in the year 2008

6.3 An impact indicator for agri-environmental measures targeting farmland birds

The problem

Over past decades, farmland birds have declined drastically across Europe. This is also the case in Flanders, and species that once were common, such as tree sparrow, partridge and corn bunting, are now much less widespread or even rare. It is well known that the collapse of farmland bird populations is due to the agricultural intensification that has taken place since the end of World War II. Modern agriculture is characterised by intensive mechanisation, the use of pesticides and fertilisers, changes in the crops grown and in the timing of sowing and harvesting, the rise of monocultures, increased density of grazing animals, changes in groundwater levels and the loss of small landscape elements like hedgerows and small ponds. For most farmland birds, these changes imply a loss of suitable nesting sites and a lack of food, resulting in a spectacular decline in their numbers and distribution.

As is shown in Figure 6.3, since 1980 the decline specifically in farmland bird populations (index based on a count of 36 species) has been sharper than that in common forest birds (based on 29 species), or all common species of birds (based on 136 species). In the course of various reforms to EU agricultural policy, measures to promote biodiversity have been introduced For example, it is now possible for farmers to join agri-environmental schemes in which they are paid a fixed amount in exchange for carrying out prescribed conservation actions on their lands, some of which are targeted to improving the rural habitat for non-farmed species.

Figure 6.3. Population index (1980=100) of common birds, forest birds and farmland birds in Europe, 1980-2007

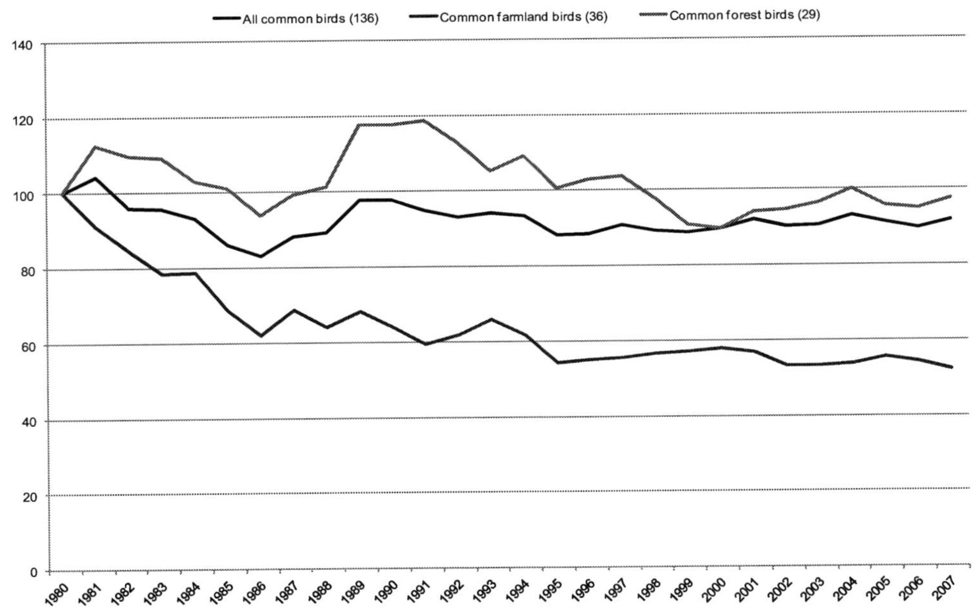

Source: EBCC/RSPB/Bird Life/Statistics Netherlands.

The evaluation approach

Currently, at least in Flanders, it is unclear what the impact of these measures is, as there are no scientifically sound monitoring programmes in effect. In order to evaluate the current implication of agri-environmental measures in Flanders, a study was carried out by the Institute for Nature and Forestry Research (INBO) to develop an appropriate monitoring scheme and to present a first assessment of farmland biodiversity in relation to these measures. The study was carried out as part of the so-called on-going evaluation of Rural Development Programme 2007-2013, and was specifically triggered by RDP Impact indicator 4: Reversing Biodiversity Decline; Change in trend in biodiversity decline as measured by farmland bird species population.

There were three major components of the study:

- a literature study intended to identify the agri-environmental schemes with a potential impact on biodiversity of farmland birds;
- analysis of the effect of agri-environmental schemes on bird abundance and diversity making use of an existing monitoring network set up to monitor breeding birds in Flanders; and
- creation of a new monitoring network in 14 areas of Flanders and analysis of the first phase of measurements. This new monitoring network is specifically designed to measure net effects of agri-environmental schemes and, more specifically, of agri-environmental schemes that aim to maintain habitats favourable for the preservation and species-diversity of farmland birds.

The scientific question to be answered was: Is there a difference in density or breeding success of birds between plots and areas with and without management agreements?

To answer the question, monitoring over time is needed and this requires appropriate time series data. Time series of the occurrence of species are not yet available in Flanders. However, baseline data of species occurrence are available as well as geographical information on the application of agro-environmental measures and geographical information of habitat characteristics. The method used to analyse these data is "spatial pattern analysis." A major challenge facing the study was that of distinguishing between general habitat characteristics and their trends, and the impact of applying RDP agri-environmental measures (AEM). Below we report the initial findings of the study.

Literature study

Based on studies of comparable agri-environmental measures in foreign countries, the AEM were classified according to their expected effects on farmland bird populations: direct effects, indirect effects and no effect. In Flanders, there is one AEM that was specifically designed to enhance farmland bird abundance and diversity. Obviously, this AEM was identified as having a direct effect on biodiversity. Besides this measure, the following AEM were classified in the group with an expected direct effect:

- field margin management;
- recovery, development and maintenance of small landscape elements;
- botanical management; and
- adoption of organic production methods.

The following AEMs were classified in the group with expected indirect effects:

- erosion control management agreement;
- mechanical weed control; and
- green cover.

Analysis of data of the common breeding birds monitoring network in Flanders

This monitoring network was developed in 2007 to track the evolution and spread of 101 common breeding birds in Flanders. It consists of 1200 sample areas of 1 km², of which 500 are under agricultural land use, distributed randomly in Flanders. The whole monitoring network is sampled every three years. With the data collected across Flanders, the evolution over time of the population size of individual species, the relative population size of species groups (meadow birds, birds typical for arable land and so on), occupancy (number of sample areas where a species is present) of species or species groups and species diversity (diversity indices) can be followed.

It must be pointed out that this network was not designed specifically to evaluate the impact of agri-environmental measures. The primary objective of its design was to permit the analysis of how different habitat parameters *not* exclusively linked to the application of AEM's or the net effects of AEM applications affect bird populations.

The following habitat parameters were analysed.

- Habitat suitability prediction, on the basis of "breeding bird atlas data:"
    - Breeding bird atlas data is available before 2007. It is the precursor of the new general monitoring network of breeding birds in Flanders, as mentioned above. These data were used to predict the number of species present in a sample area as well as the probability

of occurrence of an individual species. This prediction served as a measure of habitat suitability of a particular sample area;

- Landscape characteristics:
  - area of small landscape elements;
  - habitat and crop heterogeneity index;
  - landscape fragmentation: number of parcels;
  - landscape openness: average distance to vertical structures; and
  - percentage of cropland/grassland in measuring buffer.
- Parcel characteristics:
  - area;
  - area of small landscape elements;
  - landscape openness: average distance to vertical structures;
  - parcel type: cropland or grassland;
  - drainage class: indication of soil moisture content;
  - type of grazing (cattle, sheep, horse); and
  - crop category.

Table 6.1 summarises the most important results of the analysis. A multivariate analysis was used to relate the biodiversity index (measuring diversity and abundance) of the three bird categories to the density of RDP measures per plot, as well as a set of landscape, habitat and other variables. The bottom line of the table shows the total percentage share of the variability in the indicator across the plots that can be attributed jointly to the explanatory variables. It is striking that, in the case of meadow birds, nearly 50% of the variation across plots can be explained by these factors. In the preceding rows of the table, the share of the variation attributable to individual factors is shown, but only if that factor was statistically significant in the regression. Hence, the sum of the individual shares is smaller than the total share of all the explanatory variables in explaining biodiversity variation.

Table 6.1. Explanation of biodiversity of bird categories by selected explanatory variables, percentage of variation attributed to each and to all factors

	Breeding birds	Birds typical of arable land	Meadow birds
Density of Flemish RDP measures, direct effect	2.6	2.2	
Habitat suitability prediction, all birds	7	1.1	
Habitat suitability prediction, meadow birds	2.2		21.4
Openness	- 5.3	1.7	9.4
Density of the agricultural area			1.5
Number of parcels			- 1.9
Density of maize	- 3.3	- 4.1	
Density of summer grain		1.7	
Density of grassland			8.2
Density of fruit			3.3
Density of cabbage			- 1.8
Other variables		2.2	1.5
Total	20.4	13.0	49.0

Table 6.1 shows that the biodiversity indicators for breeding birds and for birds typical of arable land are positively related to the density of RDP AEMs, even after controlling for habitat and other relevant factors. However, the density of AEMs does not contribute to the explanation of meadow bird biodiversity. In addition to the effects of policy measures, a number of habitat variables also play a significant role in explaining bird biodiversity. The habitat prediction indicators based on the breeding bird atlas data contribute positively to biodiversity of several birds categories. As might be expected, landscape openness reduces the biodiversity index of breeding birds, but increases that of the other two bird categories, particularly meadow birds. The density of particular crops also helps to explain variations in bird biodiversity, especially for meadow birds. Maize cultivation, where significant, has a negative impact on biodiversity.

In conclusion, a successful habitat model was created for the three biodiversity indicators and, after taking into account differences in habitat quality, RDP AEMs with an expected direct impact are indeed positively correlated with biodiversity of breeding birds in general and of 'birds typical of arable land', although not with that of meadow birds. However, even in the first two cases, the contribution of the direct AEMs is rather limited, accounting for about 13% and 17%, respectively, of the total explanation.

New monitoring network in 14 areas in Flanders, focus on RDP evaluation of AEM "management schemes to enhance biodiversity of farmland birds"

Fourteen agricultural measuring areas across Flanders were selected t" form the network. Among them were areas with a low density of agri-environmental measures and others with a high density of such measures, and all typical farmland habitats were represented. These areas varied in size from 170 to 275 ha, and the number of birds breeding in these areas was quantified from March to July 2010, using the habitat mapping method (Van Dijk, 2004) (four visits were made to each of the 14 study areas). When agri-environmental measures have the desired effect, more species or more breeding areas are expected on parcels of land where measures are implemented compared to land parcels managed under traditional agricultural practices. In the analyses, the habitat quality of individual parcels was also assessed in order to ensure that differences in biodiversity between parcels were attributable to the agri-environmental schemes and not to differences in habitat quality.

The results indicate that, after accounting for differences in habitat quality between parcels, more species of birds and more breeding territories were present in areas with a higher density of agri-environmental schemes aimed at conserving meadow birds. Note that a positive correlation was found between bird abundance and diversity, and the presence of agri-environmental schemes, only if there was a density of these measures in the landscape surrounding a land parcel. Thus, introducing conservation measures on single parcels does not seem to influence bird biodiversity, but the results do suggest that as the proportion of agriculture land under agri-environmental management in an area increases, so too does bird biodiversity. Agri-environmental measures aimed at conserving birds associated with arable land do not correlate with bird diversity or bird abundance. However, in contrast to meadow bird measures, which were first introduced in 1999, measures for birds typical of arable lands became operational only in 2009.

As there is often a time lag between changes in the environment and the response of bird populations, it is most probably too early to evaluate the effectiveness of these measures. Also, as in this study, only data from one census year were available, it was necessary to control statistically for the effects of habitat quality. In order to unambiguously assess the effectiveness of agri-environmental measures, longer-term data on population trends are indispensable, as the analysis of such time trends allows a direct comparison of biodiversity trends on plots with and without conservation schemes.

An important recommendation of the study was that in the coming years, the 14 areas designated in this study should be sampled yearly. If longer-term data confirm the positive effect of agri-environmental schemes on biodiversity, it should be assessed how much of the agricultural land that should be managed in order to preserve farmland bird population across whole Flanders.

6.4 Conclusions

This chapter has reported the results of evaluating two different sets of measures implemented in Flanders under the EU Rural Development Programme. First, to evaluate the environmental impact of investment support, environmental impact studies of best available techniques from the Flemish Institute for Technology Research were used as a starting point for developing an appropriate set of environmental indicators. The investment-specific indicators that were developed are situated on the output indicator level. These output indicators were added to an administrative database. From the output indicators, it was possible to calculate different impact indicators.

The following results were obtained: farm investment support for the 2007-mid-2010 period has resulted annually in energy savings of 609 GWh (7.5% of the total energy use for the agricultural and horticultural sectors in Flanders in 2006), a saving in tap water consumption of 993 000 m^3 (1.5% of the total water consumption for the Flemish agricultural and horticultural sectors in 2006), a reduction in ammonia emissions of 670 000 kg NH_3 (1.6% of the total ammonia emission of the agricultural sector in Flanders in 2006), production of renewable energy of 55 000 MWh (0.7% of the total energy consumption of the entire agricultural and horticultural sectors in Flanders) and a saving in greenhouse gas emissions of 541 000 tons of CO_2 equivalents (5.6% of the total greenhouse gas emission in 2006 by the Flemish agricultural and horticultural sectors).

Second, we reported results from the on-going evaluation of the impacts of various on-farm conservation measures on farmland biodiversity, in particular on farmland bird populations. The results so far indicate that, after accounting for differences in habitat quality between parcels, the presence of agri-environmental schemes have a positive impact on bird abundance and diversity only if there is a density of these measures in the landscape surrounding a monitored land parcel. In order to assess unambiguously the effectiveness of agri-environmental measures, longer-term data on population trends are indispensable, as the analysis of such time trends allows a direct comparison of biodiversity trends on plots with and without conservation schemes.

Analysis of the common breeding birds monitoring network in Flanders in relation to the use of RDP AEMs also suggests that the diversity of breeding birds in the countryside is positively affected by measures with an expected direct effect on overall biodiversity (field margin management; recovery, development and maintenance of small landscape elements; botanical management; application of the organic production method).

Besides the "common breeding birds monitoring network," a new monitoring network has recently been set up and a first measurement round has taken place to evaluate trends in the biodiversity of farmland birds. This new network consists of 14 test sites, chosen with a specific focus on the AEM type "management schemes to enhance the biodiversity of farmland birds." Analysis of the first measuring cycle shows that parcels under "meadow bird managemen"' have higher species diversity and abundance than other parcels. The analysis shows, however, that this higher abundance and diversity is mainly associated with the density of meadow bird measures in the landscape around a parcel, rather than with the parcel having meadow bird management itself.

The level of complexity of the evaluation of impacts is not equal in the two cases. The first case demonstrates that with a well-defined set of output indicators for each type of investment, it is possible to calculate the environmental impact. In some cases, however, this approach can measure only part of the environmental impact because possible scaling effects are not included in the calculation. The missing scaling effects may either enhance or reduce the measured impact. For example, a low ammonia emission stable leads to ammonia reduction compared to a normal stable but if the support gives rise to an increase in the number of animal places the positive environment impact of ammonia reduction per animal place can be mitigated by other (negative) environmental impacts due to this scaling effect.

The evaluation of agri-environmental measures targeting farmland birds is at a higher level of complexity. As a result of the many intervening factors determining the habitat quality, only a well-defined experimental design is able to isolate the effects of the agri-environmental measures. The study also demonstrates that the statistical power of spatial analysis with one year's data is rather low and multi-annual measurement with a monitoring network, specifically designed to evaluate agro-environmental measures, is necessary.

Note

1. Ministry of the Flemish Community, Brussels, Belgium.

References

Dumez, L., M. Van Zeebroeck (2011), *Vlaams Programma voor Plattelandsontwikkeling 2007-2013*, Jaarverslag 2010, Departement Landbouw en Visserij, afdeling Monitoring en Studie, Brussel (concept).

Midterm evaluatie van het Vlaams Programmadocument voor Plattelandsontwikkeling 2007-2013, uitgevoerd door Idea Consult, Universiteit Gent, Soresma en VUB in opdracht van de Vlaamse Overheid, Departement Landbouw en Visserij.

Platteau J., T. Van Bogaert (2010), *Agriculture and Horticulture in Flanders 2009,* Pocket Agricultural Indicators.

Strubbe D., P. Verschelde, M. Hens, C. Wils, D. Bauwens, M. Dermout and L. De Bruyn (2010), *Impact van PDPO II maatregelen op de biodiversiteit. Studie uitgevoerd door het Instituut voor Natuur- en Bosonderzoek (INBO)* in opdracht van het Departement Landbouw en Visserij, afdeling Monitoring en Studie, Brussel. 102 blz + bijlagen.

Van Dijk, A. J. (2004) Handleiding Broedvogel Monitoring Project (Broedvogelinventarisatie in proefvlakken). SOVON Vogelonderzoek Nederland, Beek-Ubbergen.

Van Gijseghem, D., S. Danckaert, M. Van Zeebroeck, E. Maertens (2010), *Agri-environmental indicators in relation to rural development policy in Flanders*, Belgium. Department of Agriculture and Fisheries, Brussels, Belgium.

Chapter 7

Evaluation of cross compliance in England

Agri-Environment Analysis Theme Group, Farming and Food Group
DEFRA, United Kingdom[1]

This evaluation covers the first four years of the application of cross compliance conditions to all farmer recipients of the Single Farm Payment (SFP) under Pillar 1 of the EU's Common Agricultural Policy. The main findings are that the compliance level is generally high and that some measures have stimulated significant changes and benefits, although lack of additionality was noted for one measure. The lessons learnt include the need for farmers to be convinced of the rationale for and the public good benefits of certain measures, greater clarity in formulating requirements, more help to farmers with some record-keeping tasks, more care to avoid potential overlaps with Pillar 2 measures, and a separate inspection process, outside the mandatory 1% inspection monitoring fraction, for reported breaches of standards.

Cross compliance was introduced in 2005, setting baseline standards that farmers must respect in order to receive their Single Payment. There are two elements to cross compliance: Good Agricultural and Environmental Condition (GAEC) standards largely relating to the protection of soils, habitats and landscape features; and Statutory Management Requirements (SMRs), which are either pre-existing legislative requirements or those that Member States must implement under EU law. SMRs cover environmental, public, plant and animal health and, from 2007, animal welfare objectives.

This evaluation was commissioned in September 2008, and had to address the following questions.

- How effective is cross compliance in England in meeting its objectives?
- What is the nature and magnitude of the costs imposed on farmers and any others in meeting cross compliance conditions?
- Does the policy represent good value for money?
- Are there any unintended consequences?
- Has there been a change in farmer behaviour in response to the introduction of cross compliance?

7.1 Method

There were three main stages to the work.

- Review of secondary evidence, in particular, the published literature, Rural Payments Agency (RPA) monitoring data and Farm Advisory System (FAS) survey reports.
- Collection of primary evidence, namely a representative farmer survey (300 respondents), two farm advisory workshops, interviews with Technical Advisory Panel (TAP) members and consultation with Defra and staff from key agencies.
- Evaluation of effectiveness and value for money, which involved quantifying the costs and benefits of meeting CC standards, was based on benefits transfer data (from the Defra Environmental Accounts and other sources).

These three stages were reported separately as the project progressed and were brought together in the final report.

7.2. Results

Effectiveness

The research evidence and monitoring data highlighted generally high levels of compliance but some considerable variation across the measures. Table 7.1 summarises the effectiveness and other aspects of certain SMR and GAEC requirements.

Generally, standards relating to legislation that had been in existence for some time were well observed. However, where there were on-going problems of non-compliance – notably SMR 7 and 8 (Cattle ID) but also GAEC 8 (public rights of way) and GAEC 11 (control of weeds) – CC had nevertheless increased awareness and, in some cases, resulted in action, associated with the threat of penalty through deduction of a proportion of Single Payment. For other standards (GAECs with no supporting legislation), CC represents the main means of securing environmental protection, and the impacts were greater. However, there are issues of lack of clarity in terms of what is required (GAECs 9 and 12) and some resistance to compliance from farmers.

Table 7.1. Effectiveness of certain SMRs and GAEC requirements, England[1]

Measure	Level of compliance	Applicability	Level of change	Impact	Overall effectiveness
SMR					
4	*	M/H	M	M	M
6	-	L	L	M	M/L
7 & 8	++	M	L	M	M
8a	*	M	L	M	M
16	No evidence	L	L	L	L
17	No evidence	L	L	L	L
18	No evidence	H	L	L	L
GAEC					
1	H/some issues	H	M	L	L
2	H	M	M	L	L
3	H	H	M	L	L
4	H	M	L	L	L
8	H/some issues	H	L	M	M
9	H	M	L	L	L
11	H/some issues	H	L	M	L
12	H	M/L	M	H	M
13	H	M	L	L	L
14	H/some issues	H	H	H	H
15	H	H	M	H	H

Notes:
1. See Table A in Annex 7.A for a description of each SMR and GAEC.
* Not significant; + moderate positive impact; ++ significant positive impact; – moderate negative impact.
H = high; M = Medium; L = low.
Source: Tables 26 and 27 of the full report.

While the leverage provided by the Single Payment Scheme (SPS) has ensured that CC is very effective insofar as farmers are willing to comply, it has relied too much on this at the expense of genuine engagement with farmers on the rationale for sustainable farming. This has created some problems of whole-hearted willingness to comply, with implications for embedding desired behaviour.

Cost to farmers

In terms of the cost to farmers of meeting CC requirements, the main evidence came from the farmers' survey.[2] Farmers were asked if they had made changes in response to the policy. Those that did were further questioned to provide estimates of direct cost, time input, any income forgone and any costs saved. The data were gathered for groups of standards across eight key themes and aggregated to give an overall net cost per farm. Two estimates were calculated relating to GAEC only and to GAEC and SMRs, where compliance with the latter had substantively changed as a result of cross compliance. The results are reported in Table 7.2.

The estimates of cost were in line with the Regulatory Impact Assessment (RIA) at GBP 163 and GBP 289 per farm for GAEC, and for GAEC plus SMR 4 and SMR 6-8, respectively. These estimates were then scaled up to England level on the basis of the number of farmers who need to comply, using SPS claimants as a proxy. The aggregate cost at England level is estimated to range from GBP 8.7 million to GBP 15.5 million for full-time farmers but increases to GBP 17.8-GBP 31.5 million if all farmers (including part-time) are counted.

Table 7.2. Estimated total farmers' cost of cross compliance in England

	Full-time farms claiming SFP (excluding farms with <0.5 SLR)*		All farms claiming the SFP	
Number of farms subject to CC	53 492		108 924	
Land covered by CC	7.7 mn ha		8.5 mn ha	
	GAEC only	**GAEC and SMRs**	**GAEC only**	**GAEC and SMRs**
Per farm costs	GBP 163	GBP 289	GBP 163	GBP 289
Aggregated farm costs	GBP 8.7 mn	GBP 15.5 mn	GBP 17.8 mn	GBP 31.5 mn

* 1 SLR (Standard Labour Requirement) is equal to 1 900 hours of labour per year.

Source: Table 46 of the full report.

Value for money

The context for this policy intervention is payment of a direct payment (the Single Farm Payment, SFP) to farmers under the Single Payment Scheme (SPS) of the CAP, subject to farmer compliance with key elements of legislation and good practice as a condition. While the cost of the SFP is very substantial (GBP 1.45 bn in England in 2007), value for money relates only to the public benefits resulting from the policy (i.e. the additional public goods it stimulates) and the direct costs of implementing it.

The valuation of the public benefits delivered by CC is a very broad brush estimate due to difficulties of quantifying benefits relating to the scheme (i.e. after removing the effects of other factors) and the ambitious use of benefits transfer methodology to value these benefits. The estimated value of benefits ranges from GBP 24 million to over GBP 40 million annually. This compares with policy costs of GBP 8.3 million.

While there is always scope for greater efficiency, it would be difficult to reduce the public cost of implementing CC significantly as it is driven by procedures required by EU regulations. Therefore, the main scope for improving value for money lies with improving the scheme's impact.

Unintended consequences

The main unintended impacts (both desirable and less so) of CC have been:

- additional engagement of farmers with advisors,
- increased awareness of existing legislative requirements,
- disproportionate impact on small farms (fixed cost component),
- unnecessary costs incurred by some farmers who over-react to standards, e.g. GAEC 9; and
- risk-taking behaviour by some farmers who, given the limited scale of penalties, opt to risk being caught not complying rather than comply, notably where compliance involves a high capital cost, e.g. in NVZs.

Farmer behaviour

The key behavioural issue is the negative attitude to CC by some farmers as evidenced by our review of media articles and feedback from industry advisors. While many farmers have incurred some additional costs as a result of CC, these costs are generally low in relation the scale of SFP payments. Where high costs were reported, they related largely to compliance with the underlying (pre-existing) regulations, rather than with CC *per se*, which indicates a lack of understanding of this distinction. This finding highlights a need for much more attention to the principles of CC in the provision of support (via the FAS) and better links with the inspection agencies to ensure a more balanced view of the policy and its implementation.

Despite our use of a typology of farmer behaviour, there was no clear correlation between farmer type and attitudes to CC or to the level of breaches. However, it must be stressed that we did not use a random sample; rather, the sample was entirely drawn from willing respondents to the annual ADAS Farmers Voice Survey and consisted of full-time farmers only.

7.3 Summary and recommendations

While compliance rates are high for most standards (>95%), environmental and welfare benefits are maximised by embedding the spirit as well as the letter of the rules. This relies on a clear understanding of the purpose of CC and effectively linking farm practice to desired outcomes. Improvements in this respect have nothing to do with increasing the scope of the standards, but rather with developing a more positive and open relationship with farmers in order to engage them more fully with scheme objectives, rules and benefits. The Farm Advisory System has the role of helping with the aspect of CC performance. However, there remain a number of issues concerning the scope of the policy, understanding of individual requirements and policy implementation. These issues are considered in the following sub-sections, and detailed recommendations are made for delivering improved public benefits at existing cost.

Policy scope

A major problem for cross compliance policy relates to farmers not being convinced of the benefits of the standards with consequent partial – or reluctant – compliance. Given this, there are two clear messages that need to be sent effectively. First, compliance is a *prerequisite* for receipt of the SFP, and second, there are actually good reasons for the rules e.g. enhancement of public goods such as water quality and access to the countryside, or "weakest-link" public goods such as preventing animal disease or weed spread. Although the link to SPS is stated in first paragraph of the General Information section of the Cross Compliance Guide, there is considerable scope for improving effectiveness through clarification of the rationale for a number of the standards, both SMRs and GAECs.

Recommendation 1: *Place greater emphasis on presenting the case for cross compliance standards, even where they are supported by legislation. This should be across all communications with the industry, but particularly at face-to-face events such as FAS workshops where the rationale can be presented interactively.*

The evaluation has found that CC has been effective in increasing awareness and delivering compliance in most situations, but there is considerable scope for improving effectiveness through clarification of the rationale (GAEC 1, 2, 3, 9, 12, 14). Where there are issues of perceived impracticality, it may be necessary to consult with the industry to find more practical means of delivering the legislation.

Recommendation 2: *Continue to review the implementation protocols where there are problems of observance, particularly relating to record keeping, to make it easier for farmers to comply without compromising delivery of intended environmental standards.*

Some standards have potential overlap with agri-environmental schemes (Pillar 2) and it is important to distinguish clearly between cross compliance, which sets the baseline for the Environmental Stewardship (ES) schemes in England and the schemes themselves. This applies to GAEC 15 (Hedgerows, cutting date element) and GAEC 14 (protection of hedgerows and watercourses). Where possible, clear principles should separate the two policy approaches, including the proposed new Environmental Management condition.

Recommendation 3: *Define clearly where the cross compliance baseline stops and that for incentive-based management starts. Review the case for existing and new standards to ensure a consistent adherence to this principle.*

Individual standards

The case for changes to individual standards cuts across the design and implementation of the programme. However, it is perhaps best to make the case for change at individual standard level. Below, we have set out the eight groups of standards and presented the conclusions and recommendations for change relating to each.

Soil management and protection

Compliance levels for standards in this group are high. Although this group of standards has raised awareness of soil management, there are some issues with respect to record keeping (GAEC 1). The Soil Protection Review (SPR) form and process is viewed as having little or no practical value by farmers. Failure to comply with GAEC 1 is attributed to:

- farmers not persuaded that the SPR has any purpose;
- high investment in time; and
- problems in carrying out the review and identifying soil types.

There are few issues with GAEC 2-4 since, in practice, erosion and loss of soil organic matter is not an issue for all farmers. Nonetheless,

- GAEC 2 and GAEC 3: Although there are few compliance issues, the scope for impact relies on farmers recognising the need for action. There is a private incentive to manage soil well but farmers need more information and advice on best practice e.g. through knowledge transfer activities to highlight scope for change. Linking these standards to the GAEC 1 process would provide a basis for recording decisions and actions and increase the relevance of GAEC 1.
- GAEC 4: The standard is well embedded in existing practice and there is no additional impact CC.

These findings indicate that more training and advice may help to enhance the acceptance and effectiveness of the SPR.

Recommendation 4: *Review the GAEC 1 form and process to make it a more useful decision-tool for farmers.*

Recommendation 5: *Bundle GAEC 1 together with GAEC 2, 3 and 4 to make an integrated soil protection and management standard.*

Recommendation 6: *Initiate a soil management educational programme under FAS. Link it where possible to other relevant initiatives such as the EA "Think Soils" programme.*[3]

Water quality

Compliance levels were high but inclusion of these standards in cross compliance had a significant impact on awareness for SMR 4 and SMR 2. Twenty two per cent of respondents in the farmer survey had made changes to comply with the water quality SMR since the introduction of CC. Most of the changes related to SMR 4 (47%) and SMR 2 (44%).

This picture was reinforced by the practitioner workshops and TAP interviews. However, concerns were expressed about the difficulties of completing records and complying with the underlying regulation, notably SMR4 (NVZs). Given the need for capital investment, some farmers could opt for non-compliance with the wider Nitrates Regulation and risk suffering a penalty if inspected.

For most farmers, however, cross compliance raises awareness of and provides a financial incentive to adhere to legislation on water quality. Farmers need more help with the paperwork, notably from SMR4 (NVZs), which is a new requirement for many farms following extension of NVZs from 2009.

***Recommendation** 7: Ensure that a good level of administrative support is available to farmers on compliance with SMR4 (NVZs), in particular record keeping, through the FAS.*

Historic and landscape features

- GAEC 8 (public rights of way): It appears that, in spite of being a regulatory reinforcement measure, the inclusion of public rights of way as a cross compliance requirement has an impact on a minority of farmers who were not fully observing the regulations but were not being prosecuted by local authorities. However, it is difficult to respond to all referrals in a timely manner through the 1% compliance audit.
- GAEC 13 (stone walls): This is the only form of protection for stone walls and is likely to have prevented the removal of stone walls in some cases, although it is difficult to ascertain the extent to which this applies.
- GAEC 15 (hedgerows): It is difficult to determine the precise impact of CC here because of the application of similar rules to the large proportion of ELS[4] agreement holders who have taken up hedgerow management options. Nevertheless, evidence indicates that a substantial proportion of farmers have amended their practice on cutting dates with just over half of the farmers in the survey making changes relating to GAEC 15.
- There is little evidence of compliance issues for GAEC 16 and 17.

Standards relating to historic and landscape features could be grouped together in order to improve presentation and acceptance. The element of GAEC 15 (Hedgerows, cutting dates) which relates to the timing of hedge cutting is in effect a biodiversity action and would sit more comfortably in the "Habitats and Wildlife" group of standards in terms of presentation. It is not backed by legislation but has been effective in changing practices. GAEC 13 (Stone walls) is not backed by legislation and while evidence of an impact is limited, it is appropriate to include it in cross compliance to protect stone walls against removal.

***Recommendation 8:** Group GAEC 7 (Scheduled monuments), GAEC 8 (Public rights of way), GAEC 13 (Stone walls), GAEC 15 (Hedgerows) part, GAEC 16 (*Felling *of trees) and GAEC 17 (Tree Preservation Orders) under a "protection of historic and landscape features" banner to help present the rationale for these standards.*

***Recommendation** 9: Subject to the decision of the European Court of Justice, GAEC 8 (Public rights of way) should be retained in cross compliance but a* separate *inspection process established to deal with referrals (also for other breaches where referrals are* *significant). This would allow more timely responses to breaches and focus on this rather than being a full cross compliance inspection.*

Habitats and wildlife

Most of the GAEC and SMR standards in this category have a high level of compliance but there are some issues of effectiveness.

- GAEC 9 (Overgrazing and supplementary feeding): there is considerable confusion over the requirement of this standard, notably "unsuitable supplementary feeding." In practice, issues of overgrazing may be less relevant going forward due to the decoupling of subsidy and falling livestock numbers but in the absence of Cross Compliance, there is no other provision for protection at present.
- GAEC 11 (Control of weeds): compliance issues are limited but relate disproportionately to small farms. Enforcement is difficult as the regulation relates to preventing spread of weeds rather than their presence. Lack of effective enforcement by Local Authorities causes resentment from neighbouring farms.
- GAEC 12 (Eligible land not in agricultural production): rules are badly written and there is considerable confusion over the requirement of this standard, with some farmers using set aside rules.
- GAEC 14 (Protection of hedgerows and watercourses): Awareness of requirements is good, in part due to the media attention that it has received but there is limited understanding of environmental benefits and some resistance to the value of 2 m strips. In practice, little management is required and crop yields and quality from the outer metre or so of the field are poor, thus little income is likely to be foregone. However, this is not necessarily the perception of farmers, and greater provision of information and advice about the rationale for and benefits of the measure may foster more positive attitudes.

For many of the other standards in this category, there are low levels of non-compliance although it is likely that the introduction of Cross Compliance has raised farmers' awareness of legislation, notably Environmental Impact Assessment Regulations (GAEC 5).

There is a need to

- clarify the rules (GAEC 9 and 12);
- respond directly to breaches (GAEC 11);
- promote the private and public benefits to farmers; and
- link with ELS options to extend buffer width (GAEC 14).

***Recommendation 10**: Clarify the rules for GAEC 5, 9 and 12 through development of case studies and FAS activities.*

***Recommendation 11**: Improve effectiveness of GAEC 11 by responding directly to reported breaches, outside the 1% audit if feasible.*

***Recommendation 12**: Revise GAEC management rules in line with set-aside rules where this is appropriate and promote to the industry through FAS.*

***Recommendation 13**: Make more explicit links to ELS field margin options through FAS to improve the environmental effectiveness of GAEC 14.*

***Recommendation 14**: Add GAEC 15 (cutting dates) to this group of standards.*

Recommendation 15*: Bundle GAEC 5, 6, 9, 10, 11, 12 and 14 together with SMR1 and SMR 5 under a single "habitat and wildlife protection" banner to help present the rationale for these standards.*

Animal identification

Animal identification SMRs represent the main area of non-compliance among all standards. The percentage of animals failing inspection ranged from 8.7% to 9.8% between 2005 and 2007 with an overall failure rate for inspections of around 50%. This is of concern given the timescale over which the legislation has been in place and the inability of cross compliance to impact on the extent of breaches. It is at least in part because, while farmers understand the broad principles of traceability and managing disease spread, they do not give sufficient priority to day-to-day actions to meet the requirements of the SMR. Many do not realise the potential for BCMS[5] links while there is also an issue with record keeping. There is a need to reinforce the purpose of and public good argument for SMRs 7 and 8, to ensure the process is as clear and simple as possible and to change behaviour. The latter might involve, for example, more FAS workshops on record keeping or referring those who fail inspections to the FAS programme.

Recommendation 16*: The RPA Inspectorate needs to analyse and highlight the key issues, which relate to common breaches, and work effectively with FAS advisors to identify actions that will help all farmers to comply with SMRs 7 and 8 (Cattle ID).*

Control of chemicals, food and feedstuffs

SMR 9-11 relate to observation of legislation through good practice and evidenced by record keeping. Compliance levels are high but inclusion on the list helps to increase compliance amongst occasional users of pesticides such as livestock farmers using products like sheep dips and herbicides, and who may be less aware of the pertinent rules and regulations.

Cross compliance has improved the observance of correct practice, notably with regard to pesticide application (SMR 9).

Recommendation 17*: Bundle the SMRs relating to chemicals, food and feedstuffs into a single "control of chemical substances" banner to help present the rationale for these standards.*

Animal disease control

No recommendations.

Animal welfare

SMRs 16-18 relate to existing welfare legislation and while non-compliance is significant, this often relates to minor breaches such as failing to record deaths of lambs or piglets. However, the inspection agencies have to work within the EU requirements and farmers need to recognise the rules and implement change where this is required. As with animal ID, non-compliance here is in part an issue of awareness and support, and again there is a significant role for FAS to play in promoting the principles as well as the rules. Consultees raised an issue of overlap with private Quality Assurance Schemes (QAS) which is seen as unhelpful. As with environmental and food safety legislation, CC requirements should set the baseline with additional welfare demands being rewarded by the market. As such it should be possible to have consistency between QAS and CC records and inspections.

It is too early to make a full impact assessment of SMR 16 (Welfare of calves), SMR 17 (Welfare of pigs) and SMR 18 (Welfare of farmed animals), since they were only introduced in 2007 and there are differences in inspection assessments from previous on-farm welfare inspection. Cross compliance inspections need to be able to accommodate referrals on welfare issues and there is a case for a separate inspection process outside the 1% audit. In practice, Animal Health already selects the maximum feasible proportion of inspections on the basis of risk, and follows up all referrals it receives by carrying out on-farm checks that do not form part of the 1% inspection target. The fact that additional inspections were triggered in 2008 (from breaches found during the random and scored-risk parts of their selection) suggests that additional effort needs to be made in this area.

Recommendation 18: *RPA and Animal Health need to continue to work closely with increased support from FAS to ensure farmers are aware of the SMR baseline for animal welfare and that breaches are reduced. Referrals for breaches need to continue to be followed up outside the 1% inspection audit as part of this effort.*

Recommendation 19: *Treat membership of Quality Assurance Schemes as evidence of reduced risk when selecting claimants for inspection; both are based on EU animal welfare legislation, with cross compliance representing the baseline standard for QAS.*

Policy implementation

The FAS is specifically tasked with supporting farmers to meet CC and it is clear that much remains to be done. While this is partly about policy design, there is a need for increased emphasis on education and knowledge transfer, linking requirements with best farming practices to help farmers understand how best to meet requirements and to recognise when and why legislation is relevant to them e.g. GAEC 1-4 (Soil management) and GAEC 12 (Land not in agricultural production).

Recommendation 20: *Focus FAS activity on those standards and industry segments where there is most uncertainty and use knowledge transfer to link requirements with best farming practice.*

In terms of farmer behaviour, a key issue is that of negative attitudes associated with cross compliance, both in concept and application. Fundamentally, this relates to the risk of penalties and additional costs but it also denotes some failure to communicate the rationale and the detail of the standards. It is linked to the perception that public subsidy through the SPS is "of right" rather than a payment for public goods. Contrary to some media comment and feedback from some consultees, most feedback on the inspection process itself is positive. It would therefore be helpful to have better links between policy support (through FAS) and the inspection process so that this issue is addressed explicitly.

Recommendation 21: *Review the extent of partnership working between the FAS and inspection bodies and ensure the rationale for CC and the positive feedback on inspections is communicated widely to the industry.*

Increased targeting would improve the effectiveness of CC based on reported breaches of legislative requirements e.g. GAEC 7, 8, 13 and SMRs. While all referrals to RPA and Animal Health are dealt with through the targeted element of inspection, many breaches require a prompt response and are often temporal in nature. A separate process outside the 1% compliance inspections could address the breach specifically, without need for a full inspection and would allow a more timely response.

Recommendation 22: *Research the case for a separate inspection process, outside the 1% inspection, for reported breaches of standards.*

7.4 General conclusions

This evaluation summarised above was performed in England towards the end of 2008, the fourth year after cross compliance conditions became attached to the receipt of CAP direct income support paid to farmers. It evaluated the "pure" cross compliance component of the package, assembling evidence on the extent to which CC objectives were achieved and relating this at least notionally to the direct costs (by farmers and public administrators) incurred as a result of the cost compliance component only.

While we have reported that there is only limited scope to reduce the public cost of cross compliance, it is clear that a more effective approach to promoting the conditions to farmers and providing well targeted support through FAS would reduce unnecessary farmer costs as a side effect.

Notes

1. This contribution to the Workshop consists of the Executive Summary of the report *Evaluation of Cross Compliance*, prepared by outside experts for the Department for Environment, Food and Rural Affairs (DEFRA) in 2009. Some additional material from the full report has been added by the editor to improve the clarity of the summary as a stand-alone text. The full report can be found at *archive.defra.gov.uk/evidence/statistics/foodfarm/enviro/observatory/research/documents/Xceval_mar09.pdf.*
2. Using a stratified sample of 300 respondents. Aggregates are obtained using weights appropriate to each farm profile.
3. Programme of the UK Environmental Agency, see *publications.environment-agency.gov.uk/?lang=_e.*
4. ELS = Entry Level Stewardship. With nearly 60% of England's agricultural land in Entry Level Stewardship, this is the basic underlying scheme open to all farmers and land managers in England. ELS agreements are for five years. See *www.naturalengland.org.uk/ourwork/farming/funding/es/els/default.aspx*
5. British Cattle Movement Service – government register of stock movements, herd changes.

Annex 7.A

Table 7A. List of SMRs and GAEC standards for England

Standard Number	Description of the standard SMR	Standard Number	Description of the standard GAEC
1	Wild birds	1	Soil Protection Review
2	Groundwater	2	Post-harvest management of soils
3	Sewage sludge	3	Waterlogged soils
4	Nitrate Vulnerable Zones (NVZs)	4	Burning of crop residues
5	Habitats	5	Environmental assessment
6	Animal identification – pigs	6	SSSIs
7, 8	Cattle identification	7	Scheduled monuments
8a	Animal identification – sheep and goats	8	Public rights of way
9	Plant protection products	9	Overgrazing/unsuitable supplementary feeding on natural or semi-natural grassland
10	Restriction on substances having hormonal or thyrostatic action and beta-agonists	10	Heather and grass burning
11	Food and feed law	11	Control of weeds
12	TSEs	12	Eligible land not in agricultural production
13	FMD	13	Stone walls
14	Certain animal diseases	14	Protection of hedgerows and watercourses
15	Blue tongue	15	Hedgerows
16	Welfare of calves	16	Felling of trees
17	Welfare of pigs	17	Tree preservation orders
18	Welfare of farmed animals		

Source: Appendix 1 of the full report at: *archive.defra.gov.uk/evidence/statistics/foodfarm/enviro/observatory/research/documents/Xceval_mar09.pdf.*

Chapter 8

A policy evaluation of Environmentally Friendly Direct Payment Programme in Korea

Chang-Gil Kim and James Banfill[1]

Korea's Environmentally Friendly Direct Payment Programme (EFDPP) provides an incentive and transitional support for farmers who switch to environmentally friendly farming methods. As such, it has made a positive contribution towards preserving the environment in Korea. However, as payments to individual farms cease after three years, it does not provide a permanent on-going reward for the greater provision of agri-environmental public goods once the switch is complete. This chapter reviews the background and objectives of the EFDPP, and its impacts. Since its introduction in 1999, farmers and policy administrators surveyed have evaluated it highly as a programme for promoting environmentally friendly farming. The analysis is then used as a basis for suggesting improvements in the current EFDPP.

Agriculture is an industry based on continuous resource renewal and has historically been an industry in harmony with the environment. However, continued heavy use of chemical inputs, including fertilisers and pesticides, often results in environmental problems like soil degradation and deterioration of water quality, which in turn present obstacles to continued cropping and threaten the sustainability of agro-ecosystems. Accordingly, it is necessary to promote environmentally friendly (EF) farming, and in particular lower levels of chemical inputs, as a solution to environmental problems in the agricultural sector. Most farmers are in favour of the practice of EF farming. However, many farmers are reluctant actually to implement these practices due to the perceived risk of lower yield and income resulting from the adoption of environmentally friendly, and often unfamiliar, farming practices.

In these circumstances, the South Korean government has implemented several policy measures for promoting environmentally friendly agriculture on a large scale since the mid-1990s. These measures culminated in the Environmentally Friendly Direct Payment Programme (hereafter referred to as the EFDPP), introduced in 1999, which provides incentives for farmers to switch to EF farming. This programme offers a subsidised direct payment to compensate for any decreases in income associated with farmers switching to EF farming practices during a three-year transitional period. Farmers who participate in this programme receive a subsidy subject to their compliance with the requirements of the programme. The payment ceases after three years, and farmers cannot reapply for it.

The adoption of EF agriculture will initially result in both increases in labour input and decreases in yield compared to conventional farming until a technically stable situation is reached. In addition, it may also cause a considerable decrease in income until a differentiated sales network for environmentally friendly farming products can be accessed. The payments made under the EFDPP act essentially to cover adjustment costs and additional risk during transition.

At the same time, scientific analysis and on-site research have confirmed that the continuous practice of EF farming has improved the ecological environment in the regions concerned by helping to restore harmony within agro-ecological systems. As the positive externality of environmentally friendly practices in the agricultural sector cannot be traded using market mechanisms, this is a case of market failure that can justify government intervention to correct it. Since EF farming practices generate positive effects on agro-ecological systems on a permanent, long-term basis when compared to conventional farming practices, government intervention beyond the transitional period could be justified based on externality theory.

In reality, however, the EFDPP payments offered to farmers who adopt certified EF farming, are intended to cover adjustment costs and compensate them during a transition period when their products can still only be sold on conventional markets (that is, without any organic or EF premium incorporated in the price). Lee *et al.* (1998) laid the basis for the framework and the implementation of the EFDPP through their survey of EF farming practices and the benchmarking of European cases. They suggested KRW 524 000[2] per ha as the amount of direct payment required to cover the income difference between conventional and low-pesticide rice farming practices.

The need to develop and evaluate the EFDPP has led to research efforts aimed at expanding EF farming practices. Huh (2000) assessed the performance of the agri-environmental programmes using a survey of programme participants in specific regions around the country. The survey results showed concerns among farmers regarding what was seen as a low level of direct payment. The programme participants' desired amount of direct payment was found to be about KRW 1 000 000 per ha for environmentally friendly rice farming practice. Kim *et al.* (2003) also evaluated agri-environmental measures using a criterion-based survey of policy authorities and policy beneficiaries. They used evaluation criteria such as appropriateness, adequacy, satisfaction, and feasibility in evaluating the policy programme.

As environmentally friendly agriculture development is emphasised as a growth engine for future agriculture in an era of market liberalisation, a systematic evaluation of the EFDPP is an important task in establishing environmentally friendly agricultural system in Korea. Following the studies cited above, this chapter will specifically focus on evaluating the EFDPP using the evaluation criterion of policy performance in order to identify directions for improving the programme.

8.1 Theoretical background for agri-environmental payments

The theoretical framework underlying direct payments that reward farmers for producing environmental public goods comes from welfare economics and concerns externalities attributed to market failure.[3] Farming activities can affect – positively or negatively – the welfare of other economic agents due to non-marketable outputs or consequences. When an externality is generated, its production either does not reach or exceeds social optimum level. In the first case, it is a positive externality (that is, the affected party benefits from it and if he could pay for it through a market transaction, he would demand more), and in the second case a negative one (for example, pollution). In both cases, there are no markets in which third parties can buy more of the positive externality or buy from polluters some of their rights to produce a negative externality. Especially in the case of intensive conventional farming using high levels of chemical inputs, higher farm production is usually associated with higher social costs due to more pollutants being discharged into the environment. However, the resulting external costs, including the treatment costs of pollution sources, are not included in the farmer's production cost and so he takes no account of them. By contrast, environmentally friendly agricultural practices improve the quality of agro-ecological systems and thus generate a positive externality.

If we can measure the effect of environmental quality improvement generated in an agro-ecological system by EF farming practices, we can correct for its sub-optimal production level by making a direct payment to the farmer that is equal to the value conferred on it by society. Farmers will enhance the environmental performance of the agricultural sector if they are provided with a subsidy as an economic incentive to cover the environmental costs and benefits drawn from their production activities. In practice, the larger the payment, the greater is the range of practices likely to be adopted and the higher the number of likely participants. However, the subsidy programmes may be expensive for taxpayers to fund because participation will increase as payment rates rise. The underlying theory of market failure and using taxes, subsidies and direct payments to correct for it, is explained in detail in OECD (2001, 2010).

8.2 Implementation status of the Environmentally Friendly Direct Payment Programme

Background and objectives of the EFDPP

The EFDPP compensates those farmers who comply with the requirements of the programme. The implementation of the policy has its legal basis in Article 11-2 of the *Special Law regarding the Compliance of World Trade Organization Agreement* and the Article 13 and 23 of the *Enforcement Regulation on the Direct Payment Programme Implementation for the Agricultural Producers*.

The specific objective of the EFDPP is to encourage the preservation of the agricultural and rural environment together with the production of safe agricultural products by supporting farmers who have converted their farming to EF farming through a direct subsidy payment that compensates them for a part of the decrease in their income associated with this transition.

Results of policy implementation

The programme content has been continuously revised over time according to changes in political circumstances (policy targets, budget constraint, politicians' need and social demand). Table 8.1 shows that, during the first phase of the EFDPP in 1999-2001, the targets for the programme were farmlands in environmentally sensitive areas such as water source protection districts and natural parks, where the degree of potential future environmental improvement is relatively large and the potential for local support is high. The farmers eligible for the benefit of the programme were those engaged in farming and tree-planting in the target regions, who introduced environmentally friendly agriculture on an area of farmland larger than 1 000m². The target products were all agricultural products, excluding livestock and forest products.

Table 8.1. Support policy targets and payment levels of the EFDPP

	1999-2001	2002	2003	2004-2011
Policy targets	Water source protection districts, other environmental control areas	**Upland**: low-pesticide[1] **Paddy**: no-pesticide[1] **Env-regulating area**: over low-pesticide[1]	Low-pesticide[1]	No-pesticide[1]
Payment level (KRW 1 000)	524/ha (same unit amount of payment in **upland** and **paddy** fields)	524/ha (same unit amount of payment in **upland** and **paddy** fields)	**Upland**[2] • organic :794 • no-pesticide: 674 • low-pesticide: 524 **Paddy**[2] • organic:770 • no-pesticide: 650 • low-pesticide: 500	**Upland** same as in 2003 **Paddy** • organic : 824-924 • no-pesticide: 739-839 • low-pesticide: 649-749

Notes:

1. The scope of "low-pesticide" in policy targets denotes the certified environmentally friendly farmers who meet the low-pesticide standard, or exceed the standards specified by no-pesticide and organic farming methods. Similarly, "no-pesticide" is specified as an upper stage, which covers no-pesticide and organic farmers, but not low-pesticide farming.

2. The basic payment for paddy = 524 (upland) 500 (paddy); this is topped up by incentive payments of 270 for organic or trans-organic production, or 150 for no-pesticide production.

Source: MIFAFF (2011a).

From 2002, the EFDPP was improved and extended to all certified farmers who adopted EF farming. The aim was to increase programme participation and make a clear distinction with the basic direct payment system for rice paddy farming. The target area for the programme was extended from limited environmental control regions, such as water source protection districts, to nationwide. Eligibility for the direct payment scheme was limited to farmers with farmland exceeding 1 000m² and revenues from environmentally friendly agricultural products of more than KRW 1 million a year. For a farming household, the level of the subsidy was KRW 524 000 per ha. In addition, within the environmental control regions, the farmers with certified low-pesticide farming were also eligible considering the importance of environmental preservation.

In 2003, for farmers eligible for the subsidy based on low-pesticide farming, the amount of the subsidy was differentiated in proportion to the expected decrease in income depending on the type of environmentally friendly agriculture undertaken. In addition, among the farmers who obtained the certification for low-pesticide farming, incentives based on the stage of the certification were paid on top of the basic subsidy for rice paddy and upland farming. Basic amounts for the direct payment are KRW 524 000 per ha for upland farming and KRW 500 000 per ha for paddy farming (the basic subsidy amount of direct payment for rice farming). Incentive payments in the case of organic farming were KRW 270 000 per ha, 150 000 per ha for no-pesticide farming. There was no incentive payment in the case of low-pesticide farming.

In 2004, target farmers were limited to those who obtained the certification for low-pesticide farming. The period of support for farmers who were selected as the target for the certification for low-pesticide farming and continued to use low-pesticide practices was limited to three years, including the year of initial selection. The unit amount of subsidy for upland farming was the same as in 2003, but for paddy fields it was increased from KRW 500 000 to KRW 532 000. For organic and transitional organic farming households, the subsidy per ha was KRW 802 000 and KRW 682 000 in the case of no-pesticide farming practices.

The entire amount of subsidy payments came out of national treasury funds. As shown in Table 8.2, the record of actual direct payment for the period from 1999 to 2010 was on average KRW 15 billion per year covering approximately 36 000 ha of cultivation for certified products. The number of farming households eligible for the direct payment was approximately 45 000. In 2002, the number of farming household that obtained certification was significantly lower and thus the total of direct payments for that year decreased to approximately KRW 3 billion, almost half the annual average of previous years. The number of farming households participating in the programme also fell sharply to 6 589 households, covering 5 274 ha of cultivated land. The reason for these falls was the stricter eligibility criterion for the programme, which required certification equal to or exceeding no-pesticide standards for paddy farming.

Table 8.2. Implementation of the EFDPP

	1999	2000	2001	2002	2003	2004
Total paid (million KRW)	5 667	5 730	5 724	2 757	6 426	8 120
Area receiving payments (ha)	10 269	10 459	10 480	5 274	10 459	13 698
Number of farm households	17 436	18 697	18 806	6 589	12 195	14 520
Average payment based on total money paid (1 000 KRW/ha)	552	548	546	523	614	593
	2005	**2006**	**2007**	**2008**	**2009**	**2010**
Total paid (million KRW)	7 703	14 055	17 525	26 282	40 868	37 608
Area receiving payments (ha)	20 780	34 896	45 434	72 444	98 849	93 305
Number of farm households	22 119	45 567	60 090	87 416	115 300	116 385
Average payment based on total money paid (1 000 KRW/ha)	458	403	386	363	413	403

Source: MIFAFF (2011).

However, since the beneficiaries' requirement was relaxed to include low-pesticide farm households in 2003, the number of participating farming households significantly increased to 12 195 households covering 10 459 ha of cultivated land, thereby expanding the budget for the EFDPP to approximately KRW 6.7 billion. Eligibility conditions were expanded to include no-pesticide farm households in 2004, and the 24% increase in programme participants resulted in a budget of approximately KRW 8.1 billion, 14 520 participating farming household and 13 698 ha of farmland (Table 8.2).

Table 8.3. Participation in the EFDPP among certified environmental farming households

Classification			2008	2009	2010
Total number of EF farming households	Certified EF farming households	*Farm households (number)*	172 553	198 891	183 918
		Area (ha)	174 107	201 688	194 006
	Participating households	*Farm households (number)*	96 771 (56.1)	112 409 (56.5)	116 382 (63.3)
		Area (ha)	76 352 (43.9)	90 132 (44.7)	93 318 (48.1)
Organic farming households	Certified EF farming households	*Farm households (number)*	8 460	9 403	10 790
		Area (ha)	12 003	13 343	15 518
	Participating households	*Farm households (number)*	2 782 (32.9)	2 653 (28.2)	2 856 (26.5)
		Area (ha)	2 349 (19.6)	2 246 (16.8)	2 207 (14.2)
No-pesticide farming households	Certified EF farming households	*Farm households (number)*	45 089	63 653	83 136
		Area (ha)	42 983	71 039	94 533
	Participating households	*Farm households (number)*	22 274 (49.4)	30 448 (47.8)	36 448 (43.8)
		Area (ha)	16 173 (37.6)	23 484 (33.1)	29 520 (31.2)
Low-pesticide farming households	Certified EF farming households	*Farm households (number)*	119 004	125 835	89 992
		Area (ha)	119 136	117 306	83 954
	Participating households	*Farm households (number)*	71 715 (60.2)	79 308 (63.0)	77 348 (85.9)
		Area (ha)	57 830 (48.5)	64 401 (54.9)	61 592 (73.4)

Note: The figures in parentheses show the percentage of farm households that benefitted from the EFDPP among the total certified EF farming practices.

Source: MIFAFF (2011b).

In 2010, 183 918 farming households obtained certification for environmentally friendly agricultural products for an area of 194 006 ha. The percentage of farming households participating in the programme was 63.3% of those with qualifying certifications. These households accounted for 48.1% of qualifying cultivated land. That means that over half of all farming households that obtained the certification for environmentally friendly agricultural products did not get the benefit of the EFDPP even though they obtained the certification (Table 8.3). Regarding environmentally friendly certification, about 63% of total certified farming households participated in the programme, which represents about 26% of the total area of farmland involved in organic farming, approximately 44% of the total certified farming households and the size of farmland in the case of no-pesticide farming, and approximately 86% of total certified farming household in the case of low-pesticide farming.

8.3 Policy evaluation of the Environmentally Friendly Direct Payment Programme

Criteria for policy evaluation

Policy evaluation analyses the extent to which the originally intended effects of the policy in question were achieved, and the criterion of effectiveness is a central concept of this evaluation. The purpose of policy evaluation is to provide objective information for rational decision making on the scope for policies to enhance the effectiveness of limited government budget resources, and also guidance for the revision, supplementation or abolition of policy schemes.

In most cases, the policy maker is responsible for the contents of policies, including policy objectives and policy implementation. As the purpose of policy evaluation is to identify problems in the current situation and to explore areas of improvement, policy evaluation may become a threat to the person in charge. It is therefore necessary for staff involved in the monitoring and evaluation of policies, as well as researchers, to participate from the start of the evaluation. This would enhance the relevance of the evaluation, by improving the appropriateness of the method and the survey respondents, and by facilitating communication (Oskam *et al.*, 1998).

Evaluation of policy is based on criteria for judging the quality of the policy, which can be classified according to various dimensions but can be largely divided into two main categories in terms of contents and procedures.[4] This chapter has adopted *effectiveness* and *appropriateness* as the criteria for evaluating the evaluation of actual contents of the EFDPP. Effectiveness is the criterion for evaluating the degree to which policy objectives are met. Appropriateness measures the effectiveness of the budget resources applied, and is the criterion for judging the *realistic* possibility of accomplishing the policy objectives under the given conditions and constraints.

Evaluating the performance of the EFDPP

A total of KRW 178 billion was input into the programme carried out for the years 1999-2010 over a total of 426 347 ha, which represents an average subsidy of KRW 483 000 per ha (Table 8.2). The average areas of farmland for a farming household receiving a subsidy of KRW 524 000-794 000 per ha according to farming method was approximately 0.5-0.7 ha, which means a subsidy of KRW 500 000-600 000 per household. The amount of subsidy differs over households depending on input costs, and in most cases the subsidy can only cover the expenses for purchasing materials for environmentally friendly agricultural farming. Accordingly, these subsidies are insufficient to serve as a proper incentive for income compensation to the farming household that implements EF farming.

For the evaluation of the programme, an in-depth survey was conducted through site visits to the beneficiaries and officers in charge of the schemes (Kim *et al.*, 2003; Kim *et al.*, 2009). We obtained the list of farmers who actually participated in the policy programme and selected the 61 survey respondents from among them using purposive sampling, which is a subjective sampling method. Officers in charge of administering the policy were selected from among the officers in charge of policy in the Environmentally Friendly Agriculture Department of the Ministry of Agriculture and Forestry, and officers in charge of relevant administration tasks in each province, city and county office. Fifty-eight officers in charge of environmentally friendly agriculture policy, who were involved in the establishment and execution of the policy, were selected nationwide as survey respondents for policy evaluation.

The average age of officers in charge of policy was 46 years, and their break-down according to the length of time they had been assigned to environmentally friendly showed that more than 50% of them had been involved in environmental agriculture-related assignments for over two years (Table 8.4).

The average age of programme participants was 51 years, and the shares according to the length of time spent in the programme increased sharply with longer duration, with over two-thirds having participated for three years or more. Participants' recognition of the difficulties of practicing environmentally friendly agriculture compared with conventional farming showed that for nearly three out of four of them, these difficulties had been overcome after an initial phase, which means that the skills to practice EF farming are now well established for this large majority of the survey targets. The most difficult EF practice for farmers to manage is weed control. On the feasibility and longer-term prospects for practicing EF farming, 92% of total survey targets expressed the opinion that "the programme is necessary for continuous management of agriculture even though income is lower", and only 8% thought that "it is difficult to adopt the new farming programme as its influences on yield as well as income remain uncertain," which indicates a large majority who recognise and accept the necessity of EF farming for the longer term.

Table 8.4. Summary of survey results on policy officials and beneficiaries

Respondents' characteristics and responses	Policy officials[1]		Policy beneficiaries[1]	
For policy officials: length of time in involved; for farmers, length of time participating				
• less than 1 year	12	(20.7)	7	(11.5)
• over 1 year – less than 2 years	16	(27.6)	7	(11.5)
• over 2 years – less than 3 years	12	(20.7)	4	(6.5)
• over 3 years	18	(31.0)	43	(70.5)
Viewpoint on the future of EF agriculture				
• core part of future agriculture	38	(65.5)	42	(68.8)
• limitation on our agricultural circumstances	19	(32.8)	12	(19.7)
• uncertain about the future of EF agriculture	1	(1.7)	7	(11.5)
Difficulty in practicing environmentally friendly farming				
• difficulties in comparison with conventional farming	-	-	16	(26.2)
• difficulties at the beginning but are now stabilised	-	-	45	(73.8)
Viewpoint on environmentally friendly farming practices				
• necessary for sustainable management even though income becomes a little lower	-	-	56	(91.8)
• difficult to adopt EF farming due to uncertainty of income and yields	-	-	5	(8.2)

Note:

1. Percentages of each group are given in parentheses.

Source: Kim *et al.* (2009).

The result of the survey of the authorities in charge of the policy showed that, among the officials, 44.6% believed that "the programme is necessary for promoting environmentally friendly farming households, but supplementation of the policy is required because farming households' dependence on the government subsidy" is increasing, 41.1% considered that "the programme is an appropriate means for the expansion of environmentally friendly farming households,". and 12.5% believed that "it does not seem to be desirable policy as the fiscal burden is too high." On the other hand, in the group consisting of the policy recipients, 85% expressed the opinion that "the programme is a very appropriate means for expanding the number of environmentally friendly farming households" although 11.7% said that they were not well informed about the contents of the policy (Table 8.5).

Table 8.5. Survey results concerning the performance of the EFDPP

Respondents' characteristics and responses	Policy officials[1]	Beneficiaries[1]
Evaluation of effectiveness of EFDPP		
• appropriate policy measure for expanding EFDPP	23 (41.1)	51 (85.0)
• necessary policy measures for promoting EFDPP, but supplementation of the policy is required due to dependence on subsidy	25 (44.6)	1 (1.7)
• undesirable policy measures due to heavy financial burden	7 (12.5)	1 (1.7)
• not well informed about the contents of policy programme	1 (1.8)	7 (11.7)
Appropriateness of the unit amount of the payment		
• appropriate increase of the payment in 2009	20 (35.7)	36 (60.0)
• greater increase of payment needed in 2009	34 (60.7)	21 (35.0)
• smaller increase of payment appropriate in 2009	1 (1.8)	-
• uncertain about the unit amount of payment scheme	1 (1.8)	3 (5.0)

1. Percentages of each group are given in parentheses.

Source: Kim *et al.* (2009).

In relation to the appropriateness of the unit amount of direct payment, a surprising result is that a larger share of officers in charge of policy than of participating farmers expressed the opinion that "the amount (already) adjusted upwards in 2009 needs to be increased again" (61% as against 35%) and these proportions were reversed when it came to those in the two groups who considered the amount in 2009 was appropriate. It could be interesting to explore whether these differences are linked to respondents' age, length of time associated with the programme, size of farm and so on. However, the small sample sizes would preclude drawing strong conclusions from any findings on these points.

Problems associated with the Environmentally Friendly Direct Payment Programme

Farming households that are eligible for the direct payment programme are limited to those producing certified environmentally friendly agricultural products with a low-pesticide rating or above. However, the menu for the policy appeared to be too simple and the policy does not seem to have reflected the changes in the actual conditions of EF farming. Accordingly, the development of a direct payment programme with a variety of measures, which can contribute to the preservation of environment in agricultural sector, will be necessary in order to promote healthy environmentally friendly agriculture with objective set toward the harmony of agriculture and environment.

The current unit amount for the EFDPP is insufficient incentive for risk management faced by the participating farming households. For most farming households considering switching to EF farming, a major deterrent is the decrease in income due to the uncertainty about yield and price. Therefore, the appropriate level of direct payment is one that covers the risk to the farming households that implement EF farming.

As the current EFDPP does not differentiate the rate of subsidy unit according to the degree of transition during the implementation stage, it cannot yet serve as an aggressive incentive to attract farming households to opt into EF farming. Accordingly, in the future programme, it is desirable to differentiate the amount of subsidy by the stage of implementation taking account of differences in technology employed and purchasing at different stages.

The establishment of a follow-up control system for monitoring the implementation by the beneficiaries of the EFDPP, is also insufficient at the current time. In the case of the farming household, which implements EF farming, it is necessary to prepare farming administration records and establish databases of pertinent data in order to establish a proper monitoring system for implementation, and also to introduce appropriate penalties for those participating farming households that do not comply with the requirements.

8.4 Directions for improving the Environmentally Friendly Direct Payment Programme

Increase of subsidy rate and differentiated payment according to year

The current unit amount of the EFDPP subsidy is based on the difference between the *revenues* of conventional farming and EF farming practices. However, in the current situation this revenue gap between conventional and EF farming practices is gradually reducing even though there is a need for further increases in the unit amount of the direct payment. Therefore, the method for calculating the unit amount for the subsidy under the EFDPP, which is based on the revenue gap only, is insufficient. The basis of calculation for the unit amount for the payment will have to be changed to a method that comprehensively considers the elements such as production cost, income and net income together. This would still be consistent with WTO definitions of green box direct payments.

In addition, the current subsidy rate of KRW 824 000 was based on the revenue difference with that of conventional farming in 2004, and should be adjusted upwards based on the latest status survey.

The difference in gross margins per ha between conventional and organic farming practices is KRW 2 500 000 in the 1st year, KRW 2 050 00 in the second year, KRW 1 440 000 in the third year and KRW 370 000 in the fourth year. However, organic farming gross margin is KRW 550 000 higher than conventional one in the fifth year. In the no-pesticide farming case, the difference would be KRW 510 000 to 2 340 000 depending on the year. Full compensation for the difference in gross margins during transitional period would imply a very large budget. Based on compensating half the average difference in gross margins would be more realistic (Figure 8.1).[5]

On the technological level, conversion from conventional farming to organic farming requires 3-5 years and therefore subsidies designed to cover adjustment costs should be paid up to a maximum of four years. However, when EF farming is completely established, there will still be various positive effects to the preservation of soil, water quality and various microbes, and therefore it will reasonable to make direct payment for a certain fixed amount per ha in recognition of the environmental benefits and the income foregone by famers adopting EF practices. Annual payments could be graduated into three stages: 1-2 years, 3-4 years and from five years onwards using five years as the basis for implementation. We consider benefits to biodiversity and GHG reduction become observable from organic farming after four years and we therefore propose a new payment scheme should be introduced at that point. This scheme is intended to compensate farmers for the costs related to biodiversity-friendly or low-carbon practices. However, a more systematic and detailed review of the subsidy rate by stage may be necessary as implementation progresses. Figure 8.1 illustrates the hypothetical payment scheme that embodies this principle.

Among the countries that implement a direct payment programme to promote organic farming, France, Denmark, Switzerland and Norway are paying differentiated amounts for subsidies. Leading countries in developing sustainable agriculture, such as France and

Denmark, pay direct payments for conversion over five years dividing the five years into three stages. After five years, subsidy payments are still made for maintenance and administration. Other countries, including Germany, Switzerland and Norway, pay subsidies for three years to those farming households that obtained the certification for organic farming, while paying only basic payment after three years (USDA, 2001; Park *et al.*, 2004; Stolze and Lampkin, 2009).

Figure 8.1. A hypothetical five-year differentiated payment system of EF rice production

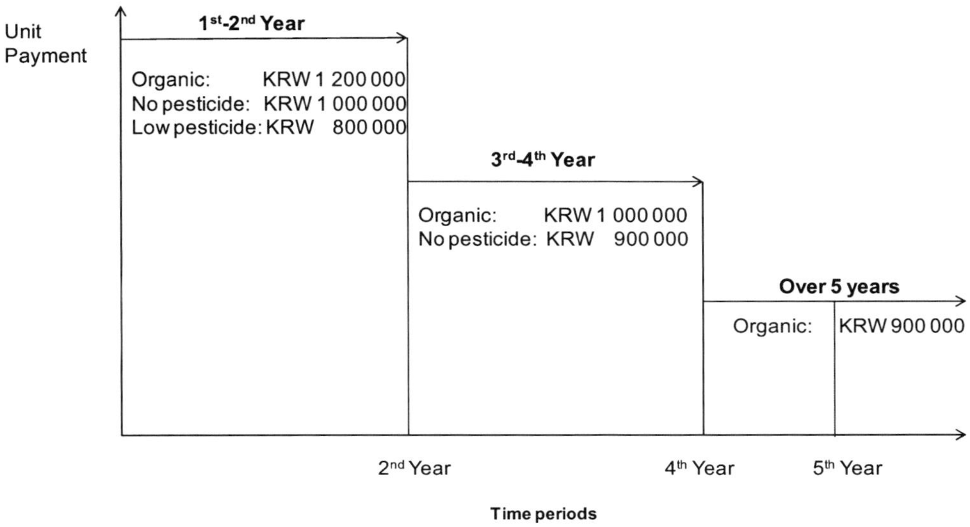

Establishment of a proper monitoring system

The establishment of proper monitoring system for farming households that participate in the EFDPP will be a key to extending the subsidy on a mid- to long- term basis and in securing systematic justification for the system. In the event that direct payments are to be made for farming households certified for EF farming, such as organic farming and no-pesticide farming, there will be no problem in monitoring the farming households concerned as the certifying authority has to issue a certification mark based on implementation status every year. However, if the number of farms implementing EF practices increases as well, major monitoring efforts would be needed regarding participation and payments.

The establishment of a database of eligible farming household will provide very important basic data in the future on various aspects like production processes, management of environmentally friendly agricultural practices and the amount of farm support.

For the healthy development of EF agriculture in the future, an authority with an extensive remit for overseeing EF agriculture and food produced using EF practices would be needed. Such an authority is operational in some countries (e.g. Denmark). Such an authority could oversee the labelling of food products and guarantees to consumers regarding the environmental friendliness of the products. As the authority would have to continuously check and control the status of farming households involved in this programme, it may be necessary to expand the resources of the National Agricultural Products Quality Management Service, which already takes care of certification, in order to administer the programme.[6]

Necessity for introducing direct payment programmes with menu types

The EFDPP is targeted to a switch in farming methods towards environmental friendly practices. However the Korean government is currently considering extending this programme so as to directly target biodiversity, landscape and low-carbon practices.

As the ultimate objective of EF farming is the "creation of harmony between agriculture and the environment", the activities for healthy maintenance and preservation of agro-ecological system can be regarded as the activities of EF farming as well. Accordingly, we will have to develop and implement a policy programme with diversified types of measure for achieving this healthy maintenance and preservation of agro-ecological system. The EFDPP with diversified types of measure would mean a programme in which farmers can voluntarily select, from among various EF alternatives eligible for the direct payments, specifically those measures that it is possible for them to put into practice, given regional and local conditions. For example, farming practices like the implementation of crop cover in winter, the cultivation of water quality purification trees, and use of techniques for preventing soil erosion on slopes can contribute to the enhancement of multiple eco-system functions, such as the maintenance of healthy agro-ecological system and the preservation of the landscape.

8.5 Concluding remarks

Positive environmental externalities produced by agriculture cannot be stimulated by price signals transmitting societal demand, since markets do not exist for these services. The evidence provided in this chapter indicates that the three-year transitional payments are offered to farmers as an incentive for them to switch to environmentally friendly farming has had a significant response in Korea. The payment ceases after three years, and yet presumably the farmers who switched continue to provide environmental public goods that they would not be providing had they remained within a conventional farming system. It follows that, although they are willing to continue producing the EF benefits even without a subsidy once the EF system is established, the level produced is below the social optimum since the value of the additional positive externality is not reflected in their remuneration. A payment system extending beyond the transitional period would undoubtedly provide a greater incentive for switching and would have more beneficial effects on the agro-ecological system. The precise justification for this payment, however, would have to be carefully studied since the figures quoted in this chapter indicate that by the fifth year after conversion, EF farming is already more profitable (in terms of gross margin per hectare) than conventional farming. Hence, the WTO-compatible rationale for the payment as compensating farmers for income foregone does not apply.

In its current form as a transitional payment, the EFDPP payment qualifies for green box status as a decoupled payment for environmental preservation. Moreover, in so far as it is more closely targeted to environmental and consumer needs than other policy options that might achieve similar effects, it is more efficient when compared to other policy options.

Since the EPDPP was introduced in South Korea in 1999, it has been highly evaluated by farmer recipients and by the officials in charge of policy administration, as a positive promotion programme for environmentally friendly farming. However, systematic programme evaluation has also revealed the need to increase the rate of subsidy, differentiate payments by year of implementation and establish a proper system for monitoring participants.

Welfare economics shows that the increased provision of positive externalities by means of a subsidy from the national treasury increases social welfare. If farmers can be incentivised by direct payments to implement EF farming, and we can get verifiable results in terms of improvements in the quality of the agro-ecological system, agriculture can be solidly established as trusted industry by consumers. Moreover, if the EFDPP works as a valid catalyst for the conversion from conventional farming to EF farming, the EF farming in the agricultural sector of South Korea will be established earlier than planned and thus agriculture will be acknowledged for its new value as a bio-industry in harmony with the environment and national land environment preservation industry, instead of an industry that increases environmental burden. However, it is important to be aware that, as the environmental effects due to the implementation of environmentally friendly farming will be generated in the mid- to long term, public expenditure on these objectives may be regarded as a political cost burden in the short term.

Notes

1. Korea Rural Economic Institute, Seoul, Korea.
2. KRW = South Korean won. In May 2012, USD 1 = KRW 1 175 (approximately).
3. An externality is a direct effect of the action of one person or firm on the welfare of another person or firm, where no market exists to compensate or reward the two parties. The theory of an externality corrected by a subsidy is explained by Baumol and Oates (1988) and Carlson *et al.* (1993).
4. In this case, "the criteria in terms of contents" are the same as "the criteria for the results." They are the basis for judging whether the results that flowed from the execution of the policy were desirable or not, and serves as the basis for evaluating policy contents in accordance with the objectives, means, target and policy situation. "Criteria in terms of procedure" are the criteria for judging whether the decision making processes for policy and policy execution that generated the policy results are desirable or not. They may be broken down to analytical reasonableness and political acceptability. For a more detailed exposition of these evaluation criteria, see Jeong *et al.* (2002).
5. The suggested unit payments for EF rice farming were drawn from the average of the revenue stream considered during the conversion period. For more detailed exposition on revenue change over time in environmentally friendly rice production, see Kim and Kim (2003).
6. See *www.naqs.go.kr/english/index.jsp.*

References

Baldock, D. and K. Mitchell (1995), *Cross-Compliance within the Common Agricultural Policy: A Review of Options for Landscape and Nature Conservation*, London: Institute for European Environmental Policy.

Baumol, W.J. and W.E. Oates (1998), *The Theory of Environmental Policy*. Englewood Cliffs, N.J.: Prentice- Hall, 2nd edition.

Carlson, G.A., D. Zilberman, and J.A. Miranowski (1993), *Agricultural and Environmental Resource Economics*. New York, United States: Oxford University Press.

Horan, R.F., J.S. Shortle, and D.G. Abler (1999), "Green Payment for Nonpoint Pollution Control", *American Journal of Agricultural Economics*, Vol. 8, pp. 1210-1215.

Huh, J. (2000), "An Empirical Assessment of Environment-Friendly Agricultural Program (2000)", *Korea Rural Economic Review*, Vol. 23-1, pp. 17-36.

Jeong, J.-G., K.-T. Seong, J. Lee and Y.-S. Lee (2002), *Policy Evaluation: Theory and Application*, Seoul: Parkyoungsa.

Kim, C.-G., S.-I. Oh, and T.-Y. Kim (2003), *Evaluation and Development Directions of Environmentally Friendly Agricultural Policies* (in Korean). Research Report C2003-4. Korea Rural Economic Institute.

Kim, C.-G. and T.-Y. Kim (2003), *A Comparative Analysis of Production Costs and the Revenues between Conventional and Environmental Friendly Agricultural Products* (in Korean), Research Report C2003-36. Korea Rural Economic Institute.

Kim, C.-G., H.-K. Jeong, J.-K. Jang, H.-M. Kwon and D.-H. Moon (2009), *Improving Direct Payment System for Environment-Friendly Agriculture and Introducing Environmental Cross Compliance Programs*. Research Report C2009-63. Korea Rural Economic Institute.

Kim, C.-G.(2001), "Policy Development for Integrating Agriculture and the Environment", *Journal of Rural Development*, Vol. 24, pp. 247-271.

Lee, K.-C., E.-S. Kim, S.-B. Jeong, S.-M. Sohn, W.-B. Yook, B.-S. Ham, C.-H. Jang, S.-J. Kim and D.-S. Kim (1998), *Studies on Direct Payment Programs under the Less-Favored Area and Environmental Conservation* (in Korean), Research Report C98-4-3, Korea Rural Economic Institute.

Ministry of Agriculture and Forestry (MAF) (1998), *Collections for Materials Related to Environmentally Friendly Direct Payments Program.*

Ministry for Food, Agriculture, Forestry and Fisheries (MIFAFF) (2011a), *Guidelines for Agricultural and Forestry Policy Programs in 2011.*

Ministry for Food, Agriculture, Forestry and Fisheries (2011b), *Internal Material for Environmentally Friendly Direct Payment Program.*

OECD (2001), *Multifunctionality: Towards an analytical framework*, OECD Publications, Paris.

OECD (2002a), *Inventory of policy measures addressing environmental issues in agriculture.* OECD internal document, Paris.

OECD (2002b), *Evaluating agri-environmental policy measures*, OECD internal document, Paris.

OECD (2010), *Guidelines for cost-effective agri-environmental policy measures*, OECD Publications, Paris.

Oskam, A.J., R.A.N. Vijftigschild, and C. Graveland (1998), *Additional EU Policy Instruments for Plant Protection Products*, The Netherlands: Wageningen Pers.

Park, D.-G., C.-G. Kim, S.-S. Lim, M.-R. Song, B.-S. Kim and K.-C. Park (2004), *Research on the Expansion Measures for the Medium-and Long-term Direct Payments System*, Research Report C2004-6, Korea Rural Economic Institute.

Stoltze, M. and N. Lampkin (2009), "Policy for Organic Farming: Rationale and Concepts", *Food Policy*, Vol. 34, pp. 237-244.

United States Department of Agriculture (USDA) (2001), "Agri-Environmental Policy at the Crossroads: Guideposts on a Changing Landscape", *ERS Agricultural Economic Report* No. 794, January.

IV. NEW METHODOLOGIES AND EVALUATION APPROACHES

Chapter 9

Evaluating agri-environmental schemes using a spatially explicit agent-based modelling approach

Marleen Schouten, Nico Polman, Eugène Westerhof and Paul Opdam[1]

Networks of nature reserves are being proposed as a solution when the degree of fragmentation is considered to endanger the long-term persistence of species diversity. Agri-environmental schemes are supposed to make a positive contribution to these networks. The spatially explicit agent-based model presented in this chapter combines spatial dynamics in land ownership, land use and the importance of agri-environmental schemes in conserving biodiversity by capturing the heterogeneity of individual farms as well as their dynamics over time, in a spatially explicit landscape. The chapter evaluates the effects of two different agri-environmental policies at landscape level, and shows that agri-environmental schemes with flexible payments based on a spatial landscape configuration can be valuable for agri-environmental policy development.

One of the greatest challenges facing the global agricultural community is the provision of sufficient food for an expanding population while maintaining the supply of environmental and social services that lie beyond routine commodity production (Hajkowicz *et al.*, 2009; Whittingham, 2011). These services include protecting biodiversity, improving long-term soil productivity, enhancing water quality, sequestering greenhouse gases and improving the visual landscape. This has led to the emergence of agri-environmental schemes (AESs). AESs are designed to secure environmental and social services from farmed countryside. They typically involve either direct or indirect (e.g. tax breaks) payments to farmers to supply those services (OECD, 2005). In the European Union (EU,) some AESs are designed to enhance, directly or indirectly, levels of biodiversity on farmland (Whittingham, 2007).

A basic principle of AESs in the EU is that the participation of individual farmers is voluntary. Many studies focus on the characteristics of farms and farmers who conclude AESs (e.g. Crabtree *et al.*, 1998; Beedell and Rehman, 2000; Wynn *et al.*, 2001; Vanslembrouck *et al.*, 2002; Wenum, 2002). Van Huylenbroeck *et al.* (2000), Peerlings and Polman (2004) and Havlík *et al.* (2008) developed simulation models to evaluate the impact of AESs on farm production and economic results, in order to better explain contract choice. Our chapter adds to this literature by including spatial and institutional dynamics in land ownership and intensity of land use among the factors influencing the uptake of AESs. For this purpose, we developed an agent-based model (see Parker *et al.*, 2003) to capture heterogeneity between agents (farmers) as well as dynamics in a spatially explicit model, specifically designed for simulating the effects of agri-environmental policies at agricultural landscape level. Agent-based models (ABMs) within the specific agricultural context were pioneered by Balmann (1997) with the Agricultural Policy Simulator (AgriPoliS). ABMs allow economic and social systems to be represented as the result of individually acting agents. When applied to agriculture, they can simulate, at micro level, the behaviour of individual farmers, without the need to define groups of farms as "representative" agents, and then generate the macro (aggregate)-evidence. Furthermore, ABMs can catch the interactions of the heterogeneous farms when competing over common finite resources, such as land (Lobianco and Esposti, 2010).

This chapter looks at how contracts with individual farmers contribute to the spatial cohesion of landscapes in terms of habitat network patterns. The importance of spatial habitat network patterns is widely accepted among ecologists (see, for instance, Opdam *et al.*, 2003) and is also important in the European policy context as shown by the Natura 2000 networks. Where nature conservation is one of the functions competing for space, quantitative tools that link spatial conditions in the landscape to conservation goals are needed (Opdam *et al.*, 1995). Because appropriate data are often not available, planning procedures need tools that are independent of actual species distribution data. Therefore, it is necessary to be able to assess a specific landscape pattern for the potential to conserve biodiversity.

The dilemma is that we must be able to "read" the landscape pattern for its potential to conserve biodiversity, whereas species differ greatly in the spatial scale at which they respond to landscape features, as well as in the features they are responsive to (Andrén, 1996; Vos *et al.*, 2001; Fahrig, 2001; Kleijn *et al.*, 2006). This implies that there is no simple and direct way to transform landscape features into an index of conservation potential. Existing tools with predictive power are either at the species level and too complex to apply in multi-species planning, or they depend on distribution data (empirical regression models) and are difficult to generalise.

Faced with these difficulties, we introduce a landscape cohesion method based on data that are available: size of the area and spatial configuration. This allows economic governance and planning to be combined with ecological objectives. It also provides a context in which the following research question can be formulated: What is the contribution of agri-environmental schemes to landscape cohesion in spatial habitat network patterns under different economic governance structures?

The rest of this chapter is organised into four sections. Section 9.1 describes the methodological approach underlying the proposed spatially explicit agent-based model. After a short introduction of agent-based modelling applied to agricultural landscapes, the section focuses on two key modelling issues: modelling farmers behaviour and making space explicit; we then describe how the model is structured. A case study is presented in section 9.2, and results of this application are discussed in section 9.3 where the model is applied to two alternative scenarios. We conclude in section 9.4 with a discussion of the methods applied in this chapter.

9.1 The agent-based model

Conceptual framework

The core of the model discussed in this chapter is the understanding and modelling of an agricultural landscape as an agent-based system, which takes into account both the farmers' behaviour and the spatial configuration of the landscape. The model focuses on an actual agricultural region, and comprises a large number of individually acting farms that operate in the region, as well as farmers' interactions with each other and with parts of their environment. This model adds to existing agricultural agent-based models in that it provides a spatially explicit landscape in which land ownership and (intensity of) land use are based on empirical data. Empirical data on individual farms and the existing regional landscape spatial structures have been initialised in the model. Extending the model so as to include an application to AESs is also new, and to the best of our knowledge this has previously not been done. The software code of this model is written in the object-oriented programming language Java using the open-source agent-based modelling framework *Recursive Porous Agent Simulation Toolkit Symphony* (REPAST, *repast.sourceforge.net/*). Those interested in the model code may directly contact the authors. The following section presents a basic overview of the model.

The farm agent and the auctioneer

The current version of the model allows for three classes of agents, the *TraderAgent,* the *Auctioneer* and the *Government.* Our model contains one type of *TraderAgent*, the farmer. Every farmer has a *Valuation Strategy* that he uses to determine a (private) price for the goods he wishes to trade. Currently, the only tradable goods in the model are farmlands. The strategy used is organised according to decision rules that keep track of the total number of parcels in use, the farmer's age and expectations about future land prices, as well as a number of financial indicators and changes as a result of the farm agent's actions. Each farm agent keeps track of the farm's nitrogen and feed production through farm-level balances. The most important decision rule of every farm agent is to calculate each of his land parcels' contribution to farm income, given limited rationality of farm agents. According to Happe *et al.* (2006), this set of assumptions is reasonable for agricultural enterprises in Western Europe where farming systems that follow different behavioural objectives such as subsistence farming play only a minor role.

Different implementations can be used in the model for different aspects of the agent's "daily operations." The farm agent decisions are based exclusively on their own situation and on their expectations about land prices. When the profit contribution of a specific parcel is known, firstly decisions can be made by the farm agent with respect to trading land. Secondly, farmers who own land that is eligible can submit a tender for enrolling in an agri-environmental scheme. They base their tender price on opportunity costs.

The second agent currently in the model is the *Auctioneer*. The *Auctioneer* is a mediator between traders and may represent an actual person or organisation, or – in a more abstract manner – a market. The *Auctioneer* "requests" traders to make offers to either express their willingness to buy or sell a good. The *Auctioneer* "uses" a mechanism to match bids and asks to clear the auction. Currently, the model contains a mechanism that uses a heuristic to clear the auction in a number of iterations. It presumes that multiple buyers and sellers are present and parcels are heterogeneous (characterised by multiple attributes).

At the start of each auction, the auctioneer informs the traders that the auction is open. Based on the outcome of the farm agent decision-making rules (does the agent want to buy or sell?), traders can respond by expressing interest in the auction. Next, the auctioneer requests all interested agents to provide the parcels they would like to sell with a related reserve price for these parcels (denoted as "asks"). This reserve price is determined by the valuation strategy the agent is applying. Once all asks have been identified, the auctioneer requests the interested agents to provide bids for the parcels on offer. A prospective buyer evaluates all available goods and is allowed to create one bid for the parcel that he values the most. Again, this is decided by the agent's valuation strategy.

After all bids have been collected, the auction mechanism matches bids and asks so as to maximise the surplus of buyers and sellers (difference between bid price and reserve price). The auctioneer will inform the traders involved in an accepted bid, who then complete the transaction and are asked to provide new offers, or can update or retract their open bids and asks in the auction, based on their valuation and decision-making rules.

If there are still unaccepted asks left after the matching process, a new cycle or iteration of the auction is started, in which all participating agents are again asked to provide a bid for one of the remaining asks. The process continues until there are no asks left, or no more bids are made. The auctioneer will then inform all interested traders that the auction is closed. In order to calculate the transaction prices for all matched bids in the auction, the auctioneer uses a pricing policy in which the surplus is equally shared.

Spatial representation and use of the spatial cohesion Reilly index

The spatially explicit landscape is represented by modelling actual parcels in the region studied. Within this spatially explicit environment, several institutional and biophysical attributes are associated with each of these parcels: for each parcel the ownership is known, as are the parcel size, current land use and the possibilities for AESs. Decisions by government on the eligibility of parcels for AES are exogenous in the model. Also the parcel quality for farming is known and provides information about soil quality and crop suitability as well as ground water tables. In the model, we distinguish between three different types of land, namely grassland, maize land and parcels with AESs. For each parcel, the distance to the agent's farmstead is taken into account in the model.

Decision rules for the government agent on accepting parcels are included in the model. The government agent can either accept or reject an offer of a farmer to be contracted. The government can apply different strategies for accepting parcels. It can accept every parcel offered by farmers for AESs, which is the current policy standard. An alternative decision rule could be based on specific characteristics of parcels or bids of farmers, which will be discussed below.

The potential of the parcel to conserve biodiversity by means of its location and the landscape configuration is taken into account. For each parcel, either under conventional farming techniques, already with AESs or with the possibility for AESs, the spatial cohesion Reilly index is calculated (see the Annex for more details). In this way, information is provided on the (potential) contribution of the parcel to the long-term persistence of network populations within habitat networks in the landscape (Opdam *et al.*, 2003). To be able to assess the potential of a specific landscape pattern for conserving biodiversity, we introduce a method for calculating the importance of individual plots for landscape cohesion based on spatial data. For this chapter, we want to assess the specific AES sites for their biodiversity conservation potential, thereby taking into account their spatial configuration in the surrounding landscape, as a way of dealing with the spatial effectiveness of AESs. A number of recent studies have highlighted the importance of the surrounding landscape for the effectiveness of AESs. Whittingham (2011) demonstrates that at landscape scale, the effect on farmland biodiversity of adopting an AES at a specific site is positively related to the extent of the nature conservation area and land under AESs in the surrounding landscape.

An AES site located near or in a nature conservation area has a higher spatial cohesion Reilly index score than a site that is located further away. Moreover, larger sites result in a higher spatial cohesion Reilly index compared with smaller sites. In Section 9.2, the index is integrated into a spatially explicit agent-based model framework. This model captures both the spatial dynamics in land ownership and land use on the uptake of AESs, but also contributes to the sustainable management of biodiversity in agricultural landscapes by making use of the spatial cohesion Reilly index described in this section. Finally, it may be that there are parcels with a higher spatial cohesion Reilly index than those within a designated area for AES. In those cases, other variables not included in the spatial cohesion Reilly index could have been taken into account. As can be seen in Section 9.2, this information can be used for policy evaluation, i.e. to adjust levels of compensatory payments for AESs or in other words the valuation function of the government.

Model flow for one simulation period

Figure 9.1 provides an overview of the dynamics of the model, and the course of events during one simulation period. The model consists of an *initialisation module* in which data are conditioned to be used in the model, a *farm module* that allows the calculations of the farm income contribution, a *land lease market module* distributing the land among farmers, and an *output module*. The *initialisation module* contains exogenous agricultural census data (reference year 2008). The attributes on farm level are the farm structure, namely age, type of farm, size and the total number of owned and rented parcels. At parcel level, attributes are soil quality, crop suitability and land use. At landscape level, attributes are the number of farms in the region, spatial land characteristics, size and distance from the parcels to the homestead. These attributes do not change during the simulation period. In the *farm module* each farm agent is equipped with a behavioural model that determines whether conventional farming or an AES is chosen. This module keeps track of the farm management decisions, thereby taking into account attributes such as age, location, farm size, whole-farm feed and nutrient balances and farm business succession. According to their behavioural models, the individual farm agents evolve subject to their current state of attributes and to changes in their environment.

The results of the farm module serve as input for the *land lease market module*. A description of the land lease market module was given in the previous section. Finally, the function of the *output module* is the conditioning of the model results for the next simulation period. Results at farm level and at regional level are used to update farm attributes and regional attributes in the next period.

Figure 9.1. Course of events during one simulation period

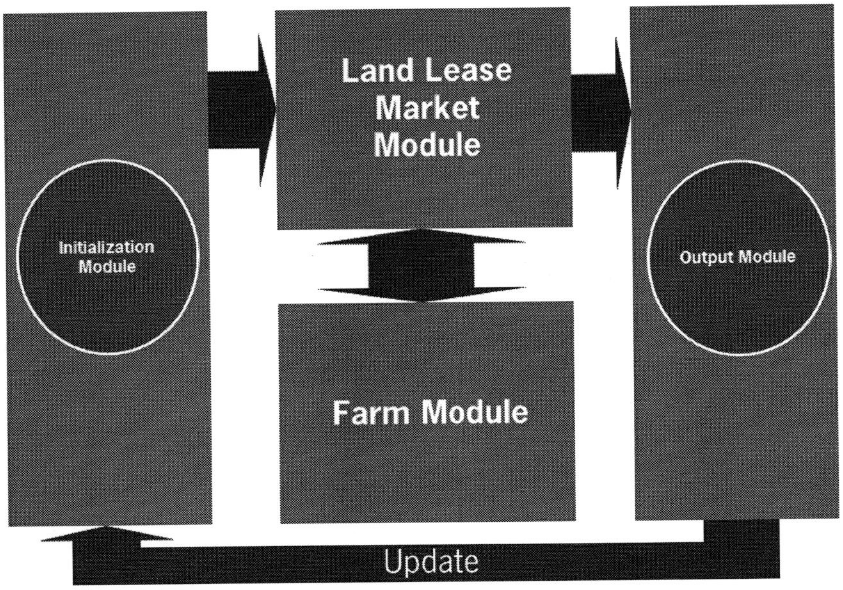

9.2 Empirical data and model initialisation

The study region, Winterswijk

We adapted the model to the agricultural region Winterswijk, which is located in the eastern part of the Netherlands. From a landscape perspective, the area represents a cultural-historic landscape where small-scale agriculture and nature conservation areas are closely inter-linked, thereby providing particular cultural, recreational, ecological and economic value to the region (Provincie Gelderland, 2005). The spatial structure of the landscape attributes are characterised as small fields surrounded by hedges or wooded banks (Mastboom, 1996). Large parts of the region contain important nature conservation areas that belong to the National Ecological Network (NEN), which is part of the European Natura 2000 network. In the 1990s, the Dutch government launched the NEN as a structure of existing nature areas that was to be made more robust and cohesive by enlarging areas, improving environmental quality, and developing new areas and local ecological corridors (Opdam *et al.*, 2008). In this way, the NEN is contributing to the development of biodiversity in the Netherlands (Lammers and Zadelhoff, 1996).

Figure 9.2 gives an overview of the study region, showing that nature conservation areas and designated areas for AESs are concentrated in the southern part of the region. Areas not included in the model are coloured white and include small villages. The main urban area is the city of Winterswijk.

Figure 9.2. The study region Winterswijk

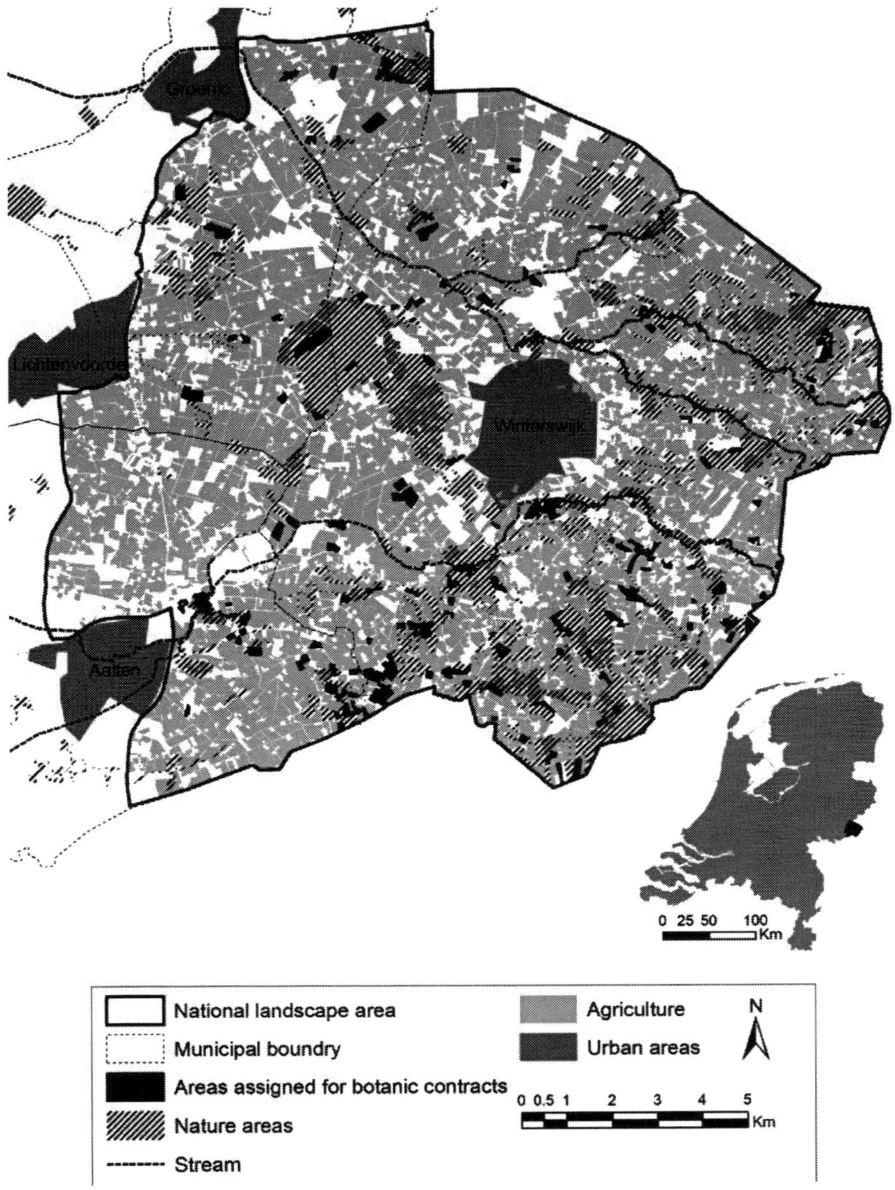

Source. Adapted from an original GIS map provided by the Dutch, Ministry of Economic Affairs, Agriculture and Innovation.

Model initialisation

This study concentrates on dairy farms, both specialised dairy farms and mixed dairy/pig fattening farms. Data on 206 individual farms were taken from the Agricultural Census. The model initialisation uses farm-level data on their current number of dairy cows, farmer's age and land use, and also data at parcel level on ownership, size and distance to the farmstead. These parcel-level characteristics are derived from Cadastral GIS maps. GIS maps on land use, soil quality, crop suitability and water tables were used to integrate the production characteristics of individual parcels in the model. These dairy farmers are typical for the region; in aggregate, they represent 13 150 hectares (5 846 parcels), and cover 60% of the main production area in the region. The size of the nature conservation areas in the region is 3 565 ha (289 parcels).

It is assumed that the farms use production techniques that are considered to be typical for the region. The required coefficients regarding production, calculations of marginal values and income contributions are derived from FADN data. Regarding AESs on grassland, the designated area has a size of 128 ha, consisting of 63 parcels, for the farms in the sample. Data on this matter was distributed by the Dutch Ministry of Economic Affairs, Agriculture and Innovation by means of GIS-maps with designated contract area for the year 2008. Whenever there is an uptake of AESs, the farmer commits himself for a period of six years.

Policy scenarios

As stated in Section 9.2, the potential, in terms of its location and the landscape configuration, of a parcel to conserve biodiversity is parameterised in the model by means of the spatial cohesion Reilly index. It is assumed that the maximum budget available for AESs on 128 ha in the study region is approximately EUR 130 000. This amount is calculated as the sum of the assigned parcels for AESs multiplied by the compensatory payment per hectare. Currently, the compensatory payment is a fixed amount per hectare, independent of location, parcel quality or spatial configuration in the landscape. For this chapter, we calculate the spatial cohesion Reilly index for each individual parcel with AESs or the potential for an AES. The total number of spatial cohesion Reilly points assigned to the parcels is about 62 000. From the perspective of landscape cohesion and the contribution to spatial cohesion of individual parcels, it is beneficial to link payments to the spatial cohesion Reilly index. We calculate the compensatory payment per individual Reilly point by dividing the total budget by the total number of assigned Reilly points. For this chapter, we define two policy scenarios to be simulated in the model:

- *Base scenario: Fixed AES compensatory payments*

  For the *base run scenario* we assume a fixed annual AES compensatory payment per hectare, independent of location and spatial configuration in the landscape. This scenario is in line with current EU AES programmes. The government agent decision rule is to accept every parcel offered.

- *Spatially differentiated scenario: Flexible compensatory payments based on contracted Reilly points*

  For the *alternative scenario*, we assume a flexible compensatory payment per hectare, based on the Reilly points for the particular contracted parcel. In this way, information is added with respect to the contribution of the parcel to the long-term persistence of populations within habitat networks in the case study region. This contract type allows for higher payments for plots that contribute more to the habitat networks. It is assumed that every eligible farm agent tenders for a contract. The spatially differentiated government decision rule is to select those bids that maximise Reilly points.

We simulate different levels of fixed compensatory payment per hectare by running the model for different budget sizes. For a range of budget sizes, we analyse the contribution to landscape cohesion and habitat networks by showing the average percentage of Reilly points on the contracted parcels in the simulation period for both scenarios.

Simulation results

The result of the simulations are shown in Tables 9.1 and 9.2. Table 9.1 reports both the base-run scenario and the alternative scenario for the average percentage of contracted AES area, thereby taking into account the designated AES area of 128 ha (=100%) after a simulation period of 25 years. We calibrated the model on the current contracted area in the region, namely 60% of the designated AES area.

Table 9.1 shows that the base scenario results in a higher contracted AES area. When budget expenditure increases by 50%, there is a 30% increase in the area contracted when payments are fixed, whereas the area increases almost by 50% when the payment is spatially differentiated. If the budget is half of the current budget, the area contracted declines by slightly more than 50% in the base run and a little less than 50% in the spatial differentiated scenario.

Table 9.2 gives an overview of the percentage of total Reilly points contracted in the two scenarios. It shows that the alternative scenario, based on the spatially differentiated payment per hectare, results in a higher percentage of Reilly points contracted. It can therefore be concluded that the alternative scenario results in a higher contribution to landscape cohesion. When the budget increases by 50%, the effect on percentage Reilly points contracted is relatively larger in the base scenario than with the spatially differentiated payment. When the budget decreases by 50%, 10% Reilly points are lost in both scenarios (a smaller *percentage* change in the alternative scenario).

Table 9.1. Average percentage of AES-eligible area contracted for base run with fixed AES payment and alternative with spatial differentiated payments[1]

Scenario	Current budget*	Budget plus 50%	Budget minus 50%
1 Fixed AES payment	60	81	28
2 Spatially differentiated payment	25	38	14

1. Under the current budget and a budget increase and decrease for a simulation period of 25 years.
* Calibrated on current contracted area.

Table 9.2. Average percentage of Reilly points contracted for base run with fixed AES payment and alternative with spatial differentiated payments[1]

Scenario	Current budget*	Budget plus 50%	Budget minus 50%
1 Fixed AES payment	65	85	55
2 Spatially differentiated payment	71	84	61

1. Under the current budget and a budget increase and decrease for a simulation period of 25 years.
* Calibrated on current contracted area.

The results show that a flexible compensatory payment rate based on spatial configuration and size can result in higher gains for habitat networks in agricultural landscapes, at each level of budget expenditure. It can therefore be assumed to make a greater contribution to the development of biodiversity in the studied region.

9.3 Conclusion and discussion

This chapter shows how the use of spatially explicit agent-based models can contribute to the evaluation and development of policies with regard to AESs. The model provides a better understanding of the social-ecological system dynamics, and the role of individual decision making for landscape management. The model can assist in the identification, design and evaluation of policy interventions and can inform the governance processes that manage AESs.

The model can contribute in different ways to the process of policy evaluation, either *ex ante* or *ex post*. First, it allows a comparative analysis of cost effectiveness by simulating alternative policies and calculating the effects in terms of Reilly points. Moreover, the method allows the impacts on both spatial landscape configuration and biodiversity to be taken into account at the same time. Second, it helps to simulate the effects of land use trajectories initiated by different policies in the long run even after the proposed programme is finished. The results reported above indicate that, for this region, when policy makers aim to maximise the area contracted to an AES, independent of spatial configuration, the current fixed compensatory payments are preferable. However, if policy makers want to use AES policy to maximise the contribution to the spatial habitat network, they should consider spatially differentiated payments. The reported results give an example of how this model could be helpful in the evaluation of policies with respect to AES.

Further developments of the model are desirable to improve the practical use of its results for policy evaluation. Some caveats should be expressed regarding the way farm agents' behaviour and the spatial configuration of AES area are modelled. First, potential public and private transaction costs of schemes (Mettepenningen *et al.*, 2011) are not taken into account. Second, it is assumed that all farmers with parcels that are eligible will tender at their opportunity cost. The model could be extended by including auction mechanisms that depend on Reilly points (see, for instance, Glebe, 2008). With regard to farm agents' behaviour, the model assumes that their behaviour is one of "limited rationality", meaning that a farm agent's decision making process is path-dependent and not globally optimising. A further caveat is that investment activities as well as off-farm labour activities are not included in the model.

With respect to the spatial configuration of AESs in the model, it would be a valuable model extension to remove constraints on the assigned locations of parcels for AESs. It would be interesting to see what the behaviour of farm agents would be if all parcels in the case study area could be contracted. Another interesting model extension might consider the spatial cohesion Reilly index. Currently, the spatial cohesion Reilly index is calculated once for each parcel. It would be interesting to see what happens if we re-calculate the Reilly index after each simulation period, thereby taking into account the dynamics of other AES parcels and their location with regard to nature conservation areas within each run. We also should mention that the landscape cohesion method used in this chapter is pretty rough and should not be used when there is a lot of detail required on, for example, the role of habitat quality of particular species. By using the proposed method, much detail is exchanged for simplicity and generality. However, for most regional planning and governance issues, this is probably sufficient. Finally, thorough calibration and sensitivity analysis are part of the future work.

Note

1. Marleen Schouten, Agricultural Economics and Rural Policy Group, Wageningen University, Netherlands.

   Eugène Westerhof, Agricultural Economics Research Institute (LEI), The Hague, Netherlands.

   Paul Opdam, Land Use Planning Group, Wageningen University, Netherlands

   This research is part of the strategic research programme "Sustainable spatial development of ecosystems, landscapes, seas and regions" which is funded by the Dutch Ministry of Economic Affairs, Agriculture and Innovation and carried out by Wageningen University and Research Centre. We are indebted to many of our colleagues for discussions and ideas that are reflected throughout this chapter.

References

Andrén, H. (1996), "Population responses to habitat fragmentation: statistical power and the random sample hypothesis", *Oikos* Vol. 76, pp. 35-242.

Balmann, A. (1997), Farm-based modelling of regional structural change: A cellular automata approach. *European Review of Agricultural Economics,* Vol. 24, pp. 85-108.

Beedell, J. and T. Rehman (2000), "Using Social-psychology Models to Understand Farmers' Conservation Behaviour", *Journal of Rural Studies*, Vol. 16, pp. 117-127.

Cotteleer, G. (2008), *Valuation of Land Use in the Netherlands and British Columbia; a Spatial Hedonic GIS-based Approach*, Wageningen University, Wageningen.

Crabtree, B., N. Chalmers and N. Barron (1998), "Information for Policy Design: Modelling Participation in a Farm Woodland Incentive Contract", *Journal of Agricultural Economics,* Vol. 49, pp. 306-320.

Fahrig, L. (2001), "How much habitat is enough", *Biologial Conservation* Vol. 100, pp. 65-74.

Glebe, T.W. (2008), "Scoring two-dimensional bids: how cost-effective are agri-environmental auctions?" *European Review of Agricultural Economics*, Vol. 35, pp. 143-165.

Hajkowicz, S., K. Collins and A. Cattaneo (2009), "Review of Agri-Environment Indexes and Stewardship Payments", *Environmental Management*, Vol.43, pp. 221-236.

Happe, K., K. Kellermann and A. Balmann (2006), "Agent-based analysis of agricultural policies: An illustration of the agriculutural policy simulator AgriPolis, its adaptation and behavior", *Ecology and Society*, Vol.11, available at: *www.ecologyandsociety.org/vol11/iss1/art49/*

Havlík, P., G. Enjolras, J. Boisson, F. Jacquet, M. Lherm and P. Veysset (2008), "Environmental good production in the optimum activities portfolio of a risk averse-farmer", *Review of Agricultural and Environmental Studies*, Vol. 86, pp. 9-33.

Kleijn, D., R.A. Baquero, Y. Clough, M. Díaz, J. De Esteban, F. Fernández, G. Gabriel, F. Herzog, A. Holzschuh, R. Jöhl, E. Knop, A. Kruess, E.J.P. Marshall, I. Steffan-Dewenter, T. Tscharntke, J. Verhulst, T. M. West, J.L. Yela (2006), "Mixed biodiversity benefits of agri-environment schemes in five European countries", *Ecology Letters* Vol. 9, pp. 243-254.

Lammers, G.W. and F.J. Zadelhoff (1996), "The Dutch national ecological network", in P. Nowicki, P., G. Bennet, D. Middleton, S. Rientjes and R. Wolters (Eds.), P*erspectives on ecological networks*, ECNC Publications Series on Man and Nature, Volume 1. European Centre for Nature Conservation, Tilburg, The Netherlands.

Lobianco, A. and R. Esposti (2010), "The Regional Multi-Agent Simulator (RegMAS): An open-source spatially explicit model to assess the impact of agricultural policies", *Computers and Electronics in Agriculture*, Vol. 72, pp. 14-26.

Mastboom, J. M. J. (1996), "Protoindustrialization and agriculture in the eastern Netherlands", *Social Science History*, Vol. 20, pp. 235-258.

Mettepenningen, E., V. Beckmann and J. Eggers (2011), "Public transaction costs of agri-environmental schemes and their determinants - Analysing stakeholders' involvement and perceptions", *Ecological Economics*, Vol. 70, pp. 641-650.

OECD (2005), *Evaluating agri-environmental policies: design, practice and results*, OECD Publications, Paris.

Opdam, P., R.F.B. Foppen, R. Reijnen and A. Schotman (1995), "The landscape ecological approach in bird conservation, integrating the metapopulation concept into spatial planning". *Ibis*, Vol. 137, pp. 139-146.

Opdam, P., R. Pouwels, S. van Rooij, E. Steingröver and C.C. Vos (2008), "Setting biodiversity targets in participatory regional planning: Introducing ecoprofiles", *Ecology and Society*, Vol. 13.

Opdam, P., J. Verboom and R. Pouwels (2003), "Landscape cohesion: An index for the conservation potential of landscapes for biodiversity", *Landscape Ecology,* Vol. 18, pp. 113-126.

Parker, D.C., S. M. Manson, M. A. Janssen, M.J. Hoffmann and P. Deadman (2003), "Multi-agent systems for the simulation of land-use and land-cover change: A review", *Annals of the Association of American Geographers*, Vol. 93, pp. 314-337.

Peerlings, J. and N. Polman (2004), "Wildlife and landscape services production in Dutch dairy farming; jointness and transaction costs", *European Review of Agricultural Economics*, Vol. 31, pp. 427-449.

Provincie Gelderland (2005), *Streekplan Gelderland 2005: kansen voor de regio's.*

Reilly, W.J. (1931), *The Law of Retail Gravitation,* W.J. Reilly, Inc., New York.

Van Huylenbroeck, G., G. Jacobs and P. Vanrolleghem (2000), "A simulation model to evaluate the impact of environmental programmes on dairy farms", *International Transactions in Operational Research*, Vol. 7, pp. 171-183.

Vanslembrouck, I., G. Van Huylenbroeck and W. Verbeke (2002), "Determinants of the willingness of Belgian farmers to participate in agri-environmental measures", *Journal of Agricultural Economics,* Vol. 51, pp. 489-511.

Vos, C.C., J. Verboom, P. Opdam and C.J.F. Ter Braak (2001), "Toward Ecologically Scaled Landscape Indices", *The American Naturalist*, Vol. 157, pp. 24-41.

Wenum, J.V. (2002), *Economics Analysis of Wildlife and Conservation in Crop Farming*, Wageningen University, Wageningen.

Whittingham, M.J. (2007), "Will agri-environment schemes deliver substantial biodiversity gain, and if not why not?" *Journal of Applied Ecology*, Vol. 44, pp. 1-5.

Whittingham, M.J. (2011), "The future of agri-environmental schemes: biodiversity gains and ecosystem service delivery?" *Journal of Applied Ecology*, Vol.48, pp. 509-513.

Wynn, G., B. Crabtree and J. Potts (2001), "Modelling farmer entry into the environmentally sensitive area schemes in Scotland", *Journal of Agricultural Economics*, Vol.52, pp. 65-82.

Annex 9.A

The Reilly index derives from Newton's law of gravitation, where gravity is stronger for larger "bodies" and gravitational strength is inversely related to the distance between "bodies." It was originally applied to the study of retail markets (Reilly, 1931) to reflect the attractiveness of different retail areas (cities) in terms of the trade-off between consumers' travel costs and the size of alternative retail areas. We modify the Reilly index to calculate the impact of surrounding nature conservation areas on the potential for biodiversity conservation by sites with AESs. We employ distance to nature conservation areas. Rather than population, we use the size of the nature conservation areas (measured in square meters).

Equation (1) gives the formula for calculating the spatial cohesion Reilly index. The calculation of the index starts at the point where the site (measured in square metres) is located. After that, the size of the nature conservation areas (NCA) within a certain radius (i.e. 5 km) is determined, as well as the size of the AES site. Based on the sum of all the distances (measured in metres) of the site to the nature conservation areas located within the chosen radius, and on the size of the nature conservation areas and AES sites, the spatial cohesion Reilly index can be calculated.

Spatial cohesion landscape Reilly index for AES site $_i$ =

$$\sum_{j=1}^{J} \frac{\text{Size of NCA j (within radius)} + \text{size AES site i}}{(\text{distance of site i to NCA})_{ij}^{2}}. \qquad (1)$$

The index captures, in one number, the size of the nature conservation area in proximity to the AES site, and the distance from the site to certain nature conservation areas (Cotteleer, 2008). Strong points of the spatial cohesion Reilly index are the combination of distance with size, and the fact that nature conservation areas located further away or which are smaller in size are weighted less. As such, the spatial cohesion Reilly index is a measure of the share of land used for a certain land-use function in the surroundings of a specific location.

We illustrate the calculation of the spatial cohesion Reilly index in Table 9.A1 and Figure 9.A1 for the location of two AES sites, A and B. The two sites (A and B) are heterogeneous in size and are situated in the proximity of four different nature conservation areas. The size of the four nature conservation areas is also given. Figure 9.A1 shows the two sites, and their location in relation to the four nature conservation areas. The arrows in Figure 9.A1 give the distance to the four nature conservation areas. The size and distance correspond with Table 9.A1.

Figure 9.A1. Graphical presentation of the spatial cohesion Reilly index

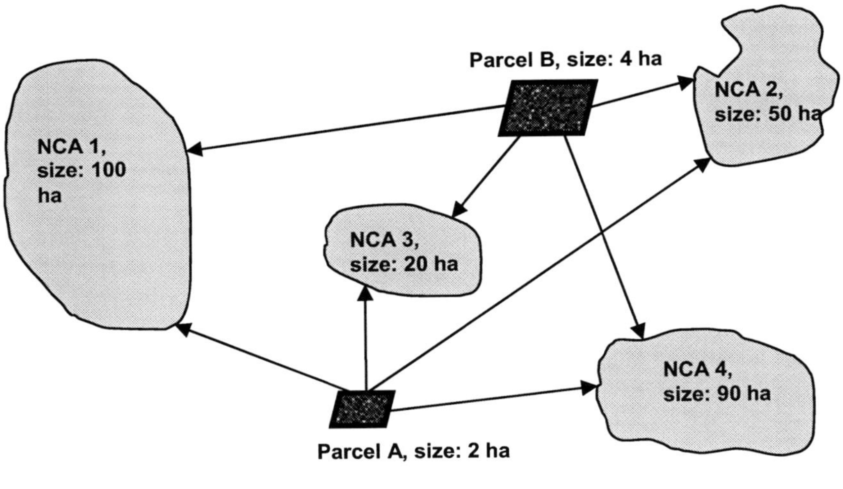

Table 9.A1. Spatial cohesion Reilly index for two AES sites given the size of sites and NCA and the distance to the NCA

NCA	NCA size (m^2)	Site A: Size site A (m^2)	Site A: Distance to site A (m)	Site A: Size / $(Distance)^2$	Site B: Size site B (m^2)	Site B: Distance to site B (m)	Site B: Size / $(Distance)^2$
1	1 000 000	20 000	1 000	1.02	40 000	1 400	0.53061
2	500 000		2 100	0.11791		400	3.375
3	200 000		600	0.61111		700	0.4898
4	900 000		1 200	0.63888		900	1.16049
Spatial cohesion Reilly index			2.38791			5.5559	

Source: Adapted from Cotteleer (2008, p. 101) and adjusted.

From Table 9.A1 and Figure 9.A.1, it is apparent that for site B, the spatial cohesion Reilly index is much larger than for site A, because site B is located closer to two of the nature conservation areas. Although location 2 of the nature conservation area is not the largest area, the shorter distance from site B to this area is largely responsible for the larger Reilly score for this site.

Chapter 10

Econometric methods for estimating the additional effects of agri-environmental schemes on farmers' practices

Sylvain Chabé-Ferret and Julie Subervie[1]

Agri-environmental schemes (AESs) that remunerate farmers who volunteer to adopt practices that are more favourable to the environment are increasingly important policy measures in both the United States and the European Union. Cost-benefit evaluation of an AES requires estimates of the additional impact of the AES and of the extent of windfall effects. This chapter defines these notions and discusses the biases of naive ways of estimating them. We then present an overview of the econometric methods that can be used to estimate additional effects. We illustrate them with examples taken from original results on the evaluation of the French AES programme implemented between 2000 and 2006.

Payments for environmental services are widely used to improve environmental outcomes. Agri-environmental schemes (AESs) that remunerate farmers who volunteer to adopt practices that are more favourable to the environment are increasingly important components of environmental and agricultural policy in both the United States and the European Union. A complete cost-benefit evaluation of AES requires estimates of the additional effect of the AES and of the extent of windfall effects. We define the additional effect of the AES programme as the difference between the practices of participants after enrolment in the programme and what their practices would have been had they remained outside the programme (i.e. the counterfactual situation). The counterfactual level of practices is also a direct measure of the windfall effect. Farmers indeed receive payments for the overall level of their practices, thereby receiving payments also for adopting practices that they would have adopted even in the absence of the payments.

When trying to estimate the additional or causal impact, a major problem arises in that the counterfactual situation cannot be observed and thus has to be estimated using observed data. Conventional estimates suffer from various kinds of bias, whose magnitude may be large. We present a set of econometric methods aiming at getting rid of selection bias. We illustrate them with examples taken from our own work on the evaluation of the French AES (Chabé-Ferret and Subervie, 2010). The interested reader is referred to Greenstone and Gayer (2009) for a more rigorous presentation of these methods in the context of the evaluation of environmental policies. Even more detailed presentations of the methods quickly introduced here can be found in papers in labour economics (Angrist and Krueger, 1999; Heckman, Lalonde, and Smith, 1999; Todd, 2007).

This chapter is organised as follows: Section 10.1 shows why additional and windfall effects are crucial parameters for cost-benefit analysis. Section 10.2 presents the fundamental problem we face when trying to estimate additional effects. Section 10.3 presents an overview of econometric methods that can be used to estimate additional effects and Section 10.4 discusses areas for further research.

10.1 Additional and windfall effects are crucial to perform a cost-benefit analysis

Our current example is an AES aiming at increasing the planting of cover crops during winter – the so-called AES 0301 in the French AES programme implemented between 2000 and 2006. This AES consists in paying farmers a fixed amount, C, per hectare planted in cover crops. The duration of the contract is five years. The total cost of subsidising one farmer is thus the area planted to cover crops (noted Y^1) multiplied by the per hectare payment (C).[2] The social benefit of subsidising the farmer is the improvement in environmental quality brought about by decreasing nitrogen leaching from the field thanks to the planting of Y^1 hectares of cover crops.[3] We suppose that this per hectare benefit is constant and equal to B. Then, the direct cost of subsidising a given farmer is $C\,Y^1$ and the direct benefit is $B\,Y^1$. In order to perform a cost-benefit analysis of the programme, it would seem natural to compare these two quantities and to decide that subsidising this farmer is socially beneficial if benefits exceed costs. This leads to a very simple criterion: the AES is welfare-enhancing if $B>C$, in which case the critical parameter to estimate is the social benefit, B, of planting one hectare of cover crops.

This approach implicitly assumes that there would be no planting of cover crops at all if farmers were not subsidised for doing so. But there are various reasons why farmers may well decide to plant some cover crops even in the absence of any subsidy: it may decrease erosion, help to control weeds or improve nitrogen use on the field. Farmers may thus have private incentives to plant cover crops that may lead to the planting of some cover crops even in the absence of the AES under study. We call the area that would have been planted to cover crops by a participating farmer the *counterfactual level* of cover crops, and we denote it by Y^0.

Figure 10.1 shows the area planted to cover crops by the average participant over time. This farmer entered the scheme subsidising the planting of cover crops sometime between 2000 and 2005. The observed planted area (continuous line) increases sharply between 2000 and 2005. But in the absence of the AES, the farmer would still have planted a non-negligible area of cover crops (dotted line). In the absence of the AES, the social benefit from cover crops would not have been zero since the average participating farmer would have planted the counterfactual area. Therefore, by using only the observed planted level in a cost-benefit analysis, we implicitly attribute all the planting of cover crops to the effect of the AES, and thereby overestimate its impact.

The correct cost-benefit approach is to compare total benefits net of costs when the programme is in place with the total benefits had the programme not been implemented. The AES under study is welfare-enhancing if it yields a higher level of social welfare relative to the no-AES baseline. What is really gained from implementing the AES comes from the increase in the area planted in cover crops above the counterfactual level. This difference between the observed level of practices of a participating farmer and the counterfactual level of practices is called the additional, or causal, effect of the AES on the practice of this farmer. When measured for the average participating farm, this effect is generally called the average treatment effect on the treated (ATT).[4] On the cost side, the total payment received by the farmer is made up of two distinct parts: the payments compensating the additional planting, and the "windfall" payment, subsidising the counterfactual level of the practice that would have taken place even without the AES.[5] The cost-benefit analysis of an AES critically hinges on the relative extent of the average additional effect (ATT) vs. the average windfall effect (W). To be more formal, the social benefit from the additional planting of cover crops on the average participating farm is ATT×B and the cost of obtaining this additional planting is (W+ATT)×C. In our framework, whenever the benefits from implementing an AES are superior to their costs (i.e. when ATT×B ≥ (W+ATT)×C), the AES is welfare-enhancing.

In order to calculate the cost-benefit result, we need estimates of these four parameters. C, the per unit subsidy, comes from administrative data on the programme. B, the monetary value per unit of the environmental benefit can either be elicited by willingness-to-pay experiments, or estimated indirectly from estimates of the effect of the agricultural practice on the environment and then welfare (through health or other consequences). For example, if cover crops prevent the leaching of 20 kgN/ha, and if the social cost of leaching is EUR 0.7 /kgN (Grinsven, Rabl, and de Kok, 2010), then the estimated social benefit of cover crops is EUR 14 /ha.

In discussion, we focus on estimating ATT and W. As can be seen from Figure 10.1, ATT and W are closely related: their sum is equal to the observed level of the practice on the average participating farm. Thus, once we have estimated one of these two parameters, the other can be easily deduced from observed data. In our work (Chabé-Ferret and Subervie, 2010), we estimate that AES 0301 has triggered the planting of 10.66 additional hectares of cover crops on average among enrolled farmers. We also observe that participating farmers planted on average 17.24 ha of cover crops, so that the estimated average windfall effect is 6.58 ha. Because the per hectare payment for this AES is of EUR 68, the total cost of the programme is thus 17.24×68= EUR 1172 per farmer whereas the estimated social benefit is equal to 10.66×14= EUR 149.24 per farmer, indicating that this programme was not cost-effective. In Chabé-Ferret and Subervie (2010), we estimate the additional effect of an AES subsidy for converting to organic farming to be 50.82 ha. At the same time, we observe that farmers enrolled in this AES cultivated 54.71 ha under organic farming. The windfall effect is thus estimated to be rather small (3.89 ha). As enrolled farmers received EUR 162 per ha,[6] total spending on this subsidy is thus 54.71×162=EUR 8 863 per farmer. Sandhu *et al.* (2008) estimate that the average social benefit of organic farming at EUR 540 per ha. The additional benefit from this AES is thus 50.82×540= EUR 27 542 per farmer, which makes it highly cost-effective.

Figure 10.1. Additional and windfall effects for the average participating farmer

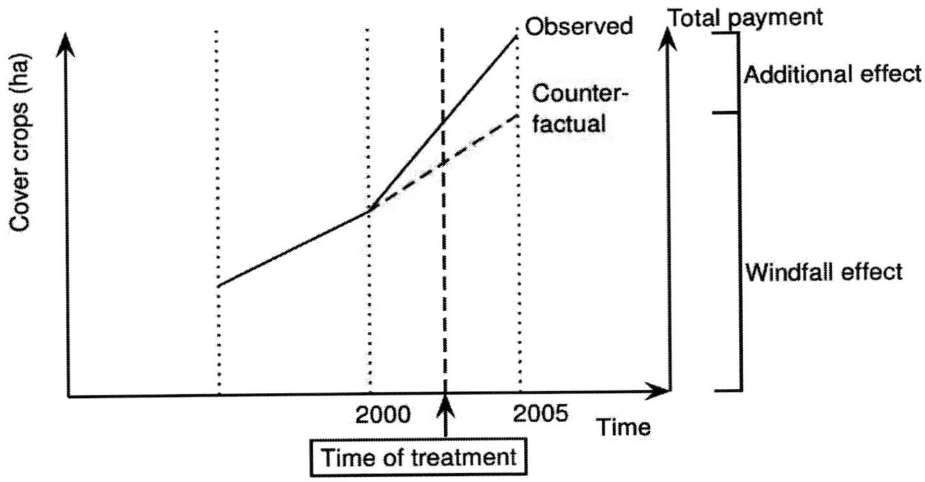

10.2 The fundamental causal inference problem: Why it is difficult to estimate additional effects

When trying to estimate the causal or additional effect, we face the fundamental problem of causal inference (Holland, 1986): the counterfactual situation cannot be observed. Therefore, it has to be approximated on the basis of observed data. Conventional estimates suffer from various kinds of bias, whose magnitude may be large.

The comparison of participants' practices before and after joining the programme suffers from a "time trend bias." It is very likely that practices would have changed over time even in the absence of the programme, since other determinants of farmers' practices like input and output prices may well have changed between these two dates, as illustrated in Figure 10.2.

However, if time is held constant and participants' practices are compared with those of non-participants, the resulting estimate suffers from another kind of bias, namely "selection bias". It is likely that participants who self-select into the programme would have adopted greener practices than those of non-participants had the programme not been implemented. Figure 10.2 also illustrates this second type of bias: in the absence of the AES, those who volunteer for it would have been using practices more consistent with the AES than those who did not volunteer. This is because complying with the requirements of the AES is less costly for those who would adopt more environmentally favourable practices even in the absence of the AES.

Selection bias is due to the fact that treated and untreated farmers differ in intrinsic characteristics that determine their agricultural practices, *including* their predisposition to volunteer for an AES. These characteristics may either be observed by us (like education, type of farm, capital or land, and so on) or unobserved (like environmental preferences or managerial ability). Selection bias may accordingly be divided into two types: selection on observables and on unobservables.

Figure 10.2. Selection and time trend biases

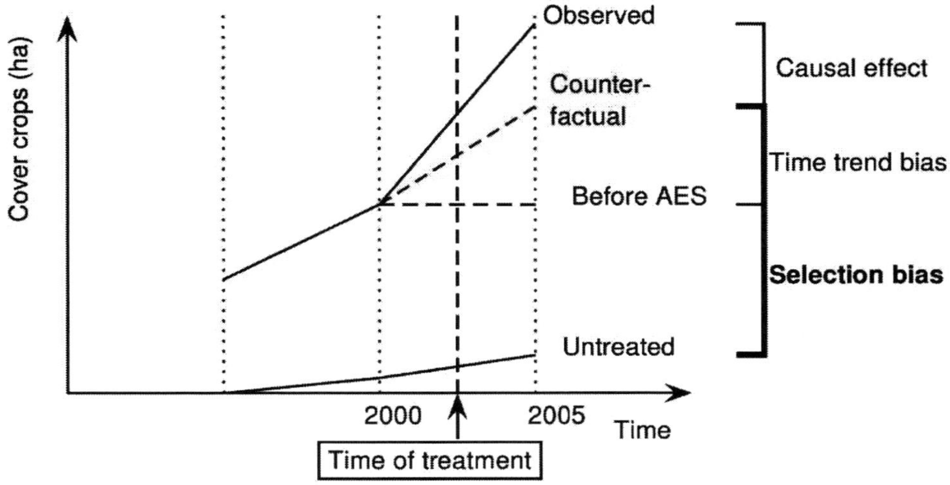

10.3 Econometric methods for estimating additional effects: An overview

This section presents a brief overview of the econometric methods that have been developed to perform causal inference, i.e. in order to estimate causal or additional effects. We provide illustrations from our work on evaluating AESs. Four types of estimators are presented: matching estimators, which aim to control for selection bias by controlling for observable factors; DID matching estimators, which use both observable factors and unobservable time-invariant factors to control for selection bias; the instrumental variables method, and the regression discontinuity method, which apply to settings with selection on unobservable factors.

We also discuss randomised control trials as a way of estimating additional effects. For the matching and DID-matching approaches, we provide concrete examples of the application of these methods to the evaluation of AES 0301, taken from Chabé-Ferret and Subervie (2010).

Matching estimators

If we believe that factors creating selection bias are all observable – meaning that we can measure all of these factors through available data – we can use matching estimators to estimate the additional effect of an AES. The method of matching gets rid of selection bias due to observables by comparing treated farmers to "twin" untreated farmers that have the same observed characteristics (Imbens, 2004). For example, we may want to find farmers who have the same education level, age, farm structure and equipment, but who differ in treatment status. We can then form the difference in outcomes between the treated farmer and his twin. By doing this for all treated farmers and taking the average of these differences, the average additional effect of the AES on participating farmers (ATT) can be estimated.

Figure 10.3 presents our application of matching to AES 0301. On average, treated (untreated) farmers planted 17.24 ha (1.12 ha) of cover crops. A direct comparison between treated and untreated farmers would lead to an estimate of the average causal effect of 16.12 ha of additional area planted to cover crops because of the AES. But this approach neglects the fact that treated and untreated farms have different characteristics even before the introduction of the AES.

Figure 10.3. Example of matching and DID matching

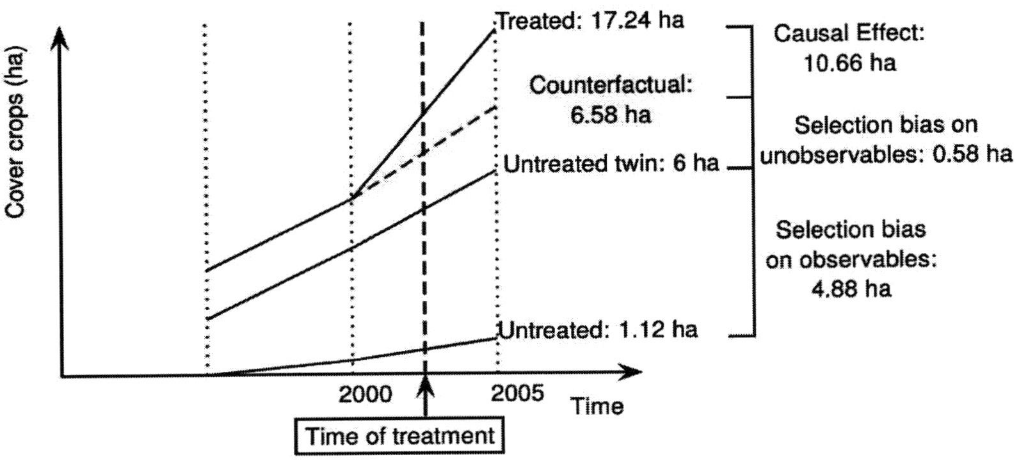

We thus compute the average level of cover crops planted by untreated farmers similar to the treated farmers in terms of observed pre-treatment characteristics. These "twin" non-participating farmers planted 6 ha of cover crops. The matching estimate of the additional effect of AES 0301 on treated farmers (ATT) is thus 17.24-6=11.24 ha of additional planted cover crops due to AES 0301. This is 4.88 ha lower than the raw with/without comparison, because twin untreated farmers have planted more cover crops than the average untreated farmer. This difference is a measure of selection bias due to selection on observables.

We select the set of control variables among variables that have been observed prior to the implementation of the AES under study. By doing so, we ensure that these variables have not been altered by the policy. We include all the variables that we suspect determine at the same time agricultural practices and enrollement in the AES.[7] The set of observable variables we use is extracted from the 2000 Census of Agriculture. The richness of the information in this database enables us to control for most of the important determinants of input choices and selection into the programme listed in our theoretical model: production factors (equipment, buildings, herd size and composition, composition and size of UAA, size of the labour force, age and education level of farm associates, etc.), and factors on the consumption side (composition of the household, the main non-farm activity of the farmer and his spouse, etc.). The dataset also includes measures of technical orientation of the farm, labels of quality, past experience with the previous AESs (1993-99) and other agricultural policies. Finally we complete the dataset with variables measuring altitude, slope, agro-environmental zone and soil carbon content at the commune level.

Matching gives an unbiased estimate of the ATT under three key assumptions that are discussed in Chabé-Ferret and Subervie (2010). First, it is assumed that the treatment received by one farmer does not affect outcomes for another farmer. This assumption is referred to in the literature as the Stable Unit Treatment Value Assumption (SUTVA) (Rubin, 1978). In our setting, this means that non-participants' practices must not have been altered by the existence of the AES programme. This rules out imitation effects or diffusion effects. This assumption seems plausible because imitators would also be likely to apply for an AES to get compensated. This assumption also rules out effects of the AES on input or output prices, which is reasonable for AESs that alter choices of inputs and outputs whose prices are determined on the world market (cereals, fertilisers), but much less so for AESs that may alter the prices of goods that are sold locally (land). AES 0301, for example, subsidises the planting of cover crops during the winter and has a limited effect on land. On the other hand, we observe that participants in AES 20, which subsidises extensive herding on grasslands, exhibit a sharp increase in farmland area. We interpret this as evidence that the AES has altered the local land market by encouraging non-participants to sell grassland to participants. If that is the case, we thus suspect that SUTVA does not hold. That is why we cannot estimate the effect of this AES (Chabé-Ferret and Subervie, 2009). All the other methods presented in this chapter rely on this assumption.

Second, another assumption of selection on observables assumes that, beyond the observed characteristics, there are no unobserved characteristics that simultaneously determine both the area planted to cover crops in the absence of the AES and entry into the AES. This means that the area that participating farmers would have planted to cover crops in the absence of the AES (counterfactual) is equal to the area planted to cover crops by the "twin" untreated farmers. Unless we can test the validity of this assumption, which is possible when data exist both before and after the treatment,[8] it is usually difficult to argue that no characteristic likely to generate selection bias has been omitted from the estimate, if only because key factors such as managerial ability are generally not measured in farmer surveys. Figure 10.3 shows that there is a difference as early as 2000 between the future participants in AES 0301 and their untreated "twins" (0.58 ha). Thus. there seems to be selection on unobservables.

Finally, we suppose that for each participant there exists at least one "twin" non-participant farmer having the same observed characteristics (common support assumption). However, some treated farmers have characteristics that make them literally "unmatchable" with any untreated farmers. When this occurs, these farms are dropped and matching is performed over the region of common support only. Empirical methods for determining the region of common support are given in Smith and Todd (2005). We followed exactly these procedures in our analysis of AES 0301 (planting of cover crops during winter), the estimated number of treated farmers on the common support, i.e. effectively used for estimation, being 1 617 out of 1 811 beneficiaries. But when it comes to AES 20 subsidies for extensive herding, we find that most of the participant farmers do not have a suitable non-participant twin. This means that among farmers complying with the requirements of this AES, almost all of them opted to join the scheme. It is thus impossible to estimate the causal effect of this AES.

It may seem counterintuitive to look for twin farmers with different treatment status. If they are twins, why are they not both participants, or both non-participants in the AES? This may happen because when we perform matching we get rid of endogenous sources of treatment variability only, not of the exogenous ones. This means that, beyond observed characteristics, other factors influence adoption of the AES. However, these factors (called instruments) must only determine entry, not outcomes (e.g. area planted to cover crops), or else they would create not only common support but also selection bias.[9] For example, in the case of the AES 0301, we argue that farmers' participation is partly driven by the different level of assistance farmers received from local advisers when filling in the application forms for the AES.

DID matching estimators

For a variety of reasons, there may be systematic differences between participant and non-participant outcomes, even after conditioning on observables. Treated and untreated farmers may also differ according to unobserved dimensions like managerial ability or environmental preferences. If we do not take these characteristics into account, the comparison between participants and matched non-participants will lead to a biased estimate of the treatment effect, as illustrated in Figure 10.3: The agricultural practices of the untreated "twins" are closer to the counterfactual ones, but some difference remains that would lead to overstate the causal effect of the AES. For example, treated farmers may be more environmentally aware or more productive and thus adopt better practices in the absence of the AES. But environmental awareness or managerial ability is not measured in our dataset and thus cannot be controlled for when using matching.

If we believe that the effect of these unobservable factors on practices is constant through time, we can estimate selection on unobservables by comparing the practices of the participants before they enter the AES to the ones of their untreated twins at the same date. We then subtract the difference in practices estimated by matching before the AES has been implemented from the difference estimated after. This method is thus called Difference-in-Difference (DID) matching (Heckman *et al.*, 1997).

The analysis of AES 0301 in Chabé-Ferret and Subervie (2010) again provides a good example of the amount of selection on unobservables.[10] Before the AES was implemented, treated farmers already differed from their untreated twins. We calculate that treated farmers planted 3.36 ha of cover crops in 2000, whereas untreated twins planted 2.78 ha of cover crops the same year. Thus, even before entering the AES, treated farmers planted more cover crops (0.58 ha) than their untreated twins. Supposing that this difference is constant through time, the difference in practices between treated farmers and their twins after the AES has been introduced (11.24 ha) has to be decreased by 0.58 ha to get an estimate of the ATT of AES 0301. This correctly yields the estimate of 10.66 ha.

DID matching also takes care of time-trend bias. As shown in Figure 10.3, untreated twins increased their area planted to cover crops by 3.22 ha between 2000 and 2005. This serves as an estimate of the increase that would have occurred on participating farms in the absence of the AES. It can thus be used to correct the simple "before/after" comparison of 13.88 ha to obtain 10.66 ha as an additional effect.

Assuming that selection bias on unobservables is fixed through time is a rather important assumption. It also amounts to assuming that the evolution of practices in the absence of the treatment would have been the same for the average treated farmer and his average twin, an assumption often called "the common trend assumption." In our example of AES 0301, this assumption seems quite plausible because unobserved determinants of participation are more likely to be constant through time (farmers' productivity and environmental awareness). It is also possible to test this assumption by performing a so-called placebo test, which consists in applying the DID matching estimator using, as a treatment group, a group of farmers known to be unaffected by the AES programme. In our running example, this "fake" treatment group includes farmers who did not participate in AES 0301 in 2003, but will enroll after this date. If the DID estimate in 2003 is different from zero, we can conclude that the trends are not parallel, and that our original DID estimate for the year 2005 is likely to be biased. In Chabé-Ferret and Subervie (2010), we implement this test and find evidence supporting the common trend assumption.

Note finally that there should be no remaining difference in pre-treatment practices if we control for pre-treatment practices when implementing the matching procedure (i.e. if we compare enrolled farmers to non participants planting the same area of cover crops). As a consequence, the DID step would be redundant. Chabé-Ferret (2010) acknowledges this problem and suggests that DID matching *without* controlling for pre-treatment practices is performed as a robustness check. We do so in Chabé-Ferret and Subervie (2010) and find the same results.

Instrumental variable methods

In cases where it is thought that there could be selection on unobservables, we may not have access to pre-treatment data, or the assumption of parallel trends may be rejected by the data. In that case, it may be possible to exploit some feature of the design or implementation of the policy, or both, in order to recover an average causal effect. In an instrumental variable strategy, we can, for example, make use of differences in the costs of entering an AES that remain unobserved in the matching procedure (Angrist and Krueger, 2001). For example, when joining the AES programme in France, farmers could receive support from advisers belonging to farmers' unions (*chambres d'agriculture*) (CA) in order to prepare their application files. However, some farmers may live further away from the local headquarters of the CA, and thus face a higher transaction cost of receiving support and information when considering applying for the AES programme. This means that the *net* amount of support received by farmers varies. For the sake of the example, we suppose that there are two types of farmers in terms of distance to the local CA headquarters: farmers living far away and farmer living close by. We expect that for farmers living far away, the net value of the scheme is less, and that, as a consequence, they will be less numerous in applying and then joining an AES than farmers living close to the CA headquarters. We thus expect that the proportion of participants decreases with the distance to the CA headquarters.

What is crucial for the instrumental variable strategy is that farmers' location relative to the CA headquarters is as good as random.[11] This amounts to assuming that the distance to the CA headquarters is not correlated with agricultural practices in the absence of the AES. If CA proximity directly alters farmers practices even in the absence of the AES (for example because CA counsellors generally promote greener practices), then it does not meet the criteria for an instrumental variable.

Adopting an instrumental variable strategy, we form the difference between the average area planted in cover crops by the farmers living close to the CA (participants and non participants)and the average area planted in cover crops by the farmers living far from the CA headquarters (participants and non participants). This difference is called the Intention to Treat Effect (ITE). If the AES has no effect on the planting of cover crops, this difference should be zero. It would indeed be equal to the average difference in practices in the absence of the AES, which is zero under the exogeneity assumption. If the ITE is positive, and both the exogeneity and SUTVA assumptions are valid, this can only be due to a positive causal effect of the AES on the planting of cover crops. Because treated farmers represent a higher share of farmers living close to the CA headquarters, this translates into a higher average area planted to cover crops among those farmers.

The problem with this approach is that it does not recover the ATT without additional assumptions (Heckman, 1997). This is mainly because a change in the instrumental variable (distance to the CA headquarters) only affects the participation decision of a subsample of all farmers. For example, there may exist farmers that enter the AES programme despite living far from the CA headquarters. This may be because they are highly motivated, because the programme is really beneficial to them, or because they have lower costs of going through the application process. These farmers will always participate in the programme (they are generally called "always takers"), whatever their distance to the CA headquarters, and thus it will be impossible to estimate the causal effect the AES has on their practices. The instrumental variable strategy only estimates the causal effect of the AES on the subgroup of farmers that decide to participate when they live close to CA headquarters and do not participate when they live far from CA headquarters ("compliers"). We generally assume that there are no farmers that are deterred from participating if they have the opportunity of receiving assistance (i.e. there are no "defiers").

The additional effect of the AES on compliers is also called the Local Average Treatment Effect (LATE) in the literature. The LATE can easily been derived by dividing the ITE by the difference in the proportion of participants between these two groups of farmers (Imbens and Angrist, 1994). This very simple estimator is called the Wald estimator.

The LATE is usually not the parameter we need in order to perform a cost-benefit analysis (Heckman and Smith, 1998). There are three solutions to this problem. The simple one is just to assume that causal effects are constant, so that the effect of the treatment on compliers (LATE) is equal to the effect of the treatment on all participants. This assumption is very unlikely to hold, as we know that farmers self-select into the programme based on their expected profits from doing so, and always-takers are expected to have higher profits and lower costs from entering the treatment than compliers have. The second solution is to change the decision problem: instead of comparing the situations with and without the AES, we might want to estimate the effect of opening CA outlets so that more farmers can live closer to CA advisers. The ITE is the measure of additionality required to compute the cost-benefit estimates in this case.[12] The third way around this problem is to use a continuous instrumental variable instead of dichotomous (distant/nearby) one. A natural candidate is the distance from CA headquarters. If there is a distance sufficiently high such that no farmer participates in an AES, then it is possible to recover the ATT by using the local instrumental variable method of Heckman and Vytlacil (1999).

Regression discontinuity designs

Regression discontinuity designs (RDD) make use of features governing eligibility to the programme or the level of payments. RDD rely on the existence of a discontinuity in programme eligibility that is governed by a so-called "running variable" (Imbens and Lemieux, 2008). For example, suppose that farmers having more 1.6 LU/ha (roughly, number of cattle divided by grassland area) in the previous year cannot receive payments for extensive herding today. Suppose also for the moment that farmers cannot choose in advance their position relative to the threshold. Then, farmers located just above the 1.6 threshold are very similar to farmers located just below (they just ended up at these respective locations by chance) and they would have adopted the same practices today in the absence of the AES. We do not expect average practices today to be discontinuous in the absence of the programme in terms of practices yesterday, especially at the 1.6 threshold. If we do observe a discontinuity in average practices around this threshold today, i.e. if farmers who were just below the threshold last year adopt more extensive practices than the ones who were just above, we can conclude that the AES has had a positive causal effect on practices. This particular example is problematic because, last year, farmers may have chosen their number of cattle and grassland area in order to be located below the threshold, in order to receive payments today. Thus, in this particular case, farmers located on each side of the threshold may differ because of selection bias.

RDDs are more convincing when they rely on running variables that have been determined before the policy was announced. It is also possible to test this assumption. First, one can check whether farmers' characteristics that should not be altered by the AES (education, age, etc.) change around the threshold. We can also check whether there is bunching at the threshold, with many more farmers located below than above the threshold (McCrary, 2008). Note that RDD only estimates the additional effect locally, at the threshold. It is thus not enough for a fully-fledged cost-benefit analysis.

It would also be extremely natural to apply RDDs to the evaluation of AESs granted through auctions. Take, for example, an auction using only prices bid by farmers to allocate the contracts (and payments). Farmers announce an area on which they will comply with the requirements of the AES and a level of payment per hectare. Payments are then allocated starting from the lowest offer, until the total budget is spent. If the distribution of offered payments is almost continuous, then the difference between the last farmer receiving a payment and the first farmer to be denied payments is very small. If there are enough farmers participating in the auction, this difference may very well be close to zero. Farmers on each side of the cutoff level are thus similar, and we do not expect them to adopt different practices in the absence of the payment. If we notice any difference (discontinuity) in practices around the eligibility threshold, we can be sure that this is a measure of the causal effect of the AES. This effect is only measured for the last farmers entering the auction. This is nevertheless an interesting parameter from a policy perspective, since it gives the marginal benefit of extending the size of the auction.

Randomised control trials

RCTs are based on a very simple intuition: if treated farmers are selected at random among applicants, then the practices of the untreated applicants offer a direct and accurate estimate of the counterfactual practices of the participants. Moreover, the direct comparison of the practices of the average participant to the ones of the average untreated applicant gives the average additional effect (Burtless, 1995; Duflo *et al.*, 2007). The validity of an RCT requires that randomisation is performed among a sufficiently large group of farmers, so that the law of large numbers ensures that treated and untreated farmers are identical *ex ante*. In order to ensure the policy relevance of the results of a RCT, we also need to assume that it has not disrupted the way the programme normally operates. For example, the selection of the beneficiaries and their behaviour may be altered by randomisation (Heckman and Smith, 1995). For example, in order to reach the same number of participants in the RCT as would have been reached without the RCT, we have to increase the number of applicants (by increasing incentives to participate). But at the same time, the pool of participants is altered and the additional effect of the AES on the group that has undergone randomisation may differ from the policy-relevant additional effect.

The main advantages of RCTs are that they do not require assumptions on the form of selection bias, like the ones needed to ensure that the econometric methods presented previously are unbiased. Counterbalancing this, political constraints are often raised against RCTs, because they entail randomly denying the benefit of the programme to a sub-sample of the population that would like to join it. In the case of AES, we think that this problem might be alleviated if we confine RCTs to the evaluation of new types of AESs vs. more traditional types, rather than evaluating these AES vs. no AES. Another way of mitigating this issue is to randomise an encouragement to participate in a given AES (receiving a letter explaining the merits of the AES, for example), while allowing everyone to enter each scheme. The policy-relevance of the evaluation is, however, reduced because we can only estimate the effect of the scheme on those that have been encouraged to join it (compliers).

10.4 Conclusions and directions for further research

In this section, we discuss the possibility of extending the methods used so as to evaluate the effects of changes in some parameters of the schemes. Second, we discuss the merits of experimental evaluations of the AES.

Simulating the effect of altering parameters of the AES

The previous discussion focused on a single AES. In Chabé-Ferret and Subervie (2010), we develop a framework allowing for participation of a single farmer in multiple AESs and we implement tests of the possible complementarities between AESs. It could also be interesting to study the effect of suppressing one AES: in that case, farmers that take this AES may join the next best alternative. To perform such an evaluation, we would thus have to predict their choice. Another extension would entail predicting the effect of alterations in the price and the requirements of a given AES. This requires variations in these parameters when the actual policy implementation.

Another possible extension would be to consider alternative allocation mechanisms of the payments for the AES. The French AESs are allocated under a uniform payment mechanism: all farmers joining an AES are paid roughly the same amount per hectare of agricultural practice subsidised. This leaves a lot of scope for windfall effects: farmers with zero or low costs of complying with the AES requirements receive the same compensation as farmers with high costs of coping with the requirements. One way of mitigating these effects is to condition entry and/or payment on farm characteristics that proxy costs, but there remains room for windfall effects even after conditioning on these observed characteristics. Another way to curb these windfall effects is to auction AESs. Auctions are theoretically more efficient than unique payments for allocating AES payments because payments to farmers are closer to their unit costs of delivering the service. To our knowledge, there has been no work trying to compare auctions to unique payments on *ex post* data.

Improving integration of the treatment effects framework with cost-benefit analysis

The very simple cost-benefit framework presented in Section 10.1 can be extended in three directions. First, we do not explicitly consider producer surplus in our calculations. This would entail estimating the effects of AES constraints on farmers' profit. Second, the environmental benefit from better practices could be modelled in a more realistic manner. For example, the marginal environmental value of the subsidised practice may not be constant: it may depend on the actual level of the practice, or on its spatial location. This would entail estimating the effect of the AES on the distribution of the practices, unconditionally or across space. Third, the link between practices, the environment and consequences on human life (landscape valuation, biodiversity, health effects) has to be better understood. Klein *et al.* (2006) offer a very nice synthesis of the effects of AESs on biodiversity. More work combining economic analysis of farmers' decisions with their effects on the environment remains to be done.

Notes

1. Cemagref, Aubière, France and INRA, Montpellier, respectively.
2. We disregard administrative costs and deadweight losses due to taxation.
3. We adopt a pure taxpayer perspective here, and do not include farmers' profit in the cost-benefit analysis. Because entry into AESs is voluntary, we expect the total net benefit to a participating farmer to be positive, and thus our approach gives a sufficient condition for the AES to be welfare-enhancing.
4. Because these concepts are brought from the experimental biology literature, the policy under study is generally referred to as a treatment.
5. Although a windfall gain to the farmer, in terms of the programme budget, this payment is an unnecessary cost. Hence, in the terminology of the EU's Common Monitoring and Evaluation Framework, the farmer's windfall gain is called a "deadweight cost."
6. In reality, they received payments on a lower area because of budget limits.
7. Chabé-Ferret and Subervie (2010) derive the set of control variables from a model of an agricultural household deciding whether or not to enroll in an AES.
8. Such a test is called a placebo test.
9. Contrary to the instrumental variables method, when applying matching estimators, we do not need to observe these instruments.
10. See also Pufhal and Weiss (2009) for an application of this method to the evaluation of the German AESs.
11. Instrumental variables are also called "natural experiments."
12. The LATE cannot be used directly because it is impossible to recover the windfall effect for compliers. It is nevertheless possible to recover the windfall effect of opening new CA outlets: it is simply the average area of cover crops planted by farmers living far from CA headquarters.

References

Angrist, J.D. and A.B. Krueger (1999), "Empirical Strategies in Labor Economics", in Orley Ashenfelter and David Card (ed.), *Handbook of Labor Economics*, Elsevier Science, North-Holland, Amsterdam, New-York and Oxford, pp. 1277-1366.

Angrist, J.D. and A.B. Krueger (2001), "Instrumental Variables and the Search for Identification: from Supply and Demand to Natural Experiments", *Journal of Economic Perspectives*, Vol. 15, No. 4, pp. 69-85.

Burtless, G. (1995), "The Case for Randomized Field Trials in Economic and Policy Research", *Journal of Economic Perspectives*, Vol. 9, No. 2, pp. 63-84.

Chabé-Ferret, S. (2010), "To Control or Not to Control? To Control or Not to Control? Bias of Simple Matching vs Difference-In-Difference Matching in a Dynamic Framework".

Chabé-Ferret, S. and J. Subervie (2009), "Estimation des effets propres des mesures agroenvironnementales du PDRN 2000-2006 sur les pratiques des agriculteurs", Technical report, Cemagref UMR Metafort. *agriculture.gouv.fr/estimation-des-effets-propres-des*

Chabé-Ferret, S. and J. Subervie (2010), "How Much Green for the Buck? Estimating Additional and Windfall Effects of the French Agro-Environmental Schemes by Difference-In-Difference Matching".

Duflo, E., R. Glennerster and M. Kremer (2007), "Using Randomization in Development Economics Research: A Toolkit", in T. Paul Schultz and John A. Strauss (ed.), *Handbook of Development Economics*, Elsevier, pp. 3895-3962.

Greenstone, M. and T. Gayer (2009), "Quasi-experimental and Experimental Approaches to Environmental Economics", *Journal of Environmental Economics and Management*, Vol. 57, No. 1, pp. 21-44.

Heckman, J.J. (1997), "Instrumental Variables: A Study of Implicit Behavioral Assumptions Used in Making Program Evaluations", *Journal of Human Resources* Vol.32, No. 3, pp. 441-462.

Heckman, J.J., H. Ichimura and P.E. Todd (1997), "Matching as an Econometric Evaluation Estimator: Evidence from Evaluating a Job Training Programme", *The Review of Economic Studies*, Vol. 64, No.4, (Special Issue: Evaluation of Training and Other Social Programmes), pp. 605-654.

Heckman, J.J., R.J. LaLonde and J.A. Smith (1999), "The Economics and Econometrics of Active Labor Market Programs", in Orley C. Ashenfelter and David Card (ed.), *Handbook of Labor Economics,*Elsevier, North Holland, pp. 1865-2097.

Heckman, J.J. and J. Smith (1995), "Assessing the Case for Social Experiments", *Journal of Economic Perspectives*, Vol. 9, No.2, pp. 85-110.

Heckman, J.J. and J. Smith (1998), "Evaluating the Welfare State", in S. Strom (ed.), *Econometrics and Economics in the 20th Century*, Cambridge University Press, New York.

Heckman, J.. and E.J. Vytlacil (1999), "Local Instrumental Variables and Latent Variable Models for Identifying and Bounding Treatment Effects", *Proceedings of the National Academy of Sciences*, Vol. 96, No.8, pp. 4730-4734.

Holland, P.W. (1986), "Statistics and Causal Inference", *Journal of the American Statistical Association*, Vol 81, pp. 945-970.

Imbens, G.W. (2004), "Nonparametric Estimation of Average Treatment Effects Under Exogeneity: A Review", *The Review of Economics and Statistics*, Vol. 86, No.1, pp. 4-29.

Imbens, G.W. and J.D. Angrist (1994), "Identification and Estimation of Local Average Treatment Effects", *Econometrica*, Vol. 62, No.2, pp. 467-476.

Imbens, G. W. and T. Lemieux (2008), "Regression Discontinuity Designs: A Guide to Practice", *Journal of Econometrics*, Vol. 142, No.2, pp. 615-635.

Kleijn, D., R.A. Baquero, Y. Clough, M. Diaz, J. Esteban, F. Fernandez, D. Gabriel, F. Herzog, A. Holzschuh, R. Johl, E. Knop, A. Kruess, E.J.P. Marshall, I. Steffan-Dewenter, T. Tscharntke, J. Verhulst, T. M. West and J. L. Yela (2006), "Mixed Biodiversity Benefits of Agri-Environment Schemes in Five European Countries", *Ecology Letters* Vol.9, No.3, pp. 243-254.

McCrary, J. (2008), "Manipulation of the Running Variable in the Regression Discontinuity Design: A Density Test", *Journal of Econometrics*, Vol. 142(2), pp. 698-714.

Pufahl, A. and C.R. Weiss (2009), "Evaluating the Effects of Farm Programmes: Results from Propensity Score Matching", *European Review of Agricultural Economics* Vol. 36, No. 1, pp. 79-101.

Rubin, D.B. (1978), "Bayesian Inference for Causal Effects: The Role of Randomization", *The Annals of Statistics* Vol. 6, No.1, pp. 34-58.

Sandhu, H. S., S.D. Wratten, R. Cullen and B. Case (2008), "The Future of Farming: The Value of Ecosystem Services in Conventional and Organic Arable Land. An Experimental Approach', *Ecological Economics* Vol. 64(4), pp. 835 - 848.

Smith, J.A. and P.E. Todd (2005), "Does Matching Overcome LaLonde's Critique of Nonexperimental Estimators?" *Journal of Econometrics*, Vol 125, No.1-2, pp. 305-353.

Todd, P.E. (2007), "Evaluating Social Programs with Endogenous Program Placement and Selection of the Treated", in T.P. Schultz and J.A. Strauss (ed.), *Handbook of Development Economics*, Elsevier, pp. 3847-3894.

van Grinsven, H., A. Rabl and T. de Kok (2010), "Estimation of Incidence and Social Cost of Colon Cancer due to Nitrate in Drinking Water in the EU: a Tentative Cost-Benefit Assessment", *Environmental Health*, Vol. 9, No.1.

Chapter 11

Application of the Agri-Environmental Footprint Index to assess agri-environmental policies in Greece

Stamatios Christopoulos and George Vlahos[1]

The Agri-environmental Footprint Index (AFI) aims to assess the environmental performance of farms under agri-environmental schemes (AESs) by combining existing agri-environmental indicators and multi-criterion decision analysis. A variant of the AFI approach, developed to address AESs in Greece, was applied to two different farming systems under AES regimes (organic farming in extensive olive groves and nitrate pollution reduction in intensive arable crop cultivation), to compare the environmental performance of participating and non-participating farms. No significant differences in environmental performance between the two groups of farms were found. Moreover, the AESs in both cases appear to lack full additionality. When AES outcomes are assessed against the environmental objectives pursued, outcomes are in line with the policy aims in the case of organic farming, whereas for the arable farms, any benefits accruing seem to be mainly collateral.

11.1 Evaluation of agri-environmental schemes

The first attempts to introduce incentives for environmental friendly farming in EU Member States (MS) coincided with the first concise version of rural development policy (RDP) measures under Reg. EEC/797/85. Since then, a number of milestones in the evolution of agri-environmental schemes (AESs) in the European Union can be identified. The establishment of an obligation for MS to implement AESs as accompanying measures in the 1992 CAP reform, drawing the relevant resources from the core of the CAP financing instrument, was one of these milestones (Baldock and Lowe, 1996; Buller, 2000; EEA, 2006) since by the end of the first implementation period 18% of the EU-15 agricultural area was under an AE agreement (EC, 1998). The incorporation of AESs as an integral part of the second pillar of the CAP, as RDP came to be known after the 1999 reform, marked the start of the second period of implementation of AESs (2000-2006). By the end of this period, 54% of the Utilised Agricultural Area (UAA) of EU25 was covered by an AE agreement (EC, 2009). The third implementation period for AESs, currently underway as part of the 2007-2013 Rural Development framework, will complete two decades of formal implementation of AESs in the European Union.

During these two decades, many attempts to evaluate the performance of AESs have been made. As part of the RDP, these policies are required to comply with a medium-term programming procedure as well as undergo a formal evaluation process. MS must perform evaluations *ex ante* (currently in the form of Strategic Environmental Assessment), at mid-term, and *ex post* at the end of the implementation period. Within these evaluations, environmental assessment of AESs, which is the main focus of the present contribution, has been an increasingly important issue. EU-level evaluation exercises within the EU policy evaluation procedures have also been undertaken, based mainly on formal national AE programmes evaluations.

A goal of these EU-level assessments was to compile national reports into a single document (EC, 1998, 1999, 2006; Oréade Brèche, 2005). This task proved to be quite difficult to achieve, not least because the reporting frameworks used by MS were not always harmonised. Recognising these difficulties and the resulting lack of clarity, a great effort has been made over a number of years to formulate a common evaluation framework for all national RDPs (EC, 2000a, 200b, 2006). These successive frameworks have become increasingly elaborate and detailed (Primdahl *et al.*, 2010). Environmental evaluation of *all* RDP measures as an omnipresent criterion, but also the need for a more efficient evaluation specifically of AESs, have led several EU services to focus their interest on agri-environmental indicator systems in order to facilitate the process. Hence, based on work done at OECD (see OECD, 1997, 1998, 1999, 2000, 2003; Peschard *et al.*, 2004) and since 2000 in European institutions (see EC, 2000c, 2001; EEA,1999, 2005a, 2005b, 2006,) much effort has been dedicated to these issues.

The evaluation of AESs in environmental terms has also been a high priority in the academic research agenda during these two decades (see, for example, Damianos and Giannakopoulos, 1999; Peco *et al.*, 2000; Louloudis *et al.*, 2000; Kleijn and Sutherland, 2003; Primdahl *et al.*, 2003; Kleijn *et al.*, 2006; Finn *et al.*, 2007, 2008, 2009).

11.2 Challenges in environmental evaluation of AESs

The problems identified during the above-mentioned exercises can be classified into three main categories. The first has to do with problems inherent in environmental evaluation *per se*, the second category consists of the problems created by the approach selected for the implementation of EU agri-environmental measures, and the third category relates to the specific situation at the MS level.

One of the major difficulties is due to the complexity of the interface between agricultural activities and the environment. Land use and management practices are diffuse and variable, both in spatial terms and time scale. In a relatively small area, a number of farmers and farm operators, i.e. farm-level decision makers, can interact with the environment through individual decisions such as fertiliser application or biocide use. These decisions are normally taken independently of each other, and yet they all contribute to the combined environmental impact of farming in that area. Moreover, farming interactions with the environment vary in intensity as well as in the very nature of the impacts, which can have a seasonal[2] or sequential dimension. For example, tree farmers in Mediterranean regions apply fertilisers during late winter-early spring and the possible impact of erroneous use is mainly nutrient loss and water pollution. The same farmers use insecticides during late spring, over the summer and sometimes well into autumn. In that case, the focus of an impact assessment should be on biodiversity effects as well as on product safety rather than on water quality. At the same time, the timing of insecticide application is crucial, since spraying at the correct time can minimise adverse biodiversity effects while earlier or later application may result to both a damaged crop and a degraded environment.

Another important challenge facing an environmental evaluation is the variety and heterogeneity of causal mechanisms involved in environmental issues, particularly with respect to their local or regional relevance and type of impact (Stoate *et al.*, 2009; Primdahl *et al.*, 2010; Cooper *et al.*, 2010). For example, a specific farming practice, grazing, and the main pressure associated with this practice, namely an excessive number of animals grazing an area (*overgrazing*), expressed as livestock units per hectare, can have entirely different impacts depending on the agro-ecosystem concerned. In northern or north-western Europe, overgrazing of bovine animals typically affects water quality, whereas in the case of most Mediterranean pastures, overgrazing of sheep and goats is a principal cause of soil erosion.

The second group of issues identified in AES assessments is due to complexities raised by the implementation approach adopted at EU level. The multiple and often inter-related rural development objectives enshrined in Pillar 2 of the CAP can be summarised under the three pillars of sustainability, namely economic, social and environmental (Buller, 2000; Huylenbroeck and Whitby, 1999; Lowe *et al.*, 1997; Park *et al.*, 2004).The rationale for including AESs as part of rural development policy has been their potential for promoting simultaneously, or at least not acting against, the a multiplicity of these objectives. Furthermore, within the environmental domain, most of the implementing authorities have chosen to apply broad and shallow types of schemes instead of an approach where each specific environmental objective is separately targeted (Andersen *et al.*, 1999; European Parliament, 1998; European Commission, 1998). This choice, of striving to achieve multiple objectives with one (or several) measures, has added considerable complexity to the assessment exercises.

The RD regulations place an obligation on both the national authorities and the European Commission to evaluate RD measures. Nevertheless, despite the two decades of RD implementation in the European Union, the problem of the time-frame for the evaluations remains, rendering all official evaluations of limited scope within the implementation period examined. Given that there is always a delay in setting up the measures, since all RDPs have to be negotiated and approved by the Commission services, there is only limited data available for mid-term evaluations – indeed, in most cases, only monitoring data are available. Going back to previous implementation periods of the same measure is not within the terms of reference of the mid-term evaluation, hence a discontinuity is created in assessments. Furthermore, *ex post* evaluations are usually made available only long after the policy following the one evaluated has been formulated. As a consequence, the design and implementation of AESs, and of RDP in general, are based on a very poor evaluation input, even as regards each MS's own implementation experience, let alone the experience of other

MS, since the EU-wide compilations of the national evaluation reports are issued even later. In that sense, it is no surprise that AE policy formulation does not benefit from a learning process (Finn *et al.*, 2009; Primdahl *et al.*, 2010).

A further complexity has been caused by the approach adopted for calculating AE payments. This can be clarified using the terminology suggested by Oñate *et al.* (2000) that divides the effects of AESs into performance and outcome effects. Performance effects concern the impacts on land use or management practices triggered by the AES under examination. Performance effects in turn influence the pressures exerted on agro-ecosystems. Measuring the way these pressures are modified by performance effects provides estimates of outcome effects. The WTO Agreement on Agriculture allows AESs to be classified as 'green box' payments as long as the farmer's compensation does not exceed income forgone and the implementation costs incurred (WTO, 1994). The amount of AE payments is, thus, based on the performance effects of AES and evaluations focus strongly on these effects. As a consequence, there is little incentive for evaluators to focus on outcome effects, nor for policy makers to facilitate the provision of information on outcome effects, since these are not decisive for calculating the budget cost of the measure.

By contrast, the performance effects of the measure would give a better idea of the value society gets from the AES. Following this line of reasoning, performance effect indicators *could* provide satisfactory estimates for the actual outcome effects, if a very well established, quantitative impact model were available. However, this is not the case for the majority of the AESs implemented across the European Union. In a study of 60 AESs, only 15% of the 93 management packages comprising these measures were found to be based on quantitative impact models while more than half of them seem to have been based on intuitive models (Primdahl *et al.*, 2010).

Finally, we can describe some of the problems arising from the specific MS implementation approaches and procedures in the local context. The most immediate problem is the lack of sufficient appropriate data, i.e. data measured at the required spatial levels, with appropriate frequency, and at the necessary points in time. In some respects, these deficiencies may be somewhat alleviated when the evaluation is performed within a research context, but here there is always the problem of limited resources. When resources are limited, sample sizes and numbers of case studies are small, and the specificities already described render generalisations based on relatively few observed cases potentially spurious. The result is that the formulation of general, scientifically-based conclusions and proposals for policy improvement are not feasible (Carey *et al.*, 2002, 2003; Finn *et al.*, 2008, 2009).

One should also observe that, from the definition of AE policy objectives negotiated with the commission by regional or MS authorities down to policy-induced changes in farming practices, there are many factors and actors that influence farmers' performance and hence the outcome of the measures. In fact, one could argue that the greater the distance between the design and the implementation levels, the more likely one is to find differentiations and distortions due to different policy agendas at different levels of the policy complex (Paniagua, 2001; Juntti and Potter, 2002; Juntti and Wilson, 2004). Differing degrees of administrative efficiency, deficient knowledge of local conditions as well as the existence of individual farm and farming household perceptions, needs and strategies are some of these factors (Damianos and Giannakopoulos, 2002).

11.3. Methodology

General introduction to the AFI

The Agri-environmental Footprint Index (AFI) was developed in 2005-2008 as a tool to quantify and evaluate the environmental performance of farms under AES, and to evaluate the effectiveness of those policy schemes in terms of environmental benefits. The AFI can measure the outcomes of agri-environmental policies at farm level in the form of a customisable index with the potential to quantify the environmental status of individual production units (Knickel and Kasperczyk, 2009; Mauchline *et al.*, 2007; Purvis *et al.*, 2009, Vesterager *et al.*, 2010). The methodology combines the use of agri-environmental indicators and multi-criterion decision analysis (MCDA) in a way that enables it to address any environmental issue via the involvement of local stakeholders and agricultural or environmental experts.

The study reported below was designed to test a variant of the methodology on two different farming systems under two AES regimes, chosen to represent the reality of AESs in the Greek context. Through this chapter we intend to address the following questions as a means of testing the usefulness of the AFI:

- Is the AFI methodology appropriate for evaluating the environmental performance of farms in a Greek context?
- Does the AFI methodology have good potential for evaluating AESs against the three dimensions of the evaluation of AESs (i.e. general, administrative, and scientific)?
- Can the AFI provide relevant information not only for *ex post* policy evaluation, but also at the stage of designing AESs?
- If so, what does it reveal about the extent to which the policy design was appropriate for the stated environmental objectives of the two schemes?

AFI variant for application in the Greek context

The AFI approach is based on a selection of environmental issues related to the application of the AES in question. Stakeholder groups are selected to be appropriate to the specific scheme, whereas the issues represented in the evaluation cover all the environmental aspects expected to be affected by the application of the AES and the farming practices in the case study areas. This set of environmental issues, hereafter called "sub-issues", can result in a wide assessment of a farm's environmental performance. Sub-issues consist of two categories. The first category contains the sub-issues related to the environmental objectives explicitly set by the scheme during its design phase, and they are used in such a way that each sub-issue is linked to one clear policy objective. The second category includes the sub-issues perceived by the stakeholders as relevant to the AES's application despite their not being explicitly linked to the scheme's stated objectives. These two complementary categories result in a wide assessment of a farm's environmental performance. The comparison contrasts the environmental performances of farms under an AES regime and non-AES farms.

The current AFI approach can be divided into two distinct levels of evaluation. The first level looks at the environmental problems related to agricultural activities at regional or local level. Local stakeholders including scientists identify and prioritise the agriculturally-related environmental problems of the area in question, enabling the evaluators to check the relevance of the overall programme objectives to the problems identified. This identification process enables a comparison of the specific environmental problems at local level against the objectives of the AES in question. Hence, this participatory process facilitates an assessment of the extent to which the specific policy measures and the issues they address are relevant to the actual environmental issues of the area concerned. In this way, the current approach, through a simple but precise participatory procedure can provide a preliminary evaluation of the design of the policy measure before the development stage of the AFI.

The second level of evaluation looks at the appropriateness of the agri-environmental indicators used to address the pre-selected agri-environmental issues, and of the harmonised quantification of the outcomes in order to render the environmental issues comparable to each other. At this stage, the stakeholders again have a crucial role in validating that the overall outcome is relevant to the current state of environmental affairs of the area in question. Thus, the second level aims to evaluate what has actually been done by AES participants in terms of environmental change at farm level. Hence, in principle, while the first level addresses the subject at the macro or regional level in terms of policy design, the second level deals with the actual implementation of the policy at the micro or farm level. In that sense, the two different levels of evaluation facilitate not only the assessment of the appropriateness of the policy design to address certain necessary environmental issues, but also assemble the information required for judging whether the policy objectives were actually served.

Addressing the problems of AES evaluation

General issues

As shown in previous work on AFI development, the major advantage of the methodology is that it can address an increased number of environmental issues taking into account their local relevance and priority (Purvis *et al.*, 2009, Vesterager *et al.*, 2010). Moreover, if developed appropriately, it could address policy measures with multiple objectives, like those addressed in the current chapter, while also investigating the complex interface between agricultural activities and the natural environment in their spatial and temporal reality (Mauchline *et al.*, 2011). The AFI, if suitably designed, can also be applied in diverse administrative structures including those with questionable effectiveness.

Administrative issues

The problem created when the mid-term reviews of the programmes are being prepared in the very early stages of AESs implementation might be mitigated by the AFI's two-level structure of evaluation and the relatively quick results produced by the first level. Hence, the first level evaluation (FLE) could help to build a more concise mid-term review.

As shown by previous research conducted by Primdahl *et al.* (2010), the design of most AESs is based on intuitive and common sense impact models that do not incorporate relevant indicators, thus increasing the distance between the design phase and the actual implementation of the policy. The AFI method could facilitate the development of impact models with the help of indicators that could enhance AES efficiency. Moreover, limited knowledge of local specificities in the design phase of top-down AESs, could be increased through the participatory dimension of the approach, by engaging local stakeholders to contribute their knowledge to the process.

Research or scientific issues

Previous applications of the AFI approach, in different national contexts, have shown that there are huge insufficiencies in terms of necessary data (Mauchline *et al.*, 2011, Purvis *et al.*, 2009). Most previous attempts at AES evaluations were based on case studies of particular areas or single measures, with only a few trying to apply a more holistic or harmonised approach that could evaluate whole sets of measures. The AFI could be used in order to reveal specific needs in data or other informational gaps. Therefore, it could be used to identify necessary information or to stimulate further data collection. It can be argued that increasing development and use of this tool would facilitate a harmonised approach to data collection systems across Europe (Purvis *et al.*, 2009).

11.4 Results

First case study: Messinian Mani

The Organic Plant Production Scheme is very widely implemented in Greece, with organic olive holdings accounting for over 50% of the total area under organic farming. Messinia has the fourth largest area under organic oleiculture (8% of the total organic olives) among 54 prefectures in Greece. Moreover, Mani is one of the first areas in Greece were olive farmers have converted to organic, making this area ideal for testing the ability of the AFI methodology to determine whether the environmental performance of olive farms participating in the Organic Plant Production scheme differs from that of non-participating farms. The AFI was used to assess environmental performance corresponding to objectives directly targeted by the scheme as well as other impacts related to non-stated objectives.

The farm survey took place during 2007 in the area of Mani that lies in the Messinia Prefecture (NUTS3) around 300 km from Athens. The Messinian part of Mani is considered to be an area of natural beauty, attracting many tourists, with Mount Taygetos dominating its east and the Messinian Gulf the west. Above the olive zone (more than 700 m in altitude), the area belongs to the Natura 2000 network, since it hosts a large variety of biotopes providing habitat for indigenous Greek animal species. Mani is mainly characterised by oleiculture, which accounts for 1 270 out of 3 550 ha (36%) of UAA in the area. The 130 olive farms in the organic scheme cover an area of 280 ha (22% of the oleicultural area).

The survey was conducted on 39 organic farms and 11 conventional ones, selected by stratified random sampling. The stated objectives for the case of 'Organic Plant Production' scheme were *reduction in pollution* caused by agriculture, *biodiversity conservation* of agricultural ecosystems and *sustainable soil management*, focusing on soil fertility and organic matter.

The comparisons between AFIs for participating and non-participating farms were limited to the Total AFIs and "natural resources" (NR) AFIs for both cases, while "Biodiversity" (B) AFIs were compared only with respect to fulfilling stated objectives and "Landscape" AFIs for not-stated objectives (Table 11.1). As Table 11.2 shows, participating farms score better when it comes to environmental effects derived from the policy objectives in all comparisons. However, the differences in results in this category are statistically significant only when it comes to the biodiversity-related stated scheme objectives. On the other hand, in the second category, non-participating farms seem to score better when it comes to "natural resources" only, but none of the differences for the non-intended environmental effects are significant[3].

Table 11.1. Issues and sub-issues per category – Messinian Mani case study area

Issue	Sub-issue	Status in stated objectives Mentioned=S/Not mentioned=NS
Natural resources	Water quality	S
	Soil quality	S
	Erosion	NS
	CO2 emissions	NS
Biodiversity	Species	S
	Ecosystem	S
Landscape	Landscape	NS

Source: Christopoulos (2011).

Table 11.2. Messinian Mani case study area: AFIs for participants and non-participants, by effect category

	Overall effects				Mentioned in stated objectives				Not mentioned in stated objectives			
	Total	NR[1]	B[2]	L[3]	Total	NR	B	L	Total	NR	B	L
Participants	6.60	7.13	5.58	5.62	7.88	8.19	5.58	-	6.77	6.56	-	5.62
Non-participants	6.29	7.06	4.49	5.00	7.06	7.41	4.49	-	6.70	6.80	-	5.00

1. Natural resources. 2. Biodiversity. 3. Landscape.

Source: Christopoulos (2011).

Second case study: Larissa

Cotton cultivation is a leading example of intensive production in Greece. Furthermore, the Nitrate Reduction Scheme is one of the first AES implemented in Greece, targeted initially at Thessaly (a Nitrate Vulnerable Zone (NVZ) under the Nitrates Directive (EEC/91/676)), and then expanded to other areas. In the prefecture of Larissa alone there are approximately 50 000 ha under an AES agreement within the Nitrate Reduction Scheme, predominantly cotton farms.

In order to test the AFI methodology with this case study, we had to determine whether the agri-environmental performance of farms participating in the Nitrate Reduction Scheme differs from that of non-participating farms in the Larissa region. The AFI was used to assess environmental performance corresponding to objectives directly targeted by the scheme as well as other impacts related to non-stated objectives.

The scheme for reducing nitrate pollution from agricultural sources was targeted in a double way. It was targeted spatially, since for the 2000-06 period was implemented in three specific areas. These were the plains of Thessaly, the Lake Kopais area, and the Pineios river area in the prefecture of Ileia. It was also targeted in terms of the objectives set. The scheme was designed to introduce or maintain nitrate-reducing farming practices concerning irrigated arable crops in areas with high concentration of nitrates in their groundwater or in NVZs under Directive EEC/91/676. Payments were made to farmers in order to apply nitrate-reducing farming practices described in the scheme methodologies found in the Greek Rural Development Programme, and in a special set (Agri-environmental) Codes of Good Agricultural Practices (GAP).

The farm survey took place during 2007 in the prefecture of Larissa (a NUTS3 region) around 380 km north of Athens. Larissa is one of the four prefectures of Thessaly. The prefecture of Larissa is second (out of 54 Greek prefectures) in size and first in total Utilised Agricultural Area (UAA). It is mostly a plain area, where agriculture has been traditionally the main economic activity. The previous "coupled" CAP commodity support schemes led farmers to shift towards highly intensive cropping patterns, in which cotton predominated. Larissa retains 164 000 ha of arable land out of which 28% is under agreement within the Nitrate Reduction Scheme. The survey covered 40 farms participating in the Nitrate Reduction Scheme and ten non-participating farms, selected by a stratified random sampling procedure.

The stated objectives for the Nitrate Reduction Scheme are protection of water resources from over extraction, restoration of quality of ground water and improvement in soil fertility.

The composition of environmental issues in terms of sub-issues is shown in Table 11.3. For the case of Larissa, the "natural resources' issue is the only one involved in the "intended effects" category, while all other issues are represented in the 'non-intended' category. Table 11.4 shows the AFI scores for participants and non-participants for both environmental effects categories in the sample.

As far as the environmental effects of participants and non-participants derived from the stated objectives of the scheme are concerned, the first seem to score higher both in the total AFI and in the "natural resources" Issues, which solely represents this category, but these differences are not significant. For environmental effects not related to stated objectives, participants score better in the two issue level AFI and subsequently in the total AFI. All differences in the category of effects not directly targeted by the policy were significant.

Table 11.3. Larissa Case Study Area: Issues and sub-issues

Issue	Sub-issue	Status in stated objectives Mentioned=S/Not mentioned=NS
Natural resources	Water quality	S
	Water quantity	S
	Soil Quality/fertility	S
	Erosion /desertification	NS
	CO2 emissions	NS
Biodiversity	Species	NS
	Ecosystem	NS
Landscape	Landscape	NS

Source: Christopoulos (2011).

Table 11.4. Larissa Case Study Area: AFIs for participants and non-participants, by effect category

	Overall effects				Mentioned in stated objectives				Not mentioned in stated objectives			
	Total	NR[1]	B[2]	L[3]	Total	NR	B	L	Total	NR	B	L
Participants	4.91	5.45	4.88	1.56	5.46	5.46	-	-	4.89	5.41	4.88	1.56
Non-participants	4.11	5.00	3.61	0.15	4.99	4.99	-	-	4.13	5.04	3.61	0.15

1. Natural resources. 2. Biodiversity. 3. Landscape.

Source: Christopoulos (2011).

11.5 Discussion

The conventional olive groves in Mani were already managed in a very extensive way even before the implementation of the organic farming scheme, because of the steep and hilly terrain and the advanced age of the farmers due to outmigration of the younger population. Consequently, AES-induced changes in input use, especially in this area where irrigation is not a common practice, have not been significant.

In the case of Larissa, although the stated objectives of the AES were clearly targeted exclusively towards "natural resources," the differences in environmental performance between participant and non-participant farms, as measured by the AFI methodology, were *not* statistically significant in relation to these stated objectives, while they were significant in relation to other environmental impacts.

It may be that the stated objectives are not addressed with sufficient precision by this particular policy. The non-significant differences in the natural resources AFI may be due to the fact that the NR-related practices encouraged by the scheme (largely input reduction) were also followed by non-participants for other reasons. The survey took place during the second year of implementation of the new CAP decoupled payments, which removed the incentive for farmers to follow intensive production patterns. Thus, input reduction was a strategy followed by both groups of farms.

On the other hand, AFI comparison suggests that the AES under examination had a positive effect on biodiversity and landscape, although these outcomes were not directly targeted by the scheme's stated objectives. The conclusion that the AES is having beneficial effects on biodiversity and landscape coincides with stakeholder perceptions: "*the fields are greener now*" (wheat, barley and other autumn crops) "*in contrast to black*" (fallow during the winter sown to spring crops).

For most scheme evaluations, the participatory process provides a means of describing the hierarchy of environmental priorities in a transparent manner, information that is often lacking in scheme literature. The participatory element and stakeholder consultation lends credibility to an evaluation. However, the problems related to the selection of stakeholders for the consultation process and the possible bias associated with it are still a major unsolved problem of the methodology. Furthermore, the probability of strategic behaviour of the selected local stakeholders is increased, since they are asked to evaluate, even if indirectly, the application of an AES that could be a considerable financial support for the farming sector and the economy in their region, as was the case in Larissa. This could lead to results of limited reliability.

The first-level evaluation (FLE) can identify the level of relevance between the policy measure objectives and the local or regional environmental problems. The value added through the involvement of local stakeholders rather than, or as well as, national stakeholders could be seen in that the former are usually better placed to appreciate the effective implementation of a measure (Mauchline *et al.*, 2011) and can identify geographical hot spots for action (Penker, 2009). Nevertheless, one should be cautious about the results of such an exercise, since in quite a few cases, some of the important environmental issues are either not perceived as such by local stakeholders or, although their importance is admitted, they are not associated with farming practices. This could be due either to the absence of an environmentally sensitive agency, in the form of an NGO or a research institution, or to the importance of agriculture in the area both in economic as well as in social terms. An example of that would be the case of an area characterised by a highly intensive monoculture where biodiversity is not seen to be of much interest. Excessive use of pesticides would be perceived as a problem only if resistance to certain pesticides developed or beneficial organisms were damaged, while the effects of pesticides on wildlife flora and fauna would usually be considered as secondary.

The Nitrate Reduction Scheme, in Larissa, failed to produce significant environmental effects regarding the stated objectives, indicating a lack of additionality as far as these objectives are concerned. Together with the beneficial collateral environment impacts not directly targeted by the design of the measure, these results suggest that the design of this measure should be seriously questioned.

The second-level evaluation (SLE), by zooming in on the stakeholder groups related to specific indicators, can give a clearer picture of the environmental state of affairs in the area concerned. It is through this approach that the actual implementation of the measure is put under the microscope, making visible the specific actions or farming practices applied. In that sense, the SLE, as part of the AFI participatory method, should help to reduce the distance between the policy making authorities at EU, MS, and regional level, communicating relevant information in a clear cut and quantified way between the afore-mentioned authorities.

In cases where robust impact models are lacking, an additional value of the process is that the method analysed strengthens the linkages of farming practices with the environmental outcomes. However, even in the cases where experts are asked to establish such a relationship, one cannot exclude the possibility of strategic behaviour. Hence, one could suggest that the use of the AFI approach could be a possible provisional alternative in the absence of quantified and reliable impact models but only up to a point.

The AFI has been implemented in 14 different agri-environmental contexts so far (Mauchline *et al.*, 2011). This chapter illustrated the use of the methodology for evaluating the environmental performance of farms for two AESs and in the two areas reported here. In the first case study, it showed that the policy design was insufficient to deliver the environmental objectives, since there was no noticeable difference between participants and non-participants. In the second case study, it revealed that the environmental benefits were of a collateral nature and the policy design did not fulfil the stated environmental objectives. Through the two distinctive parts of the method, the FLE and the SLE, the AFI can make a useful input into the designing process of an agri-environmental policy measure through swift relay of clear cut information among the competent authorities, while still in the phase of policy design. In that sense, the current chapter argues that it the use of participatory approaches would be essential for the development of an adequate and efficient *ex ante* evaluation mechanism. The informational and temporal gaps in the policy cycle, as applied in the case of agri-environmental policy measures, could be closed or shortened to a certain degree through use of the AFI methodology as a participatory, multi-criterion and indicator-based assessment tool, with attributes that make it a good candidate for such use.

Notes

1. Stamatios Christopoulos, MTT Agrifood Research Finland / Economic Research Unit and George Vlahos, Department of Agricultural Economics and Rural Development, Agricultural University of Athens.

2. This is also frequent in other sectors. For example, pollution caused by transport is more intense at peak periods.

3. Conclusions regarding significant differences between the two groups are based on a 2-sided *t*-test of the difference between their means, at the 5% significance level.

References

Andersen, E., J. Primdahl, J.J. Oñate, B. Peco, C. Cummings, J. Aquirre, J. Schramek, and K. Knickel (1999), "Environmental effects of Agri-environmental Measures Implemented under Reg. 2078/92", in: Schramek, J., Biehl, D., Buller, H., Wilson, G. (Eds.), *Implementation and effectiveness of Agri-environmental schemes established under Regulation 2078/92*. Final Consolidated Report. Project FAIR 1, CT95-274, Vol.1. Institut für ländliche Strukturforschung, Frankfurt, pp. 135-162.

Baldock, D. and P. Lowe (1996), "The Development of European Agri- Environment Policy", in Whitby, M. (eds.), *The European Environment and CAP Reform: Policies and Prospects for Conservation*, CAB International, Wallingford, pp. 8-25.

Buller, H. (1999), "Regulation 2078: patterns of implementation", in H. Buller, G.A. Wilson, and A. Höll (eds), *Agri-environmental policy in the European Union*. Aldershot: Ashgate, pp. 219-253.

Carey, P.D., C.Short, C. Morris, J. Hunt, A. Priscott, M. Davis, C. Finch, N. Curry, W. Little, M. Winter, A. Parkin, and L.G. Firbank (2003), The multi-disciplinary evaluation of a national agri-environment scheme, *Journal of Environmental Management,* Vol. 69, pp. 71–91

Christopoulos, S. (2011), "Contribution to the development and trial of a pilot system for the evaluation of agri-environmental measures in Greece", unpublished PhD thesis, University of the Aegean, Department of Environment, Mytilene (in Greek).

Cooper, T., K. Hart, and D. Baldock (2010), *The provision of public goods through agriculture in the European Union*, Report prepared for DG Agriculture and Rural Development, Contract No. 30-CE-0233091/00-28, Institute for European Environmental Policy: London.

Damianos,D. and N. Giannakopoulos (2002), Farmers participation in agri-environmental schemes in Greece. *British Food Journal*. Vol. 104, pp. 261-273

European Commission (1999), *Impact of agri-environment measures*, Collated by Frank Fay, *ec.europa.eu/agriculture/envir/report/ en/2078_en/report.htm.*

European Commission (1998), *State of application of regulation (EEC) No 2078/92: Evaluation of Agri-Environment Programmes*, DGVI Commission Working Document, VI/7655/98, European Commission, DG Agriculture, Brussels.

European Commission (2000a). *Common Evaluation Questions with Criteria and Indicators Part A*, European Commission, DG Agriculture, Brussels.

European Commission (2000b). *Common Evaluation Questions with Criteria and Indicators Part D*, European Commission, DG Agriculture, Brussels.

European Commission (2000c). *Indicators for the integration of environmental concerns into the common agricultural policy* (COM (2000) 20 Final). Communication from the Commission to the Council and the European Parliament. European Commission, DG Agriculture, Brussels.

European Commission (2001), *Statistical information needed for indicators to monitor the integration of environmental concerns into the common agricultural policy* (COM (2001) 144 Final), Communication from the Commission to the Council and the European Parliament. European Commission, DG Agriculture, Brussels.

European Commission (2006), *Rural Development 2007-2013 Handbook on Common Monitoring and Evaluation Framework*, Guidance document, European Commission, DG Agriculture, Brussels.

European Commission (2005), *Agri-environment Measures. Overview on General Principles, Types of Measures and Application*, Directorate General for Agriculture and Rural Development. Unit G-4 - Evaluation of Measures applied to Agriculture, Studies. March 2005.

European Commission (2009), *Agriculture in the European Union - Statistical and economic information 2008*, Brussels.

European Environmental Agency (2005a), *Agriculture and environment in EU-15 – the IRENA indicator report*, Report No.6/2005, European Environment Agency, Copenhagen.

European Environmental Agency (2005b), *IRENA Indicator Fact Sheet, IRENA 1 – Area under agri-environment support*, European Environment Agency, Copenhagen.

European Environmental Agency (2006), *Integration of Environment into EU Agricultural Policy – the IRENA indicator-based assessment report*, Report No.2/2006, European Environment Agency, Copenhagen.

European Parliament (1998), *Report on the report from the Commission to the Council and the European Parliament on the application of Council Regulation (EEC) no. 2078/92 on agricultural production methods compatible with the requirements of the protection of the environment and the maintenance of the countryside* (COM 97-620 final), European Parliament, Brussels.

Finn, J.A., F. Bartolini, D. Bourke, I. Kurz, and D. Viaggi (2009), "*Ex post* environmental evaluation of agri-environment schemes using experts' judgments and multi-criteria analysis", *Journal of Environmental Planning and Management*, Vol. 52, pp. 717-737.

Finn, J.A., D. Bourke, I. Kurz, and L. Dunne (2007). Estimating the environmental performance of agri-environmental schemes via use of expert consultations Final report of the ITAES project. *merlin.lusignan.inra.fr/ITAES/website/Publicdeliverables*.

Finn, J.A., Kurz, I. and D. Bourke (2008). Multiple factors control the environmental effectiveness of agri-environmental schemes: implications for design and evaluation, *Irish Journal of Agri-Environmental Research*, Vol. 6, pp. 45-56.

Juntti, M. and C. Potter (2002). Interpreting and Reinterpreting Agri-environmental policy: Communication, trust and knowledge in the implementation process. *Sociologia Ruralis*, Vol. 42, pp. 215-232

Juntti, M., and G.A. Wilson (2004), "Actor networks and the implementation of policies affecting desertification in Southern Europe", in G.A. Wilson and M. Juntti (eds.), *Unravelling desertification. Policies and actor networks in Southern Europe*. Wageningen Academic Publishers, 191-221.

Kleijn, D., F. Berendse, R. Smit and N. Gilissen (2001). "Agri-environment schemes do not effectively protect biodiversity in Dutch agricultural landscapes", *Nature*, Vol. 413, pp. 723-725.

Kleijn, D., W.J. Sutherland, (2003), "How effective are European agri-environment schemes in conserving and promoting biodiversity?" *Journal of Applied Ecology*, Vol. 40, pp. 947-969

Knickel, K. and N. Kasperczyk (2009), The Agri-environmental Footprint: Assessing the agri-environmental performance of farms in participatory and regionally adaptive ways. *Outlook on Agriculture* 38, 195-203.

Louloudis, L., N. Beopoulos and G. Vlahos (2000). Greece: late implementation of agri-environmental policies, in H. Buller, G. Wilson, and A. Höll (eds), *Agri-environmental policy in the European Union,* Ashgate, Aldershot, pp. 71-93.

Lowe, P., J. Clark, S. Seymour and N. Ward (1997). *Moralising the Environment: Countryside Change, Farming and Pollution*. Routledge, London.

Mauchline, A., J. Park, D. Westbury, G. Purvis, G. Louwagie, G. Northey, J. Finn, J. Primdahl, H. Vejre, L. Kristensen, J.P. Vesterager, K. Teilman, K. Knickel, N. Kasperczyk, K. Balázs, L. Podmaniczky, G. Vlahos, S. Christopoulos, L. Kröger, J. Aakkula, A.Y. Viikari, S. Mortimer (submitted 2011), "The value of a harmonised, participatory approach to the evaluation of agri-environmental schemes: Testing the Agri-Environmental Footprint Index", *Journal of Land Use Policy*.

Mortimer, S.R., J.R. Park, A.L. Mauchline, K.A.Haysom, D.B. Westbury, G. Purvis, G. Louwagie, G. Northey, J.A. Finn, K. Knickel, N. Kasperczyk, J. Primdahl, H. Vejre, J. Vesterager, L. Kristensen, K. Teilman, L. Podmaniczky, K. Balázs, G. Vlahos, S. Christopoulos, L. Kröger, J. Aakkula, A. Yli-Viikari and J. Peltola (2009), *The Agri-environmental Footprint Index: User's Manual* (Available from *www.footprint.reading.ac.uk/en/publications_en.html*)

Oñate, J.J., E. Andersen, B. Peco, and J. Primdahl (2000), "Agri-environmental schemes and the European agricultural landscapes: the role of indicators as valuing tools for evaluation", *Landscape Ecology*, Vol. 15, pp. 271-280

Oréade Brèche (2005), *Evaluation of Agri-Environmental Measures*, Auzeville, France, available at *ec.europa.eu/agriculture/eval/reports/measures/ex_sum_en.pdf*.

OECD (2003), *Multifunctionality. the policy implications*, OECD Publishing, Paris.

OECD. (1997), *Environmental indicators for agriculture - Volume 1: Concepts and framework*, OECD Publishing, Paris.

OECD (2000), *Environmental indicators for agriculture - Volume3 : Methods and results*, OECD Publishing, Paris.

OECD (1998). *Towards sustainable development environmental indicators*, OECD Publishing, Paris.

OECD (1999). *Environmental indicators for agriculture - Volume 2: Issues and design*, OECD Publishing, Paris.

Paniagua Mazorra, A. (2001), Agri-environmental policy in Spain. The agenda of socio-political developments at the national regional and local levels, *Journal of Rural Studies*, Vol. 17, pp. 81-97

Park, J.R., M.J. Stabler, S.R. Mortimer, P.J. Jones, D.J. Ansell and G.P.D. Parker (2004), "The use of a multiple criteria decision analysis to evaluate the effectiveness of landscape and habitat enhancement mechanisms: an example from the South Downs," *Journal of Environmental Planning and Management*, Vol. 47, pp. 773-793.

Peco, B., F. Suárez, J.J. Oñate, J.E. Malo, and J. Aguirre (2000), "Spain: first tentative steps towards an agri-environmental programme", In: Buller, H., Wilson. G.A. and A. Höll (eds), *Agri-environmental policy in the European Union,* Aldershot: Ashgate.

Penker, M. (2009), "Landscape governance for or by the local population? A property rights analysis in Austria", *Land Use Policy* Vol. 26, pp. 947–953.

Peschard, D., M.B. Galan and H. Boizard (2004), "Tools for evaluation the environmental impact of agricultural practices at the farm level: analysis of five agri-environmental methods", OECD expert meeting on farm management for agriculture and the environment, New Zealand 8-12 March.

Primdahl, J, B. Peco, J. Schramek, E. Andersen and J.J. Oñate (2003), "Environmental effects of agri-environmental schemes in Western Europe", *Journal of Environmental Management,* Vol. 67, pp. 129-138

Primdahl, J., J.P. Vesterager, J.A. Finn, G. Vlahos, L. Kristensen, and H. Vejre (2010), "Current use of impact models for agri-environment schemes and potential for improvements of policy design and assessment", *Journal of Environmental Management*, Vol. 91, pp. 1245-1254.

Purvis, G., G. Louwagie, G. Northey, S. Mortimer, J. Park, A. Mauchline, J. Finn, J. Primdahl, H. Vejre, J.P. Vesterager, K. Knickel, N. Kasperczyk, K. Balazs, G. Vlahos, S. Christopoulos, and J. Peltola (2009), "Conceptual development of a harmonised method for tracking change and evaluating policy in the agri-environment: The Agri-environmental Footprint Index", *Environmental Science and Policy,* Vol. 12, pp. 321-337.

Smeets, E and R. Weterings (1999), *Environmental indicators: Typology and overview*, Technical Report No 25, European Environment Agency (EEA), Copenhagen.

Stoate C., A. Baldi, P. Beja, N.D. Boatman, I. Herzon, A. van Doorn, G.R. de Snoo, L. Rakosy and C. Ramwell (2009), "Ecological impacts of early 21st century agricultural change in Europe – A review", *Journal of Environmental Management,* Vol. 91, pp. 22–46.

World Trade Organisation (1994), *Uruguay Agreement: Agreement on Agriculture: Annex 2,* Washington, D.C.

V. MARKET-BASED SOLUTIONS TO AGRI-ENVIRONMENTAL POLICY

Chapter 12

Cost effectiveness of CAP greening measures: An *ex ante* evaluation in Italy

Andrea Povellato and Davide Longhitano[1]

A new policy tool that creates a market for ecosystem services provided by agriculture is analysed, and compared with mandatory requirements targeting the provision of these services. We quantify the potential regional supply curve of ecosystem services, using as a proxy the amount of carbon that could be sequestered by permanent grassland. A minimum data approach is used to integrate the spatial heterogeneity of the agro-systems with economic data collected through FADN in a case study area (Veneto, Italy). Results suggest that tradable permits (floor and trade) could be more efficient than policy based on direct payments or mandatory standards, although the largest provision of ecosystem service (carbon sequestered) is achieved with mandatory mechanism.

The identification of policy measures with good cost effectiveness is a priority in the discussion of future scenarios for agriculture and rural development. Within the framework of agri-environmental policies, several analyses and proposals have tried to identify new tools to ensure the provision of environmental goods and services at a reasonable cost to society as a whole. The actions proposed, other than regulatory standards, are: 1) proportionate incentives to achieve measurable environmental results, 2) selection of farmer participants who provide greater environmental benefits, or who require less compensation for the same environmental service, 3) additional taxes on the use of potentially polluting products, 4) creation of new markets through tradable permits (Cooper *et al.*, 2009; RISE, 2009). Interest is growing in the last-mentioned approach among stakeholders and policy makers due to its potential for more effective provision of public goods, taking into account the different profitability levels of various farm typologies. On the other hand, there are often limitations to its use, mainly due to the administrative burdens resulting from the large number of farms involved. Although these limitations could increase private costs, it is of interest to analyse the overall cost effectiveness of these new market-based instruments relative to that of more traditional policies such as regulation and agri-environment payments.

In this chapter, we examine the likely consequences of implementing different policy mechanisms designed to promote the production of ecosystem services in a case study area, the Veneto region in Italy. As a proxy for ecosystem services, the analysis uses the amount of carbon sequestered from the atmosphere through less intensive farming systems such as hay meadows and grazing land (MG) in comparison to more intensive arable cropping systems (AC). Meadows and grazing systems represent the most extensive form of forage farming and they are often confined to areas not well suited to other agricultural land uses or where their environmental and landscape benefits are emphasised. Meadows and grazing land play important ecological roles linked to the fact that they are dynamic and complex natural systems and reach a high degree of biodiversity (many species of plants living in balance with the mineral substrate). In particular, these systems are characterised by their ability to sequester atmospheric CO_2 and store it directly in soil.

In recent years, the decoupling of CAP farm payments has slowed down the previous trend observed in Italy towards arable crop cultivation in order to receive direct payments. Meadows and grazing land have therefore been under less pressure. However, the gradual intensification of crop production remains a latent threat. In fact, in the most fertile plains it is becoming very rare to find MG, which are concentrated in marginal areas that have no alternative profitable use, such as mountain (Povellato, 2010). Against this background, we investigate the potential impact on land use of implementing three different policy measures: 1) an "agri-environmental scheme" in which farms voluntarily allocate a minimum area of farmland to those crops with targeted payments; 2) a mandatory scheme, assuming that the obligation to allocate farmland to meadows and grazing must be fulfilled by all farms that do not reach a minimum threshold; 3) a permit trading scheme where a tradable permit mechanism reallocates among farms the obligation to allocate a total amount of farmland to meadows and grazing. The analysis is based on the FADN database and restricted to the Veneto region.

12.1 The minimum data approach and the supply of ecosystem services

The theoretical framework

"Ecosystem services" (ES) have been defined as *the conditions and processes through which natural ecosystems, and the species that make them up, sustain and fulfil human life* (Daily, 1997). The Millennium Ecosystem assessment has classified the ES into four categories: provisioning, supporting, cultural and regulating services (Zhang *et al.*, 2007). Examples of ecosystem services could be the detoxification of harmful molecules (e.g. phytoremediation), air and water purification, soil fertility enhancement, climate mitigation, natural pest control and so on (Salzman *et al.* 2001). From this point of view, ES are public goods justifying public policy to increase their production. Agriculture is an activity that can produce ecosystem services, particularly as a function of the way it uses land resources (Antle, 2007). In theory, an efficient agri-environmental policy should aim to increase the provision of ecosystem services by imposing changes on farming practices while limiting the impacts on agricultural production. Maximising the value of the resource occurs where the marginal increase in the value of ecosystem services just balances the marginal loss in the market value of agricultural production (Antle, 2007), and this point may well be reached at positive levels of agricultural output. Finally, an efficient policy should also take spatial heterogeneity into account, because ES are site-specific and are linked at peculiar features such as land, climate and distance to market.

In this study, we consider the supply of ecosystem services provided by agriculture in the form of atmospheric carbon sequestered in agricultural soils, considering that this service is a function of various site-specific parameters like soil type and vegetation cover, cultivation practices used, topography, history of land use and microclimate. We assume that, given two alternative land uses – intensive arable crops (AC) and meadows and grazing systems (MG) – the transition from one system to another implies a change in the amount of carbon stored in soils. More precisely, the carbon sequestered by MG is significantly greater than that of intensive arable land[2]. As reported in the literature, the soil occupied by permanent forage systems in Europe shows a positive average estimated annual value of 0.52 tonnes of carbon stored per hectare, compared with the negative value of -0.84 tC/ha^{-1} y^{-1} in intensive arable land (Vleeshouwers and Verhagen, 2002).

Antle and Valdivia (2006) introduced a simple method for estimating the approximate value of the expected supply of ecosystem service provided by agriculture. Their *minimum data approach* (MDA) calculates the supply of ES in a given region by combining site-specific biophysical aspects with more general information on economic characteristics of agricultural systems. In this chapter, we try to apply an empirical analysis based on the MDA described in Antle and Valdivia (2006) and developed in several other recent works (Claessens *et al.*, 2009; Noalukenge *et al.*, 2009; Stoorvogel *et al.*, 2009; Antle *et al.*, 2010). We consider that each production system has a specific production of ES, and we assume that an increase in ES supply involves shifting to a more eco-efficient system, implying a specific opportunity cost for each management choice. From the spatial distribution of these opportunity costs, it is then possible to derive the expected supply of ES.

We estimate the potential supply of carbon sequestered in the Veneto region. The approach is based on a static analysis that estimates the proportion of farmers responding positively to incentives to convert to MG from AC, subject to an initial mandatory area threshold (e.g. 5% of total UAA). In the initial, no-policy situation, the choice whether to cultivate AC or MG depends on the profitability of alternative land uses. For simplicity, we assume here that there is no additional cost to switching from one farming system to another[3]. On this basis, the farmer chooses between the AC and MG systems as a function of return per unit (e.g. gross margin per hectare). An increase in the supply of ecosystem services can lead to important losses in agricultural productivity with a direct impact on farm income. Because of this, without policies that provide specific incentives, ES would be provided only by farms for which MG represents the most profitable form of farming (e.g. livestock farms). The supply of ecosystem services in this "private equilibrium" is thus associated with the provision of market goods and does not take into account their additional value to society. Only an appropriate intervention (e.g. payments offered to farmers) would stimulate an increase of the ecosystem services (Nalukenge *et al.*, 2009).[4]

Assuming that the choice can only occur between two agricultural systems, such as AC and MG, in analytical terms the private equilibrium is based on maximising expected profit expressed by $v = v(p, g, s)$, where p is the vector of output and variable input prices, g is the geographic location and s is the index comparison of the agro-systems (i.e. s_1 for intensive arable land and s_2 for meadows and grazing), and the management decision will be taken on the basis of opportunity cost (oc) for each farm considered, where

$$oc(p, g) = v(p.g.s_1) - v(p, g, s_2). \tag{1}$$

If $oc \geq 0$, land will be allocated to AC, otherwise it will go to MG. A *caveat* is required concerning the simplifying assumption of only two agricultural systems, which aggregate several crops with different gross margins. Furthermore, in the case of MG, the land allocation is made mainly in connection with the livestock production system. Therefore, opportunity cost should not be interpreted in terms of the market price of fodder only, but has also to be based on the processing value, where that value is given by the difference between the final products market value (e.g. dairy production) and the amount of the production costs. These considerations imply the existence of part-allocation in some farms, where AC and MG coexist, even when opportunity cost is non-zero.

By extending the analysis to all the farms in the regions spatially defined, the spatial distribution function (density function) of the relative opportunity costs at a given price can be determined:

$$r(p) = \int_{-\infty}^{0} \varphi(oc) doc, \tag{2}$$

where $0 \leq r(p) \leq 1$ is the share of land allocated to MG in the private equilibrium (Antle and Valdivia, 2006; Antle *et al.*, 2010). The expected value of the overall regional supply of ES [$S(p)$] in a given period (one year in this case study) and in a given area of H hectares can be derived from this function:

$$S(p) = r(p)H.e(g), \tag{3}$$

where $e(g)$ represents the amount of carbon sequestered annually from the atmosphere and stored in agricultural soil when is occupied by meadows and grazing systems for each site considered.

Assuming now the existence of a measure that encourages farmers to increase the supply of ES, such as represented by the additional payment per unit of ES product (p_S), a new equilibrium can be reached and equation (1) becomes

$$oc_{ES}(p, g) = v(p, g, s_1) - [v(p, g, s_2) + p_S e(g)]. \tag{4}$$

Equation (4) indicates that farmers convert arable land to grassland if and only if $oc_{ES} < 0$. The spatial distribution of opportunity costs in the presence of specific incentives, expressed by price p_S, is now given by

$$r(p, p_S) = \int_{0}^{p_S} \varphi(oc) doc, \tag{5}$$

where $r(p, p_S)$ represents the share of land allocated to MG when the opportunity cost is between zero and p_S. The resulting value of the supply of ES is

$$S(p, p_S) = S(p) + r(p, p_S)H.e(g), \quad (6)$$

which represents the total amount of ES corresponding to the range of incentives p_S. The value of the function is the sum of all units of services produced (tonnes of carbon sequestered) on the additional land units converted from intensive arable land to meadows and grazing. The properties of the curve $S(p, p_S)$ are determined by the shape of the density function of opportunity costs and the quantity per unit of ecosystem services provided (Antle *et al.*, 2010). In the farming context, therefore, three cases may occur in the formation of ES supply:

- $oc < 0$, so the allocation of MG area is preferred to AC without specific incentives,
- $oc_{ES} < 0$, meaning that AC are lower-cost than MG and so land use is changed only in the presence of an incentive,
- $oc \geq 0$ and $oc_{ES} > 0$, so that AC is always lower-cost than MG for the entire range of expected payments.

Assuming a range of payments per unit of ES produced, the analysis was repeated for each value derived from the corresponding expected values of land converted to MG and then the potential supply of ecosystem services in each provincial zone was obtained separately. The slope of the curve obtained is positive, because for each specific increase in the incentive price there is an increase in farmer willingness to participate in such contracts, according to the technical potential of their land opportunity costs incurred (Antle and Stoorvogel, 2006).

The case study

The research was based on knowledge of the average carbon fluxes for each farming systems and the opportunity costs derived from the difference between gross margin in both activities. The biophysical data on the flows of carbon sequestered by various land uses in Europe have been taken from the results of the CESAR model (Vleeshouwers and Verhagen, 2002; Freibauer *et al.*, 2004; Sousanna *et al.*, 2004),[5] while the economic information necessary to simulate the decision model is derived from the FADN sample for the Veneto region in the year 2007. More precisely, the farm sample contains 540 observations and it has been selected according to altitude limit of the Veneto plain. The spatial dimension of reference has therefore been created by layering the sample on the basis of belonging to the province of farms creating six groups (Verona, Vicenza, Treviso, Venice, Padua and Rovigo). As mentioned, in order to limit the analysis to agricultural systems for herbaceous cropping systems to intensive arable land and grassland, the farms sampled include only those with utilised agricultural area (UAA) devoted to herbaceous crops. The systems considered were built on two macro-aggregates. The first system (s_1) includes acreage for cereal, legumes, industrial crops, vegetables, flowers, alternated fodder and field crops in general, while the second system s_2 is based on the UAA devoted to hay meadows (monophyta and polyphyta), permanent pasture and pasture-fallow production. For each macro-aggregate we computed economic parameters, such as the aggregate output for each activity, the quantities sold and the respective monetary values, the variable costs of management (including the expenditure items for seeds, fertilisers, pesticides, rental farm equipment, irrigation and other expenses), and on-farm use of farm output. The variables are the average yields unit, the unit explicit costs, average prices and therefore the overall gross income. Finally were weighted appropriately and extended to the entire population of regional farms considered.

The main assumption regards the requirement for all farms must have a sufficient area to permanent grassland managed according the standards of good and sustainable agricultural practices. On this basis, in Veneto, limiting the analysis only to the agricultural land devoted to herbaceous crops in lowland areas, 91% of the farms do not have permanent forage crops, while about 9% have meadows and grazing systems. The farms that adopt MG in their land use plan devote a large share of the UAA, due to the presence of livestock breeding.

Payments for ecosystem services

The MD approach was implemented assuming a 5% increase of UAA allocated to MG. The knowledge of the unit values of costs and average yields allowed us to revise the gross margins on new configurations of crops and then the opportunity costs calculated as the difference between the first and second system. As explained above, the profitability of two systems can be given by the difference in opportunity cost, which is heterogeneous and spatially explicit.

In this step, we estimated the opportunity costs, determining the associated spatial distributions function (density function) and the spatial distribution of opportunity cost per unit of ecosystem service (tonnes of carbon sequestered) in the Veneto region. From this distribution function, we derived the potential supply of land convertible to MG systems expressed in terms of the range of payments per unit of carbon stored in soil. The sensitivity analysis was conducted based on the threshold of payment ranging from EUR 50-EUR 350/t of carbon, with intermediate steps of EUR 50/t.

Figure 12.1. Regional land supply at different ecosystem service prices

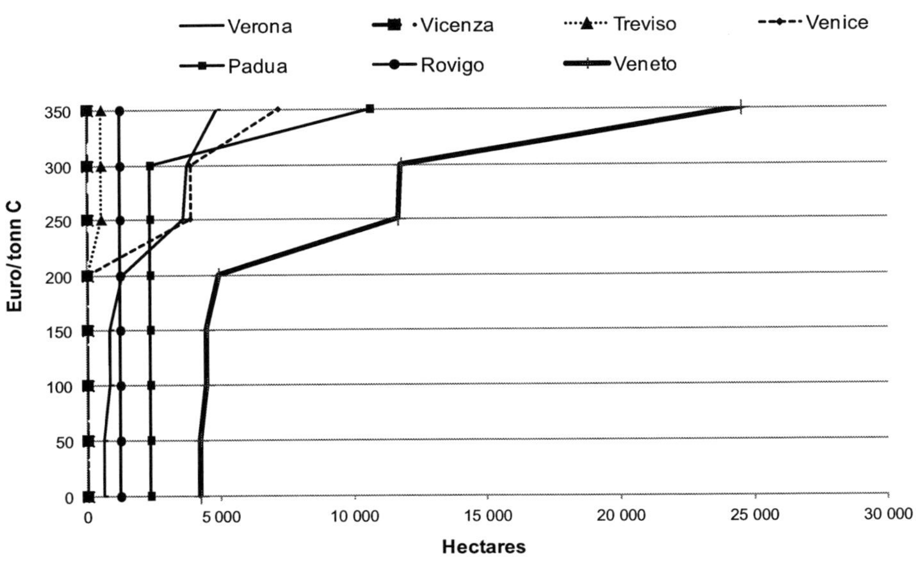

The results show that in the baseline case (without incentives) the share of farms that find it profitable to switch to a system producing more MG in Veneto is quite negligible, which in terms of area is little more than 4 000 hectares. In the presence of a policy based on payments per unit of ES provided, the amount of UAA converted to MG increases. Assuming a maximum ecosystem service price of EUR 350 t, the area converted reaches almost 25 000 hectares with an increase from baseline measured as 480% (Figure 12.1). At level of the six selected provinces, the results highlight some very interesting variations, due to the strong spatial heterogeneity discussed above. In particular, in the provinces Vicenza and Rovigo, there is no conversion for any size of payment in the range assumed. The level of EUR 200/t acts as a threshold: below this level, only in Verona is there a small amount of conversion whereas beyond which conversion in three provinces starts to be marked. For the Veneto region as a whole, supply of ES becomes relatively elastic to the payment above this level.

12.2 The floor-and-trade mechanism

Among the tradable permit instruments, the floor-and-trade (FT) mechanism has been proposed for the first time by the *Country Land and Business Association* (CLA, 2009; RISE 2009). Given a minimum quantity of environmental goods that must be provided by each farm to meet its obligations with respect to sustainable farming,[6] the FT mechanism allows each farm to provide the environmental good or to buy the share of environmental goods from other farms that have any surplus, according to which is more profitable.

In the example analysed here, with a FT mechanism, each farm would be free to decide whether to provide the environmental good (MG land) directly itself or, if other productive land-uses are more profitable, to buy its share of public good provision from other farms that produce a surplus. The introduction of this obligation associated with the possibility of trading with other farms creates a new market for environmental goods provided by agriculture. When the amount of a given environmental good produced by a farm exceeds the required minimum amount (*floor*) a "credit" is generated that can be traded (*trade*) with farms that, under the intensive and specialised production, need to comply with the minimum requirement. The system is flexible in allowing the production of environmental goods to be allocated on the basis of their opportunity costs, thereby in theory achieving a more efficient factor allocation.

This mechanism is similar to the "cap-and-trade" measure implemented in recent years for the emissions of greenhouse gases by some industrial sectors in Europe (Emission Trading System) and since the seventies in the United States for the control of air pollution. There are several pre-conditions for the establishment of a market for tradable permits: there must be a surplus of tradable goods, trades must be legally applicable and enforceable, the market must be permanent and the environmental goods must be quantifiable (Tietenberg, 2004, p.271). The measurability of the good subject to FT mechanism is particularly important for agricultural activity, which has various external effects (positive and negative) that are not easily quantifiable as in industrial production.

The quantification of the environmental good can be proxied by the area occupied by particular land uses, possibly related to compliance with certain standards of management. An example of this type of obligation is the "*ecological compensation areas*" or "*ecological priority area*" introduced some years ago in Switzerland as part of cross compliance. Farmers are required to keep part of their land in the form of ecological compensation areas as a condition for receiving direct and ecological support payments (Cooper *et al.*, 2009).

Several European environmental associations have suggested that ecological priority areas should be also included among the environmental standards that farmers must comply within EU countries (BirdLife, 2008). There seems currently to be a gradual recognition in European legislation of the need to preserve natural habitats on farms. First, meadows and grazing lands have been included since the EC Regulation 1782/2003 among the compliance cross requirements for the Single Farm Payment, and this is maintained in EC Regulation 73/2009. Moreover, among the mandatory requirements of compliance, there is an obligation to maintain the "landscape features, including, where appropriate, hedges, ponds, ditches, trees in rows, in groups or isolated and margins fields" and the "creation and/or preservation of *habitat*" has been included as an optional requirement. Thus, it looks as if environmental standards for biodiversity will have an increasingly important role, especially if they involve re-establishing the ecological network composed of semi-natural elements and areas under permanent grassland that in recent decades have undergone a dramatic reduction in Italy as elsewhere in Western Europe (Farmer *et al.*, 2008).

Considering the need to increase the supply of ecosystem services provided by agriculture, we could envisage an obligation for each farm to identify "areas of ecological priorities" at least equivalent to a minimum percentage of UAA (e.g. 5% or 10%). In these cases, the FT mechanism could be used to allow farmers to adopt the most appropriate solution for themselves in terms of land allocation, thus ensuring that the effect of the obligation on farm income is minimised. The level of the threshold values is crucial not only for creating the conditions for exchanging permits, but also for the cost effectiveness of the measure. In fact, the increase in (private) costs incurred by farmers (whether because of direct provision or purchasing credits) should be compared with the (social) environmental benefits achieved in rural areas.

The spatial design of tradable permit mechanisms is another important aspect. As already noted in the case of cap-and-trade applied to specific cases of pollution, farms located in protected areas or high nature value areas should not be allowed to compensate the lack of "ecosystem services credits" on other farms that are outside of these areas. Equally important is the choice of the size of areas that, if very large, may allow substantial inter-zonal reallocation (mountain areas with the most credits could easily offset the more intensive lowland areas), while greater segmentation would lead to a better distribution of ecosystem services within zones (e.g. a certain threshold must be met within the lowland areas). These last two examples are not neutral in terms of the environmental effects achieved and therefore the effects on environmental quality of areas should be carefully considered.

Finally, from an economic viewpoint, in the presence of a FT mechanism, a farm decides to fulfil the mandatory requirement only if the difference between the loss of traditional agricultural production income and the opportunity cost of maintaining these ecological priority areas is lower than the cost of acquiring this ecosystem service from other farms. Since the ecological priority areas cover a very limited area, it should be assumed that there are no large structural changes and then there is no change in fixed costs. This leads us to think that gross margin is the most appropriate indicator to evaluate opportunity costs.

The potential impact of ecological priority areas in Veneto

Starting from the FADN data used in the earlier analysis, we now investigate the impact of introducing "ecological priority areas" under two alternative policy mechanisms: the mandatory approach and the floor-and-trade (FT) approach. The mandatory approach involves the obligation to allocate a minimum area of land to MG systems on each farm, changing current land use if this is necessary. The FT mechanism allows the introduction of a market in tradable ES permits, which refer to minimal areas of meadows and grazing. The simulation assumes three MG thresholds at farm level (5%, 10% and 15%). In all, these assumptions provide six alternative scenarios, which are compared to the baseline.

Table 12.1 shows that in the Veneto, on a currently utilised agricultural area of about 545 260 ha, only 6% is occupied by MG (32 715 ha). For the three minimum thresholds given above, the required MG land should be 27.263, 54.526 and 81.789 hectares, respectively. Hence, in the case of the 5% threshold, no further conversion from AC to MG is needed, while in the cases of higher thresholds an additional share of MG must be provided. These same thresholds apply with both approaches. However, the two approaches could have different results in terms of farm-specific land use allocation. With the mandatory approach, each single farm must meet the threshold, while in the FT scenario the single farm can also sell or buy the option to cultivate MG on the basis of its opportunity cost. The introduction of the new standard leads to the creation of two different farm typologies: farms with a MG deficit and farms with a MG surplus.

Our investigation of the floor and trade instrument analyses the decisions of farmers either to self-produce MG or to contract MG in the market according to differences in opportunity costs between individual cropping systems (see the previous section). Any transaction costs between farmers trading permits also have to be taken into account.[7] Therefore, the choice of how much MG to produce is a function of the agricultural system gross margins, transaction costs and minimum thresholds.

In the FT scenario, the final income of the farm may also depend on payments or receipts from trading MG services with other farms. By contrast, in the mandatory scenario, the situation is simpler because there is only a (potential) reallocation of land use on-farm for those farms with a MG deficit, followed by adjustments in gross income. When the threshold is set at 10% or 15%, the situation is complicated because in the presence of FT the problem is not only primarily redistributive, but also implies the need for a proper reconfiguration of the scheme for allocating land. However, in this case also, farmers' decisions regarding how much of their land to devote to MG still depend on opportunity cost, transaction costs and the threshold. In our survey, farms were separated from those in deficit and surplus of MG according to their mandatory share (floor), while the choice between converting own land and trading on the permit market was driven by cost minimisation.

Table 12.1. Distribution of farms and land area in Veneto through meadows and grazing classes on the herbaceous UAA

MG classes	Number of farms	UAA total	AC	MG	Mandatory share	Area of MG deficit on deficit farms	Area of MG surplus on surplus farms
		ha	ha	ha	ha	ha	ha
Minimum threshold: 5% UAA							
without MG	37 272	479 917	479 917	0	23 996	23 996	
MG < 5% UAA	60	1 256	1 216	40	63	23	
MG ≥ 5% UAA	3 755	64 087	31 412	32 675	3 204		29.470
Total	41 088	545 260	512 545	32 715	27 263	24 019	29.470
Net deficit or surplus							5.452
Minimum threshold: 10% UAA							
without MG	37 272	479 917	479 917	0	47 992	47 992	
MG < 10% UAA	505	10 215	9 455	760	1 022	261	
MG ≥ 10% UAA	3 310	55 127	23 173	31 954	5 513		26.442
Total	41 088	545 260	512 545	32 715	54 526	48 253	26.442
Net deficit or surplus						21.811	
Minimum threshold: 15% UAA							
without MG	37 272	479 917	479 917	0	71 988	71 988	
MG < 15% UAA	553	11 331	10 435	896	1 700	803	
MG ≥ 15% UAA	3 262	54 012	22 193	31 818	8 102		23.717
Total	41 088	545 260	512 545	32 715	81 789	72 791	
Net deficit or surplus						49 074	

Note: AC arable crops land, MG meadows and grazing land.

Source: Based on FADN data.

In order to characterise the opportunity cost of producing intensive crops or meadows and grazing in the presence of FT, and identify the point of equilibrium between farms in effective deficit and surplus of MG, we determined the cumulative land distribution functions and then identified the equilibrium (price of ES and quantity traded) as the point of their intersection (Figures 12.2 and 12.3). At this point the opportunity costs (OC) of the two sides of the market in producing MG are equal. This break-even point identifies the price at which it could become profitable for farms in debit (credit) to buy (sell) permits of use in MG in the presence of FT.[8] The area traded is the difference between the obligation required (floor) and the requirements needed to satisfy by the reallocation "intra-farm" because the opportunity cost is less than or equal to the market equilibrium price.

Figure 12.2. Relationship between opportunity cost per marginal hectare and traded area, under FT (10%)

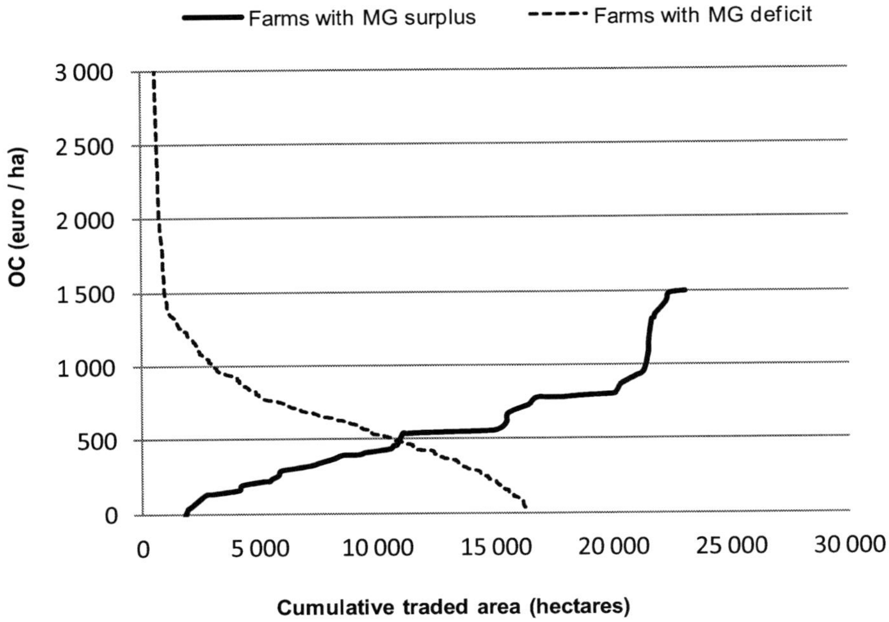

Figure 12.3. Relationship between opportunity cost per marginal hectare and traded area, under FT (15%)

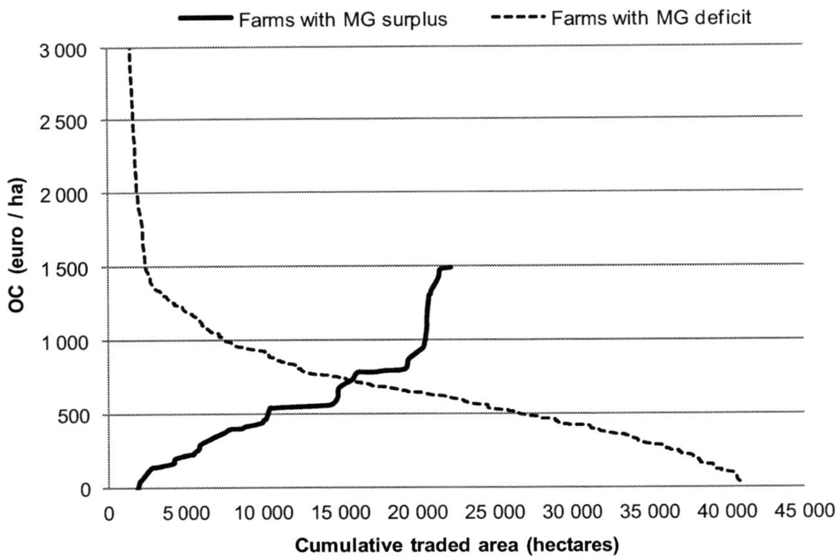

Table 12.2. Results for three scenarios: baseline, floor-and-trade and mandatory

				Baseline		Floor-and-trade scenario				Mandatory scenario			
	Threshold	Number of farms	MG mandatory share	MG land	Gross farm income	MG *Ex post*	Gross farm income			MG *ex post*	Gross farm income		
							Level	Difference from baseline			Level	Difference from baseline	
			ha	ha	EUR mn	ha	EUR mn	EUR mn	%	ha	EUR mn	EUR mn	%
Farms with MG deficit	*5%*	37 332	24 059	40	793	2 768	794	0.1	0.0	24 059	770	-24	-3.0
	10%	37 777	49 013	760	806	11 093	800	-6	-0.8	49 013	759	-47	-5.9
	15%	37 826	73 687	896	807	34 897	786	-22	-2.7	73 687	736	-72	-8.9
Farms with MG surplus	*5%*	3 755	3 204	32 675	65	32 675	65	1	1.0	32 675	65	0	0.0
	10%	3 310	5 513	31 954	52	42 818	56	4	7.8	31 954	52	0	0.0
	15%	3 262	8 102	31 818	51	47 580	58	7	14.7	31 818	51	0	0.0
Total	*5%*	41 088	27 263	32 715	858	35 442	859	1	0.1	56 733	834	-24	-2.8
	10%	41 088	54 526	32 715	858	53 911	856	-2	-0.2	80 968	810	-47	-5.5
	15%	41 088	81 789	32 715	858	82 477	844	-14	-1.6	105 506	786	-72	-8.3

Table 3. Comparison of carbon net flow between floor-and-trade and mandatory scenario for each MG threshold

			Floor-and-trade scenario				Mandatory scenario			
	Threshold	Carbon flow *ex ante*	Carbon flow *ex post*	Carbon net flow	Difference from baseline	Gross income ÷ carbon net flow	Carbon flow *ex post*	Carbon net flow	Difference from baseline	Gross income ÷ Carbon net flow
		000 tonnes	000 tonnes	000 tonnes	%	EUR /ton	000 tonnes	000 tonnes	%	EUR /ton
Farms with MG deficit	*5%*	-404	-400	4	1	26	-371	33	8	-724
	10%	-411	-397	14	3	-438	-345	66	16	-723
	15%	-411	-365	46	11	-466	-312	99	24	-723
Farms with MG surplus	*5%*	-9	-9	27	0	0	-9	0	0	0
	10%	-3	12	15	519	274	-3	0	0	0
	15%	-2	19	21	1 022	346	-2	0	0	0
Total	*5%*	-414	-410	4	1	197	-381	33	8	-724
	10%	-414	-385	29	7	-73	-348	66	16	-723
	15%	-414	-346	68	16	-209	-315	99	24	-723

With regard to effective surplus MG, two different situations may arise. The first is where the opportunity cost of using own land for MG is less than or equal to the equilibrium price, so the farm allocates all its farmland to MG, while in the second case, when the price is higher than the equilibrium opportunity cost, it sells only the MG that is surplus with respect to the threshold. For the new farmland configuration resulting from all reallocations and trading, we calculated final gross margin of the farm, also taking account of permit transactions. At the end of each simulation run (per scenario and per threshold), the amount of carbon sequestered was also computed, according to the coefficient given below.

Figures 12.1 and 12.2 show the supply and demand curves on the permit market for each of the thresholds, 10% and 15%, and the determination of the equilibrium trading price in each case. As might be expected, permits representing a much greater area are traded, and at a higher price, with the higher of these two thresholds.

Table 12.2 shows that the results in terms of land allocation are different in the two scenarios. The mandatory scenario implies that even in the case of 5% threshold, some farms in deficit must convert their AC land to MG land, and hence the total MG area increases by over 21 000 ha to 56 733 ha. With the 10% and 15% thresholds, the total MG area is 80 968 and 105 506 ha, respectively. In the FT scenario, the total land devoted to MG is less than the corresponding threshold in the mandatory scenario (respectively 35 442 ha, 53 911 ha and 82 477 ha), due to the additional possibility to activate an exchange between the two types of farm (Table 12.2).

Table 12.2 also shows the economic impact of the simulations. In the FT scenarios, changes in farm income for deficit farms are relatively low (-2.7% at most), while the situation for those in surplus could bring significant income improvements, estimated at 8% and 15%, respectively, for the 10% and 15% thresholds. With the mandatory scenario, the losses are more substantial, though limited and less than 10%. This outcome suggests that tradable-permit-based measures can minimise income losses and achieve a "win-win" solution.

The verdict changes, however, when we consider the amount of additional ES provided (Table 12.3). In fact, while the threshold of 5% of UAA leads to an estimated extra 8% of sequestered C in the mandatory scenario, in the FT scenario it is just 1%. With the threshold at 10% (15%) of UAA, the carbon sequestered in the mandatory case attains 16% (24%), while is only 7% (16%) with the FT mechanism.

In terms of cost effectiveness, the floor-and-trade mechanism appears more effective than the mandatory tool, considering that around EUR 723 per ton of carbon is the cost of the implementation at farm level in the case of the mandatory scenario, while the loss of income per ton of carbon is much less in the case of FT scenario, although increasing for higher threshold, as expected (EUR 73 per tonne with 10% threshold and EUR 209 per ton with 15% threshold)[9].

12.3 Concluding remarks

The ecosystem services provided from agriculture and classified by the recent Millennium Ecosystem Assessment depend in turn upon a web of supporting and regulating inputs to production (e.g. soil fertility and pollination). Our analysis shows how ecosystem services can be managed using the floor-and-trade mechanism for tradable permits, and that this policy is more efficient and effective than policy based on mandatory requirements alone. This is because tradable permits can achieve a win-win solution, satisfying the interests of both farmers and society, although the higher provision of ecosystem service (i.e. carbon sequestered) could have been achieved with a wholly mandatory mechanism.

The overall results show that, even without payments (first step), a certain percentage of farmers already adopt more eco-efficient practices, providing some ecosystem services. An open question is the assessment of proper transaction and adoption costs (Stoorvogel *et al.*, 2009). As these costs may have a significant impact on the interpretation of the results, we also took them into account (second step). In the FT scenario, farmers with low opportunity costs have an incentive to provide ES because they can sell permits on the market, while farmers for whom MG activity is expensive have an incentive to maintain alternative and intensive cropping systems and will prefer to buy off-setting permits. Hence, in principle, permit markets provide an incentive for landowners to use their land in such a way that a cost-effective allocation of land-use types emerges. In fact, because carbon can only be released if carbon of equivalent value is stored, the ecological effectiveness of the instrument is ensured. There are various advantages from a FT system. In fact, the supply of permits may come from private farmers but also from state authorities and conservation groups that own agricultural land. Ecological consultancies may also buy land to dedicate to providing ecosystem services or cooperate with other farmers (Wissel and Watzold, 2010).

The starting point of the case study is the spatial distribution of opportunity costs, the ecosystem services measured with carbon sequestered in function of different land uses and the reference to the FADN database. In this approach, there are also many weaknesses linked to uncertainty about the effective quantity of carbon sequestered (which depends closely on various site-specific parameters such as soil type and vegetation cover, farm practices, topography, history of land use and microclimate), data accuracy, output and variable input prices, management styles and whether or not livestock are present on the farm. Nevertheless, as a first assessment of the impact at farm level, this study can demonstrate some of the features of a floor-and-trade instrument that make it attractive in the transition of agricultural systems towards a greater degree of sustainability.

It is clear that the implications of the implementation design (threshold values, defined areas, aspects of redistribution, the impact on business costs and so on) have to be studied in more depth. But it should be stressed that the FT mechanism has been proposed by an organisation close to farmers that is very active in seeking win-win solutions that achieve environmental goals while ensuring the income of farms and simplified administrative procedures (CLA, 2009). In other words, environmental organisations need not be the exclusive proponents of eco-friendly proposals; stakeholders from agriculture (e.g. professional organisations, farmers themselves) may also find that they serve their purpose.

There are still many aspects that need to be explored. In Italy, the current availability of data from statistical sources (FADN, ISTAT census and sample surveys) or from administrative sources is such that many studies may already be made.

Notes

1. Istituto Nazionale di Economia Agraria (INEA), Rome.

2. The functional relationship between stored carbon and soil type is generally non-linear, depending on a number of other biophysical parameters. For simplicity, we adopt a linear relationship (Antle *et al.*, 2003).

3. In general, adjustment costs include capital investment, management learning costs and various transaction costs, as well as costs directly related to behavioural and institutional factors that influence the willingness of farmers to change land use (Fuglie and Kascak, 2001; Sunding and Zilberman, 2001). In addition, if the processes that govern the supply of ecosystem services are spatially dependent, more efficient provision may require cooperation between groups of farmers giving rise to coordination costs, which depend on factors like the number of farmers participating and the size of the area. All these additional costs, if they arise, should be included in the computation of opportunity costs.

4. Some processes that determine the provision of ecosystem services like carbon sequestration by agricultural land are spatially independent while others, such as biodiversity or water quality, can be spatially dependent. In these cases it is important to take spatial dependencies into account in the design of an efficient mechanism for providing the same services (Nalukenge *et al.*, 2009). Spatial dependence is also relevant when there are positive externalities affecting opportunity costs (e.g. related to learning associated with the adoption of alternative management practices).

5. The simulation model CESAR (Carbon Emission and Sequestration by Agricultural Land Use) uses a system of carbon balance, which recognises not only the inputs of carbon in plant biomass due to photosynthesis, but also the organic matter accumulated in the soil in quantities related to site-specific soil and weather conditions.

6. These environmental goods are currently provided insufficiently and perceived as scarcest and needful from the society. The "minimum quantity" of these goods could take the form of a share of the agricultural area devoted to permanent grassland, hedges or a certain amount of CO2 stored in soil or biomass.

7. In order to avoid additional complex calculation, we make a simple assumption about transaction cost. Based on some empirical investigation, we assume a cost of EUR 30 per hectare of contracted MG land, without taking into account possible economies of scale due to different size of the contracts.

8. According to our analysis, the equilibrium prices are EUR 490/ha in the case of FT (10%) and EUR 750/ha for FT (15%).

9. The positive figure in the case of 5% threshold refers to a very small amount of carbon flow.

References

Antle, J.M. (2007), *Payments for Ecosystem Services and U.S. Farm Policy. The 2007 Farm Bill and Beyond: Summary for Policymakers*, American Enterprise Institute Agricultural Policy Series (AEI) Press. Washington DC. (available on *www.aei.org/docLib/20070515_antlefinal.pdf*)

Antle, J.M., R.O. Valdivia (2006), Modelling the supply of ecosystem services from agriculture: a minimum-data approach, *The Australian Journal of Agricultural and Resource Economics*, Vol. 50, pp. 1-15.

Antle, J.M., B. Diagana, J.J. Stoorvogel, R.O. Valdivia (2010), "Minimum-data analysis of ecosystem service supply in semi-subsistence agricultural systems", *Australian Journal of Agricultural and Resource Economics*, Vol. 54, pp. 601-617.

Antle, J.M., J.J. Stoorvogel (2008), "Agricultural carbon sequestration, poverty, and sustainability", *Environment and Development Economics*, Vol. 13, pp. 327-352.

BirdLife (2008), "BirdLife International's response to the Commission public consultation on the Issues Addressed in the "Health Check" Communication", BirdLife International, Brussels.

CLA (2009), *Private solutions to public problems. Developing environmental markets*. Country Land and Business Association (CLA), London.

Claessens, L., J.J. Stoorvogel, J.M. Antle (2009), "*Ex ante* assessment of dual-purpose sweet potato in the crop–livestock system of western Kenya: A minimum-data approach", *Agricultural Systems*, Vol. 99: 13-22.

Cooper, T., K. Hart, D. Baldock (2009), *The Provision of Public Goods Through Agriculture in the European Union*, report Prepared for DG Agriculture and Rural Development Contract No 30-CE-0233091/00-28, Institute for European Environmental Policy. London.

Daily, G.C. (ed.) (1997), *Nature's Services: Societal Dependence on Natural Systems*, Island Press, Washington DC.

Farmer, M., T. Cooper, D. Baldock, G. Tucker, R. Eaton, K. Hart, J. Bartley, M. Rayment, K. Arblaster, G. Beaufoy, P. Pointereau, F. Coulon, M. Herodes, L. Kristensen, E. Andersen, R. Landgrebe, S. Naumann, A. Povellato, A. Trisorio, R. Jongman, B. Bunce (2008), *Final Report – Reflecting Environmental Land Use Needs into EU Policy: Preserving and Enhancing the Environmental Benefits of Unfarmed Features on EU Farmland*, Contract No. ENV.B.1/ETU/2007/0033, report for DG Environment (IEEP). London.

Freibauer, A., M.D.A. Rounsevell, P. Smith, J. Verhagend (2004), *Carbon sequestration in the agricultural soils of Europe. Geoderma*, Vol. 122, pp. 1-23.

Fuglie, K.O., C.A. Kascak (2001), "Adoption and Diffusion of Natural-Resource-Conserving Agricultural Technology", *Review of Agricultural Economics*, Vol. 23, pp. 386-403.

INEA (2010), *Annuario dell'agricoltura Italiana*, Volume LXIII, 2009, Edizioni Scientifiche Italiane, Napoli.

Nalukenge, I., J.M. Antle, J. Stoorvogel (2009), "Assessing the Feasibility of Wetlands Conservation: Using Payments for Ecosystem Services in Pallisa, Uganda", in L. Lipper, T. Sakuyama, R. Stringer, D. Zilberman. (eds.), *Payment for environmental services in agricultural landscapes: economic policies and poverty reduction in developing countries,* FAO/Springer, Rome.

Paustian, K., J. Antle, J. Sheehan, E. Paul (2006), *Agriculture's Role in Greenhouse Gas Mitigation*, Pew Center on Global Climate Change, Arlington, VA.

Povellato, A. (2010), "Floor and Trade": un nuovo meccanismo per incentivare la sostenibilità in agricoltura?" *Agriregionieuropa*, Vol. 6, pp. 39-42.

RISE (2009), *Public goods from private land. Rural Investment Support for Europe Foundation (RISE)*, Brussels.

Soussana, J.-F., P. Loiseau, N. Vuichard, E, Ceschia, J. Balesdent, T. Chevallier, D. Arrouays (2004), "Carbon cycling and sequestration opportunities in temperate grasslands", *Soil Use and Management*, Vol. 20, pp. 219-230.

Stoorvogel, J.J., A.J. Temme, J.M. Antle, L. Claessens, J.M. Schoorl, J.M. (2009), *A novel site-specific methodology to assess the supply curve of environmental services*, Proceedings of the Conference on Integrated Assessment of Agriculture and sustainable Development; Setting the Agenda for Science and Policy (AgSAP 2009), 10–12 March, Wageningen.

Sunding, D., D. Zilberman (2001), "The Agricultural Innovation Process: Research and Technology Adoption in a Changing Agricultural Sector", in B.L. Gardner, G.C. Rausser (eds.), *Handbook of Agricultural Economics*, Elsevier, Amsterdam.

Tietenberg, T. (2004), *Environmental Economics and Policy*, Pearson Addison Wesley.

Vleeshouwers, L.M., A. Verhagen (2002), "Carbon emission and sequestration by agricultural land use: a model study for Europe", *Global Change Biology*, Vol. 8, pp. 519-530.

Wissel, S., F. Watzold (2010), "A Conceptual Analysis of the Application of Tradable Permits to Biodiversity Conservation" *Conservation Biology*, Vol. 24, pp. 404-411.

Zhang, W., T.H. Ricketts, C. Kremen, K. Carney, S.M. Swinton (2007), "Ecosystem services and dis-services to agriculture", *Ecological Economics*, Vol. 64, pp. 253-260.

Chapter 13

Socio-political conditions for successful water quality trading in the South Nation River Watershed, Canada

Dennis O'Grady[1]

Ontario's South Nation River watershed has a regulated water quality trading programme. Legally, wastewater dischargers must not discharge any increased loading of phosphorus (P) into receiving waters. New wastewater systems are now choosing trading instead of traditional P removal technology, whereby point source dischargers buy P credits from rural landowners, primarily farmers. These credits are generated by constructing nonpoint source pollution control measures, and science-based formulae are used to calculate the credits of P removed by each measure. The chapter identifies the conditions necessary for the success of such a programme, drawing on ten years' experience of this established scheme. An independent evaluation showed higher opinions of the programme had enhanced participants' opinions of the broker and regulatory agency, and most farmers were willing to, or had already, recommended the programme to other farmers.

A point-to-nonpoint trading programme exists in the South Nation watershed. South Nation Conservation, a community-based watershed agency, acts as a broker for the programme. Wastewater treatment plants are required, by regulation, to discharge 0 kg of phosphorus (P) for new or expanded wastewater treatment plants. The amount of phosphorus removed is calculated using mathematical formulae, and dischargers must remove 4 kg of phosphorus for every 1 kg discharged into watercourses. The use of a trading programme improves water quality compared with traditional wastewater treatment since other pollutants are removed by the nonpoint pollution control methods, and not just phosphorus. It also reduces costs to all levels of government since a trading programme is a low cost alternative to phosphorus removal. Finally, trading puts more money into the hands of farmers to improve the environment.

The agricultural community had initial reservations about the programme, since they felt they would be blamed if phosphorus reduction targets were not met. A signed agreement (SNC, 1997) between farmers and regulators placed full responsibility for P reductions with the wastewater discharger. The programme is field-delivered by full-time farmers, who perform most interactions with other farmers, including site visits explaining the technical and grant details for various best management projects. All decisions are made by a multi-stakeholder Clean Water Committee.

Establishing a trading programme is not an easy task. There are many obstacles: financial (Fang *et al.*, 2005), institutional (EPA, 2008), legal (Siems, 2006), and scientific (Policy Research Initiative, 2005), to name a few. In many cases, a major problem is the simple absence of willing buyers and sellers (King, 2005). This has not been a problem in the South Nation watershed, where 269 verifiable trades were completed between 2000 and 2009.

A review of the South Nation River watershed's trading programme shows that eight conditions have helped create trading success. As cited above, a number of publications in the mid-2000 era and beyond examined trading successes and failures. SNC's trading programme became successful prior to most of this literature being published, and the conditions listed in this chapter hold up well to the scrutiny of the conclusions reached in these papers.

These eight conditions are a combination of social, political, and economic factors: community agreement on process, legislative backing for trading, credit certainty (science-based measurement), cost and revenue certainty for both the buyers and sellers of credits, longevity and credibility of a broker, written instruments for trading processes and verification, and finally legal liability protection. When looking at other initiatives that had difficulty implementing a similar programme, it appeared that one or more of these conditions were absent, making for a less than successful programme.

This is confirmed by the research done by the World Resources Institute (Selman *et al.*, 2009). In their assessment of water quality trading programmes, there were five key factors that stakeholders felt important for success. These factors are:

- strong regulatory and non-regulatory drivers to create a demand for water quality credits,
- minimal potential liability to regulated community from meeting regulations through trades,
- robust, consistent, and standardised estimation methodologies for nonpoint source actions,
- standardised tools, transparent processes, and online registries to minimise transaction costs, and
- buy-in from local and state stakeholders.

While not exactly mirroring the conditions in the South Nation River watershed, they are quite similar. This strongly supports the view that, even though the conditions established by SNC were put in place in the late 1990s, they appear to be relevant today.

13.1 SNC: Watershed management

South Nation Conservation (SNC), established in 1947 under a Provincial statute, The Conservation Authorities Act, is a community-based watershed organisation set up to manage the natural resources of the South Nation River watershed and adjacent tributaries. During the last several years, SNC paid over CAD 1 million in grants to rural landowners for various nonpoint source pollution control projects. It also manages 70 000 acres of sustainable forest, certified by the Forest Stewardship Council (*www.fsccanada.org*), on behalf of local municipalities. SNC prepares fisheries management plans, conducts intensive water quality and quantity monitoring and reviews development proposals to ensure environmental protection. SNC has regulatory power to prevent alteration to waterways, construction in flood plains and destruction of wetlands. SNC does not have regulatory power over water quality; that remains with the Provincial government and any regulatory issues surrounding trading is within their purview.

The South Nation River watershed is located southeast of Ottawa, Ontario Canada (Figure A in the Annex). The 4 146 sq. km. under its jurisdiction has a population of about 150 000 located mostly in small rural towns and villages. Agricultural activity can be characterised as mixed farming with dairy, cash crop corn and soybeans predominant. There are currently 16 wastewater lagoons in the watershed (14 municipal, 2 industrial). Provincial guidelines allow the lagoons to discharge their effluent at peak flows, primarily in the spring, for dilution of effluent to meet Provincial water quality guidelines. There are no load based limits in the watershed, only concentration limits.

SNC is governed by a 13 member Board of Directors, appointed by the 15 municipalities that comprise South Nation Conservation. These 13 are mostly farmers and politicians who ensure that SNC provides programmes geared to what the local watershed residents want.

13.2 Community agreement for trading

SNC's trading programme began with discussions amongst various government agencies in 1996. While some trading design work was going on concurrently in Ontario (Draper, 1997), water quality trading became a reality only in the SNC watershed. Some of the reasons for this include the SNC having an on-going grant programme to landowners for nonpoint source control, the fact that there were high levels of P throughout the watershed, and that several wastewater treatment plants were expanding or being built for the first time.

The early stages of the programme saw a number of conflicts dealing with the understanding of what trading was trying to accomplish. At public meetings held by SNC with the primarily agricultural community in the watershed, statements were made that could have easily stopped the programme because of the potential conflict. Internal SNC notes from these meetings recorded comments such as, "Lets municipalities off the hook", "Makes rural landowners appear to be the polluters," "Designed to save urban people money and not clean up the river."

Local newspapers covering the meetings ran headlines such as, "Municipalities could possibly be getting away with murder" (McKibbon, 1997), "Phosphorus program not sinister scheme" (Van Dusen, 1997), and "Plan to pay farmers to clean up could start a dangerous trend" (Editorial, 1997).

As proponents of the trading programme, both SNC and the Ontario Ministry of Environment (MOE) had difficulty comprehending these issues. The programme would give hundreds of thousands of dollars to farms at a time when there were not many programmes funding agricultural nonpoint source control measures. In addition, tax payers and industry would benefit from lower taxes with less costly infrastructure.

It was clear, after two years of public debate, that the programme lacked community support and would not proceed. SNC decided to put a full stop to the trading programme until the community supported the programme and the farm issues were fixed. In order to accomplish this, the Board of Directors of SNC initiated a number of steps.

First, no new programmes related to trading would start without farmer buy-in, that is, farmers' agreement to the programme is a pre-condition. SNC asked for Ontario's Ministry of Agriculture and Food (OMAF), which had the confidence of the agricultural community, to take the lead on finding a solution, if indeed one could be found. As trading was considered Provincial Policy under the MOE, it was incumbent upon its sister Ministry (OMAF) to try and find a solution. Consultation by OMAF included SNC's Clean Water Committee, which had delivered best management practices (BMPs) for nonpoint source control for several years, several farm organisations, municipalities, industry, provincial government ministries, and individual landowners.

The extensive consultation by OMAF achieved a consensus with the various partners involved in the trading programme. This consultation produced a key document, the "Statement of Roles and Responsibilities," (SNC, 1997) which helped achieve a successful trading programme. This document stated agreed-to facts, such as recognition of the trading programme as a pilot, the need for more flexible approaches to pollution control and the ability to achieve greater reductions in contaminant loading. It was signed by local agricultural organisations, the Provincial government and SNC.

The Statement also set out a 4:1 offset ratio for the first time. In theory, a discharger that contributes 1 kg of P from their wastewater treatment plant into the river must only remove 1 kg of P from nonpoint sources to achieve the new regulatory standard of no increase in P discharge (i.e. a 1:1 ratio). However, in reality each practice has variable results in removing P, and offset ratios are used to account for this uncertainty. In SNC's case, 4 kg of P must be removed for every 1 kg discharged by the plant to mitigate the variability of the practice adopted.

In an earlier agreement on trading in the watershed, finalised prior to this consultation beginning, the Ministry of the Environment had agreed to a 2:1 offset ratio. There was still scepticism about trading, since SNC's trading programme was one of the first large-scale attempts at trading. There was also a lack of science on how much P is first transported, then delivered to watercourses. There were no scientific studies to verify the need for a 4:1 *vs.* 3:1 or some other ratio. Rather it was a feeling from the farm community that a higher ratio would be more likely to achieve the required reduction in P loading required for every new or expanding wastewater treatment plant. It would allow a buffer, should any of the P reduction measures fail or not produce the designed P reduction. Farmers did not want to be blamed for any degradation in water quality and they were successful in negotiating a higher level of P reduction from the point source dischargers.

The Statement also gave municipalities the option of either implementing nonpoint source control measures or using higher levels of wastewater treatment to achieve the P reduction targets. The MOE made it clear that they were not dictating the method to use for P reduction. It was entirely up to the discharger, through the provincially required environmental assessment process designed to examine P reduction alternatives, to determine which method was most appropriate.

During the consultation by OMAF, many questions were asked about the true cost of the P reduction programme, including who would pay for the costs of water quality monitoring, reporting to municipalities and the public, public communications, programme evaluation and so on. The intent of the programme was to ensure that dischargers paid for these costs, as well as the cost of BMPs for P reduction. Therefore, higher costs were agreed to for each kilogramme of P removed, as the consultation showed that the true costs of implementing BMPs was higher than originally calculated.

The Statement went on to lay out specific roles and responsibilities for the MOE, municipalities and industries, SNC, the Ministry of Agriculture and Food, and landowners. Prior to this consultation, there were no agreements on the responsibility of landowners who accepted funding to complete nonpoint pollution control projects: it was not clear whether they would be blamed if P loadings were not reduced. Similarly, there were no stated responsibilities for the case where the wastewater dischargers did not achieve the legislated reduction.

The key phrase in the final Roles and Responsibilities document was, "Landowners are not bound, legally or otherwise, to attain the predicted phosphorus offset through the establishment of a BMP on their property." This was the final piece of the puzzle needed to allow trading to begin, as all responsibility for achieving load reduction rested with the dischargers.

The consultation process also expanded the role of, and farmer representation on, SNC's multi-stakeholder Clean Water Committee, which had been in existence for several years. This Committee is composed of farmers, industry, municipalities, farm organisations and SNC. BMP funding comes to SNC from several different sources, all with slightly different funding criteria, and the Committee then decides if the landowner project meets the criteria for one or more of the grant programmes. All criteria, grant rates, programme eligibility and other water quality decisions are made by the Committee, and not SNC. One key aspect of the Clean Water Committee is the lack of vetoes; decisions are made by consensus or votes, and no one agency or individual can stop the process.

With several granting sources, accurate record keeping is critical to ensure compliance with the different programmes and their conditions. SNC maintains these records for each field project, detailing which grant source is applied to which project. Year-end reports to the different granting agencies ensure proper recording of the grants and project costs, and both internal and external audits prevent duplication of grants and grant confusion. Section 13.8 of this chapter also discusses the necessary paper trail to avoid confusion and ensure the wastewater plants both pay for the quantity of P contributed and receive proper certification for the P credits paid for. Perhaps one of the most important factors to prevent confusion is the local knowledge of the farmer field representatives, who are active in project follow-up and report any unusual circumstances regarding project funding.

This process of consultation and full participation in decision making allowed other aspects of the trading programme to succeed. While there are various degrees of participation in decision making, ranging from tokenism to full citizen control (Goodey, 1981), it appears that a high level of local participation and sharing of responsibility in decision making is one of the most important elements in influencing changes of attitudes and behaviour (Dimock, 1977). The two-year participation process undertaken by SNC and MOE, where local control of the programme design was undertaken, resulted in a complete turnaround in attitudes amongst the farm community, and therefore a successful trading programme.

13.3 Legislative backing for trading

The surface waters in the South Nation watershed can register two to four times Provincial surface water quality guidelines for P, which is currently 0.03 mg/l (MOE, 1994). Annual mean P concentrations for the main South Nation River are 0.07 mg/L in the upper reach, 0.126 mg/L in the middle, and 0.129 mg/L in the lower reach of the River (Memo from MOE, Eastern Region, to SNC. Eastern Region Position on Total Phosphorus Management. Undated.)

A watershed study completed by SNC (SNC, 1993) shows that over 90% of the P load comes from nonpoint sources (NPS). While questions remained unanswered on the type of P, and whether all the P can be attributed to nonpoint sources, no further studies were undertaken to explore this.

The Provincial MOE is responsible for regulating water quality and licensing the operation of wastewater treatment in the Province. According to provincial policy, where surface water quality does not meet provincial standards for a specific contaminant, no further degradation of water quality will be allowed for that contaminant (MOE, 1994). However, in the past MOE gave dischargers a permit to discharge P from their plants into the South Nation River and its tributaries, even though the receiving watercourses did not meet provincial water quality objectives. Most often, these deviation permits were justified on the basis of the high cost of treatment to reach an amount of P delivery. Without this permission, secondary treatment lagoons that are the norm in the watershed would need extensive upgrades, resulting in huge financial burdens for small (less than 3 000 people) municipalities.

For example, the Village of Casselman's Environmental Assessment, which examined expansion alternatives, stated that with pre-treatment and polishing lagoons, river water quality can meet Provincial Water Quality Objectives, "with the exception of P" (Village of Casselman, 1996). The consulting engineer noted that increased contributions of P were small, and therefore an exemption from MOE's policies was justified. Recent construction costs in the South Nation watershed show new tertiary treatment plants to be CAD 20 million or more (in 2010 dollars) (Village of Russell, 1997). Even minor treatment upgrades to existing secondary lagoons for alum batching, aeration, sand filters and so on can cost several million dollars (Village of Casselman, 1996).

Beginning in 1998, the Ministry stopped issuing these "deviation from policy" permits and required all dischargers to have "no further increase in phosphorus loadings" from the establishment or expansion of industrial or municipal sewage systems discharges (Memo from MOE, to SNC. Eastern Region Position on Total Phosphorus Management. Undated). MOE imposed this standard on new plants and expansion of existing plants only. Any plants that continued to operate according to their current regulatory permits required no changes to P loadings.

One motivation for MOE's position was the desire to attain overall better water quality. Another was that of being in compliance with Provincial Policies. With 90% of P coming from nonpoint sources, MOE did not see the logic in spending huge amounts of tax dollars upgrading wastewater plants when they were only contributing 10% of the problem.

In recognition of the high cost of treatment, MOE allowed wastewater treatment plant operators to try a new, innovative trading solution to remove P contributed by wastewater dischargers. Locally called Total Phosphorus Management (TPM), it allows dischargers to contribute P from their treatment plants, in contravention of provincial policy, if they offset this increased P load by controlling P from nonpoint sources (NPS). To reduce P, the point sources must buy P credits from nonpoint sources of pollution.

In a logical approach, MOE treats the watershed as a unit. Since P is contributed throughout the watershed, and P concentrations exceed provincial standards throughout the watershed, MOE allows the TPM programme to remove P anywhere in the watershed. Therefore, a treatment plant discharging P in the lower reaches of the watershed can pay for reduced P in the upper reaches of the watershed. MOE also allows trading as one of many options to control P, and not the only means. Table 13.1 shows a cost comparison of using the TPM programme versus upgrading lagoons.

Table 13.1. Cost comparison, TPM *vs.* lagoon treatment

Municipality	TPM removal target	TPM cost	Approximate cost for treatment for phosphorus removal	TPM cost savings
	kg/year	CAD, '000	CAD, '000	CAD, '000
North Stormont – Finch	225	80.4	225.0	144.6
North Dundas – Winchester	640	192.0	640.0	448.0
Casselman	1 282	384.6	1 200.0	815.4
Nation — Limoges	772	127.6	1 500.0	1 370.0

Source: SNC, 2009.

13.4 Credit certainty

For trading to succeed, there must be certainty amongst regulators and both, point and nonpoint polluters that there will be enough P credit to satisfy the regulatory requirements for reduction. For this to occur there must be good science to back the measurement of P reduction and knowledge of the numbers and types of projects that need to be completed.

The number of kilogrammes of P to be "bought" depends on two factors. The first is the amount of P that the discharger contributes. For example, Casselman's current population of about 2 500 contributes annually about 491 kg of P into the river. Any increase in the design capacity of the treatment lagoon will have to maintain a standard of no net annual increase of P.

Since 1993, and before trading began, SNC completed over 600 nonpoint source projects in the watershed. With this expertise, it could reasonably predict the numbers and types of BMPs those landowners might complete in the future. To date, there have always been more projects than money, and every year has waiting lists that are carried forward to the following year.

With the large numbers of completed projects, SNC used existing mathematical formulae published in scientific literature from Ontario and elsewhere (Batchelor, 1999) prior to beginning the trading programme to determine the kilogrammes of P that were removed by these nonpoint source best management practices. This historic experience gave SNC the ability to predict that it could meet the P reduction targets of the wastewater treatment plants.

Table 13.2 shows that the numbers of projects and kg of P removed per year varies, but are still sufficient to meet the P reduction targets. The annual fluctuations are the result of who applies: if there were no applications for particular type of project type, there will be zero for that project for that year. Moreover, since there was limited money each year, projects were ranked on water quality improvement. Some project types may have been ranked too low to quality for the limited funding.

P reduction targets are shown in Table 13.3.

Table13.2. Annual phosphorus reduction (kg/year) by project type

Project type / Year	Septic systems	Manure storages	Milkhouse wastewater	Barnyard runoff control/clean water diversion	Livestock access restriction	Total
2000	15	213	0	0	7	235
2001	2	881	530	16	15	1 444
2002	48	784	245	7	71	1 155
2003	6	2 678	204	81	141	3 110
2004	26	396	162	47	63	693
2005	8	1 450	317	0	0	1 775
2006	7	565	197	19	22	810
2007	17	931	588	23	114	1 673
2008	21	433	0	0	71	525
2009	24	215	58	118	8	423
Total P removed (kg, 2000-9)	174	8 546	2301	311	512	11 843
Total number of projects completed	88	85	42	17	37	269

Table 13.3. Target phosphorus reductions and annual budget

	1	2	3	4	5
	Projects	**P reductions generated**	**Target P reductions**	**TPM grant budget**	**TPM delivery budget**
	Number	kg/year	kg/year	USD	USD
2000	8	235	42	10 000	2 500
2001	26	1 444	704	143 861	32 775
2002	42	1 155	808	183 195	37 828
2003	39	3 110	712	156 023	24 371
2004	33	693	279	62 405	21 009
2005	24	1 775	349	74 623	30 353
2006	15	810	86	20 517	5 129
2007	32	1 673	60	16 875	5 625
2008	19	525	67	17 178	5 726
2009	31	423	60	23 724	7 908
Totals	269	11 843	3 167	708 403	173 225

Notes:

1. Eligible TPM projects that generate a phosphorus reduction (manure storage, milkhouse wastewater, clean water diversion/barnyard runoff control, fencing, septic installations).
2. Total phosphorus reduction estimates, using the TPM science-based calculations, for above projects.
3. Required number of kg/yr of phosphorus reduction to meet the TPM agreements for the year.
4. TPM Program grant dollars: Clean Water Program project grants (landowner grant payment).
5. TPM Program delivery dollars: Clean Water Committee, Program Representatives, outreach/education, staffing to administer grants.

When SNC enters into a P reduction programme with a wastewater discharger, it has the discretion to decide over how many years it wants to achieve the reductions. Agreements typically run from one year to a maximum of five, and total payments of CAD 500 000 or more for P control may be spread over this time frame. If a wastewater discharger has only a small amount of P to offset, it may pay the amount in full. SNC limits the time frame to achieve the P reductions to a maximum of five years because of the unpredictability of BMP project supply, and hence P reduction supply. Most agreements are for three years or less.

Any P credits generated are treated by the Ministry of the Environment as permanent removal of P from the watercourse. As discussed previously, the 4:1 offset ratio accounts for any uncertainty that may exist with the science, or with failed or poorly operating BMPs.

Should there be changes in the markets that affect BMP project supply, the Clean Water Committee can manipulate the market through either increasing maximum grants or increasing maximum grant rates. For example, manure storages currently have a maximum grant rate of 50%, and a maximum grant of CAD 10 000, even though costs can run CAD 30 000 or more. Should more manure storage projects be needed, either the grant rate or the grant maximum could be increased, thereby increasing the demand for projects and the possible amount of P available for removal. The extra funds for such changes, if required, would come from the contributions of the wastewater treatment plants.

The experience of SNC shows that high grants or grant rates are not necessary for project success. The grants paid by SNC are not a result of definite criteria, but rather it is a combination of a number of factors considered by the Clean Water Committee[2]. As most of the Committee are full-time farmers, they use their own professional experience as a guide when determining grants. The grants are an incentive to do clean water projects, but the farmer must match some portion of the grant. The Committee does not want to fund projects where the main rationale from the farmer is "they're paying me to do it." They would prefer the landowner do the project completely on their own, but many cannot afford to do so, and a small incentive is enough for the landowner to do the project.

Also, the Committee knows they are using public funds, and they are accountable for their use. They know there is a limit on the amount of public money available, and the Committee wants to spread the grant around to as many landowners as possible. Finally, the incentive grant from SNC is sometimes also enough for the farmer to secure bank funding for the project, where otherwise financing would not be available.

While the wastewater dischargers paid for the full cost of the TPM programme, the landowners do not receive 100% funding. The programme was initially set up, after consultation with landowners, to have the discharger pay for the full costs of their discharge, monitoring, etc. However, there was no debate on how this money was to be allocated. This was a decision all agreed to leave to the Clean Water Committee. To date, there is no concern expressed by any sector about this approach. If a concern arises, it would go to the Clean Water Committee for resolution.

Other funded projects considered by the Clean Water Committee include septic system upgrades, milk house wash water treatment, barnyard runoff control, livestock access and buffer strips. A new project, soon to be added to the programme, is a controlled tile outlet. Current research by Agriculture and Agri-Food Canada in SNC's watershed shows significant reductions in P using controlled tile discharge. This science is not yet published and the formulae are still under review (as of May 2012), however the Clean Water Committee wants to include this project type as soon as the data is published. More information on the project can be found on the Federal government website (Agriculture and Agri-Food Canada, 2010).

Currently, the amount of P contributed by various nonpoint sources is determined by formulae derived from studies in Canada and elsewhere. A study of the scientific literature

(Alway, 2003) showed that the range in results for individual practices is quite large and the results are highly variable since calculating P lost or saved by agricultural management practices is complicated and not easily measured. Since 2003, other studies have been published on P reduction using various BMP measures, and these will be evaluated by SNC in the near future. However, there is a reluctance to alter the current formulae for two reasons. First, they are accepted by the regulatory agency and any move to alter them could alter the status quo with unintended consequences. These consequences could include new regulatory requirements restricting what can or cannot be traded, alterations in offset rations, restrictions on brokers like SNC, less control for local watershed agencies, and exclusion of certain BMPs by regulators. Second, they are accepted by the nonpoint source community; alterations to the formulae or programme could affect farm operations and the success of the programme.

The reluctance to alter the formulae can also have long-term consequences. Alway (2003) showed that the older formulae, which SNC first relied upon, could be altered with no serious social, grant, or regulatory consequences. In fact, the new formulae are more precise in estimating P removed. Therefore, by not updating the formulae, SNC runs the risk of using out-of-date science, to the detriment of the programme.

A recurring question asked of SNC's trading programme is to prove that this reduction actually occurs. Most often, simple answers are sought to changes in complex ecosystems, such as the need measure year over year improvements in river water quality. However, watersheds are intricate mechanisms and changes in water quality cannot always be measured in political cycles. Over the last 30 years, SNC's water quality has improved and P levels have decreased (SNC, 2006). But was the lower P due to higher fertiliser prices, increased conservation tillage, lower planting of row crops, or farmers retiring? The standard one litre chemical bottle sent to a lab does not provide these answers: was the sample collected after a major rainfall, or after a four-week drought? The water quality will be substantially different in each case.

In measuring P reduction and water quality improvement, researchers must use many different criteria and indicators of success other than standard chemical analysis. Biological measurements, visual assessment protocols, and other methods can provide assurances that water quality has indeed improved. For example, in Connecticut (EPA, 2009), aquatic life will be measured on a rotating basis, since it is considered a good indicator of improved water quality. Other scientific methods depend on modelling and non-modelling approaches (Neilson and Stevens, undated). The common thread is to ensure a scientific approach.

Alway's paper (2003) was derived from published science. If there is agreement that the science of the P reduction formulae is based on primary research, then the formulae should be accepted as reasonable estimations of the amount of P removed permanently from a watercourse. If this premise is rejected, on what basis? Which science do we accept or reject, and why? Debate can continue on what the research shows, and these formulae are likely to change as more research is done, but they cannot be rejected based solely on personal opinion. The Ontario Ministry of the Environment has adopted SNC's trading programme and its science as official policy for the South Nation River watershed, lending further credence to the formulae.

13.5 Cost and revenue certainty

To have a successful trading programme in the South Nation River watershed, there must be cost certainty for the wastewater treatment plant and revenue certainty for the landowner.

In Ontario, wastewater dischargers have a finite amount of government grant dollars to build their treatment plants; if they exceed this, local taxpayers will pay more. Prior to construction, they also have to decide on the taxes to raise from their electorate for the costs of the treatment plant. The dischargers therefore wanted assurances that for a set price per kg of P, they will achieve their regulatory requirements and not have to contribute more funding at some future point. Dales (1970), in an early discussion of pollution markets, argues that the system of charging a uniform amount for the right to discharge wastes into natural water systems is the most efficient method. A trading programme that creates cost uncertainty also creates a lower desire by wastewater plant operators to enter into trading since it could cause them to open up new discussions with their ratepayers about paying higher more for their treatment plant, a politically undesirable consequence.

Landowners also want revenue certainty. A trading programme with revenues that vary depending on distance from stream, delivery ratio mapping changes or soil types, is technically accurate, but creates revenue uncertainty and a lower desire to enter into trading. They are paid for their projects, and not for each kg of P removed. Prior to starting a project, they want to know with certainty what their revenues will be. In SNC's programme, the grants are known well in advance of a project starting.

In SNC's programme evaluation (SNC and Kassirer, 2005), 75% of landowners constructed a project based on the grants given. This feedback shows that fixed revenue is an important factor when entering a trading programme. The dollar cost for removing each kg of P was determined by SNC based on its history of delivering projects. Using earlier trading formulae (Batchelor, 1999; Draper, 1997), it was possible to calculate the amount of P controlled for a number of projects completed by SNC prior to the trading programme starting. Since the total cost for each of these projects was known, it was possible to derive an average cost of CAD 400 (2009 figures) for each kg of P. This figure is reviewed by South Nation Conservation annually, and is generally increased by yearly inflation figures.

This CAD 400 is the cost to the discharger, and includes both the costs of constructing the BMP and the costs of project management, (paying farmer field representatives, SNC support staff, travel costs, Clean Water Committee meeting expenses, etc.), water sampling, communications to promote the grants available to landowners, and yearly reporting. SNC must complete a yearly report that is distributed to the public, the Ministry of the Environment, and the wastewater plant owner showing the amount of P controlled that year, and allocating that P to each of the TPM dischargers. Some projects are more efficient at controlling P than others; however, the CAD 400 figure is accepted by MOE, farmers and wastewater plants.

13.6 Broker longevity and credibility

Neither landowners nor dischargers in SNC want multiple brokers each trying to buy or sell their credits. The business of farming and the complexity of operating wastewater plants makes spare time a rare commodity, and for a trading programme to succeed there must be simple application and delivery processes and the broker must have the trust of both the landowner and wastewater discharger. Any grant programme or delivery agent will have different rules, forms, contracts, reporting requirements and deadlines to meet. Having one broker deliver a trading programme in a geographic area achieves simplicity by having the same processes for all landowners and plant operators.

Other trading programmes may use brokers, aggregators, banks or other third parties to deliver trading programmes (Selman *et al.* 2009). While it is difficult to determine whether trading is prone to the emergence of natural monopolies, i.e. having one broker, it is possible that for watersheds, certain objectives are not expressed adequately through market mechanisms (Baum and Allbaugh, 1961). Watershed projects do not always fit into well-defined market structures, and achieving watershed objectives may be more successful if more thought is given to institutional change rather than market conditions.

SNC is the sole broker between the point source and nonpoint sources, handles all financial transactions between the two, and reports on compliance for P control. SNC delivered nonpoint source control projects to rural landowners for 25 years prior to trading beginning. With professional foresters, planners, biologists, engineers and water quality specialists, it has worked with local landowners on a wide range of projects for over 60 years. With this experience, not only was SNC the logical broker, but its longevity was also assured. Landowners and regulators are comfortable when dealing with one agency for delivering on P load reduction and saw SNC as the natural broker. This was confirmed in the decision by all wastewater treatment plants to date to choose SNC as a broker. There is no regulatory requirement to choose SNC; each plant can hire whom they wish.

The trading programme is advertised as a straightforward grant programme. Publicity for grants is made through the local media and presentations to municipalities and farm organisations. All projects are voluntary, with no landowner forced to participate in the programme.

The key to trading success is keeping the process simple. Farmers, while aware of the P trading programme, are not concerned with where the funding comes from for their BMPs. SNC accesses several sources of grants for BMPs, each with their own rules, and blends them into one delivery programme. It is up to SNC to report back on compliance for each of the funding sources. The focus to local landowners is on BMP delivery, not a P reduction trading programme.

Simplicity in using one delivery mechanism has its drawbacks. It reduces competition for buying and selling P credits, which could increase delivery costs. It may also reduce innovation, since different methodologies for measuring and controlling P may not be sought.

As the broker, SNC agreed from the start of the trading programme to keep confidential the names and locations of the grant recipients. SNC enters into contracts with each landowner detailing the project type, costs and grants. The public is only allowed to see project types by township, and not the actual contracts. At the start of the programme, this was a non-negotiable requirement from the farm groups that were participating in the review. In the watershed, there were many farms at that time that were causing serious water quality issues. The farm organisations did not want to see the names of farmers appearing in media or government reports as examples of poor agricultural practices.

Recent shifts in public perception are changing this process. There is no appetite for what some see as secret payments, and in 2009 all landowners receiving a grant were asked to check off a box allowing their names and projects to be used in public. After SNC staff examined the grant applications, it was interesting to see that 80% of farmers receiving grants agreed to let their names be used, but only 69% of non-farmers were in agreement.

The other advantage that SNC had from the beginning in order to boost credibility was the existence of the Clean Water Committee, a sub-committee of the SNC Board. Prior to trading, it was already a multi-stakeholder committee delivering a wide range of BMPs.

There was one additional change that SNC made after the OMAF consultation that increased its credibility within the agricultural community. SNC began using farmers as field representatives to do all site visits related to trading and BMP delivery. The agricultural community expressed some concern over using SNC staff who might not understand the complex business of farming and what are commonly accepted agricultural practices. Now, when a landowner applies for a grant, they contact SNC, which then refers the call to one of several farmer field representatives who then do the field inspection. These representatives review the project and potential grants with the landowner and determine if it is eligible for grants. The representative then makes a presentation to the Clean Water Committee, which has the final say on which projects receive funding. This peer-to-peer approach is rare amongst water quality programmes in North America, which tend to use full-time professional staff to do field inspections.

Delivering grants to landowners is not a difficult task. With a minimal amount of training by SNC staff on programme requirements and grant levels, the representatives are as capable as anyone of delivering the information and making field decisions. All are full-time, or retired, farmers. Most had roles in some or all of county agricultural federations, municipal councils, and the Board of Directors of SNC. They are professionals on a par with college/university graduates.

One of the reasons for their success is their use of language common to farming. The TPM programme introduced many new words and phrases. Using words and phrases that are unfamiliar to local farmers, as technical people often do, can lead to misunderstandings and confusion. By speaking the same language, and by using farmer representatives who are leaders in their community, there is considerably more uptake and credibility in the trading programme. This peer-to-peer networking therefore improves communication and understanding of the programme.

Using farmer field representatives is also cost effective. They are paid for their time and expenses, and in one year, 110 site visits cost CAD 4 500. Using similar full time staff would cost CAD 50 000 or more. The representatives also play a secondary, perhaps more critical, role. They report that they are often told of other farm-related problems that are not connected to the trading programme or BMPs, and their experience allows them to trouble-shoot these problems. At other times, the representatives provide moral support for issues or problems that the farmer may be experiencing. None of these are ever discussed publicly, and the representatives are careful to not divulge which landowners have these discussions.

13.7 Instruments for trading process and verification

From the beginning, SNC worked on developing with the wastewater dischargers, regulators, and landowners, documents required to properly manage the programme and document the point to nonpoint trades. Legal contracts were signed by SNC with the dischargers to ensure clarity on the trading process, and what the dischargers' and SNC's responsibilities were. The legal Certificates of Approval (C of A) required by MOE to operate a wastewater discharge facility needed proper wording on P reduction targets for the plant to operate and this was incorporated. Legal mechanisms for reporting back to both the MOE and the plant operators to ensure accountability of the trades were developed.

Administration costs and overheads are kept to a minimum, and are constantly reviewed by both the Clean Water Committee and farmer field representatives for improvements. Paperwork for completed projects is sent to SNC staff to verify receipts and then issue cheques. About 10% of the projects are audited for performance to ensure that the projects are working as designed and for accuracy of construction costs. Verbal reports made by the farmer field representatives to SNC and the Clean Water Committee suggest that, with the large amount of peer-to-peer interaction, non-compliance or fraud is not a concern for the Clean Water Committee. To date, no audited project showed substantive inaccuracies from what was approved by the Committee.

As a result, annual reports, water quality summaries, project management and tracking, media releases, and so on were developed to guide the process. These instruments allow the programme to proceed without confusion of what is to be done, by whom and when. In all, over 50 separate instruments are used to administer, monitor, report and publicise the TPM programme.

13.8 Legal liability protection

These days it is a given that legal action may be taken at some point against the SNC, acting as a broker. In the "Certificate of Approval to Operate a Wastewater System" signed by the owner of the wastewater system, SNC's role is clearly defined: it must supply a certain number of P kg for the wastewater plant to be in regulatory compliance.

There is also the potential for costly enforcement actions against wastewater plant operators if they do not meet the effluent concentration conditions of their discharges (MOE, 2009) and in early discussion with the TPM programme, the nonpoint suppliers of P credits in the SNC watershed did not want to be blamed for problems with wastewater treatment plants.

The MOE recognised this complication in the "Statement of Roles and Responsibilities" when it absolved the supplier of credits from liability should the wastewater treatment plant be in non-compliance due to insufficient P credits. While SNC does not have regulatory responsibilities for surface water quality or wastewater treatment plant operations, by being named specifically in the Certificate of Approval, it is likely that SNC could be part of future enforcement issues and could be part of a legal action by the point source discharger if it failed to produce the legally required credits. Trading is not just a simple delivery of a grant programme. SNC has agreed, legally, to provide the requisite reduction in P from watercourses. Failure to do so will not only irreparably damage the organisation's reputation, but will almost certainly launch costly lawsuits.

The conclusion to be drawn from this is that, for a broker to be successful, they must have proper legal protection, including errors and omissions insurance and "save harmless" agreements that limit liability should a trading programme break down and insufficient trades occur. SNC also protects itself by knowing the market for P credits, based on previous projects completed, and an analysis of the number of potential projects in the future. Extensive consultation with the wastewater plant operator prior to their entering into a trading programme helps avoid future conflicts that could lead to a lawsuit. With this consultation, all parties enter into contracts confident about the quantity of P that can be supplied and the processes needed to get there. Finally, for the duration of the TPM agreement with the wastewater discharger, they are allowed to have a representative on the Clean Water Committee. Therefore, if a lawsuit were to be launched, they would be effectively suing themselves.

13.9 Programme evaluation

Consultation with the agricultural community called for a full programme evaluation after five years. An independent firm was hired to conduct an evaluation of the trading programme, and of 89 landowners contacted, 68 responded (SNC and Kassirer, 2005). One of the objectives of the evaluation was to determine the overall benefits of the programme, and not just as it related to achieving trading targets.

The evaluation showed that grants for all projects funded by the Clean Water Committee in the first five years totalled CAD 604 000, with the TPM portion of this being CAD 153 000. The non-TPM grants came from a variety of government and non-government programmes, and the TPM grants came solely from wastewater treatment plants. The trading programme resulted in considerable economic activity, with total construction costs for all projects being CAD 2.2 million. Any costs over and above the TPM grants were paid for entirely by the landowners.

Another question asked by the evaluator to participants in the trading programme was whether, in the opinion of the participants, the programme resulted in any other improvements. Figure 13.1 shows the results from the 68 landowner responses after a five-year period. This was an unprompted question, meaning that there were no options given and the answers were spontaneous. These responses showed lead to some surprising conclusions. A high percentage of respondents stated an improved opinion of SNC, on a par with increased respect for the environment and increased property value. This was surprising because of the negative publicity in the earlier stages of the programme design, and it gave credence to the subsequent steps SNC undertook to get the programme going. High marks were also given to the regulatory agency, MOE, which was also a surprise, as SNC's experience with the agricultural community in the 1990s suggested a very low opinion of MOE due to their regulatory charges against the farm community for manure spills, pesticide accidents and other such incidents.

Figure 13.1. Improvements noticed by landowners involved with trading

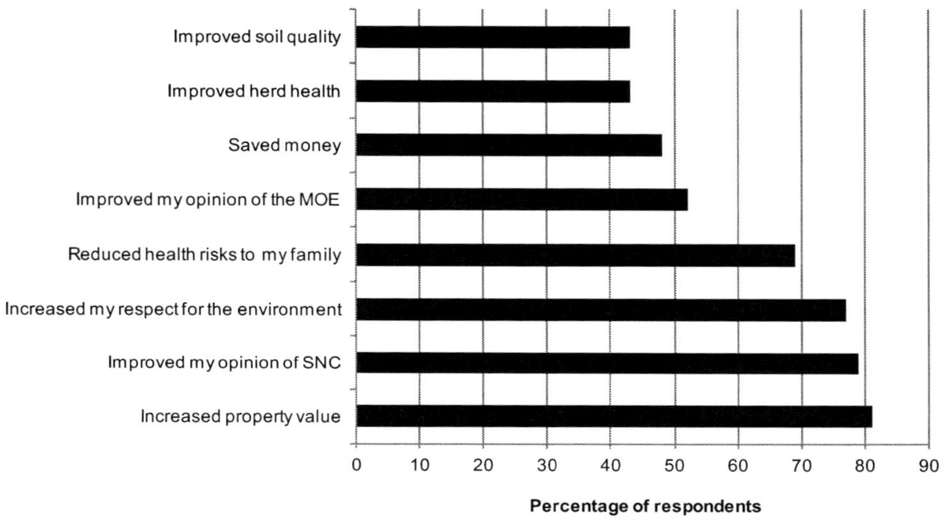

In any programme for landowners, the ultimate success has to be measured in the attitude of these landowners and their willingness to share their experiences. The evaluation showed that 90% of the respondents had already recommended the programme to a friend or neighbour.

Participants also felt that the programme built stronger relationships and engaged landowners. Improvements suggested included streamlining the administration of the programme, improved water quality monitoring and continued integration of other BMP programmes. These recommendations, and other observations, are reviewed continuously by the Clean Water Committee and SNC to improve the programme. For example, when new grants for environmental projects are announced by other agencies, a meeting is held with that agency to see if it can be integrated into one programme for field delivery.

Farmer quotes in the evaluation included, "It has made the water a lot cleaner for everybody, including the animals," "It used to be that rural areas were on their own as far as cleaning up," "It should not just be a voluntary programme … otherwise people will keep dumping into the river However, there is still some hesitancy, as noted in this quote: "How does SNC even know the project was completed…? This makes me think it is just a spend-the-money game." These comments, and others, were reviewed by the Clean Water Committee and SNC to find reasonable solutions. For example, audits were done of projects to ensure completion, and more public presentations were made on the programme's objectives and results. The Clean Water Committee also hears delegations and responds to inquiries about issues to inject new ideas and resolve complaints.

13.10 Final comments

Water quality trading is not a panacea; it does not work in all rivers, in all watersheds. The MOE recognised this when it set out the parameters of the programme (MOE, 2000). MOE would only allow trading under the following conditions: local water quality had to be protected; must be a definable net benefit to water quality, the programme must be well designed and documented to provide confidence in achieving environmental benefit and it must include monitoring and assessment to verify phosphorus load reductions. However, it is an important tool that can result in water quality improvements and watershed managers need all the tools they can get.

Trading also has the ability to clean up multiple contaminants for lower costs. In SNC, point source pollution contributed only 10% of the P problem (SNC, 1993). Yet to satisfy provincial regulations, millions of dollars were going to be spent on this small percentage. On the initiative of MOE to start a trading programme, millions of dollars in grants were redirected to rural nonpoint sources of pollution, or 90% of the P problem.

Even though large sums were spent on nonpoint source control, the total amount of funding spent to reduce P loadings was substantially smaller than if the wastewater plants themselves had to control this same amount of loading. By having a less expensive solution available to achieve equal, or better, water quality, industries, towns, and government are able to reduce their expenditures and free up funding for other priorities.

The grants given to rural landowners have the added benefit of being green payments probably not subject to international trade rules (Batie, 1999). With agricultural subsidies being scrutinised internationally (Lynn, 2007), this type of payment may be important to farmers in the future.

One important aspect of trading often overlooked is the income redistribution from urban to rural communities. All governments today are saddled with huge debts, and due to large public deficits, the future may not bode well for additional funding for government grants for either point or nonpoint source control measures. In this context it is important to stress that trading is not only cost effective, but it also allows for income to move from areas with large property tax revenues (e.g. cities) to rural areas with low property tax revenues. Wastewater plants will always be needed, or upgraded, and the use of trading allows income to shift, with resultant water quality improvements, without as much need for costly government subsidies that may be non-existent in the future.

In Canada, water quality trading is not widespread. Several jurisdictions across Canada have discussed the trading concept with SNC, and the Federal Government produced a series of papers on water markets and trading (Policy Research Initiative, 2005). SNC's personal experience leads to a belief that there is scepticism in these other areas about the science and methodology of trading. Continued education, new legislation, and positive case studies should reduce this scepticism and help establish new trading programmes.

In SNC, trading was possible only because of an interpretation by MOE of an existing policy. Until recently, no words existed in legislation or regulations to explicitly allow trading. That has now changed. In 2009, changes to the Ontario Water Resources Act RSO of 1990[3] were made to call explicitly for trading for the first time in Canada. This legislation now allows the province to state where trading can occur, the water quality parameters that can be traded, who can trade, what instruments will be allowed and who should administer the programme.

While the legislation has been passed, the regulations needed for its implementation have yet to be written. Trading rules in the SNC watershed are clear, but province-wide regulations for trading will not be completed until the conclusion of work now underway on Lake Simcoe, a large inland lake north of Toronto that must reduce its P contributions for the lake to maintain its ecological integrity. When completed, these regulations could become the future driver for many new trading programmes in Canada.

Notes

1. This chapter first appeared, in a slightly different version, as O'Grady, D. (2011), "Sociopolitical Conditions for Successful Water Quality Trading in the South Nation River Watershed, Ontario, Canada", *Journal of American Water Resources Association*, Vol. 47:39-51, *www.awra.org/jawra*. It appears here with the author's and first publisher's permission.
2. Denis Perrault, Chair, Clean Water Committee, Personal Communication, May, 2010.
3. See *www.e-laws.gov.on.ca/html/statutes/english/elaws_statutes_90o40_e.htm#BK100.*

References

Agriculture and Agri-Food Canada. *Watershed Evaluation of Best Management Practices: South Nation Watershed. www4.agr.gc.ca/AAFC-AAC/display-afficher.do?id=1228864413685&lang=eng*. Accessed May, 2010.

Alway, C. (2003), *Phosphorous Loading Algorithms for the South Nation River*, South Nation Conservation, Finch, Ontario.

Batchelor, Gwyneth (1999), *Phosphorus Loading Algorithms Used for the Clean Water Program. South Nation Conservation*, Finch, Ontario.

Batie, S.S. (1999), *Green Payments as Foreshadowed by EQIP,* Department of Agricultural Economics, Michigan State University, East Lansing, Michigan. *ageconsearch.umn.edu/bitstream/11750/1/sp99-45.pdf* Accessed June, 2010

Baum, E.L., L.G. Allbaugh, (1961), *Economics of Watershed Planning*, edited by G.S. Tolley and F.E. Riggs, Iowa State University Press, Iowa.

Dales, J.H. (1970), *Pollution, Property and Prices*, University of Toronto Press, Toronto, Ontario.

Dimock, H.G. (1977), *Factors in Working With Groups*, Sir George Williams University. Montreal, Quebec, Canada.

Draper, D.W. and Associates Ltd. (1997), *Bay of Quinte Remedial Action Plan: Phosphorus Trading Program Evaluation and Design*. Etobicoke, Ontario.

Editorial, March (1997), Plan To Pay Farmers To Clean Up Could Start Dangerous Trend. *Eastern Ontario Farmers Forum*. Ottawa, Ontario.

Environmental Protection Agency (2008), *Water Quality Trading Evaluation: Final Report, www.epa.gov/evaluate/wqt.pdf,*accessed November, 2009.

Environmental Protection Agency (2009), *Restoring Impaired Waters: Total Maximum Daily Loads (TMDLs) and Municipal Stormwater Programs, www.epa.gov/NE/npdes/stormwater/assets/pdfs/RestoringImpairedWaters.pdf.* Accessed, December, 2009.

Fang, F., K.W. Easter, P.L. Brezonik (2005), "Point-Non-point Source Water Quality Trading: A Case Study in the Minnesota River Basin", *Journal of the American Water Resources Association*, pp. 645-658.

Goodey, Brian. (1981), *Towards a Participatory Culture in the Built Environment*, Oxford Polytechnic.

Jones, C. (2005), "Legal and Financial Liability – Issues in Mitigation Banking and Water Quality Trading" in *Proceedings of National Forum on Synergies Between Water Quality Trading and Wetland Mitigation Banking*, Environmental Law Institute, Washington, D.C.

King, D.M. (2005), Crunch Time For Water Quality Trading. Choices, 1st Quarter. *www.choicesmagazine.org/2005-1/environment/2005-1-14.htm*, accessed December, 2009.

Lynn, J. (2007), *WTO launches investigation of U.S. farm support, www.canada.com/ottawacitizen/news/story.html?id=f521aafe-2339-4526-89d7-b1a716967ca4&k=86373*. Accessed June, 2010.

McKibbon, S. (1997), "Municipalities could possibly be getting away with murder", *The Chieftain*, 18 June, Iroquois, Ontario.

Ministry of Environment (1994), *Water Management Policies, Guidelines*, Provincial Water Quality Objectives, Queen's Printer. Toronto, Ontario.

Ministry of the Environment, (2000), "Draft Roles and Responsibilities", Unpublished Memorandum.

Ministry of Environment (2009), Court Bulletins, *www.ene.gov.on.ca/en/news/convictions/2009/index.php*, accessed June, 2010.

Neilson, B.T., D.K. Stevens (undated), "Issues Related To The Success Of The TMDL Program", *www.ucowr.siu.edu/updates/pdfn/V122_A8.pdf,* accessed December 2009

Policy Research Initiative (2005), *Water Quality Trading I: Scientific Considerations for Agricultural Pollutants, and Water Quality Trading II: Using Trading Ratios to Deal With Uncertainties*, Government of Canada, Ottawa, Ontario.

Selman, M., S. Greenhalgh, E. Branosky, C. Jones, J. Guiling (2009), *Water Quality Trading Program: An International Overview*, World Resource Institute, WRI Issue Brief No. 1.

Siems, A. (2006) *Establishing Water Quality Trading Banks: Opportunities and Barriers, envtn.org/uploads/Microsoft_PowerPoint_-_Antje_Siems_-_Establishing_WQT_Banks.pdf* Accessed November, 2009.

South Nation Conservation (1993), *Wastewater Assimilation Study*, Finch, Ontario.

South Nation Conservation (1997), *Statement of Roles and Responsibilities*, South Nation Conservation, Finch, Ontario

South Nation Conservation and Ministry of the Environment, (1993), *Waste Water Assimilation Study of the South Nation River Watershed*, Queen's Printer, Toronto, Ontario.

South Nation Conservation (SNC) and J. Kassirer (2005), *South Nation Watershed Total Phosphorus Management: 5-Year Program Evaluation*, South Nation Conservation, Finch, Ontario.

South Nation Conservation (2006), *State of the Nation: A Watershed Report Card*, South Nation Conservation, Finch, Ontario.

South Nation Conservation (2009), *TPM Program Summary for North Glengarry*. South Nation Conservation, Finch Ontario.

Van Dusen, T. (1997), *Phosphorus program not sinister scheme*, Agrinews, Chesterville, Ontario.

Village of Casselman, (1996), *Lagoon Discharge and Assimilation Study For The Village of Casselman*. Casselman, Ontario.

Village of Russell (1997), *Expansion of the Sewage System for the Village of Russell*. Lecompte Engineering, Ottawa, Ontario.

Annex 13.A

Figure 13A.1. Location of South Nation Conservation

Source: Natural Resources Canada.

ORGANISATION FOR ECONOMIC CO-OPERATION AND DEVELOPMENT

The OECD is a unique forum where governments work together to address the economic, social and environmental challenges of globalisation. The OECD is also at the forefront of efforts to understand and to help governments respond to new developments and concerns, such as corporate governance, the information economy and the challenges of an ageing population. The Organisation provides a setting where governments can compare policy experiences, seek answers to common problems, identify good practice and work to co-ordinate domestic and international policies.

The OECD member countries are: Australia, Austria, Belgium, Canada, Chile, the Czech Republic, Denmark, Estonia, Finland, France, Germany, Greece, Hungary, Iceland, Ireland, Israel, Italy, Japan, Korea, Luxembourg, Mexico, the Netherlands, New Zealand, Norway, Poland, Portugal, the Slovak Republic, Slovenia, Spain, Sweden, Switzerland, Turkey, the United Kingdom and the United States. The European Union takes part in the work of the OECD.

OECD Publishing disseminates widely the results of the Organisation's statistics gathering and research on economic, social and environmental issues, as well as the conventions, guidelines and standards agreed by its members.

OECD PUBLISHING, 2, rue André-Pascal, 75775 PARIS CEDEX 16
(51 2012 11 1 P) ISBN 978-92-64-17932-5 – No. 60253 2012-01